SURROGATE MOTHERHOOD:
INTERNATIONAL PERSPECTIVES

This book is a multi-disciplinary collection of essays from leading researchers
and practitioners, exploring legal, ethical, social, psychological and practical
aspects of surrogate motherhood in Britain and abroad. It highlights the common themes that characterise debates across countries as well as exploring the
many differences in policies and practices. Surrogacy raises questions for medical and welfare practitioners and dilemmas for policy makers as well as ethical
issues of concern to society as a whole. The international perspective adopted
by this book offers an opportunity for questions of law, policy and practice to
be shared and debated across countries. The book links contemporary views
from research and practice with broader social issues and bio-ethical debates.

The book will be of interest to an international audience of academics and
their students (in law, social policy, reproductive medicine, psychology and
sociology), practitioners (including doctors, counsellors, midwives and welfare
professionals) as well as those involved in policy-making and implementation.

Surrogate Motherhood:
International Perspectives

Edited by
RACHEL COOK
and
SHELLEY DAY SCLATER
WITH FELICITY KAGANAS

·HART·
PUBLISHING
OXFORD – PORTLAND OREGON
2003

Hart Publishing
Oxford and Portland, Oregon

Published in North America (US and Canada) by
Hart Publishing c/o
International Specialized Book Services
5804 NE Hassalo Street
Portland, Oregon
97213-3644
USA

Hart Publishing is a specialist legal publisher based in Oxford, England.
To order further copies of this book or to request a list of other
publications please write to:

Hart Publishing, Salter's Boatyard, Folly Bridge,
Abingdon Road, Oxford OX1 4LB
Telephone: +44 (0)1865 245533 or Fax: +44 (0)1865 794882
e-mail: mail@hartpub.co.uk
WEBSITE: http//www.hartpub.co.uk

British Library Cataloguing in Publication Data
Data Available
ISBN 1–84113–255–1 (hardback)

Typeset by Hope Services (Abingdon) Ltd.
Printed and bound in Great Britain on acid-free paper by
Biddles Ltd, www.biddles.co.uk

For Francis and George
RC

For Trey, Sophia and Alicia
SDS

For my mother, Sarah
FK

Contents

About the Contributors

Tim Appleton MA PhD ScD has a doctorate in cell biology, is an ordained Anglican priest and has worked as an independent fertility counsellor in the UK since 1982. He was asked by the pioneers of *in vitro* fertilisation (IVF), Patrick Steptoe and Robert Edwards, to become a founder member of the Bourn Hall Ethics Committee in 1981 and, for some years, was secretary of that committee. The committee explicitly considered surrogacy in 1982, and concluded that it was ethically acceptable, provided that appropriate counselling was undertaken and that each case was considered on its merits. This practice continues at the Bourn Hall Clinic, Cambridge, UK to the present day.

Eric Blyth BA MA PhD CQSW is Professor of Social Work at the University of Huddersfield, UK. He has researched extensively in the areas of involuntary childlessness, assisted conception and surrogacy. He is a member of the British Fertility Society, the British Infertility Counselling Association and the British Association of Social Workers Project Group on Assisted Reproduction. He is editor of the *Journal of Fertility Counselling*. His publications include *Truth and the Child Ten Years On: Information Exchange in Donor Assisted Conceptions* (co-edited with Marilyn Crawshaw and Jennifer Speirs, British Association of Social Workers, 1998) and *Infertility and Assisted Conception: Practice Issues for Counsellors* (British Association of Social Workers, 1995).

Peter Brinsden MBBS FRCOG is Medical Director of Bourn Hall Clinic, Cambridge, UK. He has co-authored 80 scientific papers, mainly on assisted reproduction, and authored 12 book chapters on Assisted Reproductive Technologies. He is editor of *A Textbook of In Vitro Fertilisation and Assisted Reproduction* (Parthenon, 1999).

Rachel Cook BA MA PhD CPsychol is a Senior Lecturer in Health Psychology and Field Leader at APU, Cambridge, UK. She has researched and published extensively on psychological aspects of infertility and its consequences. She was involved in the BMA working party on surrogacy and was a contributing author to its report *Changing Conceptions of Motherhood* (BMA, 1996).

Ken Daniels MA Hons, Dip Soc Sci, Dip App Soc Sci, is Associate Professor of Social Work at the University of Canterbury, Christchurch, New Zealand. He has been researching and writing in the field of assisted human reproduction for over 20 years and has published 65 papers. He has recently co-edited *Donor Insemination: International Social Science Perspectives* (Cambridge, 1998). He has acted as a consultant to government-appointed committees in Sweden, UK, Canada, Australia and New Zealand.

Shelley Day Sclater BSc PhD is a Reader in Psychosocial Studies and co-director of the Centre for Narrative Research at the University of East London. Formerly a family lawyer, she has researched a number of topics from a socio-legal perspective. Her co-edited books include *Undercurrents of Divorce* (Dartmouth, 1999), *What is a Parent? A Socio-Legal Analysis* (Hart, 1999), *Lines of Narrative* (Routledge, 2000), and *Body Lore and Laws* (Hart 2002). She is sole author of *Divorce: A Psychosocial Study* (Ashgate, 1999), and *Access to Sociology: Families* (Hodder and Stoughton, 2000). She is currently a visiting scholar at the Centre for Family Research, Cambridge.

Gena Dodd is secretary of Childlessness Overcome Through Surrogacy (COTS), the leading surrogacy support organisation in the UK. She launched COTS 1988 with Kim Cotton. COTS now has over 750 members and over 200 surrogate births. It is run without financial gain by people who have all had first hand experience of surrogacy. The prime objective of COTS is to pass on collective experience to both surrogates and would-be parents, helping them to understand the implications of surrogacy before they enter into an arrangement and to deal with any problems that may arise during it.

Robert Edelmann BSc MPhil PhD FBPsS CPsychol is a Chartered Clinical, Forensic and Health Psychologist working in private practice. He is a Fellow of the British Psychological Society. Professor Edelmann has over 100 publications, including 36 dealing with psychological aspects of infertility and the reproductive technologies. He has also authored five books. His most recent academic appointment was to the University of Surrey Roehampton where he currently holds an honorary chair.

Martin Johnson MA, PhD is Professor of Reproductive Sciences at the University of Cambridge, UK and Visiting Professor in the Department of Physiology at the University of Sydney, Australia. He was for six years until 1999 a member of the Human Fertilisation and Embryology Authority, and is a former Chair of the British Society for Developmental Biology. He is the author of numerous works on reproductive and developmental science and medicine, on bioethics and on medical education. He is co-author of the standard undergraduate teaching text on mammalian reproduction *Essential Reproduction* (Blackwell, 1999, 5th edn).

Felicity Kaganas BA, LLB, LLM is a Senior Lecturer in Law and co-director of the Centre for the Study of Law, the Child and the Family at Brunel University. She has published extensively both in the UK and South Africa in the fields of child and family law, working primarily from a socio-legal perspective. She was co-editor of *Legislating for Harmony: Partnership Under the Children Act* (Jessica Kingsley, 1995) and co-author of *Family Law, Gender and the State* (Hart Publishing, 1999).

Melissa Lane PhD is University Lecturer in History at the University of Cambridge, UK where she was awarded a PhD in philosophy, and is a Fellow of King's College Cambridge. Her books include *Method and Politics in Plato's Statesman* (Cambridge, 1998) and *Plato's Progeny: how Socrates and Plato still captivate the modern mind* (Duckworth, 2002), and she has published on and participated in media discussion of political and ethical themes including ancient philosophy, democracy, bioethics, and corporate ethics. Dr Lane co-founded the Cambridge Gender Studies Symposium and has taught on gender and feminism at Cambridge, and at Harvard as a visiting professor in 2002. She was a visiting fellow at the Research School of the Social Sciences, Australian National University, in 2001, and is on leave as Research Fellow of the Centre for History and Economics at Cambridge in 2001–04.

Derek Morgan BA is Professor of Health Care Law and Jurisprudence at Cardiff Law School and Senior Fellow at the Law Faculty, University of Melbourne. He has been a member of the British Medical Association Medical Ethics Committee since 1995 and chaired the BMA working party on Surrogacy, 1994–96. He has published widely in the area of medical law and ethics with numerous papers on surrogacy. He was editor of the BMA Report *Changing Conceptions of Motherhood: The Practice of Surrogacy in Britain* (BMA, 1996).

Claire Potter obtained a first degree in Psychology from the University of Huddersfield. She is currently engaged in PhD research at the University of Huddersfield researching drug assisted sexual assault in terms of prevalence, experience and women's 'recovery'. At the time of writing this chapter Claire was employed as a research assistant with the Assisted Conception and Infertility Research Group at the University of Huddersfield. Her interests include infertility and assisted conception, sexual violence and feminist research methods.

Heléna Ragoné BA MA PhD is a Lecturer in Anthropology at the University of Massachusetts, USA. She is the author of numerous publications. *Surrogate Motherhood: Conception in the Heart* (1994), her first book, was the first ethnographic study of surrogate motherhood. She has since co-edited three collections: *Situated Lives: Gender and Culture in Everyday Life*; *Reproducing Reproduction: Kinship, Power and Technological Innovation* (University of Pennsylvania Press, 1998); and *Ideologies and Technologies of Motherhood: Race, Class, Sexuality and Nationalism* (Routledge, 1999). Dr Ragoné is currently working on a book on surrogacy and gamete donation.

Radhika Rao AB JD is Professor of Law at the University of California, Hastings College of the Law, and a member of the California Advisory Committee on Human Cloning. After receiving a JD from Harvard Law School, she clerked for Justices Harry Blackmun and Thurgood Marshall of the US Supreme Court. Professor Rao has testified before various governmental bodies on the subjects of genetic screening and human cloning, and on the constitutionality of proposed laws regulating assisted reproduction and late-term abortion. Her research focuses upon the contours of the constitutional right of privacy as applied to legal regulation of the human body. Recent publications include 'Assisted Reproductive Technology and the Threat to the Traditional Family' 47 *Hastings Law Journal* 951 (1996); 'Reconceiving Privacy: Relationships and Reproductive Technology' 45 *UCLA Law Review* 1077 (1998); and 'Property, Privacy, and the Human Body' 80 *Boston University Law Review* 359 (2000).

Joseph G Schenker MD graduated from the Hebrew University Hadassah Medical School in 1959 and is Professor and Chair of the Department of Obstetrics & Gynaecology and a leading clinician and scientist in the fields of infertility and assisted reproduction. His scientific contribution is reflected in his membership of the editorial boards of eight international publications on human reproduction. He has been elected to the position of honorary member in numerous associations including the American College of Obstetrics and Gynecology, the Royal College of Obstetrics and Gynecology (UK), and the German Association of Obstetrics and Gynecology. In 1996, Prof Schenker was elected President of the International Academy of Human Reproduction. He is also chair of the Ethics Committee of the World Federation of Gynecologists and Obstetricians. He has served as chair and as a member of several public committees in Israel including the 'Abortion' Committee, the Public Committee for Surrogacy in Israel, and the Committee for the Investigation of the Use of Hormonal Agents during Pregnancy, the Permanent Advisory Committee of the Minister of Health. He has a special interest in surrogacy and was one of the special committee invited by the government to draw up guidelines upon which Israeli law on surrogacy is now based.

Rhona Schuz PhD studied law at Cambridge, UK and obtained her PhD in law from London University. She was a lecturer in law at Nottingham University and the London School of Economics before coming to live in Israel in 1993. She is currently a senior lecturer, teaching at Sha'arei Mishpat Law College and the Yaacov Herzog Faculty of Law at Bar Ilan University, Israel. She has published articles in the field of family law, private international law and taxation, and acted for a number of years as a consultant to the Law Commission on the Ground for Divorce. Her publications include *A Modern Approach to the Incidental Question* (Kluwer).

Lita Linzer Schwartz PhD is a Psychologist who gained her PhD from Bryn Mawr College, holds a Diplomate in Forensic Psychology from the American Board of Professional Psychology, and taught for many years at Pennsylvania State University from where she retired in 1995 as Distinguished Professor Emerita. She has written widely on aspects of infertility, surrogacy and adoption and, throughout her long and distinguished career, has published 17 books including *Alternatives to Infertility: Is Surrogacy the Answer?* (Brunner/Mazel, New York, 1991).

Marilyn Strathern PhD is William Wyse Professor in the Department of Social Anthropology at the University of Cambridge and Mistress of Girton College, Cambridge, UK. Her research interests are divided between Melanesian and British ethnography. Recent publications include the co-authored *Technologies of Procreation*; the edited volume *Shifting Contexts: Transformations in Anthropological Knowledge;* a collection of essays, *Property, Substance and Effect: Anthropological Essays on Persons and Things* and an edited volume on *Audit Culture*.

Elly Teman is currently completing her PhD in cultural anthropology at the Hebrew University of Jerusalem. Her research focuses on the experiences of surrogate mothers and commissioning couples involved in gestational surrogacy arrangements in Israel. Her areas of interest and research include the anthropology of the body, medical anthropology, the new reproductive technologies and Jewish folklore.

Acknowledgements

The idea to edit and present this collection of essays grew out of work we did and relationships we forged in meetings of the Cambridge Socio-Legal Group. Thanks are due to friends and colleagues there, particularly Martin Richards for discussions in which we received support and encouragement for our early plans. Andrew Bainham also deserves mention for the help he gave on human rights issues. We were a little daunted when we began—bringing together an international, interdisciplinary collection was never going to be an easy task. But we have managed, mostly, to make light of the difficulties, thanks to the enthusiasm, patience, willingness and sheer hard work of those who have contributed to this volume. Many are highly acclaimed scholars of international renown; we are immensely grateful to all who have shared their experience and expertise to enable us to produce this collection. We are very thankful to Felicity Kaganas whom we cajoled to join us when the workload proved too much for two; she lifted our spirits as well as lightened our load. Thanks are also due to Dr Julie Jessop and to Gavin Biggs for assisting with the copy editing, and to Nathalie Madron for proof-reading the manuscript. Without their assistance, the editorial role would have been much less manageable. We are very grateful to Richard Hart whose patience we must have stretched to its limits, yet we never felt that we lacked his support.

Rachel Cook
Shelley Day Sclater
August 2002

1

Introduction

RACHEL COOK, SHELLEY DAY SCLATER AND FELICITY KAGANAS

THIS BOOK IS about surrogacy and, more specifically, surrogate mother-hood.[1] It is a collection of chapters that aims to provide a contemporary and international picture of a practice, traceable to ancient times, devised to solve the problem of childlessness. The collection, which explores surrogacy from a variety of perspectives including law, policy, medicine and psychology, is timely. For although there is nothing new in the notion that a woman might bear a child for someone else, there is some evidence that the incidence of surrogacy is increasing[2] and technology has developed to make ever more complex arrangements possible.

The simpler process of 'partial' surrogacy involves the insemination of the surrogate mother with sperm of the 'commissioning' (or 'intended') father. By contrast, 'full' (or 'gestational') surrogacy requires medical intervention, and entails *in vitro* fertilisation (IVF) using the egg and sperm of the 'commissioning couple' (or 'intended parents').[3] While partial surrogacy can, and often does, remain a private or even secret arrangement, the involvement of medical personnel and clinics in full surrogacy has meant that the procedure has become a matter of public concern. This concern deepened in places such as the UK and the USA when surrogacy was catapulted into the headlines by a small number of contentious cases. Many commentators called for state controls to be introduced.

---

[1] **Surrogate** *n.* a substitute: . . . a person or thing standing for another person or thing, or a person who fills the role of another in one's emotional life.—**surrogate mother** a woman who bears a baby for another, esp. childless, couple, after either (artificial) insemination by the male, or implantation of an embryo from the female (*Chambers Concise Twentieth Century Dictionary*). For Warnock (1984) surrogacy was 'the practice whereby one woman carries a child for another with the intention that the child should be handed over after birth' (para 8.1:42). The difficulties associated with the terms in use in this area, and the ways in which the terms may be used, have been addressed by Morgan (1990) and Tangri and Kahn (1993), among others.

[2] See British Medical Association (1996). More than 10 years ago, Morgan (1990) reported that since 1976 there had been 'between 29 definite, 38 probably and 43 possible cases of *known* surrogacy arrangements' in Britain. It is extremely difficult to calculate the extent of surrogacy, particularly in countries where it is unregulated. There is no evidence that it is taking place on a wide scale and there seems to be no sign that 'surrogacy for convenience' is becoming common or even more common. But it is probably increasing: between two international surveys, the number of countries permitting IVF surrogacy increased overall (ASRM (1999, 2001)).

[3] While partial surrogacy of one kind or another is most commonly a private transaction and may have a long history, full surrogacy's dependence upon IVF technology meant that the first reported case was not until 1985 in the US and 1988 in the UK (Utian *et al*, 1985; Brinsden *et al*, 2000).

Committees have been set up in a number of countries to assess whether regulation is necessary and, if so, what the nature of such regulation should be. Different jurisdictions have responded in different ways to the issue. Some ban surrogacy altogether. Some have opted for partial bans while introducing rules to designate and regulate what is permissible. Some have voluntary guidelines and some have eschewed any form of regulation at all.

A recent survey gives us an idea of the current state of acceptance worldwide (American Society for Reproductive Medicine (2001), chapter 10, S26). Twenty-six of the countries or states surveyed have legislation in place which deals with aspects of assisted reproductive technology and/or IVF, eight have voluntary guidelines and eight have neither of these. More specifically, surrogacy is permitted and regulated by means of legislation in Australia (Victoria), Brazil, Hong Kong, Hungary, Israel, The Netherlands, South Africa and the United Kingdom. Australia (5 states), Korea, and some states in the USA have introduced voluntary guidelines. Surrogacy is also practised in a number of countries where no legislation or regulations, either permitting or banning it, exist: Belgium, Finland, Greece, India. Currently, IVF surrogacy is not permitted in Australia (South or West), Austria, China, the Czech republic, Denmark, Egypt, France, Germany, Italy, Jordan, Mexico, Norway, Poland, Portugal, Singapore, Spain, Sweden, Switzerland, Taiwan, Turkey, and some US states. Finally, it has been permitted in Saudi Arabia, if it took place between two wives of the same husband, but is now no longer allowed. The most severe penalty for violation of legislation is imprisonment (eg as in the UK and Norway). It has been noted that we do not see significantly different practices operating in those nations and states that do not have guidelines or legislation (ASRM (2001) chapter 1: S9).[4]

What emerges from any consideration of the ways in which surrogacy is dealt with in different jurisdictions is that a sense of profound anxiety and ambivalence has tended to pervade the thinking of professionals, policy-makers and legislators where surrogacy is concerned.

This ambivalence appears, for example, in the debates surrounding surrogacy in the UK (see Jackson (2001)). Rao (chapter 2, this volume) points to a similar ambivalence in the US. Jackson (2001:262) argues that the UK legal position is unclear and that this is, in part, attributable to a lack of clarity about the purpose of regulation in the Warnock Report, the precursor to the Surrogacy Arrangements Act 1985. The majority of the Warnock Committee apparently was of the view that surrogacy is 'almost always unethical' (Jackson (2001:262)).[5]

---

[4] The difficulty of establishing the extent to which guidelines are followed or violated is also noted (ASRM (2001) S10).

[5] 'Even in compelling medical circumstances the danger of exploitation of one human being by another appears to the majority of us far to outweigh the benefits, in almost every case' (Warnock (1984) para 8.17) and 'for the majority the use of a surrogate is classified as essentially unethical in nearly all cases' (Brazier *et al* (1998) para 2.23). It has been noted that the Warnock Report's approach to surrogacy—everything short of a total ban—was entirely different from its approach to other methods of infertility treatment, and it has been suggested that other European countries were influenced by this (eg France and West Germany) (Burke, Himmelweit and Vines (1990:263).

However, it recognised that people would continue to make 'privately arranged surrogacy agreements' and decided that children born as a result should not have their mothers 'subject to the taint of criminality' (para 8.19:47). The judgment that surrogacy was 'flawed but inevitable' says Jackson (2001:262), led to legislation with 'two disparate goals': protection of the vulnerable (primarily women and children) and the discouragement of surrogacy. Also in the UK, the more recent Brazier Report (Brazier, Campbell and Golombok (1998)), while stating that the existence of surrogacy is now 'accepted' (para 4.5) and that it had to be regulated, also expressed reservations. It indicated that 'surrogacy should remain an option of the last resort' (para 8.9) and only used where pregnancy would be impossible or very risky. The British Medical Association and the Human Fertilisation and Embryology Authority too have adopted the position that surrogacy is acceptable but only as a 'last resort' (see British Medical Association (1996) and Jackson (2001:292)).

In jurisdictions where the official policy is to do nothing, like some parts of the US and New Zealand (see Daniels, chapter 4, this volume), it appears that underlying the inaction—what Rao (chapter 2, this volume) calls 'passive resistance'—is a deep hostility towards surrogacy. In the UK, recognition of the practice has been, at best, grudging. The Warnock Report, for example, expressed fears that regulation might appear to give official endorsement to surrogacy (see Jackson (2001:281)) and the majority of the committee decided against setting up a surrogacy service lest this encourage the growth of the practice (para 8.18:47). The Brazier Report saw non-regulation as potentially problematic but opted instead for what has been described as a 'policy of "containment" ' (Brazier (1999:183)). The Brazier proposals, like the existing law in the UK as well as regulations in other jurisdictions, reflect some of the widely held concerns about surrogacy. This book is intended to inform understanding about those concerns and to explore their broader and deeper significance.

1. SURROGACY: SOLUTION OR PROBLEM?

While surrogacy is represented as a last resort medical 'solution' to the problem of infertility, the varying international responses to its regulation (or prohibition) plainly indicate that it is more often perceived as a social 'problem'. What is clear from the chapters in this book is that we cannot fully understand the 'problems' that surrogacy seems to pose for so many societies without some appreciation of the moral, social and political contexts in which surrogacy takes shape as a specific kind of 'problem'.

As Friedman and Squire (1998) remind us, we in the developed world live in an age of moral uncertainty. Where once we relied on scientific discoveries and technological advances to promise both progress and certainty, we are now finding that they might not be the answer at all. On the contrary, they are increasingly likely to be seen as bringing new problems and as raising pressing moral questions. Nowhere is this ambiguity—this moral uncertainty—more obvious, and more acute, than in the area of reproduction. Here, the combination of technological development and rapid social change have brought not certainty, but a profound unease (eg see Day Sclater (2002)). Developments in assisted reproductive technologies, coupled with the possibilities afforded by the so-called 'revolution' in human genetics, may deal the final blow to the grandest of grand narratives of Euro-American modernity—that of 'the family'. For it is in the sphere of the family that scientific, technical and social change have arguably had the most dramatic—and apparently the most worrying—impact.

For many, the alleged demise of 'family values' has been seen as signifying a moral decline, with 'civilisation' as we know it at stake.[6] Others might represent the changes in more positive terms, seeing them as signifying something less threatening—as opportunities to celebrate diversity, perhaps. It is clear, though, that we live in uncertain times and we are unsure where the road might take us. Perhaps not surprisingly there is a deep anxiety attached to this, and no dearth of attempts to frame the uncertainties in narratives that make them more manageable and less anxiety provoking. In this moral landscape, issues and events, including surrogate motherhood, become susceptible to a range of meanings.

Surrogacy is a 'problem' for so many societies because it renders the familiar ambiguous and forces us to think anew about our values, and about the basis of those values. Friedman and Squire (1998) identify surrogacy as the contemporary issue that encapsulates many of the moral ambiguities of our age. In a very obvious way, surrogacy foregrounds the shifting patterns of 'family', intimacy, parenthood, gender relations and sexuality that are the hallmark of post World War II Euro-American societies. Surrogacy is problematic for traditional notions of 'mother', 'father' and 'family' when it introduces a third (or even fourth) party into reproduction, when it introduces contractual 'public' arrangements into 'private' affairs and when it fragments motherhood. Surrogacy makes motherhood negotiable and confounds both social and biological bases of claims to parenthood. As family and kinship are increasingly being defined in terms of biology and genetic heritage, surrogacy disrupts these smooth elisions by making it possible for there to be either no biological links among family members or, alternatively, no social relations. Surrogacy both confirms notions of 'nature' and disrupts them; it occupies an uncertain place in relation to the distinction between the 'natural' and the 'artificial', opening up the possibility that we might begin to think beyond this and other similar traditional dualisms.

These ethical confusions of surrogacy are reflected in the laws and policies that seek to regulate it. In the UK, for example, the Surrogacy Arrangements Act 1985 largely side-stepped the ethical minefield and did little more than outlaw 'commercial' surrogacy. The Human Fertilisation and Embryology Act 1990 regulates surrogacy only incidentally and is, in any event, Johnson (chapter 6,

---

[6] Morgan (1996).

this volume) argues, an inappropriate means of regulation. And as Jackson (2001:262) reminds us, most surrogacy arrangements are made in a regulatory vacuum; the ease with which a woman can inseminate herself undoubtedly undermines effective legislative control.[7] In the USA, as Rao (chapter 2, this volume) shows, different laws in different states exemplify four distinct approaches to surrogacy: prohibition (sometimes including criminal sanctions), inaction, status regulation and contractual ordering. Laws and policies inevitably embody ethical uncertainties that derive from broader cultural contexts and values.

Surrogacy, then, perhaps more than any other reproductive practice, throws into sharp relief our anxieties about the future(s) of the family. It threatens accepted views of what a family is, of gender-appropriate parental behaviour, and of our ideas of what is natural in the realm of reproductive behaviour. Johnson (chapter 6, this volume) notes 'deep unease at dislocations between genetic, gestational and post-natal parenthood'. While there are variations between countries in the specifics, we see these tensions reflected worldwide. There is unease about what is seen by many as a dangerous tampering with the natural order of things. There are fears that women might be exploited or demeaned and that children might be psychologically damaged. There is disquiet about the possible potential for the commodification of women's reproductive capacity and, more worryingly for many, the commodification and trafficking of children.

2. NATURE VERSUS SCIENCE

Surrogacy evokes anxiety because it is perceived to be unnatural. First, it is the state of mind of the surrogate mother that is considered unnatural. The Warnock Report, for example, hinted at this when it in effect endorsed the opinion that when, as in surrogacy, 'a woman deliberately allows herself to become pregnant with the intention of giving up the child to which she will give birth . . . this is the wrong way to approach pregnancy' (Warnock (1984) para 8.11:45). The effect of this unnatural arrangement might, it is thought, impact on the resulting child in unforeseen and worrying ways: 'It is not known, for example, how a child will feel about having been created for the purpose of being given away to other parents' (Brazier *et al* (1998) para 4.11).

Secondly, it is the commissioning mother who may be behaving unnaturally. There is widespread revulsion at the notion that women might use surrogacy as a convenience—a 'career woman', for example, using another woman to have a

---

[7] In the UK, the Human Rights Act 1998 may have an impact on the future of surrogacy. At the time of writing, surrogacy issues had not been considered by the Commission or the Court. Swindells , Gargan, Kushner and Neaves (1999:84) point out that Art 8 (right to respect for private and family life) and Art 12 (right to found a family) could be employed in future to strengthen the position of the genetic intended parents.

baby while she continues to work. COTS (1999:11) 'considers surrogacy objectionable if used . . . as a convenience'. This anxiety is also apparent in the Warnock Report: 'As we have already noted, the Warnock Committee unanimously condemned surrogacy for convenience and the majority regarded surrogacy as intrinsically objectionable in almost every case' (Brazier *et al* (1998) para 4.2). Generally speaking, where surrogacy is permitted, it is only where there is *medically* diagnosed infertility that *treatment* is provided (see Brinsden chapter 7, this volume).[8]

Thirdly, even where medically indicated, the process and its outcome might be seen as unnatural, so warranting, at the very least, control and remedial measures. Lane (chapter 9, this volume) suggests that the exclusion of the surrogate mother after the handover of the child represents an attempt to ensure that the new family is more 'natural', presumably because it would otherwise be obviously 'unnatural'. Strathern (chapter 18, this volume) argues that it is only when science can be perceived as serving nature and society that it is not threatening. The surrogate mother, she says, is seen as assisting the 'real' mother[9] to overcome a medical impairment. In the same way, medical technology can be seen as facilitating a natural outcome—an egg is fertilised, a child is born. As long as surrogacy is 'simply giving nature a helping hand' then 'it appears as a natural resource which can be put to the benefit of society'. However, science, argues Strathern, can also be seen in a more negative light: as 'fuelling a runaway world when its aims are presented as a substitute for Society's.' An examination of the rules regulating surrogacy reveals what appears to be an attempt to rein in science so as to confine its effects to be compatible with society's dominant values and goals.

3. REGULATING THE SURROGATE FAMILY—FOR THE CHILDREN'S SAKE?

Rao (chapter 2, this volume) contends that surrogacy 'threatens the traditional understanding of families as the mere reflection of biological facts, revealing instead that they are social constructs' (see also Rao, 1996). She also notes that, by constructing the family through the marketplace rather than through loving relationships, surrogacy arrangements 'promote a world of private ordering' where family relationships are a matter of choice and so are 'contingent and revocable'. As Dewar (1998:483) says, what is 'natural' becomes an act of creation and there is a pattern of inconsistency in the law, 'reflecting wider uncertainties about what constitutes connections between individuals.'

---

[8] However, some directors of clinics consider surrogacy for convenience acceptable: Stern, Cramer, Garrod and Green's (2002) survey of assisted reproductive technology clinics in the US found that around 20% of clinic directors thought that surrogacy for convenience should be allowed.

[9] See also Teman (chapter 17, this volume) for a discussion of the strategies employed by gestational and intended mothers alike to construct the intended mother's identity as the 'real' mother.

   That surrogacy appears to provoke so much more anxiety than adoption is perhaps attributable to the perception that science may be running out of control and leaving dominant values behind. In any event, it is apparent that the law regulating surrogacy in the UK represents strenuous efforts, going beyond those relating to adoption, to ensure that the new family replicates as closely as possible the heterosexual, married, nuclear family.[10] These measures can be and are explained in terms of a particular construction of children's welfare. This is exemplified by section 13(5) of the Human Fertilisation and Embryology Act 1990 which stipulates that, 'A woman shall not be provided with treatment services unless account has been taken of the welfare of any child who may be born as a result of the treatment (including the need of that child for a father).' Section 30 HFE Act 1990[11] provides for the making of parental orders to confer parental status on the commissioning parents without the need for adoption. It limits eligibility for an order to married couples. In addition, the embryo must have been created with the gametes of either the wife or the husband or both, so ensuring a genetic connection. Similar restrictions exist in other jurisdictions. In most countries, assisted reproductive technology is used only for the benefit of heterosexual couples who are married or in a stable relationship[12] (American Society for Reproductive Medicine (2001)). For instance, Rao (chapter 2, this volume) points out that in the USA, in those states where surrogacy is regulated, there are generally limits placed on the age and marital status of the commissioning parent. There is also normally a requirement that surrogacy should be permitted only in the case of married, and therefore by definition, heterosexual, couples. In addition, many states 'valorize genetic ties' by enforcing contracts only where there is a genetic relationship with child. Schuz (chapter 3, this volume) describing the law in Israel, observes that the law promotes a two-parent heterosexual model of the family: the intended parents must be a man and a woman who are spouses. In practice, cohabitants have been approved for surrogacy arrangements but single persons have not. In addition, and for reasons dictated by religious law, the sperm used must be that of the father.[13] In New Zealand too, the draft guidelines require that one of the parents should be a genetic parent (see Daniels, chapter 4, this volume). The rules in numerous jurisdictions therefore 'radiate', as Dewar (1998:483) puts it, the message that children should be raised within the framework of a traditional family structure, preferably with genetic links with at least one parent.

---

[10] See also Dewar (1998:482).

[11] See also s 28 which seeks to attach a man as father to the child, provided he is married to the surrogate mother and consents or has received the treatment services together with the surrogate. Oddly, if no man falls within this section, it appears that the child is fatherless (see Dewar (1998:482)), with the effect that legislation at least partly concerned with the maintenance of traditional family life resulted in the creation of a new category of fatherless children.

[12] 'Stability' appears normally to be determined by a relationship's length, rather than any specific assessment of its quality.

[13] See also Schenker (chapter 16, this volume).

Paradoxically, surrogacy presents policy-makers and regulators seeking to promote the two-parent family also with another problem—the practice can create too many potential parents. The law in jurisdictions that regulate surrogacy accordingly designates one person as the 'real' mother and one as the 'real' father (see Strathern, chapter 18, this volume). In the US, the 'real' mother is usually taken to be the genetic mother. Somewhat surprisingly, given the emphasis on genetic connection elsewhere in the law, the opposite is true in the UK, perhaps in recognition of the risks undertaken by the carrying mother.[14] In the UK, section 27(1) of the HFE Act 1990 stipulates that the gestational mother is to be treated as the mother of the child while, in terms of s28, the father is her husband, provided he has consented to the arrangement. It has been argued that rather than specifying one exclusive legal mother, so reproducing the 'one mother/nuclear family construct', we should 'recognise the maternity of both the genetic mother and the gestational mother and involve them both in the child's social rearing'[15] (Kandel 1994:168). COTS (1999) maintains that there is little difference between this situation and one where parents re-marry; it is not unusual to have more than two parent figures.[16] Lane (chapter 9, this volume) in a similar vein, points out that divorce and open adoption have,

> already shown that legal systems and, to an increasing extent, public cultures can accommodate children with more than one maternal and paternal actor in their lives. What is paradoxical about surrogacy is the extent to which discomfort with it drives appeal to the most traditional of paradigms—marital privacy and all it entails—to understand and legitimate it, no matter that fewer and fewer couples marry and reproduce within that paradigm at all.

For Lane this is both a moral and experiential issue.[17] She shows that a powerful argument can be made that it is morally wrong to attempt to erase the past and to use the surrogate mother as a disposable means to an end. Moreover, to do so may harm the birth mother and her family.

However, it is perhaps unlikely that legal recognition would be assigned to both mothers, given the importance accorded to children's interests and given the dominant construction of children's welfare that prevails in the Western world. Children's well-being is seen as intimately tied up with the existence of a nuclear family unit. Even open adoption does not result in the sharing of parental status between the adoptive and biological parents. Nor does it impose enforceable obligations on the adoptive family. It seems that families which do not conform to the traditional model are viewed with suspicion. Like lone par-

---

[14] See Diduck and Kaganas (1999:111).

[15] However, noting that some surrogate mothers are motivated by a desire to enjoy pregnancy and childbirth without the responsibility of raising the child, we should ask whether surrogate mothers or intended parents would want this kind of involvement, and therefore whether it should be imposed upon them.

[16] What we may lack are suitable terms to describe these different 'mothers'.

[17] See Teman (chapter 17, this volume) for a discussion of the experiential issues based on interviews with surrogate and commissioning mothers.

ent families, families that create multiple relationships[18] are perceived as being potentially damaging to children. For example, Brazier *et al* remarked that, 'It is not known . . . what the impact of two mothers will be on [the child's] social, emotional and identity development through childhood and into adult life' (Brazier *et al* (1998) para 4.11).

4. PROTECTING THE BIRTH MOTHER

Surrogacy is seen as a risky business, not only for children but also for the adults concerned and, in particular, the birth mother. Fierce debate has raged over the ethical issues associated with surrogacy, with its connotations of baby-selling, and exploitation of host mothers.[19] Lane (chapter 9, this volume) draws our attention to a number of the arguments put forward and focuses, among others, on the feminist contributions to the ethical debate. Some feminists maintain that surrogacy commodifies women's reproductive capacity, reducing birth mothers to 'paid breeders' or even to the equivalent of prostitutes. However, as Lane points out, not all objections are confined to commercial surrogacy. Some feminist scholars assert that the arrangements dominating all forms of reproduction in modern developed societies further the ends of patriarchy by increasing control over women's reproductive powers. By contrast, there are other feminist writers who champion choice and who maintain that surrogacy could be used to transform gender relations by potentially empowering women to use their reproductive capacity as they choose. Taking on board these different views, Rao (chapter 2, this volume) points to the potential of surrogacy to both advance and undermine individual liberty.

The image of surrogate mothers as vulnerable and subject to exploitation appears to be the dominant one among policy- and law-makers. In the UK, the Brazier Report, for instance, represented surrogates as uneducated and in straitened circumstances: 'There is evidence that the majority of surrogates . . . have relatively low educational attainments. A number are unemployed, unsupported by a partner and responsible for children of their own. "Professional" surrogacy may appear to be an attractive option for women in these circumstances . . . ' (Brazier *et al* (1998) para 4.19). It goes on to say that, 'The issue of exploitation of the surrogate . . . resolves into the fundamental question of her capacity to foresee the risks entailed.' It is possible, however, that 'the force of socio-economic differentials between a surrogate mother and commissioning parents may be overplayed'; the absence of payment can be seen as similarly exploitative (Blyth and Potter, chapter 15, this volume). While the Brazier

---

[18] For full discussion of the relationships 'spawned' by a surrogacy arrangement, see Schwarz (chapter 11, this volume).
[19] See for example Arditti (1987); Lamb (1993); van Niekerk and Van Zyl (1995); Paulson (1995); Bromham (1995); Schenker and Eisenberg (1996); Schenker and Eisenberg (1997).

Report only considered exploitation in the context of payment,[20] others have pointed to the risks inherent also in 'altruistic' surrogacy:

> It is assumed that, because there is no payment no exploitation can exist. However, subtle familial pressures may be more effective than financial reward in persuading a woman to enter into an altruistic arrangement. Relegating such decisions to the family not the legislature does not guarantee protection of women's rights because women are particularly vulnerable to exploitation within families. (New Zealand Law Commission (2000) para 534:195).

Moreover, fears extend beyond the vision of women impelled to agree to arrangements against their better judgment or in ignorance of the consequences. Concern extends also to the possibility of coercion being used to compel a surrogate against her wishes to give up the child she has borne. This possibility[21] too, highlighted in the much-publicised cases of *Baby Cotton* in the UK (Cotton & Winn (1985)) and *Baby M* in the US (see Friedman and Squire (1998)) is one that is not confined to commercial surrogacy.

Schuz (chapter 3, this volume) in her analysis of the law in Israel, notes that the legislation is designed in part to safeguard the interests of the birth mother. Starting from the premise that 'potential birth mothers are not in a position to judge their own suitability', the law requires that she be assessed by medical and mental health professionals. To ensure that her consent is 'informed' and 'genuine', she must be advised by a lawyer and be questioned by committee. There are also legal measures in place intended to protect her health, her privacy and her financial position. Israel is unusual in its approach; it regulates surrogacy quite stringently but, once all the requirements have been met, the law gives the birth mother little opportunity to change her mind.

In most jurisdictions, such as the UK, while individual clinics or ethics committees may have rules in place to provide for some kind of assessment of birth mothers,[22] there has been no attempt to introduce positive protective measures. Protection is largely negative in nature and, arguably, reinforces the image of the birth mother as vulnerable to exploitation and coercion. Most importantly, the surrogate mother is free to withdraw from her agreement; surrogacy arrangements are unenforceable. This state of affairs is criticised by Lane (chapter 9,

---

[20] Given this concern with the possibility of financial pressure, a major focus for researchers has been the motivations of surrogate mothers. Findings suggest that, while financial gain may be the only or the main motivation for some, most women report a number of emotional reasons behind their decision, including a wish for enhanced self-esteem or self-worth, an attempt to resolve feelings associated with previous reproductive losses and a desire to re-experience pregnancy and childbirth without the responsibility of rearing the child (see, for example, Franks (1981); Parker (1983); Einwohner (1989); Reame and Parker (1983); MacPhee and Forest (1990); Fischer and Gillman (1991); Blyth (1994)).

[21] Jackson (2001) notes that there is not much evidence that many surrogates regret their decision: Andrews (1995) reports that less than 1% of surrogate mothers changed their minds about giving up the child and another small study of 14 women in the US reports that none of the surrogate mothers regretted their decision (Ciccarelli (1997) cited in Baslington (2002)).

[22] See Daniels (chapter 4, this volume) on the proposed measures in New Zealand.

this volume) who argues that, if women are to enjoy the reproductive freedom of engaging in surrogacy, it may be in their interests to have the protection of an enforceable contract. To ignore the agreement, she contends, is to ignore the parties' intentions. Women have several interests that need to be protected. They have:

> an interest in being treated as contracting equals; an interest in the protection which contract can afford; an interest in being in control of the experience and the crucial decisions affecting any pregnancy they may conceive, including the possibility of terminating that pregnancy; and an interest in retaining parental status in relation to any child they bear until after that child's birth. The typical public policy justification for thoroughgoing unenforceability, such as that adopted in the UK, does not take adequate account of the first two interests.

She goes on to argue, by analogy with contracts of service, that while specific performance should not be available, financial penalties should be imposed on a birth mother who fails to fulfil her promise.

Further protection is afforded by section 30 of the HFE Act. This provides that a parental order cannot be made without the informed consent of the birth mother and consent cannot effectively be given until six weeks have elapsed after the birth.[23] The legislation, says Johnson (chapter 6, this volume) is perhaps designed to discourage surrogacy by disadvantaging those who choose that route to parenthood. But it is also consistent with adoption law[24] and seems to rest on the assumption that, post-partum, women are irrational. Finally, commercial surrogacy is outlawed in the UK so that financially disadvantaged women will not be tempted into potentially exploitative arrangements for monetary gain.[25]

5. SURROGACY AS A GIFT

Ragoné notes (chapter 14, this volume) the pervasive notion of surrogacy as a gift, despite the inherent commercialism of assisted reproduction in the US. She explores how the theme of the 'gift of life' supports and reflects Euro-American cultural beliefs about pregnancy and parenthood. We see this ideal of surrogacy as a gift reflected in the Brazier Report, where it is stated: 'We believe that the core value here, on which many social arrangements in the United Kingdom are based, including blood and live organ donation, is the "gift relationship"' (Brazier *et al* (1998) para 4.36).[26] Nevertheless, as Jackson (2001:265) points out,

---

[23] See Dodd (chapter 8, this volume).

[24] See s 16(4) Adoption Act 1976.

[25] Yet this would not prevent them taking up equally exploitative work of another kind (see Blyth and Potter, chapter 15, this volume).

[26] It is worth noting however that while blood and organ donation take place within the context of the National Health Service, surrogacy in the UK essentially is located in the private sector. The tensions between the ideal of the gift and the reality of remuneration are noted by Ragoné (chapter 14, this volume) and Blyth and Potter (chapter 15, this volume).

while commercial surrogacy is forbidden, it is increasingly practised. This, she says, is because the courts are permitted to authorise payments made in contra-vention of the ban on commercial surrogacy retrospectively if it is the child's best interests to remain with the commissioning parents. The Brazier Report recommends that, at least in relation to parental orders,[27] this should change; access to such orders would be limited to those who have complied fully with the statutory rules and those rules would prohibit payment other than compen-sation for specified expenses.[28]

The Brazier Report gives a number of reasons for rejecting payments to sur-rogates other than those for expenses actually incurred. First, it suggests that children will be harmed by the knowledge that their gestational mother has been paid. Secondly, it takes the view that altruistic agreements are less likely to break down than commercial ones. Thirdly, it predicts that surrogates might extort money from commissioning parents once the pregnancy is established. Finally, it suggests that, generally, the amounts paid would increase and that surrogacy would be encouraged as a result. All these reasons are criticised as speculative by Jackson (2001:284–85), who also points out that sperm donation and egg-sharing attract payment. Ragoné (chapter 14, this volume) in turn, notes that doctors who assist infertile patients are paid and wonders why surrogate mothers cannot be paid too. COTS (1999) note that children may be 'bought' in other ways in our society: foster parents, they argue, are paid and fostering could be regarded as a profession.[29] But it is the prospect of profes-sional surrogacy that the Brazier Report deplores, noting with disapproval that, 'There is evidence that some women view surrogacy as a form of employment' (Brazier *et al* (1998) 5.17).

The revulsion provoked by the practice of commercial surrogacy appears to be rooted then not only in the perception that it demeans women, with some commentators making comparisons with prostitution, but also because it is thought to commodify, and to harm, children. Yet, as Schuz (chapter 3, this vol-ume) shows, these perceptions are not necessarily universal. In Israel, 'the effect of the law is that surrogacy will invariably occur on a commercial basis'; for one thing, a relative of the intending parents cannot legally act as a surrogate. While trade in babies is illegal, payment of surrogates is not. Guidelines set out the expenses and heads of compensation for which provision must be made in the agreement by the intended parents. These include all medical expenses, legal expenses, the cost of counselling, the cost of insurance premiums and compen-sation for pain and suffering. For Schuz, these requirements provide important

---

[27] The courts are permitted, in adoption proceedings, to authorise payments retrospectively (see s 57 Adoption Act 1976).

[28] See, for full discussion Jackson (2001:289–90).

[29] See COTS (1999) Chapter 5: 'Children are paid for every day, at IVF clinics . . . Children are also bought . . . when a child is adopted from abroad as they pay the social services or adoption agency. . . . There is also evidence that fostering is a "profession" in this country, and now couples are paid a weekly salary to adopt certain children by the Social Services' (p 17).

safeguards for carrying mothers and she points out that the courts and legislature have rejected the argument that surrogacy should not be permitted because its 'unnatural' character affects children adversely.[30] Children's interests are protected in the law and, she concludes, the Israeli experience 'suggests that non-altruistic surrogacy can work well provided that adequate safeguards are introduced.'

Stuhmcke (1996:2), in her criticism of the prohibition of commercial surrogacy in some Australian states, goes further. She rejects the distinction drawn between altruistic and commercial surrogacy. It is unclear, she says, 'when an altruistic arrangement becomes commercial—for example an arrangement may include payment of the surrogate mother's medical, travel and home-help expenses yet remain classified as an altruistic arrangement' (1996:2). She notes that the distinction between the two terms implies greater acceptability of 'altruistic' arrangements, ignoring the fact that surrogate mothers who are paid may have altruistic motivations and those who are not paid may not be altruistically motivated. She also notes that it has been argued by Anderson (1990) that the actual reasons behind surrogate mothers' behaviour—'lack of self confidence and subordination'—mean we can never term their acts 'altruistic'. More care is clearly needed in the use of these terms. Becoming a surrogate mother is complex behaviour, resulting from individual psychological factors and the social, legal and cultural context (eg see Edelmann, chapter 10; Schwartz, chapter 11, this volume). Although it might be easier for legislative purposes, it is not reasonable to accept a simplistic dichotomy between acceptable, altruistic motivations and unacceptable, commercial ones.

6. SURROGACY AND HUMAN RIGHTS

Morgan (chapter 5, this volume) makes reference to the difficulty that feminists have in addressing reproductive technology. On the one hand, as Stuhmcke suggests, assisted reproduction may be seen as implicated in the exploitation of women and in reinforcing dominant patriarchal images of motherhood. On the other hand, to see it in this way is to deny women's ability to make their own decisions and to withhold from individual women the opportunity of having a family. Surrogacy, therefore, raises important questions about reproductive rights and autonomy. Morgan examines the notion of reproductive rights and considers whether the UK law is consistent with the Human Rights Act 1998. Drawing on the work of other scholars as well as judicial pronouncements, he argues that democratic ideals demand the recognition of 'procreative liberty' and that this should not be interfered with except for good reason such as harm

---

[30] We should note that there is as yet no evidence that children suffer (or indeed benefit) as a consequence of surrogacy arrangements. The concerns expressed remain speculative (eg see Ragoné (1996); Jackson (2001)).

to others. However, he maintains, procreative liberty 'implies a negative right against state interference'; it is not a positive right to be given the means or the resources to procreate. Nevertheless, although restrictions on the availability of treatment and on commercial surrogacy may not contravene the Article 8 right to family life, the status provisions of the HFE Act might.[31]

7. SURROGACY AND THE PROFESSIONAL

Surrogacy, then, raises issues of human rights as well as the potentially counter-vailing considerations of individual protection and public policy endorsement of particular family forms. There are some clear rules in some jurisdictions limiting the availability of surrogacy on the basis of factors such as age, marital status and sexuality. However, in many cases the law or guidelines also make provision for the medical and psychological assessment of both intended parents and potential surrogates. These assessments are, it seems, intended to reduce the potential for failed arrangements and, more specifically, to protect the interests of the adults concerned as well as any child born as a result of the arrangement. The crucial role of assessment means, in effect, that while the law stipulates a few general rules, it delegates to professionals the task of deciding who is suitable in individual cases. Thus the state leaves it to the professionals to make the decisions it cannot make without the risk of being seen as trampling on individual liberties. And professionals may, in consequence, find themselves faced with the dilemma of whether, and how, to avoid becoming implicated in what might be regarded as social engineering.

Edelmann (chapter 10, this volume) describes the internationally highly visible cases of *Baby Cotton* in the UK, and *Baby M* in the US, to highlight some of the difficulties in surrogacy and the potential role for psychological assessment. He notes the need to protect the surrogate mother, the role for the psychologist or counsellor in facilitating decision-making and the development of a working relationship between the surrogate mother and the intended parents. He argues that although there are concerns about psychological issues such as the emotional stability of intended parents, it is not the role of the psychologist to act as gatekeeper and make decisions about rejection and acceptance of surrogacy participants.[32] Rather, the psychologist should facilitate decision-making and permit parties to screen themselves, consistent with the 'permissive' nature of access to surrogacy in Britain.[33] Edelmann's argument is an important one, as it

---

[31] See above, n 5.
[32] For an alternative view, see Schwartz (chapter 11, this volume). The screening of those involved in third-party assisted reproduction, including gamete donation and surrogacy, is common practice in the US (for example, see Schover, Collins and Richards (1992); Schover, Rothmann and Collins (1992); Leiblum (2000)).
[33] Identified by Brazier (1999).

highlights the blurring of the boundary between psychological 'assessment' and social 'control'[34] that also, as Cook (chapter 12, this volume) demonstrates, assumes significance in the counselling process. It is in the *psychological* arenas of 'assessment', 'support' and 'counselling' that there arises the opportunity for particular discursive constructions (such as what constitutes a 'good' parent, or an acceptable family form) to frame the practice and the experience of surrogacy. These discursive constructions may thus be said to 'govern'[35] both actions and feelings in areas where specific legal provisions would fear to tread.

As Cook (chapter 12, this volume) shows, these tensions form the inevitable backdrop of the psychological aspects of surrogacy arrangements. For some, counselling is the only appropriate way of addressing the 'emotional minefield' that surrogacy represents (Appleton, chapter 13, this volume). Dodd (chapter 8, this volume) offers another perspective on the tension when she observes that it is unlikely that individual health professionals will have experience of surrogacy, and for this reason she argues that the 'patient', in a role reversal, needs to become the 'expert'. Appleton (chapter 13) notes the difficulty of linking 'assessment' with 'counselling' and it is clear from his account of his many years of experience as a counsellor, that the counsellor will develop a view on the viability or wisdom of the arrangement, but can do no more than make recommendations. In the processes of 'assessment' and 'counselling' we see the language and the practice of (individual) psychology being used to address social issues of morality and legal issues of regulation.

8. CONCLUSION

The chapters in this volume illustrate many of the uncertainties and dilemmas of surrogacy. In them we see different societies formulating the 'problem' in different ways, and attempting to put in place 'solutions' that are appropriate for them. But these chapters make it clear that, making laws or rules, and putting policies into practice in an area that is characterised by such a profound moral uncertainty, can generate further problems that demand yet other solutions. The difficulties are undoubtedly compounded by the lack of systematic research[36] into the social and psychological aspects of surrogacy and its consequences, the ways in which laws work, and the pitfalls of translating policies into practice. Despite the acknowledgement that surrogacy agreements are fraught with psychological and social dilemmas, there has been, for example, almost no systematic research into the consequences for participants. The 1996 British Medical Association report on the practice of surrogacy drew attention

[34] See, eg: Burman (1994); Morss (1995).
[35] See Rose (1990).
[36] Until recently, most research into surrogacy was driven by practical concerns and carried out in the United States; there are notable and more recent exceptions to this (eg Blyth (1994, 1995); Ragoné (1994, 1996); MacCallum and Golombok (2002)).

to the fact that we have almost no information about outcomes for those involved in surrogacy arrangements; what little information we do have is unsystematic and anecdotal (BMA (1996)). Similarly, the recent Department of Health review of surrogacy regulation pointed to the absence of empirical data in this area, and the consequent impossibility of assessing the psychosocial consequences for those involved (Brazier *et al* (1998)). This lack of research evidence poses problems for screening, counselling and informed decision-making as well as for wider questions of legislating and policy-making. The development of policy may therefore depend upon speculation. And as Dodd shows in her chapter, the participants in surrogacy arrangements often lack accurate information about the process.

Yet, because of the moral ambiguity surrounding surrogacy, as well as the social anxieties and emotional ambivalences it provokes, it seems that we are compelled to try to tame and confine it whenever it rears its head. For this reason, much has been said about surrogacy on very tenuous empirical foundations. Surrogacy is often in the headlines, a situation that is unlikely to change in the foreseeable future. Surrogacy will continue to highlight the dilemmas of our changing relations with technological developments, our changing notions of rights and responsibilities, and our changing values of individual, family and community. Across the world, surrogacy remains a divisive issue, and there can be no recourse either to science or to any moral consensus to settle the score.

As Morgan (chapter 5, this volume) observes: surrogacy is socially and ethically divisive precisely *because* it does not attract universal opprobrium, and because it may be seen as a natural and beneficial product of the reproduction revolution as much as an unnatural and abnormal artefact of it. In short, surrogacy occupies a terrain of profound moral uncertainty, social anxiety and emotional ambivalence. The contours of this uncertain terrain are mapped out in the chapters in this book. In them we see the potential for differing and conflicting moral, legal and experiential positions that surrogacy poses. The law governing surrogacy differs between jurisdictions but, crucially, the laws of individual jurisdictions contain gaps and internal contradictions and inconsistencies that may be manifested as policies are translated into practice, and as individual surrogate mothers and intended parents negotiate the uncertain and shifting boundaries of 'family'. Dewar (1998:484) has argued that legislators, by seeking to reconstitute a sense of collective family values, has created a set of inconsistent principles, 'whether between rights and utility, or autonomy and community—while at the same time using law to give the appearance of having created shared values; and then have off-loaded the detailed working out of those contradictions to the legal system.' Indeed, in relation to surrogacy, as in other fields, the legislators have off-loaded the working out of these contradictions also onto medical and mental health professionals.

The legislation relating to surrogacy attempts to reconcile a number of conflicting principles. These include the importance of genetic links as well as the significance of social parenting; the autonomy of the family and the individual as well as the public policy implications of permitting non-traditional family forms; and the rights of individuals as well as the welfare of those perceived as vulnerable. The law, as Dewar (1998:485) says, 'seeks to describe good behaviour' by recognising some relationships while withholding recognition from others, and also by seeking to constrain the influence of the market within the family. However, ultimately, surrogacy must be a very good example of what he calls the 'normal chaos of family law.'[37]

REFERENCES

American Society for Reproductive Medicine (ASRM), 'IFFS Surveillance 98' (1999) 71 [Suppl 2] *Fertility and Sterility*.

American Society for Reproductive Medicine, 'IFFS Surveillance 01' (2001) 76 [Suppl 2] *Fertility and Sterility*.

Anderson, ES, 'Is women's labor a commodity?' (1990) 19 *Philosophy and Public Affairs* 86.

Andrews, L, 'Beyond doctrinal boundaries: a legal framework for surrogate motherhood' (1995) 81 *Virginia Law Review* 2343

Arditti, R, 'The surrogacy business' (1987, Fall) *Social Policy* 42.

Baslington, H, 'The social organization of surrogacy: relinquishing a baby and the role of payment in the psychological detachment process' (2002) 7 *Journal of Health Psychology* 57.

Beck, U and Beck-Gernsheim, E *The Normal Chaos of Love* (Cambridge, Polity, 1995).

Blyth, E, 'I wanted to be interesting. I wanted to be able to say "I've done something interesting with my life': Interviews with surrogate mothers in Britain' (1994) 12 *Journal of Reproductive and Infant Psychology* 189.

—— 'Not a primrose path: commissioning parents' experiences of surrogacy arrangements in Britain' (1995) 13 *Journal of Reproductive and Infant Psychology* 185.

Brazier, M, 'Regulating the reproduction business?' (1999) 7 *Medical Law Review* 166.

—— Campbell, A and Golombok, S, *Surrogacy: Review for Health Ministers of Current Arrangements for Payments and Regulation. Report of the Review Team.* Cm 4068 (London, HMSO, 1998).

Brinsden, PR, Appleton, TC, Murray, E, Hussein, M, Akagbosu, F and Marcus, S, 'Treatment by *in vitro* fertilisation with surrogacy: experience of one British centre' (2000) 320 *British Medial Journal* 924.

British Medical Association, *Changing Conceptions of Motherhood. The Practice of Surrogacy in Britain* (London, BMA Publications, 1996).

Bromham, DR, 'Surrogacy—ethical, legal, and social aspects' (1995) 12 *Journal of Assisted Reproduction and Genetics* 509.

Burke, L, Himmelweit, S and Vines, G, *Tomorrow's Child* (London, Virago, 1990).

Burman, E, *Deconstructing Developmental Psychology* (London, Routledge, 1994).

Ciccarelli, J, 'The surrogate mother: a post-birth follow-up' (1997) 58(3) *Dissertation Abstracts International* 1522B.

---

[37] See Beck and Beck-Gernsheim, 1995.

Cotton, K and Winn, D, *Baby Cotton: For Love and Money* (London, Dorling Kindersley, 1985).

COTS, *Surrogacy. A Workable Solution. In Response to the Review Team's Report* (1999) Available online at www.surrogacy.org.uk.

Day Sclater, S, 'Introduction' in A Bainham, S Day Sclater and M Richards (eds), *Body Lore and Laws* (Oxford, Hart Publishing, 2002).

Dewar, J, 'The normal chaos of family law' (1998) *Modern Law Review* 467.

Diduck, A and Kaganas, F, *Family Law, Gender and the State* (Oxford, Hart Publishing, 1999).

Einwohner, J, 'Who becomes a surrogate: personality characteristics' in J Offerman-Zuckerberg (ed), *Gender in Transition: A New Frontier* (New York, Plenum Publishing Corporation, 1989).

Fischer, S and Gillman, I, 'Surrogate motherhood: attachment, attitudes and social support' (1991) 54 *Psychiatry* 13.

Franks, DD, 'Psychiatric evaluation of women in a surrogate mother program' (1981) 138 *American Journal of Psychiatry* 1378.

Friedman, E and Squire, C, *Morality USA* (Minneapolis, University of Minnesota Press, 1998).

Jackson, E, *Regulating Reproduction. Law, Technology and Autonomy* (Oxford, Hart Publishing, 2001).

Kandel, RF, 'Which came first: the mother or the egg? A kinship solution to gestational surrogacy' (1994) 47 *Rutgers Law Review* 165.

Lamb, SR, 'The ethics of surrogacy: a framework for legal analysis' (1993) 31 *Family and Conciliation Courts Review* 401.

Leiblum, SR, 'Some thoughts and comments about screening candidates for third-party assisted reproduction: the clinician's dilemma' (2000) 15 *Sexual and Relationship Therapy* 79.

Leeton, J. and Dawson, K., 'A case of attempted IVF surrogacy in Victoria—breaking the law or breaking the deadlock' (1994) 34 *Australian and New Zealand Journal of Obstetrics and Gynaecology* 586.

MacCallum and Golombok, S, 'Outcomes for families created through surrogacy' (2002) paper presented at ESHRE conference, Vienna, July 2002.

MacPhee, D and Forest, K, 'Surrogacy: programme comparisons and policy implications' (1990) 4 *International Journal of Law and the Family* 308.

Morgan, D, 'Surrogacy: an introductory essay' in R Lee and D Morgan (eds), *Birthrights: Law and Ethics at the Beginning of Life* (London, Routledge, 1989).

Morgan, P 'Family crisis affects us all' in C Donnellan (ed), *Marriage and Divorce: Issues for the Nineties* (Cambridge, Independence Educational Publishers, 1996).

Morss, J *Growing Critical* (London, Routledge, 1995).

New Zealand Law Commission, *Adoption and Its Alternatives. A Different Approach and a New Framework*. Report 65. (New Zealand Law Commission, Wellington, New Zealand, 2000).

Parker, PJ, 'Motivations of surrogate mothers: initial findings' (1983) 140 *American Journal of Psychiatry and Law* 117–18.

Paulson, RJ, 'Ethical considerations involving oocyte donation and gestational surrogacy' (1995) 13 *Seminars in Reproductive Endocrinology* 225.

Ragoné, H, *Surrogate Motherhood: Conception in the Heart* (Boulder, Westview Press, 1994).

—— 'Chasing the blood tie: surrogate mothers, adoptive mothers and fathers' (1996) 23 *American Ethnologist* 352.

Rao, R, 'Assisted reproductive technology and the threat to the traditional family' (1996) 47 *Hastings Law Journal* 951.

Reame, N and Parker, P 'Surrogate pregnancy: clinical features of 44 cases' (1983) 162 *American Journal of Obstetrics and Gynaecology* 1220.

Rose, N, *Governing the Soul* (London, Routledge, 1990).

Schenker, JG and Eisenberg, VH, 'Surrogate pregnancies: ethical, social and legal aspects' (1996) 1 *Prenatal Neonatal Medicine* 29.

—— 'Ethical issues relating to reproduction control and women's health' (1997) 58 *International Journal of Gynaecology and Obstetrics* 167.

Schover, LR, Collins, RL and Richards, S, 'Psychological aspects of donor insemination—evaluation and follow-up of recipient couples' (1992) 57 *Fertility and Sterility* 583.

—— Rothman, SA and Collins, RL, 'The Personality and Motivation of Semen Donors: A Comparison with Oocyte Donors' (1992) 7 *Human Reproduction* 575–79.

Stern, JE, Cramer, CP, Garrod, A and Green, RM, 'Attitudes on access to services at assisted reproductive technology clinics: comparison of clinic policy' (2002) 77 *Fertility and Sterility* 537.

Stuhmcke, A, 'For love or money: the legal regulation of surrogate motherhood' (1996) 3 *E Law—Murdoch University Electronic Journal of Law* (www.murdoch.edu.au/elaw) 1.

Swindells, H, Gargan, C, Kushner, M and Neaves, A, *Family Law and the Human Rights Act 1998* (Bristol, Jordan Publishing, 1999).

Tangri, SS and Kahn, JR, 'Ethical issues in the new reproductive technologies: perspectives from feminism and the psychology profession' (1993) 24 *Professional Psychology: Research and Practice* 271.

Utian, WH, Sheehan, L, Goldfarb, JM and Kiwi, R, 'Successful pregnancy after *in vitro* fertilization-embryo transfer from an infertile woman to a surrogate' (1985) 313 *New England Journal of Medicine* 1351.

van Niekerk A and Van Zyl L, 'The ethics of surrogacy. Women's reproductive labour' (1995) 21 Journal of Medical Ethics 345

Warnock, M, *Report of the Committee of Inquiry into Human Fertilisation and Embryology*. Cmnd 9314 (London, HMSO, 1984).

SECTION 1

Legal Regulation, Policy and Practice

2

Surrogacy Law in the United States: The Outcome of Ambivalence

RADHIKA RAO

NLIKE THE UNITED Kingdom, there is no uniform national position on surrogacy in the United States.[1] Instead, surrogacy is governed by a patchwork of disparate state laws which fall into essentially four broad categories of legal policy: (1) prohibition; (2) inaction; (3) status regulation; and (4) contractual ordering.[2] Under the first approach, the state attempts to put an end to surrogacy, either by means of an outright ban on the practice or by imposing civil and criminal penalties on persons who enter into or facilitate surrogacy contracts. The second approach consists of a struggle to maintain the status quo: the state seeks to withdraw its support by refusing to enforce surrogacy contracts and by declining to prescribe specific rules governing the allocation of parental rights and responsibilities in this context. Under the third approach, individuals may enter into state-approved surrogacy contracts that contain mandatory terms and create preordained status relationships. This allows the state to channel surrogacy into particularly favoured forms and to encourage voluntary compliance with its regulations by facilitating legal recognition of those surrogacy arrangements that comply with the statutory requirements. This is in contrast to the fourth approach, in which the state agnostically enforces whatever individual agreements are negotiated in the free market, limiting its own role (if any) to that of enacting regulations designed to provide complete information and ensure true consent.

---

[1] In the past, several Bills were introduced in the House of Representatives that would have prohibited commercial surrogacy, but none to date have been enacted into law by Congress, thus there is no federal law on the subject of surrogacy. Even the National Conference of Commissioners on Uniform State Laws was unable to achieve any nationwide consensus on the issue. The statute that they ultimately approved, the Uniform Status of Children of Assisted Conception Act (the USCACA), sets forth two radically different and inconsistent approaches to surrogacy: one alternative would make surrogacy contracts void and unenforceable, while the other alternative would enforce surrogacy contracts so long as they comply with the statutory requirements. The choice between these two alternatives is left to the individual states, which are entirely free to adopt either version of the uniform statute or to reject both alternatives altogether.

[2] For a detailed description of several models of state policy in the surrogacy context, see US Congress, Office of Technology Assessment, *Infertility: Medical and Social Choices* (1988).

1. PROHIBITION

A few jurisdictions flatly prohibit all surrogacy, whether for compensation or not,[3] though it is unclear whether a blanket prohibition that is unaccompanied by civil sanctions or criminal penalties differs in any significant respect from the mere refusal by the state to enforce surrogacy contracts. More common are the statutes that proscribe only commercial surrogacy;[4] a number of these also impose civil sanctions or criminal penalties upon those who participate in or procure such agreements.[5]

In order to determine the legal limitations upon state actions that purport to prohibit or regulate surrogacy, it is first necessary to understand the parameters of the constitutional right of privacy. Although the US Constitution does not expressly guarantee any right to privacy, such a right has been found to be implicit in the Constitution; it has been variously located in the Due Process Clause of the Fourteenth Amendment,[6] the Ninth Amendment,[7] and the penumbras and emanations surrounding several other specific provisions of the Bill of Rights.[8] This constitutional right of privacy originated in the protection afforded to parental rights of child-rearing.[9] It has evolved into a right invoked

[3] See, eg Ariz. Rev. Stat. Ann. 25–218(A) (1995) (prohibiting all persons from entering into, assisting, or arranging surrogate parentage contracts, agreements, or arrangements); DC Code Ann. 16–401, 402 (1996) (prohibiting surrogate parenting contracts); Ind. Code Ann. 31–8–2–1 (West (1996)) (prohibiting surrogacy agreements which require a surrogate to provide a gamete, become pregnant, undergo abortion, waive parental rights, or consent to adoption).

[4] See, eg Ky. Rev. Stat. Ann. 199.590 (4) (Baldwin (1996)); La. Rev. Stat. Ann. 9:2713 (West (1997)); Mich. Comp. Laws. Ann. 722.859 (West (1993)); Neb. Rev. Stat. 25–21,200 (1995); NY Dom. Rel. 123 (McKinney Supp. 1997–98); Utah Code Ann. 76–7–204(1) (1995); Wash. Rev. Code Ann. 26.26.230 (West (1997)).

[5] Participation in or procurement of a surrogacy arrangement constitutes a civil offence in the District of Columbia, with a maximum penalty of $10,000 in fines and imprisonment for one year. DC Code Ann. 16–402. In Michigan, it is a misdemeanour to enter into a surrogacy contract, punishable by up to $10,000 in fines and up to one year in prison, and a felony to facilitate a surrogacy contract, punishable by up to $50,000 in fines and five years in prison. Mich. Comp. Laws Ann. 722.859. New York requires parties to such contracts to pay a civil penalty of up to $500, while those who broker such contracts must forfeit their fees and pay fines of up to $10,000 for the first offence, and may be guilty of a felony for subsequent offences. NY Dom. Rel. 123(2), (3). Utah makes it a class B misdemeanor and Washington makes it a gross misdemeanour to engage in or induce paid surrogacy. Utah Code Ann. 76–7–204, Wash. Rev. Code Ann. 26.26.230. In addition, as part of comprehensive statutes regulating surrogacy, New Hampshire and Virginia also forbid surrogacy brokerage, making it a misdemeanour to induce or solicit anyone to enter into a paid surrogacy arrangement. NH Rev. Stat. Ann. 168–B:16 (IV), 168-B:30 (II); Va. Code Ann. 20–165(A).

[6] See *Griswold v Connecticut* 381 U.S. 479, 500 (1965) (Harlan, J concurring) (grounding the constitutional right of privacy in the Fourteenth Amendment's Due Process Clause, which provides: '[N]or shall any State deprive any person of life, liberty, or property, without due process of law').

[7] See *ibid* at 499 (Goldberg, J, concurring) (finding support for an unenumerated constitutional right of privacy in the Ninth Amendment, which provides that '[t]he enumeration in the Constitution, of certain rights, shall not be construed to deny or disparage others retained by the people').

[8] See *ibid* at 484 (Douglas, J) (locating the constitutional right of privacy in the penumbras and emanations surrounding the First, Third, Fourth, Fifth, and Ninth Amendments).

[9] See, eg, *Pierce v Society of Sisters*, 268 U.S. 510 (1925); *Meyer v Nebraska* 262 U.S. 390 (1923).

in a wide range of cases involving individuals who seek to marry,[10] to form a family,[11] to procreate[12] or not to procreate,[13] to serve as parents,[14] to rear children,[15] and to engage in sexual activity.[16]

It follows that any law that purports to prohibit individuals from engaging in the underlying acts involved in surrogacy, such as inducing pregnancy by artificial insemination or sexual intercourse, carrying the pregnancy to term, and delivering the resulting child, is constitutionally problematic. Such intimate activities fall within the ambit of the amorphous right to privacy and thus may merit constitutional protection, at least when they occur within the context of marriage or a similarly intimate relationship, rather than as part of a commercial transaction between complete strangers.[17]

However, statutes that prohibit *commercial* surrogacy appear to be entirely constitutional to the extent that they simply prevent the contractual exchange of parental rights or preclude payment for such services. Several state courts have upheld laws that prohibit commercial surrogacy, proffering these and other rationales. In *Doe v Kelley*,[18] for example, the court considered the constitutionality of a Michigan statute prohibiting the exchange of money in connection with adoption. A married couple challenged the law on the grounds that it interfered with their right to reproduce by means of surrogacy, but the court found the law to be constitutional because it did not forbid conception of a child—it merely precluded the payment of consideration to transfer parental rights over the child:

> While the decision to bear or beget a child [is] a fundamental interest protected by the right of privacy, we do not view this right as a valid prohibition to state interference in the [parties'] contractual arrangement. The statute . . . does not directly prohibit John Doe and Mary Roe from having the child as planned. It acts instead to preclude plaintiffs from paying consideration . . . to change the legal status of the child. . . . We do not perceive this goal as within the realm of fundamental interests protected by the right to privacy from reasonable governmental regulation.[19]

In another case, *In re Paul*,[20] a New York court upheld a similar statute, basing its decision upon precisely the same rationale. *Doe v Attorney General*[21] likewise determined that a subsequent Michigan statute expressly outlawing paid

[10] See *Zablocki v Redhail*, 434 U.S. 374 (1978); *Loving v Virginia*, 388 U.S. 1 (1967).
[11] See, eg, *Moore v City of East Cleveland*, 431 U.S. 94 (1977).
[12] See *Skinner v Oklahoma*, 316 U.S. 535 (1942).
[13] See, eg *Planned Parenthood v Casey*, 505 U.S. 833 (1992); *Roe v Wade*, 410 U.S. 113 (1973); *Eisenstadt v Baird*, 405 U.S. 438 (1972); *Griswold v Connecticut*, 381 U.S. 479 (1965).
[14] See, eg *Lehr v Robertson*, 463 U.S. 248 (1983); *Santosky v Kramer*, 455 U.S. 745 (1982); *Quilloin v Walcott*, 434 U.S. 246 (1978); *Stanley v Illinois*, 405 U.S. 645 (1972).
[15] See, eg *Wisconsin v Yoder*, 405 U.S. 205 (1972).
[16] See *Bowers v Hardwick*, 478 U.S. 186 (1986).
[17] See Rao (1998:1077).
[18] 307 N.W.2d 438 (Mich. Ct. App. 1981).
[19] *Ibid* at 441.
[20] 550 N.Y.S.2d 815 (Fam. Ct. 1990).
[21] 487 N.W.2d 484 (Mich. Ct. App. 1992).

surrogacy was also constitutional, though for a different reason. The court conceded that the statute encroached upon the constitutionally protected zone of privacy, which guarantees 'freedom from government interference in matters of marriage, family, procreation, and intimate association.'[22] Concluding that 'there are compelling interests sufficient to warrant governmental intrusion into the otherwise protected area of privacy in the matter of procreation,' however, the court upheld the statute as narrowly tailored to achieve the state's interests in protecting the best interests of children, preventing them from becoming commodities, and precluding the exploitation of women.[23]

The only decision to date holding that constitutional privacy actually protects the right to enter into and enforce surrogacy contracts is the discredited trial court opinion *In re Baby M*.[24] In that opinion, which was later overturned by the New Jersey Supreme Court, Judge Sorkow reasoned: 'if one has a right to procreate coitally, then one has the right to reproduce non-coitally. If it is the reproduction that is protected, then the means of reproduction are also to be protected.'[25] Therefore, although 'a state could regulate . . . the circumstances under which parties enter into reproductive contracts, it could not ban or refuse to enforce such transactions altogether without compelling reason.'[26] To the contrary, the court suggested that a state's prohibition of money payments or refusal to enforce surrogacy contracts would unconstitutionally interfere with the procreative liberty of childless couples, which falls within the protected realm of privacy.[27]

2. INACTION

Although a number of states have proscribed and even criminalised surrogacy, the dominant attitude across the country appears to be one of passive resistance—state courts find surrogacy contracts to be legal but unenforceable, and state legislatures fail to prescribe specific rules governing the allocation of parental rights and responsibilities in this context. As a result, courts must look to background principles of family law to assign parental rights when a surrogacy arrangement sours. The paradigm example of this approach is *In re Baby M*,[28] where the New Jersey Supreme Court declined to enforce a contract that required a woman to be artificially inseminated, to carry her pregnancy to term, and to surrender her child at birth to the biological father in exchange for a fee of $10,000, concluding that surrogacy contracts are void and unenforceable as

---

[22]   487 N.W.2d 484 (Mich. Ct. App. 1992), at 486.
[23]   *Ibid* at 486–88.
[24]   525 A.2d 1128 (NJ Super. Ct. Ch. Div. 1987).
[25]   *Ibid* at 1164.
[26]   *Ibid*.
[27]   See *ibid* at 1163–64.
[28]   537 A.2d 1227 (NJ 1988).

contrary to New Jersey law and public policy. Almost all of the statutes regulating surrogacy adopt this approach in some form or another, making surrogacy agreements legally ineffectual under certain circumstances. Seven jurisdictions refuse to enforce *any* surrogacy contracts, even those that do not involve the exchange of money.[29] Paid surrogacy agreements are deemed void and thus without legal effect in four more states.[30] And even in the states that recognise and respect the right to enter into surrogacy arrangements, contracts that fail to conform to the statutory requirements are rendered unenforceable under state law.[31]

The inaction approach—in which the state allows individuals to engage in the acts underlying surrogacy but withdraws its support by refusing to enforce the terms of their contract—also appears consistent with constitutional doctrine, which generally distinguishes between negative and positive rights, here the negative right to be free from government interference with procreation and the positive right to call upon the apparatus of the state for assistance in procreation.[32] The United States Supreme Court has drawn a similar distinction in the context of abortion, holding that the constitutional right to be free from government interference with abortion does not impose any affirmative obligation upon the government to provide the financial resources necessary to exercise the right by subsidising abortions.[33] But if government need not supply the *financial* resources necessary to exercise the right to procreate, then it would seem that government need not supply the *judicial* resources necessary to exercise the right by enforcing surrogacy contracts, either.

More fundamentally, if the constitutional right to procreate did require court enforcement of surrogacy contracts, recognition of such an expansive right to procreate would diminish other constitutional rights and disregard the constitutional rights of others. As a result, the right to reproduce does not necessarily entail the right to rear one's biological child. This was the conclusion reached by the New Jersey Supreme Court in *In re Baby M*, which rejected the biological

---

[29] They include Arizona, the District of Columbia, Indiana, Michigan, New York, North Dakota, and Utah. See, eg Ariz. Rev. Stat. Ann. 25–218(A); D.C. Code Ann. 16–401; Ind. Code Ann. 31–8–2–1; Mich. Comp. Laws Ann. 722.855; NY Com. Rel. 122; N.D. Cent. Code 14–18–05 (1995); Utah Code Ann. 76–7–204(1), (2).

[30] The four states are Kentucky, Louisiana, Nebraska, and Washington. See Ky. Rev. Stat. Ann. 199.590 (4); La. Rev. Stat. Ann. 9:2713; Neb. Rev. Stat. 25–21,200; Wash. Rev. Code Ann. 26.26.240.

[31] Florida, New Hampshire, Nevada, and Virginia all fall into this category. See, eg Fla. Stat. Ann. 742.16 (West 1996); N.H. Rev. Stat. Ann. 168-B:23 (1995); Nev. Rev. Stat. Ann. 126.045(2); Va. Code Ann. 20–162(A).

[32] See Rao (1995:1485–86).

[33] See, eg *Harris v McRae*, 448 U.S. 297, 316 (1980) (holding that the constitutional right to abortion does not impose an affirmative obligation upon the government to subsidise abortions because 'although government may not place obstacles in the path of a woman's exercise of her freedom of choice, it need not remove those not of its own creation'); *Maher v Roe*, 432 U.S. 464, 473–74 (1977) (holding that the constitutional right to an abortion is only a negative 'right protect[ing] the woman from . . . interference with her freedom to decide whether to terminate her pregnancy. It implies no limitation on the authority of a State to make a value judgment favoring childbirth over abortion, and to implement that judgment by the allocation of public funds').

father's argument that his right to procreate entitled him to enforcement of the surrogacy contract, stating:

> We find that the right of procreation does not extend as far as claimed . . . The right to procreate very simply is the right to have natural children, whether through sexual intercourse or artificial insemination. It is no more than that. Mr Stern has not been deprived of that right. Through artificial insemination of Mrs Whitehead, Baby M is his child. The custody, care, companionship, and nurturing that follow birth are not parts of the right to procreation.[34]

The court proceeded to balance the parties' competing interests, ruling that a biological father's right to procreate cannot extend so far as to deprive the biological mother of her own right of procreation:

> To assert that Mr Stern's right of procreation gives him the right to the custody of Baby M would be to assert that Mrs Whitehead's right of procreation does not give her the right to the custody of Baby M; it would be to assert that the constitutional right of procreation includes within it a constitutionally protected contractual right to destroy someone else's right of procreation.[35]

In this case, protecting the parental rights of one procreator would deny the parental rights of the other procreator. Thus the court suggested that constitutional rights are qualified by their effects upon the interests of other parties, concluding that '[t]here is nothing in our culture or society that even begins to suggest a fundamental right on the part of the father to the custody of the child as part of his right to procreate when opposed by the claim of the mother to the same child.'[36] By refusing to enforce the surrogacy contract, moreover, the court obviated the need to address the biological mother's counterclaim that enforcement would violate her own constitutional right to the companionship of her child.[37] Instead, the court adjudicated the case as if it were a custody dispute over a coitally produced child, holding that the child's best interests required that she reside with her biological father, while awarding visitation rights to her biological mother.[38]

3. STATUS REGULATION

Some states have enacted comprehensive statutes that recognise and regulate surrogacy, authorising court-approved surrogacy contracts that contain mandatory terms and create preordained status relationships.[39] Most of these

---

[34]   537 A.2d at 1253.
[35]   *Ibid.*
[36]   *Ibid* at 1254.
[37]   See *ibid* at 1255.
[38]   See *ibid* at 1261–63.
[39]   These states include Florida, New Hampshire, and Virginia. See, eg Fla. Stat. Ann. 742.16 (West 1996); N.H. Rev. Stat. Ann. 168-B:23 (1995); Va. Code Ann. 20–162(A) (Michie 1995).

laws set limits upon the age[40] and marital status[41] of the parties to a surrogacy arrangement, require the intending mother to be incapable of gestating a pregnancy without physical risk to herself or the fetus,[42] and mandate that the parties be physically fit and psychologically suitable to parent a child.[43] By favouring surrogacy arrangements that satisfy these conditions,[44] such statutes systematically channel surrogacy into certain avenues, attempting to mould surrogacy into a form that closely resembles adoption. Unlike adoption, however, many of these statutes valorise genetic ties, enforcing surrogacy contracts only when at least one of the intending parents possesses a genetic connection to the child.[45] However, by limiting compensation to expenses actually incurred by the surrogate, by requiring the intending couple to undergo a home study to determine whether they will be suitable parents, and by guaranteeing the opportunity for the surrogate to change her mind and retain parental rights under certain circumstances, these laws clearly structure surrogacy along the lines of adoption.

[40] Florida requires all parties to be at least 18 years old, while New Hampshire sets a minimum age of 21 years. Fla. Stat. Ann. 742.15 (1); N.H. Rev. Stat. Ann. 168-B:17(I).

[41] Virginia mandates that all parties to a surrogacy contract be married, while Florida and New Hampshire require only the intending parents to be married. Va. Code Ann. 20–160; Fla. Stat. Ann. 742.15(1); N.H. Rev. Stat. Ann. 168-B:21(II).

[42] The Florida, New Hampshire, and Virginia statutes all contain some variant of this condition. See Fla. Stat. Ann. 742.15(2); N.H. Rev. Stat. Ann. 168-B:17; Va. Code Ann. 20–160B(8).

[43] Florida requires only the surrogate 'to submit to reasonable medical evaluation and treatment,' Fla. Stat. Ann. 742.15(3), while Virginia compels not only the surrogate mother, but also her husband and the intended parents to submit to both physical examinations and psychological evaluations by licensed practitioners, mandating that the records of these examinations be made available to the court and all of the parties, Va. Code Ann. 20–160B(7). New Hampshire goes even further, demanding that all of the parties undergo a 'nonmedical evaluation' by a licensed psychiatrist, psychologist, pastoral counsellor or social worker and specifying that this evaluation 'shall determine the party's suitability to parent' by considering not only '[t]he ability and disposition of the person being evaluated to give a child love, affection and guidance,' but also '[t]he ability of the person to adjust to and assume the inherent risks of the contract.' N.H. Rev. Stat. Ann. 168-B:18. In addition, both New Hampshire and Virginia call for home studies to ensure that all parties will make suitable parents for the child. See N.H. Rev. Stat. Ann. 168-B:18; Va. Code Ann. 20–160B(2).

[44] Florida offers an expedited affirmation of parental status for surrogacy contracts that satisfy the statutory conditions. Under the Florida statute, within three days after birth of the child, if the court determines that a binding and enforceable surrogacy contract has been entered in compliance with the statute, 'the court shall enter an order stating that the commissioning couple are the legal parents of the child.' Fla. Stat. Ann. 742.16(6). New Hampshire permits judicial preauthorisation of surrogacy agreements and provides that 'the effect of a judicial order validating the surrogacy agreement shall be the automatic termination of the parental rights of the surrogate and her husband, if any, after the birth of a child born as a result of the arrangement and a vesting of those rights solely in the intended parents,' unless the surrogate exercises her statutory right to change her mind and keep the child within 72 hours after birth. N.H. Rev. Stat. Ann. 168-B:23(IV). Virginia allows the parties to petition in court for approval of a surrogacy contract; birth pursuant to a court-approved surrogacy contract means that 'the intended parents are the parents of any resulting child,' unless the surrogate exercises her right to terminate the contract within 180 days after the last attempt at assisted conception, in which case she and her husband will be deemed the legal parents of the child. Va. Code Ann. 20–158(D).

[45] The Florida, New Hampshire, and Virginia statutes all contain this condition. Fla. Stat. Ann. 742.16(6); N.H. Rev. Stat. Ann. 168-B:17; Va. Code Ann. 20–160B(9).

There are as yet no cases challenging the constitutionality of these statutes, but it is likely that any constitutional challenges would fail. These laws appear to be entirely constitutional because they do not even proscribe surrogacy. At worst, they simply refuse to enforce surrogacy contracts that do not comply with the statutory requirements, while at best, they actually authorise and enforce state-approved surrogacy contracts, subject to mandatory terms guaranteeing the surrogate the right to change her mind and retain parental rights.

4. CONTRACTUAL ORDERING

In the absence of government prohibitions upon surrogacy, refusal to enforce surrogacy contracts, or enforcement of court-approved contracts subject to status regulation, what remains would appear to be a system of contractual ordering in which the parties are entirely free to negotiate their rights and responsibilities under the surrogacy contract. Only one state—the state of Nevada—actually comes close to such a result by enacting a law that states '[t]wo persons whose marriage is valid [under Nevada law] may enter into a contract with a surrogate for assisted conception,' so long as the agreement specifies parentage, custody of the child, and the respective rights and responsibilities of each party.[46] The statute provides that '[a] person identified as an intended parent in [such] a contract . . . must be treated in law as a natural parent under all circumstances.'[47] In so doing, it appears to authorise enforcement of any terms of the contract to which the parties agree, rather than ordaining in advance the results of all surrogacy contracts. Even in Nevada, however, this system of contractual ordering is disconnected from the demands of the market, because the statute simultaneously makes it 'unlawful to pay or offer to pay money or anything of value to the surrogate except for the medical and necessary living expenses related to the birth of the child.'[48] Moreover, no state actually permits enforcement of a surrogacy contract that is completely governed by the will of the parties. For example, it is unlikely that even Nevada would go so far as to enforce a contract that would require a surrogate to carry the pregnancy to term or force her to have an abortion upon request of the parties who intend to rear the child, for such a consequence would likely be unconstitutional. And although other states appear to achieve outcomes that are identical in their effect to enforcement of the surrogacy contract, they generally reach this result by applying principles of family law—which are largely status-based—rather than principles of contract law.

One of the foremost examples of such an approach is *Johnson v Calvert*,[49] in which the California Supreme Court confronted the question, who is the mother

[46] Nev. Rev. Stat. Ann. 126.045(1) (Michie 1995).
[47] Nev. Rev. Stat. Ann. 126.045(2).
[48] Nev. Rev. Stat. Ann. 126.045(3).
[49] 851 P.2d 776 (Cal. 1993).

of a child conceived from the egg of one woman but gestated in the womb of another pursuant to a gestational surrogacy contract? Faced with such a conflict, the Court ruled that the woman who intended to parent the child was the child's mother under California law,[50] achieving exactly the same result that it would have reached had it enforced the surrogacy contract. The Court rejected the gestational mother's argument that this result deprived her of her constitutional right to the companionship of her child on the grounds that '[s]ociety has not traditionally protected the right of a woman who gestates and delivers a baby pursuant to an agreement with a couple who supply the zygote from which the baby develops and who intend to raise the child as their own.'[51] Indeed, '[t]o the extent that tradition has a bearing on the present case,' the Court declared, 'it supports the claim of the couple who exercise their right to procreate in order to form a family of their own, albeit through novel medical procedures.'[52] The *Johnson* court acknowledged the clash between the competing constitutional interests of the parties and concluded that protecting the rights of the gestational mother would necessarily diminish the rights of the child's genetic parents: '[I]f we were to conclude that Anna enjoys some sort of liberty interest in the companionship of the child, then the liberty interests of Mark and Crispina, the child's natural parents, in their procreative choices and their relationship with the child would perforce be infringed.'[53] The Court also suggested that the choice to enter into a surrogacy contract is not part of the right to privacy, but merely the provision of a commercial service:

> [T]he choice to gestate and deliver a baby for its genetic parents pursuant to a surrogacy agreement is [not] the equivalent, in constitutional weight, of the decision whether to bear a child of one's own. . . . A woman who enters into a gestational surrogacy arrangement is not exercising her own right to make procreative choices; she is agreeing to provide a necessary and profoundly important service without (by definition) any expectation that she will raise the resulting child as her own.[54]

The Court's statement intimates that privacy does not protect an individual's right to enter into surrogacy contracts to the extent that such contracts embody commercial transactions rather than intimate associations.

5. CONCLUSION

The dominant approach towards surrogacy in the United States appears to be neither outright prohibition nor unequivocal permission, but rather passive resistance, where the state seeks to withdraw its support by refusing to enforce

---

[50] See *ibid* at 782.
[51] *Ibid* at 786.
[52] *Ibid*.
[53] *Ibid*.
[54] *Ibid* at 787.

surrogacy contracts and by declining to enact specific rules that would allocate parental rights and responsibilities. Even the statutes that simply prohibit surrogacy without imposing civil sanctions or criminal penalties are consistent with this pattern to the extent that they rely upon the state's refusal to enforce surrogacy contracts. Such an approach reveals a profound ambivalence in the American attitude towards surrogacy.

Surrogacy is fraught with contradictions in terms of its potential impact upon individual liberty, equality, and the family, and these contradictory impulses produce ambivalence. Surrogacy contracts not only pit the value of liberty against the principle of equality, but they also expose a deeper conflict over the very meaning of liberty and equality. On the one hand, surrogacy contracts may be seen to advance individual liberty—the liberty of those women who freely choose to sell their reproductive services, and the liberty of infertile couples who wish to conceive and rear biological children.[55] At the same time, surrogacy contracts may be seen to undermine individual liberty—the liberty of those women who feel compelled to enter into surrogacy contracts because of desperate financial or familial circumstances, and perhaps the liberty of infertile persons who feel pressured by their partners to accept surrogacy rather than turn to other methods of child-rearing, such as adoption. Similarly, surrogacy may empower women and enhance gender equality by allowing some women to use their reproductive capacity to earn money, while affording other women the opportunity to purchase gestational services on the market.[56] Yet surrogacy may also diminish gender equality by exploiting women, particularly those who are relatively poor and powerless, and by reinforcing women's primary role as that of child bearer, reducing women to their wombs and perpetuating patriarchy.[57] Surrogacy may even contribute to other forms of inequality to the extent that it commodifies children and reflects and reinforces racial and other hierarchies.[58]

Surrogacy also contains contradictory consequences for the family. On the one hand, surrogacy appears to reinforce the traditional family by allowing infertile married couples to create biologically-related children. On the other hand, surrogacy possesses the potential radically to destabilise and disrupt the traditional conception of the family. At the most obvious level, surrogacy

[55] See Robertson (1994: 16) (arguing that procreative liberty protects 'the freedom to decide whether or not to have offspring and to control the use of one's reproductive capacity').
[56] See Shalev (1989: 12) (arguing that it is consistent with feminism for women to be able to use their reproductive capacity to earn money and power); Shultz (1990: 303) (arguing that rules which look to individual intentions to determine the legal parents of children born of assisted reproduction enhance gender equality).
[57] See Raymond (1993) (arguing that technological and contractual reproduction result in the reproductive exploitation of women and undermine women's right to equality); Rothman (1989); Sherwin (1992).
[58] See Roberts (1996); Roberts (1995); Ikemoto (1996) (exploring ways in which infertility discourse constructs boundaries that divide women into different categories and oppress women of colour, poor women, and lesbians in different ways).

enables the formation of families by gay men, lesbians, and single people, visibly assaulting the traditional image of the two-parent, heterosexual, biologically-connected family. But even when employed by heterosexual married couples to produce families identical in all respects to the conventional model, surrogacy may insidiously undermine the traditional paradigm from within in three fundamental and potentially far-reaching ways.[59] First, surrogacy threatens the traditional understanding of families as the mere reflection of biological facts, revealing that they are instead social constructs.[60] Secondly, surrogacy destroys the traditional opposition between the family and the market by assembling families in the commercial exchange of reproductive goods and services on the marketplace, rather than forging them from the loving interchange of those entwined in close relationships.[61] And, in so doing, surrogacy contracts promote a world of private ordering, where family ties are not automatically assigned by biology, but are instead a matter of individual choice, and thus contingent and revocable.[62]

The result of all these contradictions is an impasse: state inaction. The inaction approach embodies the American ambivalence towards surrogacy: it is an attempt to permit surrogacy while simultaneously discouraging it by creating a regime in which those who enter into surrogacy contracts do so at their own peril, without any of the protections provided by state enforcement of other types of contracts. Whether such an approach ultimately succeeds in containing or limiting the incidence of surrogacy, or whether instead inaction becomes tantamount to tacit acceptance of surrogacy, remains to be seen.

REFERENCES

Ikemoto, LC, 'The In/Fertile, the Too Fertile, and the Dysfertile' (1996) 47 *Hastings Law Journal* 1007.
Rao, R, 'Constitutional Misconceptions' (1995) 93 *Michigan Law Review* 1473.
—— 'Assisted reproductive technology and the threat to the traditional family' (1996) 47 *Hastings Law Journal* 951.
—— 'Reconceiving privacy: relationships and reproductive technology' (1998) 45 *UCLA Law Review* 1077.
Raymond, JG, *Women as Wombs: Reproductive Technologies and the Battle Over Women's Freedom* (San Francisco, Harper, 1993).
Roberts, DE, 'The Genetic Tie' (1995) 62 *University of Chicago Law Review* 209.
—— 'Race and the New Reproduction' (1996) 47 *Hastings Law Journal* 935.
Robertson, JA, *Children of Choice: Freedom and the New Reproductive Technologies* (Princeton, Princeton University Press, 1994).

[59] See Rao (1996).
[60] See *ibid*.
[61] See *ibid*.
[62] See *ibid*.

Rothman, BK, *Recreating Motherhood: Ideology and Technology in a Patriarchal Society* (New York, WW Norton & Co, 1989).

Shalev, C, *Birth Power: The Case for Surrogacy* (New Haven and London, Yale University Press, 1989).

Sherwin, S, *No Longer Patient: Feminist Ethics and Health Care* (Philadelphia, PA, Temple University Press, 1992).

Shultz, MM, 'Reproductive Technology and Intent-Based Parenthood: An Opportunity for Gender Neutrality' (1990) *Wisconsin Law Review* 297.

US Congress, Office of Technology Assessment, *Infertility: Medical and Social Choices* (1988).

3

Surrogacy in Israel: An Analysis of the Law in Practice[1]

RHONA SCHUZ

1. INTRODUCTION

SINCE ISRAEL IS one of the first countries in the world to have introduced a fully fledged regulatory regime for approving surrogate motherhood agreements,[2] other countries which are considering following the same path can learn much from the Israeli experience in devising and implementing the scheme over the last seven years.[3] This essay assumes that the justification for state intervention in surrogate motherhood agreements is the need to protect those who may be affected by the surrogacy arrangement—the birth mother, the intended parents, the child to be born, and the public ('the groups'). Protection given to one group, however, may affect the interests of others. Thus, it is submitted that the test of the success of the Israeli regulatory regime is the extent to which it provides the optimal measure of protection for each group while achieving the right balance between the interests and rights of each group.

This chapter examines the Israeli scheme, the way in which it has been implemented, and the practice of the statutory Committee for Approving Surrogate Motherhood Agreements (the 'Approvals Committee').[4] We discuss the protection offered to each group and then examine the main areas of tension between the interests and rights of each group.

[1] I wish to express my thanks to my research assistants who helped on this project—Emily Cooper, Tirza Shaw and Orly Yaakov. I am also grateful to two former students, Esty Shemama and Amir Chantzinski for obtaining the relevant documentation from the Ministry of Health while preparing seminar papers. The research was funded by Law Faculty of Bar Ilan University, Israel.

[2] For the historical and cultural background to this legislation, see Schuz (1998:237–56), Shalev (1998) and Halperin-Kaddari, (1999). The latter article makes comparisons between the Israeli scheme and those in New Hampshire and Virginia which preceded it.

[3] Statistics relating to the use of the scheme are set out in Appendix 1.

[4] The Approvals Committee consists of seven members: two physicians who are specialists in childbirth and gynaecology, one physician who is a specialist in internal medicine, a clinical psychologist, a social worker, a representative of the public with legal training and a cleric in accordance with the religion of the parties. At least three of the members must be male and three female.

2. THE STRUCTURE OF THE ISRAELI SURROGACY SCHEME

The structure of the scheme can best be seen from a brief description of the main sources on which the scheme is based and the bodies involved in its implementation.

In 1992 the Aloni Commission ('the Commission') was established to consider the social, ethical, legal and religious law implications of fertility treatments involving *in vitro* fertilisation (IVF) in Israel. Reporting in 1994, their main recommendation was that surrogate motherhood through IVF should be allowed, but should be regulated primarily by the need to obtain *a priori* approval from a statutory body. This liberal recommendation reflected the belief of the majority of the Commission that principles of 'autonomy' and 'privacy' require minimum state interference in human reproduction (para 1.A.5). The Surrogate Motherhood Agreements (Approval of Agreement and Status of Newborn) Law 5756—1996 ('the Law') while adopting the Commission's recommendation for approval of agreements (para 1.B.7.4–5), diverges from the views of the majority in relation to a number of important issues. In particular, whilst the Commission envisaged that surrogacy would be largely 'altruistic' (para 1.B. 7.19–24),[5] the effect of the Law is that surrogacy will invariably occur on a commercial basis. For example, the Law prohibits relatives of the intended parents to serve as birth mothers. Further, while the Commission envisaged that the birth mother would be reimbursed for financial expenses and losses incurred during the process, but not receive any actual payments, (para 1.B. 7.23), the Law allows payments to compensate her for her time and suffering. Other fundamental differences are that the Law does not allow partial surrogacy[6] and that, while the majority of the Commission recommended that the handing over of the child to the intended parents should be sufficient to determine her/his status as their child (para 1.B. 7.31), the Law requires a parentage order to be made by a court.

In accordance with the Law, regulations were published dealing with the technical aspects of implementation of the Law and including standard forms for completion by the parties before and after the birth.[7]

The Approvals Committee has issued Guidelines to Applicants, which details the documents which have to be submitted, the forms which have to be completed and conditions which have to be included in the contract. As these

---

[5] Surrogacy is considered altruistic where the main motive of the birth mother is to help the intended couple, and non-altruistic where the main motive of the birth mother is financial gain. Usually surrogacy will only be altruistic where the birth mother is a relative or very close friend of the couple.

[6] Partial surrogacy is where the egg of the birth mother is fertilised by the sperm of the intended father, usually by Donor Insemination, whereas in full surrogacy the egg is that of the intended mother or a third party donor.

[7] The Notices, Requests and Orders Regulations 1998 (by the Minister for Employment) and the Welfare and the Registration Regulations 1998 (by the Minister of Justice).

requirements are not legally binding, the Approvals Committee has discretion to waive them and they may be judicially reviewed. Interestingly, some of the Approvals Committee's requirements and practices[8] seem to have been introduced in the light of negative experiences in the early surrogate motherhood arrangements.[9]

Shortly after the introduction of the surrogacy scheme in Israel, a number of commercial agencies were set up offering a wide range of services to intended parents including finding a suitable birth mother, assisting in the negotiation of an agreement, obtaining approval from the Approvals Committee, and on-going counselling and support to all parties until after the birth.[10] However, it seems that most of these agencies have been forced to close down because of lack of clientele.[11] One explanation for this may be the high fee demanded by these agencies compared with that demanded by the public IVF Centre at Rambam Hospital in Haifa.[12] While this centre does not actually find birth mothers for intended couples, it screens candidates brought by the couple and is involved in preparing the application for the Approvals Committee.[13] Social workers at the centre then accompany all the parties throughout the whole process. Another explanation for the closure of the private agencies is the substantial reduction in the number of intended couples showing an interest in surrogacy in the last couple of years.[14] This reduction appears to reflect the fact that in the first years after the enactment of the Law, surrogacy was seen as a solution to all those couples who had been infertile for many years. Now that these couples have either successfully entered into surrogacy agreements or discovered that it is not suitable for them, the initial 'boom' is over.

---

[8] Information about these practices was obtained through interviews with members of the Approvals Committee and with lawyers who have experience of obtaining approval from the Committee as well as from interviews appearing in the press.

[9] The first surrogate birth in March 1998 received a bad press. The intended parents complained about the birth mother's alleged instability, and the birth mother complained, on the one hand, of having been 'emotionally suffocated' by the intended parents and, on the other, of not having received sufficient support, particularly at the time of and after the birth. The difficulties of the relationship between the parties were exacerbated by the fact that the parents, concerned about the birth mother's poor financial situation and her difficulty in coping with the twin pregnancy, brought her to live in an annex to their house. Both in this case and another early case there were disputes about the sums due to the birth mother (Harel (1998)) and (Kaplan Sommer (2000)).

[10] See Kost (1997).

[11] This information is based on interviews with lawyers and social workers who work in the field and on unsuccessful attempts to contact the agencies.

[12] Around $8,000 as compared with $500.

[13] See interview with Ronit Gagin, director of the social work department at Haifa's Rambam Hospital (Kaplan Sommer, 2000:17).

[14] This phenomenon was confirmed to us by a worker at the centre at Rambam Hospital (who said that the number of couples approaching the centre had dropped from around 18 per month in the first two years after the scheme was introduced to around 4 per month in 2001), by lawyers and by the Secretary of the Approvals Committee.

3. PROTECTING THE BIRTH MOTHER

Perhaps the major concern of opponents of non-altruistic surrogacy,[15] particularly feminists, is that it constitutes 'exploitation' of vulnerable women, often in difficult financial circumstances (Shalev, 1998). The Israeli legislature clearly prefers the ideology of autonomy over this paternalistic approach.[16] Nonetheless, it is clear that one of the main *raisons d'être* of the regulatory scheme is to provide safeguards for the birth mother. Protection for the birth mother is provided by ensuring (1) her suitability (2) that her consent is voluntary and fully informed (3) protection for her physical and mental health (4) protection of her right to privacy and (5) financial protection.

Ensuring her Suitability

Part of the rationale behind regulation is that potential birth mothers are not in a position to judge their own suitability to act as birth mothers and thus, for their own protection as well as for the protection of the other parties involved, professional assessment is required. Accordingly, the Law requires that medical opinions and a psychological opinion confirming the birth mother's suitability to participate in the surrogacy procedure be filed together with the application.[17] In addition, the Approvals Committee forms its own impression of the birth mother and determines whether she is suitable.[18]

The Approvals Committee has introduced various restrictions on eligibility of a woman to act as a birth mother, which reflect its views as to suitability. Thus, it provides that a birth mother must be older than 22 and younger than 40, she must not previously have given birth more than five times[19] or have undergone

---

[15] See definition at n 5 above.

[16] We would comment that the consequences of similar paternalism in relation to men would not be acceptable. For example, it may be asked is it not exploitation to allow poor men to undertake work involving health risks (such as certain types of mining)?

[17] However, some scepticism has been expressed as to the value of these opinions. For example, Ronit Gagan, director of the social work department at Haifa's Rambam Hospital commented that most psychologists did not have any expertise in this particular area and were not qualified to determine suitability for surrogacy (Katz (1998)).

[18] We have been told that lack of suitability of the birth mother from a psychological perspective is the main reason why agreements are not approved. This caution may well be a response to the criticism the first problematic surrogacy attracted (see n 9 above). The Law does not include any procedure for reviewing the decision of the Approvals Committee. However, like any other administrative decision it is subject to judicial review in accordance with the principles of administrative law.

[19] Interestingly, the second surrogate mother to give birth in Israel was a forty-year-old divorcee who had five of her own children. According to a newspaper report, there were no complications at any stage, the relationship between the intended parents and the birth mother was excellent and she did not have any feelings of regret (Haaretz (3 May 1998)).

two Caesarian sections. Furthermore, although this is not published in its guidelines the Approvals Committee's practice is to only approve birth mothers who
have previously given birth at least once. This practice might be seen as controversial since the legislature adopted the view of the majority of the Commission
that no such restriction should be made. The reasoning of the majority of the
Commission was not only that such a restriction would unnecessarily limit the
pool of birth mothers, but also that it was undesirable to encourage mothers
of young children to act as birth mothers because of the effect on them of her
carrying a child for someone else (para 1. B. 7.12).

Apparently, the Approvals Committee prefers the minority view that a
woman who has not experienced pregnancy and childbirth cannot imagine
what is involved in handing over the child she has borne to the intended parents.
Thus, not only is the risk of a dispute increased but also the risk to the mental
health of the birth mother. These increased risks make such a woman unsuitable
to act as a birth mother. From a legal point of view, the Approvals Committee's
restriction can be justified on the basis of the requirement in section 5(a)(2) of
the Law that an agreement is only to be approved where the Approvals
Committee is satisfied that there is no risk of harm to the birth mother's health
(Shemama (2001:20)).

Ensuring that her Consent is Voluntary and Fully Informed

The Approvals Committee's guidelines for drawing up the surrogate motherhood agreement start with a clear statement that it is necessary to ensure, so far
as possible, that the birth mother understands the nature of the commitments
involved in the agreement and agrees thereto voluntarily and without coercion.
A number of the Approvals Committee's requirements are designed to further
this end.

First, the physician who examines the birth mother has to declare that s/he
has explained to the birth mother the consequences and significance of acting as
a surrogate including the risk of death, infertility and permanent disability, and
that to the best of the doctor's knowledge, the birth mother understood this.
This declaration is also signed by the birth mother. The agreement itself must
also include a declaration by the birth mother that she has received an explanation from a physician of her choice about the consequences and risks of
surrogacy.

Secondly, the Approvals Committee will not consider any application until it
is satisfied that the birth mother has obtained independent legal advice from a
lawyer who is an expert in surrogate motherhood agreements. The agreement
must provide that the intended parents will pay for this and any further legal
advice required by the birth mother in relation to the surrogacy. Thirdly, the
birth mother is interviewed separately by the Approvals Committee and will be
asked questions designed to test whether her consent is voluntary and

informed.[20] Finally, as we mentioned above, the Approval Committee's practice is only to approve birth mothers who have previously given birth. This practice can also be justified on the basis that a woman who has not previously given birth cannot truly understand the consequences of her commitments and thus cannot give true consent.

Protection for her Physical and Mental Health

In order to safeguard the birth mother's physical health, a medical examination will check that the birth mother is fit to undergo the implantation and carry the baby. Medical examinations of the intended parents include testing for HIV and other infectious diseases that could be communicated to the birth mother through the implanted embryo.[21] The implantation of the embryo has to be carried out at a recognised IVF centre. The Approvals Committee requires that the contract define the maximum period during which attempts at securing a pregnancy will be made (up to a maximum of eighteen months) and the maximum number of attempts (up to a maximum of seven). In addition, the surrogacy agreement should state how many embryos the birth mother is prepared to carry to term.

It is however not just the birth mother's physical health that might be at risk. There is a real danger to the mental health of the birth mother both during the pregnancy and after the birth.[22] The Approvals Committee requires that the agreement include provision for the birth mother and her children to receive psychological counselling throughout the process until six months after the birth at the expense of the intended parents. Protection of the potential birth mother's mental health is also the reason behind the Approvals Committee's practices of not allowing a woman to serve as a birth mother more than once,[23] and of not allowing a woman who has never given birth to act as a birth mother.[24]

---

[20] One Approvals Committee member suggested that it is more difficult to discern the birth mother's true feelings in cases where a private agency has coached her to give the 'right answers'.

[21] Where the egg is donated by a third party, the birth mother is referred to the doctor who is responsible for the health of the donor.

[22] The first birth mother reported that she was emotionally broken as a result of the experience (Yediot Aharonot, 8 March 1998). Some of the birth mothers who were interviewed by Teman (2001) reported that during the pregnancy they felt very important and became very close to the intended mother. After the birth, they felt an emotional vacuum. This was particularly acute where the intended parents did not maintain any contact with her, which tended to make her feel exploited and unappreciated. Similarly the birth mother who only got paid after her lawyer had written to the intended parents reported that her emotional problems in the aftermath were caused not by handing over the child but because she felt so badly treated by the couple (Kaplan Sommer (2000:15)).

[23] Which might prevent the birth mother from building her own life and in particular from finding a new partner (Shemama, 2001:20–21). In a case reported in the press, one birth mother whose first two pregnancies for the intended couple had ended in abortion because of defects in the embryo, declared that she was going to try again and for that reason was delaying remarrying (Maariv, 5 April 2000).

[24] See Ensuring her Suitability above.

Protection of her Right to Privacy

Section 18 of the Law specifically provides that neither the provisions of the Law nor the surrogate motherhood agreement derogate from the statutory requirements of informed consent to medical treatment and do not prevent the birth mother receiving any medical treatment including interruption of pregnancy. The Approvals Committee requires a clause in the agreement confirming that the birth mother may refuse any medical procedure during the process, and must have her dignity and privacy respected during all medical treatment. While such a clause simply reflects the general law, its inclusion in the agreement ensures that both the birth mother and the intended parents are aware of these rights. A significant consequence is that the intended parents do not have any right to be present at any examination or at the birth itself without the consent of the birth mother.[25]

Nonetheless, the birth mother's privacy is clearly compromised, *inter alia*, in the following respects. First, in the contract, the birth mother has to undertake not to have sexual intercourse for two weeks before and three weeks after the implantation and not to have unprotected intercourse throughout the whole period of the contract. Secondly, there is clearly a danger that, during the pregnancy, the intended parents—anxious to be involved with the development of their foetus in the womb—will interfere with the privacy of the birth mother. After the traumatic experiences of the first surrogacy,[26] parties are advised to agree in advance what level of contact there will be between them.[27] Thirdly, while the birth mother's privacy is protected by the statutory provision forbidding publicising any details of the parties to surrogacy arrangements,[28] the fact that her name appears in a register which can be viewed by the child on attaining majority, as well as by various officials, can be seen as a serious invasion of her privacy.[29]

Financial Protection

Perhaps the realm in which the birth mother is most vulnerable is the financial one. There is a real danger that, if she is in a desperate situation because of her financial difficulties, she may agree to inadequate compensation.

---

[25] However, Teman (2001) and other press reports show that the birth mother is usually only too happy to allow the intended mother (and sometimes even the father) to be present at all medical examinations and the birth and to share the experience with her.

[26] See n 9 above.

[27] However, in practice, the question of privacy is a function of the success of the relationship between the parties rather than the terms of the agreement. Teman's research (Teman, 2001 and Kadush, 2001) shows that in a high proportion of cases the two mothers enjoy a very close relationship and show considerable respect for each other's views. Thus one birth mother was reported as making a considerable effort to reduce her smoking because she knew it worried the intended mother.

[28] Section 19(c) of the Law.

[29] For analysis, see s 7 below.

The Law does not provide any minimum or maximum figures,[30] simply stating that the Approvals Committee may approve conditions of the agreement that concern monthly payments to the birth mother in order to cover real expenditures connected with the implementation of the agreement, including costs of legal advice and insurance, as well as compensation for inactivity, suffering, lost income or temporary loss of earning ability, or any other reasonable compensation.[31] Any deviation from the payments approved by the Approvals Committee is an offence, punishable with one-year imprisonment.[32] In practice, the Committee does not recommend specific sums and does not interfere with the sums agreed by the parties.[33] However, some of the Committee's requirements do provide financial protection for the birth mother. The agreement has to differentiate between 'compensation' and reimbursement of 'expenses' and the Committee's guidelines list the expenses and heads of compensation for which provision must be made by the intended parents. These include all medical expenses (including the cost of a second opinion where the birth mother so requests), all legal expenses in relation to the agreement; the cost of counselling for the birth mother and her children by a psychologist during and for six months after the birth, the premiums for an insurance policy which provides cover against death or injury and for inability to work during the pregnancy (a copy of the policy has to be shown to the Approvals Committee), and any additional direct or indirect costs incurred by the birth mother as a result of hospitalisation resulting from the pregnancy. Provision must also be made to compensate the birth mother for pain and suffering involved in any special procedures such as a Caesarian section, amniocentesis, or reduction of the number of embryos and termination of the pregnancy, where medically indicated.[34]

In order to ensure that the intended parents can indeed afford to make the payments to which they have agreed, the Approvals Committee requires that a sum sufficient to cover all the estimated costs be deposited with a lawyer or other trustee before it will consider the application for approval of the agreement. The trustee is required to confirm that s/he has received the sum and that s/he will pay the insurance premiums and all other sums provided for in the agreement in full and on time.[35] The Committee's guidelines state that since the

---

[30] In comparison, the Adoption of Children (Maximum Payments to a Recognised Agency) Regulations 1998 lays down a maximum fee of $20,000 for adopting a foreign baby.

[31] Section 6 of the Law.

[32] Section 19(b) of the Law.

[33] Figures appearing in newspaper reports, which were confirmed by some of our interviewees, suggest that payments to the birth mother (excluding payments of insurance premiums and professional fees) are usually in the region of US $20,000–25,000.

[34] The Committee does not issue any guidelines as to how the quantum of this compensation should be calculated.

[35] This requirement is necessary since in one early case the money was not deposited even though the contract provided for it to be so deposited. The money was not paid by the couple after the birth as promised and the birth mother only received payment after threatening legal action. She never received an extra bonus promised to her secretly by the wife (Kaplan Sommer (2000:15)).

insurance policy does not cover all possible risks, the birth mother may not waive her right to sue the intended parents.

4. PROTECTING THE INTENDED PARENTS

It may be thought that as the intended parents are the stronger party they are not in need of protection (Shalev (1998:71)). However, while they will invariably be socioeconomically stronger than the birth mother, they are often more vulnerable emotionally. Frequently, they regard surrogacy as their last hope for biological parenthood after many years of emotionally and physically draining failed fertility treatments.[36] Therefore, the assumption that they are in all respects in a stronger position and not in need of protection is too simplistic. There are three main areas in which the intended parents may need protection: protection against the birth mother reneging, financial protection, and protection for their mental health.

The Law effectively denies the birth mother the right to renege unless a court is satisfied that there has been a change in circumstances and that the welfare of the child will not be damaged thereby. We are not aware of any cases where the birth mother has requested to keep the child. One reason for this may be the screening by the Approvals Committee.[37] While, of course, we cannot be sure that there would have been problems if arrangements had gone ahead with the birth mothers rejected as unsuitable, it seems likely that the Approvals Committee is in a better position than the intended parents to judge the suitability of the birth mother both because of the professional skills and experience of the Approvals Committee members and because they are likely to be more objective. Childless couples, with limited options open to them, perhaps need protecting against possible rashness and lack of judgment in choosing a birth mother.[38]

While, as stated above, the Approvals Committee does not interfere with the size of the payments agreed between the parties, presumably the fact that the surrogate motherhood agreement has to be approved by the Approvals Committee prevents the birth mother from making outrageous demands.[39] Furthermore, intended parents should be able legitimately to resist any request

---

[36] The first intended mother had suffered eight miscarriages during twelve years of trying to have a baby (Harel (1998)).

[37] Another reason may be that social workers explain to the birth mother from the beginning how to avoid getting emotionally attached to the child, for example, by seeing themselves as 'the babysitter'. Teman (2001) analyses this detachment from the baby in terms of anthropological theory.

[38] Especially if there is a dearth of candidates. The first intended parents went to a lot of trouble to ensure that they chose a suitable birth mother including travelling all over Israel to interview in their own homes potential candidates who had answered their advertisements. However, despite these precautions, they and the professional screening failed to identify the emotional instability of the birth mother (Harel (1998)).

[39] There is some evidence that some birth mothers think that the compensation is inadequate (Kadosh (2001)).

for additional payments since they are not lawful and would expose the parties to prosecution.

Surrogacy potentially poses mental health hazards too to the intended parents.[40] Thus, they also have to be examined by a psychologist who confirms their suitability to embark upon the process (see, for example, chapters 10, 12 and 13, this volume).

5. PROTECTING THE CHILD

Some opponents of surrogacy claim that we do not know how a child will be affected by the fact that s/he has been brought into the world in this 'unnatural' way and that therefore, in accordance with the overriding principle of giving precedence to the best interests of the child, adults do not have any moral right to put a child in this position.[41] The Israeli legislature and courts[42] clearly reject this position. The imposition of responsibility on the state to protect the child's welfare in surrogacy arrangements can be justified on the basis that the risks to the child's welfare are greater than in relation to 'natural' birth, and that surrogacy involves the active assistance of the state (both in the provision of medical services and determining the status of the child). The requirements of the legislature and the Approvals Committee, which are designed to protect the child, may be divided into four categories: the child's physical health, future welfare, legal status, and right to privacy.

The child's physical health at birth is dependent on the health of the three adults on whom his/her conception and gestation was dependent as well as on the doctors who carried out the IVF and implantation.

Thus, as has been discussed, all applications for approval of agreements have to be accompanied by medical opinions and tests. As with any pregnancy, there is a potential conflict between the child's health and the mother's right to privacy. As discussed above, even where the birth mother agrees to undergo particular tests or treatment, she retains the right to refuse. However, it would seem that if her refusal is unreasonable and causes damage to the child, she may be liable in damages.[43]

---

[40] In a number of the newspaper interviews, intended mothers reported severe anxiety and other stress-related symptoms. Teman (2001) reports one case where the intended mother suffered from post-partum depression .

[41] The legitimacy of this argument rests to a large extent on the philosophical question of whether it is possible to compare non-existence with existence, which issue is outside the scope of this paper.

[42] See *CAA Nachmani v Nachmani* 2401/95 P.D. 50(4) 661 (discussed in Schuz (1998)).

[43] In tort to the intended parents and in tort to the child. This question has not yet been tested in the Israeli courts. Where a child is born naturally, there will be little point in him suing his parents because in any event they are the ones who will have to bear the expenses caused by his handicap. In the case of C.A. 540/82 *Catz and others v Zytzov and other* P.D. 40(2) 85, there was disagreement among the judges in the obiter discussion as to whether parents may be liable to the child who is born severely handicapped when they could have prevented the birth. However, liability for handicaps which could have been prevented does not raise the same moral dilemmas as liability for wrongful life.

As regards protection of the child's future welfare, the Law requires that the intended parents must be 'a man and a woman who are spouses'. It is unclear from this definition whether the parties must be married. In practice, the Approvals Committee has approved agreements where the intended parents are unmarried cohabitees. However, there is no doubt that the legislative definition excludes the possibility of a single man or woman entering into a surrogate motherhood agreement. This requirement may be seen as intended to protect the child by maximising the chances that s/he is brought up in a two-parent heterosexual environment, which is assumed to be the optimal situation.[44] Recently a single woman sought judicial review of the Approval Committee's refusal to consider her application. The High Court rejected the Respondents' claim that the best interests of the future child required that s/he be born into a two parent household as too sweeping. Thus, the need to protect the future child could not justify the blanket restriction on single women in the legislation which was discriminatory. Nonetheless, the petition was rejected because any decision to include single women should be made by the legislature in view of the novel, delicate and complex nature of surrogacy.[46]

The legislation does not proscribe any maximum age for the intended parents. However, the Approvals Committee requires that the age of the intended father should not exceed 59 and that of the mother should not exceed 48 years.[47] While the Committee does not explain these restrictions, it seems likely that their concern is that it is not in the best interests of a child to be brought up by elderly parents, who are too old to have given birth to her/him by natural means.[48]

The risk of a child born in pursuance of a surrogacy arrangement being rejected at birth by the intended parents is likely to be greater than that of a child born in the ordinary way because the intended mother does not have the same physical bond with the child as a mother who has carried and given birth to

---

[44] Where a surrogate motherhood agreement has been approved, if the marriage breaks down at any time during its implementation the Approvals Committee must be informed. It is not clear whether in the case where the birth mother had not yet become pregnant whether the Approvals Committee would revoke its approval if all the parties wished to continue with the agreement, even though the child would effectively be born into a single parent family. The question of whether being born into a single parent family is damaging to the welfare of the child was raised in the famous frozen embryo case of *Nachmani v Nachmani* (n 42 above). Justice Strasbourg-Cohen held that it should not be assumed that being born into a single parent family was necessarily contrary to the child's best interests and that in this case Rutti Nachmani's personal characteristics ensured that the child would have a good home.

[45] HCJ 2458/01 *A New Family and Plonit v The Approvals Committee, The Minister of Health and the Minister of Employment and Welfare.* (Unpublished decision of 23.12.02).

[46] The Court was clearly concerned that allowing the applicant's petition would open up the way for single men to claim that the legislation discriminates against them.

[47] Form no 2.

[48] Compare the maximum age of 51 for a woman to receive an egg donation under the Draft Law on Egg Donation and IVF 2001, and the maximum ages set by the adoption authorities (internal adoption—45 and 40 respectively; external adoption—48 years between adoptor and child).

her/him. Thus, in order to protect the child against potential rejection, the Approvals Committee requires that the intended parents undertake that they will accept and bring up the child even if s/he is born with disabilities. Furthermore, they must agree to make provision for the child if their marriage breaks down.

Rabbi Dr Halperin, a member of the Aloni Commission, in a minority opinion, opposes partial surrogacy,[49] *inter alia*,[50] because it is not in the best interests of the child to know[51] that s/he had been conceived by the birth mother purely for the purpose of being handed over to a 'total stranger' (para 3.B.7.6). The Law, adopting this position,[52] does not allow partial surrogacy and requires that the egg must be that of the intended mother or, where she cannot produce eggs, that of a donor.

The third aspect of the protection of the child relates to its legal status. The child's welfare requires that it should be clear who is responsible for her/him from the moment of her/his birth. Section 10(b) of the Law provides that the welfare officer appointed by the chief welfare officer is the **sole** legal guardian[53] of the child until a court order is made to the contrary, but that the child should be in the physical care of the intended parents who have all the parental duties and responsibilities in respect of the child. Effect is given to this legal arrangement by the formal handing over of the baby by the birth mother to the intended parents in the presence of the welfare officer as soon as possible after the birth.

Section 11(a) of the Law requires that the intended parents apply for a parentage order within seven days of the child's birth and that the court should make such an order unless it is satisfied, after receiving a report from the welfare officer, that this course of action would not be consistent with the welfare of the child.[54] As far as we are aware, a parentage order has been made without difficulty in every case. The consequence of the order is that the intended parents are the parents and sole guardians of the child for all intents and purposes.[55]

---

[49] See definition at n 6 above.

[50] He was also concerned that if partial surrogacy were allowed, there would be a temptation to achieve conception by sexual intercourse rather than through artificial insemination.

[51] There is no way of guaranteeing that the child will never find this out, even if it were thought desirable in principle to hide this from him.

[52] Although it is not clear that this reasoning was accepted. More likely, the concern was that if partial surrogacy were allowed, the Law would not be passed because of opposition by religious and conservative elements in the Knesset.

[53] The effect of this provision is to negate the natural legal guardianship of the intended father as well as that of the birth mother.

[54] In which case, the court has to make an order declaring that the birth mother is the mother of the child (s11(b) of the Law).

[55] Section 12(a) of the Law. However, s12(b) provides that this order does not affect any rules concerning capacity to marry, which is governed by Jewish law. Corinaldi (1996:98) points out that the wording of the Law differs from that of the adoption law in that the latter expressly states that the adoption order ends any legal relationship between the child and the biological parents, whereas such statement is absent in relation to surrogacy . It is not clear what is the significance of this omission since the intention of the legislature seems to have been that the surrogate mother should not have any further connection with the child. Corinaldi also points out that the equation of the intended father and mother is incorrect. The father is the natural father of the child and therefore is

As explained in detail in Professor Shencker's chapter, the status of the child in Jewish law is of significant practical importance and in particular his/her future may be severely prejudiced if s/he is classified as a *mamzer* or the identity of his/her father is unknown. A number of provisions in section 2 of the Law are designed to protect the child's future welfare by preventing doubts arising about his/her status in Jewish law. First, the requirement that the intended mother and the birth mother are of the same religion (unless neither of them is Jewish) will avoid disputes as to whether the child is Jewish. Secondly, the requirement that the sperm must be that of the intended father, and not of a donor ensures that the identity of the father is known. Thirdly, the provisions that the birth mother must not be a relative of the intended parents and that normally she should not be married prevent the risk that the child might be treated as a *mamzer*.[56]

As regards the child's privacy rights, section 16(a) of the Law provides that the parentage order should be registered in a special register. The regulations provide that the register should record the court which gave the parentage order, the number of the court file, the date of the order, the name of the child after and before the giving of the order, the date and place of birth, the identity number of the child, the child's sex, the name, religion, nationality and identity number of the birth mother and intended parents and any instructions given in the order.[57] Access to the register is restricted to the Registrar of Marriages, the Attorney General and the Chief Welfare Officer and the child her/himself upon attaining majority.[58]

The provision for a register was controversial. The majority of the Commission took the view that such a register invaded the privacy not only of the child but also of the intended parents and the birth mother. The reason for the rejection of this opinion seems to have been to appease religious factions, concerned about forbidden marriages.[59] However, the recording of the details of the birth mother may also be defended as giving effect to the child's right to know her/his origins.[60]

---

already the parent in every sense of the word since Israeli law does not distinguish between the status of a father who is married to the mother of the child and one who is not. Thus, in his view, it should be made clear that the parenthood order is declarative in relation to the father, but constitutive in relation to the mother.

[56] Under s 2(3)(a) of the Law, the Approvals Committee is given authority to sanction a married birth mother where it is satisfied that it is not possible to find a suitable unmarried candidate. In practice, all birth mothers have been unmarried (ie single, widowed or divorced).

[57] Regulation 3 of the Surrogacy Agreements (Approval of the Agreement and Status of the Child) (Registration) Regulations 1998. Under regulation 4, three additional registers must be set up in which the surnames of the child, the intended parents and the birth mothers are listed respectively in alphabetical order.

[58] This is the same as in relation to the adoption register except for the fact that the regulations give the child born from surrogacy an absolute right to look in the register whereas adopted children require the permission of a welfare officer.

[59] Although Corinaldi (1996: 67) points out that the details of the birth mother are in any event recorded in the register of births. For further discussion on the significance of religion, see Schenker, chapter 16, this volume.

[60] See, for example, the UN Convention on the Rights of the Child, Art 7. This right usually refers to the right of access to information concerning genetic parentage, but arguably also applies to information about the birth mother.

Section 19(c) of the Law provides that the publication, without permission from a court, of anything which would enable the identity of the birth mother, the intended parents or the child to be identified is a criminal offence punishable with one-year imprisonment.[61] A film was prepared documenting the first surrogacy. The intended parents and the birth mother appealed to the Family Court for permission for the film to be screened on television.[62] The application was rejected on the basis that the child's interest in privacy overrode the interest of the adults interested in publication. Moreover, the public interest in obtaining information about surrogacy could be satisfied without identification of the parties involved. Indeed, the film was screened with the faces blurred.

6. PROTECTION OF THE PUBLIC

The final group potentially affected by surrogate motherhood is the public; the public arguably needs protection against the use of surrogacy 'for convenience', the over-commercialisation of surrogacy arrangements, and against 'reproductive tourism'.[63] One of the arguments against surrogacy is that it could be used by fertile women who, for reasons of convenience, do not want to undergo pregnancy and childbirth. Such a development is seen as a perversion of nature. Moreover, while surrogacy may be justified, despite the undoubted ethical and other problems entailed, as a method of realising the infertile couple's right to parenthood,[64] such justification does not exist where that right can be realised by natural means. The Law requires that every application for approval of an agreement be accompanied by a medical opinion confirming that the intended mother is incapable of conceiving and carrying a baby, or that to do so would involve a serious risk to her health. Moreover, the practice of the Approvals Committee is not to allow couples who already have two children to enter into surrogate motherhood agreements.

We discussed above the need to ensure that the birth mother is properly compensated while at the same time protecting infertile couples from financial exploitation.[65] This issue also has a public policy aspect. Selling babies is illegal and while it might be argued that surrogacy is different because the transaction is entered into before the baby is even conceived, it is clearly in the public interest to avoid so far as possible the impression that surrogacy is a market in

---

[61] Publication of anything said at the sessions of the Approvals Committee, which are held *in camera* or any documents presented to it is also a criminal offence.

[62] *Ploni and Al Mor Communication Ltd v Attorney-General* FCA 4570/98 (unpublished decision of 5 March, 1998).

[63] This term was coined by Shalev (1998: 57).

[64] The existence of a right to be a parent was recognised by the Supreme Court in the frozen embryos case (*Nachmani v Nachmani*, n 42 above). See also Schuz (1998). However, it is far from clear to what extent if at all a positive duty is imposed on others to help realise this right as opposed to a negative duty to avoid interfering with the exercise of the right.

[65] At s 4 above.

babies. The legislature treads carefully using terminology designed to reduce the impression that the transaction is a financial one (Shemama (2001:17)). Thus, the parents are referred to as 'intended parents' and not 'commissioning parents'[66] and the money to be paid to the birth mother is not referred to as a fee, but as 'compensation'.

However, it should be noted that although the involvement of profit-making agencies might be seen as the hallmark of commercialisation, the regulation of such agencies is limited to the requirement that the agency agreement is submitted to the Approvals Committee.[67]

As regards protection for the public against 'reproductive tourism', following the Commission's recommendations (para 1.B.7.10), the Law requires that all parties be Israeli residents. Public policy requires that Israel should not be allowed to become a 'surrogacy haven' for foreigners and that foreign women should not be brought to Israel to serve as birth mothers.[68] Adopting the public law interpretation of 'residence' would include new immigrants from the date of arrival and thus open the possibility of 'sham immigration' by infertile couples intending to return to their country of origin immediately after the birth of the child (Shalev (1998:57)). However, the Approvals Committee prefers the private international law interpretation which requires that Israel is the 'center of life' and thus looks behind the public law status (Shemama (2001:23)). Evidence of this can be seen from the Approval Committee's 'guidance to applicants' which recommends that, where any of the parties are recent immigrants, applications should not be submitted until 18 months after immigration. The addition of the words 'each case will be decided on its merits' reflects the fact that a blanket restriction of this nature would be outside the Committee's authority.

7. BALANCING THE INTERESTS OF THE DIFFERENT GROUPS

Most of the criticism of the Law has centred round the restrictions which were imposed in order to avoid doubts arising as to the status of the child in Jewish law.[69] It is argued that exclusion of relatives and married women leads to the choice of the most vulnerable women as birth mothers and makes it harder for the intended parents to find a suitable birth mother. Similarly, it is claimed that the requirement that sperm be that of the father and not of a donor discriminates against couples where the man rather than the woman does not produce

---

[66] As in the draft law.

[67] This is in stark contrast to the position in some other countries, which ban commercial surrogacy agencies (see, for example, the English Surrogacy Arrangements Act 1985) and to the extensive regulation in Israel of agencies involved in inter-country adoption.

[68] Involvement of foreign residents would also make it harder to screen the parties and supervise the surrogacy process (Shalev (1998:57)).

[69] See Schenker, chapter 16, this volume, and above at s 5.

gametes. In other words, in the view of the critics, the Law has not achieved the appropriate balance between the conflicting interests of the different parties.

We would disagree and argue that the legislation has got the balance right. The welfare of the child to be born must take precedence. We cannot leave the decision as to taking risks about the status of the child to the intended parents. It would be irresponsible for society actively to sanction and facilitate the birth of children whose status in Jewish law may be problematic. Our view is strengthened by the fact that birth mothers have been found and by the evidence that most of them come out of the experience satisfied as well as in a better financial position (Teman, 2001; Kadosh, 2001).[70] While relatives and married women might be less likely to encounter some of the emotional problems described by single or divorced birth mothers, there might well be other problems which would arise as a result of the effect on the birth mother's marriage or distortion of family relationships. We do not have any evidence concerning couples who have been unable to take advantage of surrogacy because of the infertility of the husband.

The tension between the rights of the birth mother and the child also arises in relation to the question of registration. Again, we would suggest that the child's right to know his origins as well as the need to protect him from forbidden marriages override the birth mother's right to privacy. However, it would seem that the child's rights could be adequately protected without providing him with identifying information concerning the birth mother. Thus, while the Registrar of Marriages will need to ascertain the identity of the birth mother, the child should not be provided with identifying information without first obtaining the consent of the birth mother.[71]

Some have suggested that, because generally the birth mother has no opportunity to renege or have any say as to the future of the child and simply has to hand him over after birth, the physiological connection between her and the child is not recognised and her basic human rights are negated.[72] However, we have seen above that the provisions concerning handing over and the status of the child are necessary in order to protect the intended parents and the child.

Again, it seems to us that the legislation has achieved the right balance between the needs and rights of the different groups. Not only can it be argued that the birth mother knew from the beginning what her status would be within

---

[70] Most of our interviewees confirmed this conclusion. A number of the birth mothers interviewed by Teman stated that they had discovered in themselves the ability to give and that while their original motive had been financial, in retrospect the experience of giving the most valuable present in the world to another woman was worth as much if not more than the money.

[71] Arguably the child's need to make contact with the woman that gave birth to him is less than that of an adopted child whose birth mother is also his genetic mother and yet the welfare officer may refuse to give identifying information to the adopted child. On the other hand, it may be argued that the invasion of privacy of the adoptive birth mother is greater than that of the surrogate birth mother.

[72] For example, Rabbi Dr Mordechai Halperin reported in Kaplan Sommer (2000).

the relationship and entered into it of her own free will, but also that to give her enhanced status by allowing her to renege or have some part in the future of the child might well not be 'doing her a favour'. The birth mother would be torn in two, faced with an impossible dilemma. On the one hand she is attached to the child and on the other she is committed to the intended parents. Whichever path she chooses, she is likely to be filled with remorse.

Thus, it can be argued that giving her virtually no way out of handing the child over not only protects the intended parents and the child, but also the birth mother herself. Such paternalism can perhaps be justified by the highly unusual and intensely emotional nature of the decision in question.

In practice, as we have seen, this debate is largely academic as there has not arisen any problem of the birth mother wishing to keep the child. Perhaps the clear-cut nature of the legislation prevents the problem arising because the birth mother knows from the beginning that there is simply no possibility of reneging and thus avoids developing any attachment to the child. Evidence suggests that the rejection that the birth mother feels when the intended couple choose not to have further contact with her is not because she wishes to play some role in the child's life, but because she feels that her act of giving has not been recognised by the intended parents (Kadosh (2001)).

Even if it is accepted that the child has to be automatically handed over after birth, we may question the need for an emotional ceremony.[73] Such a ceremony may well be traumatic for the birth mother, who is still recovering from the birth, and certainly seems insensitive to her feelings.[74] However, it may be argued that this physical act is of critical symbolic importance not only in relation to the legal status of the child but also in helping the birth mother comprehend the finality of the situation. Thus, again it may be that the requirement is for the surrogate's long-term benefit and that this is a situation where it is necessary 'to be cruel in order to be kind'. Research into the reaction of birth mothers to this ceremony would help in clarifying this issue.

The question of whether a single woman has the right to genetic motherhood is a controversial one, which is outside the scope of this essay. Assuming that such a right is recognised, the equally controversial question arises as to whether fulfilment of this right jeopardises the welfare of the child. We would subscribe to the view that no generalisation can be made in this respect. Thus, the Approvals Committee should be relied upon to decide whether in any given case the fact that the mother is single presents a threat to the welfare of the child.[75]

---

[73] Welfare officers testify to the intensely emotional nature of this ceremony.

[74] Corinaldi (1996: 69) even considers that the requirement endangers the whole agreement.

[75] See n 44 and n 45 above.

8. CONCLUSION

In sections 3 to 6 of this chapter, we demonstrated how the Israeli legislative and administrative framework regulating surrogacy arrangements is designed to protect all the parties involved. Our analysis in section 7 shows that most of the tensions between the interests of different parties are more apparent than real and that preference has, in our view quite rightly, been given to the interests of the child to be born.

We saw that while there were some teething problems at the beginning, experience has enabled improvements to be made which have successfully increased protection and reduced pitfalls. Indeed, Teman's research (2001) together with the interviews which we conducted indicate that intended parents, birth mothers and professionals working in the field are basically satisfied with the way in which the Law is now working in practice.

Thus, the Israeli model might usefully be adopted, with appropriate modifications, by other countries interested in regulating surrogacy. While other countries will not have to face the conflict of interests caused by the need to protect the child's status in Jewish law, two lessons might usefully be learnt from the way in which this issue has been addressed in Israel. First, the approach of the Israeli system in giving priority to the interests of the child should be followed in relation to all aspects of a surrogacy scheme. The child whose involvement is involuntary is the most vulnerable of all the parties and thus his/her interests must be the main concern at all stages of the process. Secondly, the Israeli experience suggests that non-altruistic surrogacy[76] can work provided that appropriate safeguards are introduced.

However, we must add a word of caution. It is difficult to judge properly the adequacy of protection, particularly for birth mothers, without more information about the long-term effect of the experience on birth mothers and their children and on the child born as a result of the surrogate motherhood agreement. Empirical research is necessary in order to enable proper assessment of the working of the Law.

The most criticised aspects of the scheme have been the restrictions imposed by Jewish law, which are seen by feminists as perpetuating patriarchal structures and increasing the potential exploitation of the birth mother (Shalev (1998)). While it would be a major achievement if we could promote the status of women in society at the same time as providing a solution for infertile people, this is simply not realistic in the Israeli context without sacrificing the interests of the child to be born. Thus, efforts at improving the scheme should be directed not to removing the restrictions based on Jewish law, but to ensuring maximum protection through accurate screening, and effective safeguards against financial exploitation by either party or by an agency, and to developing methods of min-

---

[76] See definition in n 5 above.

imising, through social work and other professional support, the mental health risks to the parties and particularly the birth mother.

APPENDIX

The following statistics, updated to 1 June 2001, were obtained from the Ministry of Health, which is responsible for the operation of the Law.

Number of applications for approval of Agreement	109
Number of applications submitted in 2001	12
Number of applications approved	89
Number of applications under consideration	9
Number of applications rejected	11
Number of births	22
Number of children born	30
Number of birth mothers pregnant	7
Number of couples who stopped the process	36
Number of couples who succeed in having a child after approval	4

REFERENCES

Corinaldi, M, 'The Surrogacy Question in Israel: Comments on the Surrogate Motherhood Agreements Law 1996, and The Aloni Commission Report' (Hebrew) 3 (1996) *Hamishpat (The Journal of the Minhal Law School)* 63.

Halperin-Kaddari, R, 'Redefining Parenthood' (1999) 29 *California Western International Law Journal* 313.

Harel, O, 'A Womb to Rent' (Hebrew) appearing in three parts in the weekend supplement of the Hebrew daily *Maariv* 20 March 1998, 27 March 1998 and 3 April 1998.

Kadosh, R, 'We are One Body' (Hebrew) *Women's Supplement of Maariv* 2 July 2001.

Kaplan Sommer, A, 'Labor Pains' (2000) *Jerusalem Post Magazine* 7 January 2000.

Katz, A, 'Those Involved in the First Surrogate Birth in Israel Cannot Return to Normal' (Hebrew) *Maariv* 7 April 1998.

Kost, H, 'The Complete Guide to Surrogacy' (Hebrew) *Maariv Style* 23 March 1997.

Schuz, R, 'The Right to Parenthood: Surrogacy and Frozen Embryos' in A Bainham (ed), *The International Survey of Family Law 1996*, (The Netherlands, Nijhoff, 1998) 237–56.

Shalev, C, *Birth Power: The Case for Surrogacy* (New Haven and London, Yale University Press, 1989).

—— 'Halakha and Patriarchal Motherhood—An Anatomy of the New Israeli Surrogacy Law' (1998) 32 *Israel Law Review* 51.

Shemama, E, 'Surrogacy in the Eyes of the Israeli Legislature' (2001) (seminar paper on file with author).

Teman, E, 'Technological Fragmentation as Women's Empowerment: Surrogate Motherhood in Israel' (2001) 31 *Women's Studies Quarterly* 11.

4

The Policy and Practice of Surrogacy in New Zealand

KEN DANIELS

1. INTRODUCTION

THERE IS A widespread acceptance in New Zealand that surrogacy is a matter of public policy (Coney and Else (1999)). The determining of the contents and parameters of such policy seems to have been the major factor contributing to successive governments' inertia and lack of action. In this respect, New Zealand differs little from most other jurisdictions, which have grappled with this demanding and difficult issue. The Warnock Committee on Human Fertilisation and Embryology in the United Kingdom stated 'the question of surrogacy presented us with some of the most difficult problems that we encountered. The evidence submitted to us contained a range of strongly held views and this was reflected in our own views. The moral and social objections to surrogacy have weighed heavily with us.' (Warnock (1984:46)).

The strong reactions evoked by surrogacy almost certainly contribute to the challenges of determining policy. Perhaps this is why the media have taken an acute interest, which, in turn, has generated a level of public engagement that has impacted on the policy makers.

While New Zealand's policy formation has been protracted, problematic and, in the view of some,[1] inadequate, policy does in fact exist. This chapter reviews the development of that policy, placing it in the context of wider policy on assisted human reproduction (AHR). The way in which surrogacy is managed in New Zealand, and the guidelines that have been established, are discussed.

2. ASSISTED HUMAN REPRODUCTION POLICY IN NEW ZEALAND

Following the commencement of *in vitro* fertilisation (IVF) treatment in New Zealand in 1983, there were calls for the Government to establish a system for managing developments in this area. A very influential group of organisations, the Royal Society of New Zealand, the New Zealand Law Society, the Medical

---

[1] See for example, Daniels and Caldwell (2002) for arguments on this point.

Council of New Zealand, the Medical Research Council of New Zealand and the Medical Association of New Zealand approached the Government with the suggestion that it appoint a standing committee to consider the legal, moral and social issues arising from *in vitro* fertilisation, artificial insemination by donor and related developments in biotechnologies.[2] The Government's response to this and other calls was to publish, through the Law Reform Division of the Justice Department, an issues paper entitled *New Birth Technologies—An Issues Paper on AID, IVF and Surrogate Motherhood* (1984). In his introduction, the Minister of Justice stated that the object of the paper was to promote informed public debate and to ascertain the views of the public on the way in which the Government should respond to these developments.

It is important to note that the paper emanated from the Law Reform Division of the Justice Department and that it was, as the minister pointed out, mainly the work of a lawyer. If this document had been prepared by the Policy Division rather that the Law Reform Division then the direction of policy development might have been very different in that a broader perspective would have been adopted. As it was, the focus was primarily on what needed to be modified or created in terms of the law. The issues paper drew heavily on two recently published overseas reports, the Warnock Report in the United Kingdom (Warnock (1984)) and the Waller Report in the State of Victoria, Australia (Waller (1983)) and their findings were quoted extensively.

The public and interested parties were invited to make submissions and 164 were received. A further paper was issued which provided a summary of these submissions.[3] Of particular note in relation to policy development was that 15 per cent of the submissions reportedly advocated the setting up of a national body to oversee developments, such a committee to be made up of persons representing medical, legal, theological, lay and Maori interests. Telfer (1989) also analysed the submissions and concluded that 23 per cent of the submissions supported the establishment of such a body/committee.

In its summary of the responses, the Law Reform Division observed that there was little consensus on the status or purpose of such a committee and that the proposal did not therefore merit consideration. The lack of consensus was to be expected, however, as the various groups and individuals had not conferred: if they had, a consensus may well have emerged (Daniels and Caldwell (2002:205)). While the reluctance to establish an overseeing body representing different interests was to be a characteristic of New Zealand's policy development, the Government did decide to take some action. In 1986 an interdepartmental monitoring committee was established—an in-house government committee of officials—to keep a watching brief on developments in AHR. One further development was that New Zealand's only legislation specifically relating to AHR was enacted. The Status of Children Amendment Act 1987 clarified

[2] *New Zealand Medical Journal* (1985).
[3] *New Birth Technologies: A summary of submissions received on the issues paper* (1986).

the legal status of the various parties when third party reproduction was utilised within AHR. In effect, those providing gametes and those conceived as a result of these gametes would have no legal rights or responsibilities to each other.

The next major government initiative occurred in 1993 when the Minister of Justice announced the formation of a two-person (a doctor and a lawyer) Ministerial Committee on Assisted Reproductive Technologies (MCART) to investigate and report on 'options and ways ahead'.[4] The principal recommendation of the committee's report was that an advisory and overseeing body should be established. Such a council would be the focus for both government and the community on matters relating to AHR. Its functions were envisaged to include preparation of codes of practice and guidelines to assist providers, consumers and the general public. The multi-disciplinary and multi-interest council would determine and oversee policy and practice in New Zealand. The Government asked an officials committee to respond to the Report[5] and, based on its recommendations, the Government decided not to proceed with the formation of the recommended council. Again New Zealand was left with no representative forum to be either a focus for, or contributor to, thinking and policy development.

There was, however, increasing concern regarding ethical considerations in the provision of AHR services and, as a result of this, the Minister of Health established The Interim National Ethics Committee on Assisted Reproductive Technologies (INECART) in 1993. Two years later the committee was reconstituted as The National Ethics Committee on Assisted Human Reproduction (NECAHR). The members of this committee are appointed by the Minister of Health and reflect the interest areas envisaged for membership of the council proposed by MCART. This became the first and only national body with a specific responsibility for AHR issues, albeit within an ethics framework. It is this committee that has played a critical role in the determining of policy on surrogacy and other developments in New Zealand, and we shall return to this later.

Frustrated at the lack of government action in relation to legislation, an MP (Diane Yates) introduced The Human Assisted Reproductive Technologies Bill in 1996. This Private Members Bill sought to outlaw certain practices, set up an AHR authority system similar to the HFEA in the UK and establish a central register for the recording of information regarding third party reproduction. The Bill would ban commercial surrogacy. In 1998, the Government introduced the Assisted Human Reproduction Bill, which would outlaw certain procedures, set up information registries and establish the National Ethics Committee on Assisted Human Reproduction (NECAHR) on a statutory basis. This latter proposal would provide for an overseeing body, but again limited to an ethics focus rather than a broader policy focus. Extensive provisions are contained within the Bill to ensure that if NECAHR is proposing to approve some new

[4] *Assisted Reproduction—Navigating our Future* (1994).
[5] Officials Committee (1995).

procedure or research then it must advise the Government before it gives approval. This seems designed to ensure that if the Government does not approve, it may introduce and pass legislation to ban such procedures or research. The Bill defines the concept of a 'full surrogacy agreement', but otherwise does not deal with the practice.

Select committee hearings on both Bills have recently been held and, as a result, a decision has been made to ask officials from the Ministry of Health and Justice, with assistance from the Ministry of Science, Research and Technology, to look at a 'merging' of the two Bills. There are currently no indications as to what will result.

3. SURROGACY POLICY IN NEW ZEALAND

As far as can be ascertained, the first publicly reported consideration of surrogacy in New Zealand occurred at the 1981 New Zealand Law Society Conference. An American professor of law (Wadlington (1981)) mentioned surrogacy in the context of a discussion of the need for legislation in AHR. This was developed further at the 1984 and 1987 New Zealand Law Society conferences where surrogacy and AHR were discussed in greater detail (Scott (1984)). As might be expected from law conferences, the major focus was on the legal issues. In the Justice Department's issues paper[6] a definition and overview of surrogacy was provided. This was followed by a review of the New Zealand position and an outline of the arguments for and against surrogacy. Of the 164 submissions received in response to the general issues of AHR, 99 specifically commented on surrogacy. Forty-five submissions opposed surrogacy. The arguments against may be summarised as: the potential for exploitation of the women involved; surrogacy as morally wrong; the legal and ethical issues as too complex; surrogacy as not in the best interests of the child; surrogacy amounting to the buying and selling of babies; and there being sufficient children available for adoption to meet the needs of infertile couples.

While 38 submissions supported surrogacy, there was disagreement concerning the circumstances in which it should be permitted. Eleven submissions favoured allowing surrogacy arrangements to proceed without restriction, arguing that this was an area that law should not concern itself with, while the remaining 27 wanted to see restrictions imposed. The view adopted by the Law Reform Division in response to these and other submissions was that in AHR in general (encompassing surrogacy) no immediate action was needed: New Zealand, for the time being, could afford to adopt a wait and see approach.[7] In relation to surrogacy, the wait and see approach lasted only until 1992. At this time one of the health providers (Fertility Associates) approached the then Auckland Health Board's Ethics Committee seeking approval to set up a 'com-

---

[6] *New Birth Technologies: an issues paper on AID, IVF and surrogate motherhood* (1985).
[7] *New Birth Technologies: a summary of submissions received on the issues paper* (1986).

passionate surrogacy programme'. The Ethics Committee said that the request was of such significance that there was a need for national guidelines to be established and referred the request to the committee of government officials in Wellington who pointed out that their role was advisory and referred the request back to the Ethics Committee.

At this point the combined chairpersons from existing, regionally-based ethics committees proposed that the Minister of Health establish a national committee to be responsible for this specific area. The Minister of Health established the Interim National Ethics Committee on Assisted Reproductive Technologies and at its third meeting in October 1993, the Committee considered a request from Fertility Associates to commence non-commercial surrogacy by means of IVF. The Committee declined to provide ethical approval and this led to Fertility Associates reapplying and the application being reconsidered in November 1994. Again the Committee declined to give ethical approval and undertook to provide a report, which it did in 1995 (INECART (1995)). It outlined its concerns in relation to the legal—there was no specific statutory provision, which addressed surrogacy—and ethical dimensions. One of the grounds for Fertility Associates' request for reconsideration was that MCART had, in the meantime, been considering the issues. In its report, MCART said, 'We disagree with the decision of INECART to deny ethical approval for IVF compassionate surrogacy and urge a new application be made to the reconstituted national committee.'[8] MCART provided, in some detail, its reasons for disagreeing with INECART's decision. The reconstituted ethics committee (NECAHR) was established in 1995 and in 1997 this committee gave ethical approval to a general application for non-commercial surrogacy using IVF as treatment and to subsequently review applications on a case-by-case approach. A set of draft criteria was established to guide providers as they made their applications. These guidelines have been modified in the light of evolving practice—hence the use of the words 'draft guidelines' (see Appendix 1). These guidelines will be discussed later in this chapter.

Four important points need to be noted from this review of New Zealand's policy developments in relation to surrogacy: first, the management of applications for IVF surrogacy occurs within the framework of health—NECAHR is appointed by the Minister of Health. Secondly, the Committee considers only surrogacy arrangements that involve medical intervention therefore surrogacy that does not involve health providers is not covered by any committee. Thirdly, there has been considerable concern expressed (NECAHR (2000); Law Commission (2000)) about the lack of a legal framework for surrogacy. Finally, by their decision, governed by ethical considerations, NECAHR has in effect established a policy that approves IVF surrogacy. Daniels and Hargreaves (1997) have argued that in effect NECAHR became a *de facto* policy group when it approved IVF surrogacy.

---

[8] Above, n 5 at 4.

NECAHR has received 30 applications for IVF surrogacy and has approved 25 of these, declined four and one is pending. MCART (1994) noted in its report however that a limited amount of surrogacy—both natural intercourse and 'do-it-yourself' insemination—was occurring and therefore the exact number of surrogacy arrangements in New Zealand is not known. Two 'informal' cases of surrogacy have come before the courts. In the first of these[9] there was an application to adopt the child born as a result of a surrogacy arrangement. The judge approved the adoption despite the fact that the commissioning couple had paid the genetic/birth mother a sum of $15,000. Such payment is in contravention of the Adoption Act 1955. A major consideration impacting on the judge's decision seems to have been his assessment that the commissioning couples were 'fit and proper' people to be the parents. The judge did note that, 'the issue of surrogacy is one which should be addressed by Parliament.' In the second case[10] the commissioning couple had also paid the genetic/birth mother $12,000. They had not complied with the Department of Social Welfare's requirements—regarding the adoption of their child—but two years later did apply to adopt. The Department recommended guardianship rather than adoption, but the judge did not agree and granted an adoption order. His view on the payment was that this was for the surrogacy and not the adoption. His main concern was with the parents' suitability and acknowledgement of the fact that the child and its parents had lived together for two years.

Both cases have highlighted the difficulty of using existing legislation to cover a new practice. For parents to have legal custody of a child following surrogacy an adoption order must be made and the adoption legislation was not drafted with surrogacy in mind. The Law Commission has recently reviewed the current adoption legislation (Adoption Act 1955) and, in its report,[11] discusses both adoption and surrogacy: 'At present in New Zealand there is a legal vacuum, which has permitted the growth of such practices (surrogacy) before all the ethical and moral questions have been publicly debated.'[12] The Commission points out that it 'did not presume to judge. . . . the morality or virtue of surrogacy arrangements. We simply ask how best it could be regulated and whether adoption law was an appropriate mechanism by which to regulate surrogacy arrangements.'[13]

The Commission drew heavily on and was influenced by the Brazier Report (Brazier, Campbell and Golombok (1998)) in the UK. The Commission believed that 'ultimately, commissioning parents will be required to apply for an adoption order . . . however surrogacy cannot be treated in exactly the same manner as adoption. Legislation should explicitly recognise that surrogacy

---

[9]   *P (Adoption) Surrogacy* [1990] NZFLR 385 quoted in Coney and Else (1999:53).
[10] In *re G* quoted in Coney and Else (1999:53).
[11] NZLC R65, 2000.
[12] Above, n 11 at 185.
[13] Above, n 12 at 186.

involves front-end issues—it should provide a structure to regulate what occurs before the baby is conceived' (Brazier *et al* (1998:200)). They suggested that there were a number of regulatory issues at the pre-conception stage, namely: the suitability of the commissioning parents, the suitability of the proposed surrogate mother, advertising regarding surrogacy arrangements, and payment. It is these and other issues that NECAHR seeks to cover in its pre-conception approval system when surrogacy-utilising IVF is being considered, and it is to this system that we now turn our attention.

4. THE PRACTICE OF SURROGACY IN NEW ZEALAND

The practice of surrogacy takes place within a context that has the following characteristics: first, there is no specific legislation concerning surrogacy. Adoption legislation manages the legal relationships between the various parties but it was not designed for, and arguably does not deal appropriately with, cases of surrogacy. Secondly, there is an absence of guidelines/monitoring for 'private' surrogacy arrangements and, finally, a comprehensive system to manage surrogacy arrangements that includes the use of health professionals.

Clinics that provide fertility services are covered by a professional self-regulation system.[14] For a clinic to be accredited, ethical approval must be given before any new treatment is commenced. This system, which now covers both Australia and New Zealand, commenced in Australia in 1986. In Australia, clinics apply to their local hospital ethics committees, but in New Zealand a national review system has been established through NECAHR (as referred to earlier). This means that while NECAHR has no statutory or regulatory authority, its approval system is both significant and powerful: without its approval of a new treatment, a clinic or provider would not be able to obtain accreditation from the professional body.

NECAHR, following approval of a general application for non-commercial surrogacy in July 1997, produced its criteria for individual approvals in March 1998 and these have subsequently been modified. The current guidelines are attached as Appendix 1. They cover the requirements that health providers have to meet in submitting applications. These guidelines relate to the providers themselves, the commissioning parents, the birth mother and her partner, the legal advisors and the counsellors. The application, which must contain no identifying information concerning the applicant parties, may be submitted in two stages or as a complete application. This procedure is followed so that the medical reasons for the use of surrogacy are established before the more extensive and expensive aspects of legal and counselling requirements are entered into. This is because NECAHR has established that 'there should be

---

[14] The Reproductive Technology Accreditation Committee (RTAC) of Australia provides a voluntary mechanism for quality assurance of IVF and DI in New Zealand.

medical reasons for the commissioning mother not undertaking a pregnancy.'[15] The Committee's approval system therefore assumes medical rather than social indications for the use of surrogacy. The use of the word 'should' is significant, in that while the guidelines make it clear that approval is based on certain factors/conditions (eg medical rather than social reasons) there is a willingness 'to consider an application deviating from the proposed guidelines'.[16] A case has to be established for deviating from the draft guidelines. The Committee accepts that there are special cases that need special consideration and does not see the guidelines as a set of 'rules'. A recent example of such a 'deviation' was where approval was given to an application where neither of the commissioning parents was contributing gametes, even though the draft guidelines state that, 'one or both of the commissioning parents should be the potential child's genetic parents.'[17]

While the medical aspect of the commissioning mother's condition establishes the grounds for application, emphasis is also placed on the obstetric history and health of the birth mother and her partner. The draft guidelines state that the birth mother should have given birth to children and that she and her partner should have completed their family. This is thought to be important in that it is likely to contribute to a surrogate being 'more aware of the medical and psychological risks to herself.'[18] It is also stated that this may be important if a surrogate experienced medical complications as a result of surrogacy and this in turn led to complications, which may prevent a further pregnancy for her and her partner. The requirement that the birth mother's partner be screened for conditions such as HIV and Hepatitis (A & C) illustrate how the surrogacy arrangement impacts on all the adult parties entering into the arrangement. Yet another impact on the birth mother and her partner is that the provider must, in their application, refer to the discussion that they have had with the birth mother and her partner about how they will ensure that they do not conceive their own child during the IVF treatment.

All the requirements are designed to protect, as far as it is possible, the safety and welfare of all the parties and any children that result. This protection relates both to medical and what may be described as psychosocial considerations. These psychosocial considerations are, in fact, more extensive than the considerations relating to medical, legal or cultural factors. This arises from the Committee's acceptance that surrogacy arrangements raise major emotional and social issues for all parties. The management of these issues will almost certainly impact on the welfare of any future child. NECAHR requires that professionally qualified counsellors meet with the parties to ensure that they understand and are prepared for entering a surrogacy arrangement. Counsellors also have a

---

[15] For full details see Appendix 1.
[16] Above, n 14.
[17] *Ibid.*
[18] *Ibid.*

role in ensuring that participation is based on informed consent. More controversially, counsellors fulfil an assessing role in relation to all those involved, and are expected to undertake family histories.

If there are histories of, for example, psychiatric problems or substance/physical/sexual abuse which could predispose any of the applicants to risk when moving into a new situation, or which may pose a risk to the potential child, these must be referred to in the counsellor's report. Some counsellors in New Zealand have expressed reservations at conferences and workshops—and concerns about being required to make psychosocial assessments, arguing that this is not their role, that it interferes with the more important therapeutic role and that the process of assessment is problematic. Mindful of these concerns, NECAHR does not use the terminology of assessment but, as the draft guidelines clearly indicate, information is to be collected and if deemed significant is to be reported to NECAHR as part of the counsellor's report. In effect, this places NECAHR in the assessing role, but clearly it is dependent on the information reported to it and the 'professional judgments' of the counsellors. Other counsellors do not see assessment as a problem, believing that this is necessary in terms of providing for the welfare of any child as required by the Ethics Committee—and ensuring that any vulnerable persons are not exploited or made more vulnerable as a result of a surrogacy arrangement. The draft guidelines outline the areas that must be included in discussion with participants and these primarily focus on the establishment of the agreement between them. In particular there is to be a focus on issues that may not have been thought about, eg multiple births, a child born with a disability, decision-making regarding legal termination should a foetal abnormality be diagnosed.

The counselling arrangements are also covered by a set of expectations from NECAHR. Two counsellors are to be involved, one for each of the family groups. The family groups are to be seen together as a group and individually. Where there are existing children of an appropriate age, they are to be included in the counselling, eg the surrogate and her partner's 12 and 14-year-old offspring. Discussion of what happens in the event of a dispute between the parties is expected to be covered by both the counsellors and the lawyers. There is the recognition that disputes may ultimately have to be resolved by a court, but clearly this is to be avoided if at all possible and in this respect the involvement of counsellors may be quite crucial.

As with counselling, NECAHR requires that two lawyers be involved, one for each of the family groups. It is recognised by NECAHR that there are legal implications arising from the use of surrogacy and that these need to be considered as part of the process of ensuring informed consent. Surrogacy arrangements involve agreements between the various parties and important issues arise over the nature and status of such agreements. NECAHR states that it does not require a formal agreement to be entered into (it would be ruled null and void by a court) but in practice all applications have included a written agreement prepared by or with the assistance of lawyers.

The main value of a written agreement is that it ensures that all the relevant issues have been considered and the parties have clearly stated their intentions and expectations. Given the issues that arise in relation to the adoption of a child born as a result of surrogacy, lawyers are required to ensure that participants understand the legal situation regarding the status of the child and the procedures relating to guardianship, custody and adoption.

The draft guidelines seek to acknowledge and provide for the bi-culturism that is increasing at the heart of all policy development in New Zealand. In 1840 Maori, as the indigenous people, entered into a treaty (The Treaty of Waitangi) with representatives of the British Government. The Treaty established New Zealand as a British colony and in return guaranteed Maori rights in relation to lands, fisheries and forests, full political and civil rights and freedom to continue their traditional ways of life. It is the focus on the traditional ways of life that raises important issues in relation to surrogacy and AHR. For Maori there is acknowledgement that, as Metge and Durie-Hall (2002) remind us, there are two kinds of family, the nuclear family and the *whanau*. The primary meaning of *whanau* is a group of relatives defined by reference to a recent ancestor (*Tupuna*) comprising several generations, several nuclear families and several households. Nelson (2000: 4–10) has stated that children are born into their *whanau*, while Dyall points out that, 'the sharing of kin was and still is seen today by *Maori* as a *Taonga* (treasure) in which all involved have a responsibility to ensure that the interests of the child are paramount' (Dyall (1999:37)). The concept of *whakapapa* is closely related to *whanau*, in fact membership of *whanau* is determined by knowledge of *whakapapa*. *Whakapapa* is similar to the concept of genealogy in that a Maori can trace his/her origins back to the beginnings of life. Dyall (1999) has noted that this knowledge is important as *whakapapa* links determine certain entitlements such as land. She also states that, 'the ability to become pregnant, to bear children and to have and maintain *whanau* is central to *hapu*—a group of *whanau, iwi*[19] and Maori development. Any seed that is shared between people to create life is regarded by Maori as *tapu* or sacred, for it establishes relationships between people, and *whakapapa* is shared' (Dyall (1999:35–36)). This has important implications for both AHR and adoption, as it is crucial that persons know their lineage.

Another closely related concept is that of *whangai* in which a child is given into the care of relatives. In the case of an infertile couple, customary practice would have seen relatives giving birth to a child and giving the child into the care of the infertile couple. No particular formalities took place and the arrangement occurred with the express or tacit approval of the *whanau* or *hapu*. As Dyall points out, 'the children in this situation generally grow up knowing fully who they are in terms of their *whakapapa* and the reasons why their care had been shared' (Dyall (1999:37)). Nelson (2000:13) points out that this meant that the

---

[19] *Iwi* refers to larger social networks of people.

arrangement 'did not extinguish the relationship of those children with their natural parents.'

What will be clear from the above is that Maori, in terms of their customary practices, do not have difficulty with, or objections to, the concept of surrogacy. It is crucial that certain safeguards are observed and these have been outlined. It will also be obvious that Maori have considerable difficulty with the notion of anonymous gamete provision, as this prevents knowledge concerning *whaka-papa*. De Luca (2000) states that, 'For some time New Zealand stood out as one of the few countries which insisted on information sharing about biological origins being recorded and made accessible to children resulting from the application of reproductive technologies. This practice is possibly attributable to the influence of *whakapapa* in Maori culture.'[20]

NECAHR is very aware of the need to recognise not only cultural diversity but also the importance and commitments of the treaty as the founding document of New Zealand. With this in mind, applications from providers must take account of cultural differences and counselling must be culturally appropriate. Having acknowledged this position NECAHR also seeks to take account of the fact that there are many Maori who have distanced themselves from traditional values and practices[21] and that there are a variety of viewpoints among Maori[22] in relation to AHR.

5. CONCLUSIONS

Surrogacy has been established as a matter of public policy in New Zealand. Successive governments have seemed reluctant to act decisively however; developments perhaps best being described as pragmatic, piecemeal and incremental. This in part is a reflection of the complexity of the subject. It may also reflect uncertainty as to how best to develop coherent policy. Stewart (1994:138) following his analysis of one of the cases to come before the courts, concluded that 'the case signals the pressing need for legislation to address the issues.' This sentiment was supported by NECAHR in its Annual Report for 2000 (National Ethics Committee, 2000): 'NECAHR is of the view that there is a gap in the law with regard to assisted human reproduction. From time to time, it has felt that it has been forced inappropriately to take an *ad hoc* role in policy formation in the vacuum that exists.'[23] A previous minister of justice has pointed out that 'even though it (surrogacy) lacks a legal framework, it is not illegal' (Graham (1994)). New Zealand currently stands at the crossroads in relation to the enactment of legislation concerning AHR, including surrogacy. It seems highly

[20] R De Luca, quoted in NECAHR (2000:20).
[21] *Ibid.*
[22] *Ibid.*
[23] Above n 20.

unlikely that the revised Bills, which are to be presented in 2003, will ban surrogacy. It is, after all, an accepted but controversial practice. The system that currently operates is driven by concern for the ethical principles of autonomy, respect, protection of the vulnerable and accountability. It is the part that these principles, which are central only to surrogacy involving health providers, play in the broader policy and legislative framework that remains to be determined.

APPENDIX 1

Draft Guidelines
for
Non-commercial Altruistic Surrogacy
using IVF as Treatment

Prepared by the National Ethics Committee on Assisted Human Reproduction
May 2001
c/o Ministry of Health
PO Box 5013
Wellington
NEW ZEALAND

Introduction

The National Ethics Committee on Assisted Human Reproduction (NECAHR) agreed to give ethical approval to a general application pertaining to non-commercial, altruistic surrogacy using in vitro fertilisation (IVF) as treatment in July 1997 and to review applications on a case-by-case basis. The draft guidelines have been developed progressively as cases are reviewed. NECAHR will continue to notify clinics of amendments to the guidelines.

Each and every instance of this practice with which any infertility services provider wishes to proceed must be submitted individually for ethical review and will be assessed on a case-by-case basis and in relation to these guidelines.

The following issues and reporting requirements must be addressed for ethical approval of non-commercial, altruistic surrogacy using IVF as treatment.

Provider

NECAHR requires a report on the medical status of the birth mother, including the age of the mother, existing medical conditions, and the number of children. Information on the birth mother's age is necessary as the risks to the mother's health and likelihood of a less successful outcome increase with age. Information on the number of children is necessary in order to know whether the birth mother is likely to be capable of having a normal pregnancy. Also, a surrogate mother who already has children of her own is likely to be more aware of the medical and psychological risks to herself.

- The application for ethical review should be explicit about conditions that may impact on the safety of the birth mother when undertaking treatment and pregnancy and should include documentation from medical advisers.
- The treatment must be in accordance with the RTAC[24] guidelines.
- If the birth mother has a partner, the provider must discuss with the birth mother and her partner how they will ensure that they do not conceive their own child during the IVF treatment.
- NECAHR considers that screening of the birth mother's partner should be the standard screening carried out for partners of women undergoing IVF treatment, ie for HIV and Hepatitis A and C.
- NECAHR requires a provider to notify it in the case of each non-commercial altruistic surrogacy using IVF as treatment which has been approved, of:
  —when the IVF programme begins
  —when pregnancy is confirmed or the programme is discontinued
  —any adverse events
  —the outcome of pregnancy, and
  —the outcome of the adoption and guardianship process.
- NECAHR requires that the clinic's policy take account of cultural diversity.

[24] Reproductive Technology Accreditation Committee.

Commissioning parents

- The commissioning parents' use of their own gametes: one or both of the commissioning parents should be the potential child's genetic parents.
- The existence of a medical condition that precludes pregnancy or makes pregnancy damaging to the commissioning mother or the child: there should be medical reasons for the commissioning mother not undertaking a pregnancy.
- The relationship between the birth mother and the commissioning parents: NECAHR prefers that the birth mother be either a family member or close friend of the commissioning parents.
- Expenses related to pregnancy and childbirth: such recompense may be made, but no payment should be made in lieu of employment.

Birth mother and her partner

- The birth mother and her partner should have completed their family as this may reduce the likelihood that they will want to keep the child. Problems could arise if they had not completed their family or begun it, including in relation to medical complications due to the surrogacy, which then prevented further pregnancy.
- If the birth mother has a partner, the birth mother and her partner must take measures to ensure that they do not conceive their own child during the IVF treatment.

Legal advisers

- NECAHR requires a report from a legal adviser for each party, indicating that the party clearly understands the legal issues and the current environment in which surrogacy agreements are legally unenforceable. The same legal adviser must not advise both parties.
- NECAHR does not require a formal agreement. This does not preclude a statement of intent between the parties that allows them to work through the issues and clearly state their intentions and expectations.
- NECAHR advises that the parties discuss possible disputes, for example, about the custody of the child, termination of pregnancy, and life style issues during pregnancy, with their legal advisers and counsellors before the proposal is finalised. It should be noted that disputes may ultimately be resolved by a court.
- Legal advisers must ensure the parties understand that the child will legally be the child of the birth mother (and her partner if there is agreement to the surrogacy arrangement), unless adopted by the commissioning parents.
- Legal advisers must ensure that the parties clearly understand procedures relating to guardianship, custody and adoption and the requirements that adoptive parents have to meet, including the requirements of CYFS,[25] if they wish to adopt the child.

[25] Child Youth and Family Service.

Counsellors

- NECAHR requires counselling reports which confirm that the following issues raised by NECAHR have been discussed and, in the professional judgement of the counsellors, have been adequately understood. NECAHR prefers that two counsellors be involved, one for each family group.
- Counselling must be undertaken by qualified counsellors and be culturally appropriate.
- Counselling must include discussion of the following:
  —the possibility of a breakdown in the arrangement such that the birth mother wishes to keep the child, or the commissioning parents do not wish to take custody of the child
  —the position of both parties in the event of a multiple birth
  —the risk of rejection of a child for any reason, eg if the child is born with a disability or abnormality
  —the possibility of legal termination of a pregnancy if foetal abnormality is diagnosed before birth, having regard for the Contraception, Sterilisation and Abortion Act 1977
  —the possibility of the birth mother deciding against a termination in the above situation, and the subsequent care of the child
  —the amount of control that genetic parents have over the birth mother's conduct of her pregnancy
  —the availability of a permanent, accurate record of conception and gestation for the child and
  —any issues covered in a written agreement.
- NECAHR expects that the parties be counselled as two separate family groups, two family groups together, and as individuals. Existing children should be included in counselling in an age-appropriate manner.
- NECAHR prefers that there be a month free of counselling after the initial counselling period and then further counselling, to allow for the issues to be thought through without counselling intervention.
- NECAHR expects counsellors to follow the usual counselling practice of recording the family histories of those involved in the surrogacy arrangement. If there are life experiences, for example, psychiatric problems, substance/physical/sexual abuse which may predispose any of the persons to risk when moving into a new situation, or which may pose a risk to the potential child, these must be referred to in the counsellors' reports.
- A process should be set up for the resolution of disputes, for example, about the custody of the child or any other issues that arise in discussion with counsellors and legal advisers, before the proposal is finalised.

Further considerations

The Committee is prepared to consider an application deviating from the proposed guidelines. If applicants wish to deviate from any of the proposed guidelines, they should indicate this and give their reasons at the time of the application.

Please note that these guidelines that NECAHR wishes to see addressed in applications for ethical review of non-commercial, altruistic surrogacy using IVF as treatment are provisional only. NECAHR cannot at this time guarantee that the guidelines include all the issues it might wish to have addressed by applicants in such proposals. Where new issues do come to its attention, NECAHR undertakes to inform potential providers of this in as timely a fashion as possible.

The Committee welcomes comment on the proposed guidelines, to assist in the ongoing development of the guidelines. The Committee requests that previous draft guidelines be destroyed.

REFERENCES

Assisted Reproduction—Navigating our Future (Report of the Ministerial Committee on Assisted Reproductive Technologies, July 1994), Wellington, New Zealand.

Brazier, M, Golombok, S and Campbell, A, *Surrogacy. Review for the Health Ministers of Current Arrangements for Payments and Regulations. Report of the Review Team* Cm 4068 (London, HMSO, 1998).

Coney, S and Else, A, (eds), *Protecting our Future: The Case for Greater Regulation of Assisted Reproductive Technology—A Discussion Document* (Women's Health Action Trust and New Zealand Law Foundation, 1999).

Daniels, K and Caldwell, J, 'Family Law Policy and Assisted Reproduction' in M Henaghan and B Atkin (eds), *Family Law Policy in New Zealand*, 2nd edn (Wellington, LexisNexis, 2002).

Daniels, K and Hargreaves, K, 'The Policy and Ethics of Surrogacy in New Zealand: Who is Left Holding the Baby?' (1997) 6 *Otago Bioethics Report* 14.

De Luca, R, 'Issues for the NECAHR in its Review of Medically Assisted Surrogacy with Wider Implications for Ethical Review' (2000) 8 *Otago Bioethics Review* 20.

Dyall, L, 'Awhina I te hangarau whakato: Tiaki te whakapapa—Assisted Reproductive Technologies: Protecting the generations' in S Coney and A Else (eds), *Protecting our Future: The Case for Greater Regulation of Assisted Reproductive Technology—A Discussion Document* (Women's Health Action Trust, New Zealand Law Foundation, 1999).

Re G Unreported Judgment, Adopt 6/92. District Court Invercargill, 3 February 1993 quoted in S Coney and A Else, *Protecting our Future: The Case for Greater Regulation of Assisted Reproductive Technology—A Discussion Document* (Women's Health Action Trust, New Zealand Law Foundation, 1999) p 53.

Graham, D, *The Christchurch Press*, 14 February 1994.

Interim National Ethics Committee on Assisted Reproductive Technology—INECART, (1995) *Non Commercial Surrogacy by means of In Vitro Fertilisation* (15 December 1995) Wellington, New Zealand.

Metge, J and Hall, D, 'Tua tutu Te Puehu, Kia Mau: Maori Aspirations and Family Law' in M Henaghan and B Atkin (eds), *Family Law Policy in New Zealand*, 2nd edn (Wellington, LexisNexis, 2002).

National Ethics Committee on Assisted Human Reproduction (NECAHR) (2000) *Annual Report to the Minister of Health* (for the year ending 31 December 2000) (Wellington, New Zealand).

Nelson, JL, 'Reproductive Ethics and the Family' (2000) 1 *New Zealand Bioethics Journal* 4.

New Birth Technologies: An issues paper on AID, IVF and Surrogate Motherhood (Law Reform Division, Department of Justice, New Zealand, March 1985).

New Birth Technologies: A summary of the submissions received on the issues paper (Law Reform Division, Department of Justice, Wellington, New Zealand, 1986).

New Zealand Law Commission, *Adoption and its Alternatives. A Different Approach and a New Framework*. Report 65 (New Zealand Law Commssion, Wellington, New Zealand, 2000).

Officials Committee: A commentary on the Report of the Ministerial Committee on Assisted Reproductive Technologies, 1995, Wellington, New Zealand.

P (Adoption) Surrogacy [1990] NZFLR 385 quoted in S Coney and A Else (eds), *Protecting our Future: The Case for Greater Regulation of Assisted Reproductive Technology—A Discussion Document* (Women's Health Action Trust, New Zealand Law Foundation, 1999).

Scott, R, 'Discussion on Bioethics' (1984) *New Zealand Law Journal* 240.

Reproductive Technology Accreditation Committee. The Fertility Society of Australia. Code of Practice for Centers Using Assisted Reproductive Technology. (Revised March 1997).

Royal Society of New Zealand, the New Zealand Law Society, the Medical Council of New Zealand, the Medical Research Council of New Zealand and the Medical Association of New Zealand *New Zealand Medical Journal* (1985) Volume 98 pp396–8.

Status of the Children Amendment Act, 1987, Wellington, New Zealand.

Stewart, G, 'Adoption and Surrogacy' (1984) *New Zealand Law Journal* 138.

Telfer, B, *The New Birth Technologies: Analysis of a Community's Response, and an Ethical Assessment* (Unpublished MSc thesis, University of Otago, New Zealand, 1989).

Wadlington, WJ, 'When are Mothers and Fathers not Mothers and Fathers?' (1981) 140 *LawTalk* 27.

Waller, L, *Report on Donor Gametes in IVF. The Committee to Consider the Social, Ethical and Legal Issues arising from In-Vitro Fertilisation* (State of Victoria, Australia, 1983).

Warnock, M, *Report of the Committee of Inquiry into Human Fertilisation and Embryology.* Cmnd 9314 (London, HMSO, 1984).

5

Enigma Variations: Surrogacy, Rights and Procreative Tourism

DEREK MORGAN

1. ENIGMA VARIATION

SURROGACY IS ONE of the enigmas of the 'reproductive revolution'. Surrogacy contracts touch upon one of the most, if not *the* most sensitive subjects of human endeavour.[1] It is one of those kinds of concern that lie in the heartland of the ethical divide in which we also find subjects such as abortion, experimentation on human embryos, genetic engineering, cloning, and so on. And yet, as Ruth Deech, sometime Chairman of the Human Fertilisation and Embryology Authority (HFEA) writing in a personal capacity, has observed: 'when surrogacy runs smoothly, there are no objections; but if the arrangement breaks down, then surrogacy is disapproved of by the media and the general public, and the disposition of sympathy is dependent, almost entirely, on the facts of the individual case' (Deech (1998)).

Since 1985, surrogacy has undergone a number of metamorphoses, from the sexual to the medical; the private (and invisible) to the public (and intermittently visible); the altruistic to the commercial and back again; and from the contested and controversial to the accepted and clinically mediated, and back again. Surrogacy, and the various metamorphoses through which it has passed in barely two decades since it has attained public visibility, attracts controversy. In this chapter, I want to reflect briefly on two of the most recent metamorphoses to affect surrogacy, engaging what might be called 'reproductive communications'. I want to look, severally, at surrogacy and human rights and surrogacy and the internet.

The sequential metamorphoses of surrogacy can be located in the history of assisted conception. For Margot Brazier, appointed by the incoming government in 1997 to review the workings of the law in England and Wales, the fundamental issues concerned safeguarding the welfare of the child and ensuring protection of the interests of the surrogate mother. Another issue that troubled Brazier, as well as others, was the question of payments to surrogates and whether such transactions were readily distinguishable from the buying and

---

[1] *Johnson v Calvert* 851 P. 2d 776, at 787 (1993) (Supreme Court of California), per Arabian J, concurring opinion.

selling of children.[2] A further concern has been the way in which medicine is perceived in the context of surrogacy; increasingly it is linked to ideas about autonomy and rights.

Notions of autonomy and individual choice, coupled with the fervour to translate many aspects of the doctor–patient relationship into issues of human rights, lead to the fear that we might be in the process of transforming the 'therapeutic alliance' into a consumer association.

In so far as there has been a shift from power based in medicine as an art to power based in the objectives of science, medicine has changed the focus of the doctor from the uniqueness of the disease carrier in front of him to the generalisations of science. This shift to impersonal medicine has caused patients to look for their own objectivity in the relationship by the assertion of claims to self-determination. In turn, this is reinforced by modern ideas of the paramountcy of the consumer (Jacob (1988:2)).

Rights arguments, especially when developed in a sophisticated, calibrated fashion, have an important, influential rhetorical force in defining what may be achieved, and they carry that value in a way that is hard to deny, as I shall shortly review (see Kennedy (1991)). But an exclusive concern with rights, as opposed to other ethical values (for example care (Gilligan (1982) or virtue (Noddings (1978)), produces an atomised, anomised, autonomised individual rather than the community of interest in which modern medical practice is, in my view, best delivered and understood. The 'procreative tourist',[3] surfing the waves of information, is merely in the vanguard of the information activists' more settled development of the surgery, the theatre and the clinic.

Surrendering concepts of illness and according legitimacy to desire alone means, according to Brazier and Glover, that consumer protection laws could (in theory) '. . . offer sufficient guarantee of the quality of the goods supplied and standards of service provision.'[4] Such a future, where medical law is subsumed into consumer law, may be seen as a logical development of the trend that regards medical law as a sub-set of human rights law:

> Expanding definitions of illness coupled with the present tendency to prioritise self-determination as *the* basic human right in medical law, assume that health is essentially a personal concern.[5]

Ethical disagreements over surrogacy turn, first, on an acceptance or general scepticism about or rejection of the biomedical model of medicine. Secondly,

---

[2] She has declared her view that it is not: 'If an infertile couple can buy an egg, and rent a womb, why should they not buy the finished product? It will be argued of course that in purchasing gametes and/or the services of a surrogate, they are *not* buying a baby. I hope to demonstrate that that argument is specious' (1999a:345). For the view that it is possible to distinguish between the payment for the reproductive services of a surrogate which we should permit, and 'baby selling' which we should not, see Dickenson (1997:160 *et seq.*); Mason (1998:259) and Freeman (1999).

[3] See Knoppers and Le Bris (1991:333). And see Brazier (1999b) for specific examples of the use of the Internet.

[4] Brazier and Glover (2000).

[5] *Ibid*, at 375.

and possibly but not necessarily flowing from this, is an argument that centres on whether reproductive technologies are the wrong sets of responses to the wrong sets of problems, or whether at best they promise a limited set of outcomes for a very limited set of questions for a limited set of people. Surrogacy is caught up in, if not centrally implicated, in this. And even if reproductive technologies do properly have a place in westernised societies' responses in the twenty-first century to the consequences of 'infertility', there is still a third issue. There is debate about whether and to what extent these technologies should be free from explicit manipulation or control by the state to secure other, underlying policy goals that exist either for the benefit of the state or others whom it supposedly serves, rather than for the benefit of the individual users those reproductive technologies.[6]

For liberal social theorists and ethicists, such as John Robertson and John Harris, surrogacy, or 'collaborative conception', is part of a general recognition of 'reproductive rights' that calls for very special vigilance against the intrusions of the state and calls for special reasons if prohibitive intervention is to be sanctioned. The techniques and trappings of assisted conception—AI, IVF, GIFT, cryopreservation of gametes, eggs and embryos, gamete and embryo donation, and surrogacy—also challenge traditional views of procreation and parenthood, a challenge that has legal as well as ethical implications.

John Harris, a British philosopher, elegantly summarises the rights-based arguments in his recent essay *Rights and Reproductive Choice*.[7] Drawing explicitly and extensively on arguments developed in a more general context by Ronald Dworkin,[8] he has defined and described 'a vital feature of an essentially democratic approach to reproductive choices' as lying in the recognition of, and a generous reading of, the concept of 'procreative autonomy' involving much needed and much desired treatment as a legitimate extension of human choice.[9] This is a principle which, in a broad sense, is embedded in any genuinely democratic culture.[10]

Developments in reproductive technologies have demanded that questions about what ought and ought not to constrain choice in reproduction (an idea 'that is respected more in the breach than in the observance'[11]) should be brought to the bar of procreative autonomy. Specifically, we should ask of reproductive technologies: 'is their use ethical and should access to it, or use of it, be controlled by legislation, and if so how?'[12] Framing these questions is the belief that we should not ask questions of those requiring medical or other assistance, nor

---

[6] I have attempted to identify my own reading of feminist approaches to debates such as this generally in Morgan (1998).

[7] In Harris and Holm (1998:5–37).

[8] Especially in his books *Life's Dominion* (1993), *Freedom's Law* (1996), *Taking Rights Seriously*, (1997) and *A Matter of Principle* (1985).

[9] Harris, n 7 above at 5 and 37.

[10] Dworkin (1993:166–67).

[11] Harris, n 7 above, at 5

[12] *Ibid* at 34.

should we oblige them to fulfil criteria that we do not or could not be justified in asking of those who do not need such assistance. In this sense, arguments from reproductive rights based on respect for procreative autonomy demand simply that people needing help should be treated, as far as their procreative and parenting choices are concerned, in the same way as anyone else.

Dworkin has defined the 'right of procreative autonomy', in the context of the abortion debate, as, 'a right [of people] to control their own role in procreation unless the state has a compelling reason for denying them that control'.[13] Harris takes Dworkin's expression and asks whether it might properly be interpreted to include the right of procreative autonomy in what might be thought of as a more positive way (in assisted conception) rather than in the context in which Dworkin originally developed his argument. For Harris, on this analysis, the right of 'procreative autonomy' would need to encompass the right,

> . . . to reproduce with the genes we choose and to which we have legitimate access, or to reproduce in ways that express our reproductive choices and our vision of the sorts of people we think it right to create.[14]

If procreative autonomy is to be taken seriously, it should not be possible for it to be trumped easily; it is necessary for *any* democratic society (whether one with a written constitution or not) to demonstrate that it has a compelling reason before denying individual citizens control over their own reproductive choices and decisions:

> In so far as the decisions to reproduce in particular ways or even using particular technologies constitute decisions concerning central issues of value, then . . . to establish [that the state had such a compelling reason] the state would have to show that more was at stake than the fact that a majority found the ideas disturbing or even disgusting.[15]

These reproductive decisions are a central, if not a defining, part of moral responsibility; the idea that 'people have the moral right—and the moral responsibility—to confront the most fundamental questions about the meaning and value of their own lives for themselves, answering to their own consciences and convictions.'[16]

What follows from this is not necessarily an untrammelled, uninhibited orgy or assisted reproductive excess. Rather it requires a close and careful examination and explanation of what we propose to do and what we hope to achieve. The presumption, cautions Harris, should be against over-hasty prohibition; what is required and justified is dual caution. There should be caution when considering the acceptability of scientific 'advances' and the use of reproductive technologies, but equally, there should be caution against the deployment of baseless charges of unethical practices and the enactment of restrictive legislation based on such charges.

---

[13] Dworkin (1993:148).
[14] Harris, n 7 above at 34.
[15] *Ibid* at 36.
[16] Dworkin (1993:166–67).

By contrast, Robertson's[17] version of reproductive rights is grounded in the notion of what he calls 'procreative liberty'. He sees this as a negative right against state interference in procreative decisions, whether the decision is to have children or to avoid having them. Here we concern ourselves only with the former aspect of the argument. This 'liberty' is not co-extensive with everything that concerns procreation, but it is a primary liberty because it is central to personal identity, dignity and the meaning of one's life.[18] This vocabulary, perhaps first articulated in the United States Supreme Court in *Skinner v Oklahoma*,[19] has begun to take root in the United Kingdom. For example, in a recent case dealing with a claim for damages for an unwanted pregnancy, Lord Steyn indicated that the starting point for his analysis was the recognition of a right vested in parents to take decisions on family planning and, if those plans should fail, their right to make their own untrammelled decisions on how then to proceed: 'The law does and must respect these decisions of parents which are so closely tied to the basic freedoms and rights of personal autonomy.'[20]

Lady Justice Hale, writing extra-judicially, has expressed herself in similar language:

> ... The rights set out in Articles 8 to 12 of the European Convention on Human Rights form a coherent and related group; the right to respect for private and family life, home and correspondence; the right to freedom of expression; the right to freedom of peaceful assembly and free association; and the right to marry and found a family. These are the very essentials of a free-thinking and free-speaking society.[21]

Of course, what follows from this may legitimately be a source of disagreement. Hale, for example, would hardly be in agreement with the whole of Robertson's thesis. But on one specific point they are in tandem: 'procreative liberty' or the 'basic freedoms and rights of personal autonomy' are *negative* rights. The state has no duty to supply a service on demand.[22] Procreative liberty implies a right against state interference, but it is not 'a positive right to have the state or particular persons provide the means or resources necessary to have or avoid having children.'[23] Without doubt, social and economic circumstances impact crucially on the ability to access reproductive technologies—in other words, they impact on whether an individual is able effectively to exercise or to enjoy their

---

[17] Robertson (1994). Robertson's book-length treatment of procreative autonomy also contains, at pp 220—26, his reply to anticipated criticism from class, feminist and communitarian critiques of procreative liberty.

[18] *Ibid* at 24.

[19] 316 US 535 (1942). There are useful discussions of the 'right to procreate' in the British context and literature in Mason (1998:85–87); The Hon Mrs Justice Hale (1996:5–9), and in a characteristically early essay by Sheila McLean and Tome Campbell (1981:178 et seq).

[20] *Macfarlane and another v Tayside Health Board* [1999] 4 All ER 961 at 976j.

[21] Hale, n 19 above at 7.

[22] *Ibid* at 8.

[23] Robertson, n 17 above at 23. For a telling contemporary example see the High Court and then Court of Appeal decisions in *Broidy v St Helen's & Knowsley AHA* (2000) 53 BMLR 108 and (2001) 62 BMLR 1.

procreative liberty. But whether the state should alleviate those conditions 'is a separate issue of social justice.'[24]

Similarly, that a right to procreative liberty should presumptively be recognised does not mean that the fact that the impact of reproductive choices on others should be ignored, nor that those choices should never be limited. It does mean, however, that those who would limit reproductive choice '. . . have the burden of showing that the reproductive actions at issue would create such substantial harm that they could justifiably be limited.'[25] This distinct echo of Mill recalls Harris' claim that distaste or disgust are not in themselves proper grounds for state interference. In Robertson's view being unmarried, homosexual, physically disabled, of HIV+ status, or imprisoned are not sufficient grounds in themselves to override this liberty; speculation or 'mere moral objections'[26] would not suffice. In the light of these arguments, it is worth reminding ourselves that a proposal in the debates of 1989 and 1990 to limit access to assisted conception to married couples was defeated by only one vote.

The development of assisted reproduction programmes and the medicalisation of infertility have raised 'some of the most difficult questions for feminist theory and practice.'[27] According to Lene Koch, 'One of the most difficult problems that have confronted feminist critics of *in vitro* fertilisation (IVF) and the other new reproductive technologies, is the great enthusiasm for IVF among involuntarily childless women.'[28] Carol Smart has even doubted that there can there be a satisfactory feminist response to reproductive technology. On the one hand, it is possible to argue against the use of such technologies on the grounds that they contribute to and reinforce (male) dominant ideologies of motherhood and womanhood. However, to do so would be to deny individual women's experiences and announced intentions. To do so may also amount to suggesting that individual women are not able—autonomously—to choose for themselves. Such an argument casts women as incompetent, unable to weigh and balance the consequences of infertility treatments and the possible opportunity costs of the treatments and the very real costs of disappointment and 'failure' in conception. On the other hand, to argue that reproductive technologies liberate women from the consequences of either their infertility or that of their partner is to suggest an uncomfortably determinist approach to mental and physical well being and notions of personhood.[29] As Margaret Radin points out,[30] 'it should be clear that there are coherent feminist arguments on both sides.'[31]

[24] Robertson, n 17 above at 23. For a telling contemporary example see the High Court and then Court of Appeal decisions in *Broidy v St Helen's & Knowsley AHA* (2000) 53 BMLR 108 and (2001) 62 BMLR 1.
[25] Robertson, n 17 above at 24.
[26] *Ibid* at 35.
[27] Anleu (1994).
[28] Koch (1990:235).
[29] Smart (1990:223–24).
[30] Radin (1996).
[31] *Ibid* at 149.

2. REGULATING SURROGACY

Anne Maclean has identified surrogacy as complex and difficult because it raises not one issue but a cluster of issues, and issues of different sorts at that. 'It is easy to confuse considerations relevant to one of these issues with considerations relevant to another, or to misunderstand the character of a particular claim or a particular objection.'[32] She has suggested that there is no single moral issue called surrogacy; people's moral worries about surrogacy arrangements will vary greatly depending on the type of surrogacy in question, the relationships of the parties involved to one another, and whether or not it is a commercial transaction. And this moral concern will engage a variety of wider concerns too; not just about 'the family' and parenthood but also 'about one's whole attitude to what life brings.' The sorts of worries, or objections, the 'issues of different sorts' as Maclean puts it, will carry different force in different circumstances. Thus, worries about resource implications (which can of course involve ethical concerns), are very different sorts of worries from those deep, inarticulate worries about the basic legitimacy of an action or of a general attitude exemplified in an action.

Surrogacy has been used in ways that demonstrate some of the complexities that Maclean is concerned to identify and distinguish. One woman has given birth to her sister, another to her grandchildren, and another to her niece. In the light of this, it may be surprising to discover that English law on surrogacy is, at least at first sight, simple and straightforward. Surrogacy arrangements are not unlawful, nor is the payment of money to a surrogate mother in return for her agreeing to carry and hand over the child. Commercial surrogacy arrangements, however, are unlawful. The core of the Surrogacy Arrangements Act 1985 is directed towards commercial agencies. The Act does not attempt to deal with 'altruistic'[33] or family arrangements, neither does it deal with those in which the offices of a charitable organisation have assisted the establishment of the contract. The expressed reasoning behind these exemptions is to avoid the birth of a child whose mother or family are 'subject to the taint of criminality.'[34]

Although though the law prohibits neither 'altruistic' surrogacy nor surrogacy for which the surrogate is paid without the involvement of a commercial agency, the restraints on advertising surrogacy services attempt to ensure that, to all intents and purposes, surrogacy will be kept 'within the family'. Section 3 of the 1985 Act makes it an offence to advertise to act as a surrogate mother, to advertise in the search for a surrogate mother, or to say that one is willing to set up a surrogacy agreement. The prohibition is exhaustive, making it clear that it

[32] Maclean (1993:202).
[33] The term 'altruistic' surrogacy is that suggested by Singer and Wells (1984:124) in discussing the *Crozier* case in France of a twin who bore a child for her infertile sister.
[34] Warnock, *Report of the Committee of Inquiry into Human Fertilisation & Embryology* (Cmnd 9314, 1984: para 8.2).

is not only newspaper or periodical advertising that is caught, but also advertising which uses telecommunication systems or through putting a card in the local corner shop.[35] Whether this would catch the increasingly prevalent use of the Internet—to which I return, below—is a moot point. Contravention of these provisions can only be prosecuted by or with the consent of the DPP.

The Human Fertilisation and Embryology Act 1990, in establishing the HFEA to regulate certain types of infertility treatment and research, also took the opportunity to extend the remit of the HFEA to certain aspects of infertility treatment that would encompass surrogacy, and to correct certain aspects of the emergent law of surrogacy that the 1985 Act had not addressed sufficiently clearly. By virtue of a late amendment, the Act also introduced a new kind of order: the Parental Order.

It is a statutory requirement that any centre undertaking activities covered by the Act must have a licence from the authority which specifies the activities covered by the licence, the premises in which the activities may be performed and the name of a 'person responsible' under whose supervision the work must be carried out.[36] Licensed activities include the creation or use of an embryo outside the body and the use of donated eggs, sperm or embryos. Any medical treatment used as part of a surrogacy arrangement will involve the donation of sperm, eggs or embryos and thus must be carried out in a licensed centre. Under the Act's requirements, details of every treatment carried out must be lodged with the HFEA. Thus, although the Authority does not directly regulate surrogacy, licensed treatment services provided to establish a surrogate pregnancy will be carried out under its auspices.

One aspect of the HFEA's supervisory role is the publication of a code of practice that provides guidance concerning proper conduct of licensed activities. All centres providing treatment services for the purpose of establishing a surrogate pregnancy must abide by the code of practice. One of the provisions of the 1990 Act makes it a condition of all treatment licences that:

> a woman shall not be provided with treatment services unless account has been taken of the welfare of any child who may be born as a result of the treatment (including the need of that child for a father), and of any other child who may be affected by the birth.[37]

Thus all centres providing treatment services as part of a surrogacy arrangement are legally obliged to take account of the welfare of the child. This requirement is complicated by the fact that either the surrogate mother and her partner, if she has one, or the intended parents could take on the role of social parents; the centre is therefore obliged to make enquiries of both parties. The HFEA's Code of Practice advises consideration of the following factors:

---

[35] ss 3 (3), (4).
[36] Human Fertilisation and Embryology Act 1990, ss 12–15.
[37] Human Fertilisation and Embryology Act 1990 s 13(5).

The commitment of the woman, and her husband/partner to having and bringing up a child or children.

Their ages and medical histories and the medical histories of their families.

The needs of any child or children who may be born as a result of treatment, including the implications of any possible multiple birth and the ability of the prospective parents (or parent) to meet those needs.

Any risk of harm to the child or children who may be born, including the risk of inherited disorders, problems during pregnancy and of neglect or abuse.

The effect of a new baby on any existing child of the family.[38]

The HFEA also advises in its code of practice that all people seeking treatment are entitled to a fair and unprejudiced assessment of their situation and needs, which should be conducted with the skill and sensitivity appropriate to the delicacy of the case and the wishes and feeling of those involved.[39]

Those participating in a surrogacy arrangement must reach agreement between themselves as to how the arrangement will proceed. However, regardless of whether the agreement is detailed in writing and regardless of whether expenses have been paid, section 36 of the Human Fertilisation and Embryology Act renders surrogacy contracts unenforceable.[40] This means that if the surrogate mother wishes to keep the child she is entitled to do so. Equally, if the intended parents decide that they do not want the child, the surrogate mother, as the legal mother of the child, is responsible in law for its welfare. In practice, a child rejected by both its birth mother and the intended parents is likely to be placed for fostering or adoption.

A child born to a surrogate mother must be registered as her child and, if applicable, that of her partner or person treated as the father under the Act. Where a parental order has been granted under s30 by a court, the Registrar General will make an entry in a separate Parental Order Register registering the child and cross referencing it to the entry in the existing Register of Births. There is no public Parental Order Register. It is not possible to 'abolish' the original record of birth and, at the age of 18, a person who was the subject of a parental order may be supplied with information enabling him or her to obtain a certified copy of the original record of the birth. Prior to being given access to the information, the person is to be advised of counselling services available. The birth certificate includes the name of the surrogate mother. This is an exception to the general provisions that children born of assisted conception may not discover the identity of the people who were party to their conception. These 'status' provisions, as I shall show, are one of a suite of provisions of the Human Fertilisation and Embryology Act that are potentially at risk of a challenge under the Human Rights Act 1998.

---

[38] *Code of Practice*, part 3.16.

[39] *Code of Practice*, part 3.15.

[40] Human Fertilisation and Embryology Act 1990 s 36 inserts s 1A in the Surrogacy Arrangements Act 1985 and provides that 'No surrogacy arrangement is enforceable by or against any of the persons making it.'

The Parental Orders (Human Fertilisation and Embryology) Regulations 1994[41] are intended to achieve the same effect as an adoption order. The relevant provisions of those regulations are para 1(1), (2) and para 2, col 1, sch 1, sub-para 1(b), which adopts (under section 30(9) of the 1990 Act) amended provisions of the Adoption Act 1976, section 12 (1)-(3). As amended, the relevant part reads:

'(1) A parental order is an order giving parental responsibility for a child to the husband and wife, made on their application by an authorised court.
. . .
(3) The making of a parental order operates to extinguish—
(a) the parental responsibility which any person has for the child immediately before the making of the order;
(aa) any order under the Children Act 1989;
(b) any duty arising by virtue of an agreement or the order of a court to make payments, so far as the payments are in respect of the child's maintenance or upbringing for any period after the making of the order'.

Concerns, however, have arisen in connection with the section 30 procedure.[42] It does not assist those intended parents who want to ensure that, in formalising their relationship with the child, they also exclude the surrogate mother and strip her of all of her parental rights. This is indeed the effect of adoption, but not of section 30. In England and Wales, the terms of the Adoption Act 1976 sections 12 and 39, provide that adoption is the process whereby a court irrevocably extinguishes the legal ties between a child and his or her natural parents and creates analogous ties between the child and the adopters. Section 30 has only the effect that the intending social parents are registered as the child's legal parents. Two birth certificates are issued. One of these, accessible to the public, names the commissioning parents as the child's parents if they have completed the Parental Order procedure. A second register, not open to the public, names the surrogate mother. Since the HFE Act does not explicitly extinguish the parental status of the surrogate mother, it is possible that she could apply for contact with the child under the Children Act 1989, and that a court would be required to consider whether to admit such a claim.

The section 30 procedure itself also presents problems. Regulations made under section 30(9) provide that the court must be satisfied that the welfare of the child is prioritised throughout the proceedings. Some solicitors have argued that, by the time a social worker has been appointed as guardian *ad litem*[43] for these purposes, and assuming only a first hearing, the time involved could be as long as that usually involved in obtaining an adoption order. Section 30(5)

---

[41] (SI 1994/2767) (made under the provisions of the Human Fertilisation and Embryology Act 1990, ss 30(9), 45(1) and (3)).

[42] These following paragraphs are based on the evidence presented to and marshalled in the British Medical Association's report, BMA (1995).

[43] Under s 41(1) of the Children Act 1989.

further requires the consent of the surrogate mother to the making of the orders, and section 30(6) provides that her consent is ineffective if given within the first six weeks after the child's birth. Compared with the adoption process, in which any refusal of consent is open to review after consultation with social work staff, including the question of whether any consent is being unreasonably withheld, section 30 has clear and present dangers or limitations.

The restriction of section 30 to married couples caused predictable disappointment to some people, but the limitation has gone further than some could have anticipated. Section 30(1) provides that: 'The Court may make an order providing for a child to be treated in law as the child of the parties to a marriage,' if the further conditions of the section and subsequent regulations are satisfied. The phrase 'parties to a marriage' has for lawyers, of course, a particular significance. Death is one of the events that might bring a marriage to an end. In separate cases reported to the surrogacy self-help group COTS within the same week in December 1994, two women who had intended to apply with their respective husbands for Parental Orders under section 30 died. One woman was killed in a road accident and the other died of natural causes. In both cases their husbands were deprived by the death of, among other things, the ability to apply for a section 30 order. In the first case the child had been living with the couple for several years, while in the latter the child was only 12 weeks old. That father faced uncertainty in establishing a good case under the Adoption Act that he was the most fitting person to care for the child, because he had, by definition, little parenting experience.

3. SURROGACY AND HUMAN RIGHTS?

The Human Rights Act 1998 gives effect in English law to the provisions of the European Convention on Human Rights. Article 8 of the Convention provides that:

1. Everyone has the right to respect for his private and family life.
2. There shall be no interference with the exercise of this right except such as in accordance with the law and is necessary in a democratic society . . . for the protection of the rights and freedoms of others (ECHR, Art 8(2)).

The objects and scope of Article 8 have been the subject of three particularly pertinent judgments of the European Court of Human Rights where the sequelae of assisted conception in the guise of surrogacy might be concerned. In *Marckx v Belgium* the Court wrote that:

The object of the Article [8] is 'essentially' that of protecting the individual against arbitrary interference by the public authorities. Nevertheless, it does not merely compel the State to abstain from such interference: in addition to the primary negative undertaking, there may be positive obligations inherent in an effective 'respect' for family life. This means, amongst other things, that when the State determines in its domestic legal system the regime applicable to certain family ties such as those between an unmarried mother and her child, it must act in a manner calculated to allow those concerned to lead a normal family life.[44]

The Court, deciding the Diane Pretty case, has more recently held in relation to Article 8:

> It covers the physical and psychological *integrity* of a person. It can sometimes embrace aspects of an individual's physical and social identity. Elements such as, *for example*, gender identification, name and sexual orientation and sexual life fall within the personal sphere protected by Article 8. Article 8 also protects a right to personal development, and the right to establish and develop relationships with other human beings and the outside world. . . . Though no previous case has established any such right to self-determination as being contained in Article 8 of the Convention, the Court considers that the notion of personal autonomy is an important principle underlying the interpretation of its guarantees. . . . the ability to conduct one's life in a manner of one's own choosing . . . the very essence of the Convention is respect for human dignity and human freedom. . . . it is under Article 8 that notions of the quality of life take on significance. In an era of growing medical sophistication combined with longer life expectancies, many people are concerned that they should not be forced to linger on in old age or in states of advanced physical or mental decrepitude which conflict with strongly held ideas of *self and personal identity*.[45]

Now some aspects of these judgments can be overstated in relation to the substantive rights they might give rise to or support. But substitute at the end of that extract from the Court's judgment in the Dianne Pretty case the phrase:

> In an era of growing medical sophistication combined with *a strong emphasis on rights to personal autonomy* that encompass the physical and psychological *integrity* of a person, many people are concerned that they should not be forced to *live in a state of mental anxiety that conflicts* with strongly held ideas of *self and personal identity*.

Indeed, the enjoyment of the sorts of rights that the Court enumerates in its judgment in *Pretty* are not only an expression of, but are actually predicated on, a strong sense of self and personal identity, a sense—taken literally—of knowing who you are.

Support for this proposition seems to flow directly from the Court's recent decision in *Case of Mikulic v Croatia*.[46] In that case the applicant was a child born to an unmarried woman on 25 November 1996. Her mother had been trying to establish the paternity of one HP since January 1997. The application alleged breaches of Article 6—the right to a hearing within a reasonable time, which need not concern us here, and Article 8. Of the latter claim the Court said this:

---

[44]   *Marckx v Belgium* (1979) 2 EHRR 330.
[45]   *Case of Pretty v The United Kingdom* (Application no. 2346/02) (Fourth Section) judgment of 29 March 2002.
[46]   (Application no. 53176/99) (First Section) Judgment 7 February 2002.

The Court has held that the notion of 'family life' in Article 8 is not confined solely to marriage-based relationships but may also encompass other *de facto* 'family ties' where sufficient constancy is present. . . . The present case differs from the paternity cases cited above in so far as no family tie has been established between the applicant and her alleged father. The Court reiterates, however, that Article 8, for its part, protects not only 'family' but also 'private' life. Private life, in the Court's view, includes a person's physical and psychological integrity and can sometimes embrace aspects of an individual's physical and social identity. Respect for 'private life' must also comprise to a certain degree the right to establish relationships with other human beings. . . . There appears, furthermore, to be no reason of principle why the notion of 'private life' should be taken to exclude the determination of the legal relationship between a child born out of wedlock and her natural father. The Court has held that respect for private life requires that everyone should be able to establish details of their identity as individual human beings and that an individual's entitlement to such information is of importance because of its formative implications for his or her personality. . . . The applicant is seeking . . . to establish who her natural father is . . . through the establishment of the biological truth. Consequently, there is a direct link between the establishment of paternity and the applicant's private life. . . .

[P]ersons in the applicant's situation have a vital interest, protected by the Convention, in receiving the information necessary to uncover the truth about an important aspect of their personal identity. On the other hand, it must be borne in mind that the protection of third persons may preclude their being compelled to make themselves available for medical testing of any kind, including DNA testing. . . . [T]he courts are required to have regard to the basic principle of the child's interests [and the need to] strike a fair balance between the right of the applicant to have her uncertainty as to her personal identity eliminated without unnecessary delay and that of her supposed father not to undergo DNA tests.

I take it from this that Article 8(1) is engaged, and perhaps infringed: where a state prevents or interferes with a person's ability to establish the 'biological truth' of their 'social identity'; and that knowledge is important because of 'its formative implications for his or her personality'; and where preventing or refusing to facilitate this causes or has caused harm to a person's physical and psychological integrity. The potential for infringement exists whether the state is dilatory (as in *Mikulic* itself), whether it is attempting to achieve certain social goals (such as discouraging posthumous pregnancies) or through the operation of sections 27 and 30 of the HFEA. Let me explore this latter contention briefly in the light of the foregoing case analysis.

Section 27(1) of the HFE Act 1990 provides that the surrogate is *always* the child's legal mother *irrespective* of whose eggs were used. No legal mechanism for discovering an anonymous egg donor's identity exists. If the intending social father provided the sperm, he will be the child's father, *unless* section 28 of the Act applies to make someone else the legal father. Thus, if a child is born following IVF to a married surrogate mother, her husband will be the legal father unless it is shown that he did not consent to the treatment by virtue of section 28(2). There is no legal provision that acknowledges the biological father as such. Any of these provisions might be vulnerable, in an appropriate case, to an examination and possible Human Rights Act challenge.

Article 8(2) requires that, to be justified, state interference with a person's rights must be

(i) in accordance with the law;
(ii) necessary in a democratic society for a legitimate purpose set out in Article 8(2), and
(iii) proportionate.

It could be argued that the rights of all the parties in a surrogacy relationship are at stake and that the status sections of the HFE Act would be justified under the Artcle 8(2) provision allowing for the 'the protection of the rights and freedoms of others.' Whether this would succeed in pushing back the tide of European jurisprudence most recently evidenced in *Mikulic* remains to be seen.

4. SURROGACY AND PROCREATIVE TOURISM

Brazier has noted with some disquiet, the possibility of procreative tourism,

> those wealthy enough to participate in reproduction markets can readily evade their domestic constraints. If I can order sperm on the internet, or hire a surrogate mother from Bolivia, are British regulators wasting their time? The international ramifications of the reproductive business may prove to be a more stringent test of the strength of British law than all the different ethical dilemmas that have gone before.[47]

One of the most remarkable developments affecting surrogacy since it achieved public visibility has been the use of the internet. It is used to search for and to advertise surrogacy services; to provide information about services; and to record surrogates' and intended parents' own stories about surrogacy arrangements. One of the main uses of the internet for these purposes is to enable people to circumvent domestic legal regimes that are either hostile to or prohibit surrogacy; the internet is a passport for those who would wish to surf as a 'procreative tourist'. Would a supra-national response to this be possible *if* it were concluded that it were desirable? To address this, I need to turn to wider developments in medical jurisprudence and one facet of the relationship between international laws and reproductive medicine.[48]

The Council of Europe's Convention on Human Rights and Biomedicine was adopted by the Committee of Ministers on 19 November 1996 and opened for signature on 4 April 1997. The Convention sets out only the most important principles; additional safeguards and more detailed questions will be spelled out in protocols, of which the first, on the prohibition of cloning, was opened on 12 January 1998. The Convention makes provisions with regard to:

---

[47] 1999b at 166.
[48] Much of what follows in this section draws on Millns (2001) see also Millns (2002).

- The priority of the interests and welfare of the human being over those of society (Article 2).
- Equitable access to healthcare (Article 3).
- Observation of professional obligations and standards in carrying out health interventions, including research (Article 4).
- Free and informed consent by a person before an intervention in the health field (Article 5).
- Respect for a person's private life in relation to health information (Article 10).
- A prohibition on discrimination on the grounds of genetic heritage (Article 11).
- Protection against human genome modification unless for therapeutic purposes (Article 13).
- A prohibition on sex selection, unless for preventing the transmission of a serious sex-linked disease (Article 14).
- Only limited research on the human embryo and ensuring, where the law permits research, 'adequate protection of the embryo' (Article 18).
- A prohibition on the creation of an embryo only for research purposes (Article 19).
- A prohibition on the use of the human body and its parts for financial gain (Article 21).

Some member states (eg Germany) have so far refused to sign the Convention, holding that its provisions are insufficient, while some (eg the UK) maintain that it is too stringent and is incompatible with their domestic law. In both cases, incidentally, objections focus on the question of the status of the human embryo.

Article 29 of the Convention provides that the European Court of Human Rights in Strasbourg may give Advisory Opinions on the interpretation of the Convention. This, Millns has observed, begins the process of tying the Convention to European human rights jurisprudence. The provision presents the most significant opportunity yet to work towards supranational consensus on issues of assisted reproduction and of biomedicine more generally. Deep differences between different legal regimes will almost certainly preclude the achievement of consensus, but harmonisation or approximation of laws is potentially a powerful weapon against the growth of 'procreative tourism'. However, while it may be true that wise government does not always legislate at the first opportunity, it is perhaps also true that it may sometimes be desirable for individual states to act without supranational consensus, since such action might itself precipitate the desired consensus. The problem, as we have seen, is that there is often little domestic consensus on how to respond to surrogacy.

5. ENIGMA VARIATIONS

Christopher Hill has memorably remarked that it sometimes appears to be thought that the first English revolution occurred as if 'in a fit of absence of mind'.[49] It is important to recall the historical place of the development of reproductive technologies so that we do not come to believe that the 'reproduction revolution' took place in that way. Thus, we must locate the emergence of reproductive technologies in their modern form at a time when established social boundaries were disintegrating. The dominance of the traditional form of the family and of marriage was waning. The stability of the family was being questioned. There was an increase in the openness and acceptability of heterosexual partnerships without marriage and of homosexual relationships. Established social and legally enforced gender roles and stereotypes both outside and inside the home were beginning to be recast in the long shadows of feminisms and the changing expectations and demands of women. Feminist challenges were undermining established ethical principles. And finally, at the same time that traditional theological canons were collapsing, new questions were emerging concerning the methodology and epistemology of ethics and the nature of the philosophical enterprise itself. It is against these backgrounds that any examination of the regulation of reproductive technologies must take place so that they can be seen in the context of contemporary citizenship.

Against this backdrop of turbulent change, surrogacy has been both hailed as an example of scientific progress and, at the same time, has attracted criticism condemning it as evidence of a cultural malaise, as part of a culture in which anything and everything can be bought and sold. The *unique* temper of surrogacy—one of the conundrums which it displays—is that it is socially and ethically divisive *because* it does not attract universal opprobrium, because it may be seen, indeed it is seen by some, as a natural and beneficial product of the reproduction revolution as much as an unnatural and abnormal artefact of it. Surrogacy fails, in other words, to offer the cohesive function of traditional Durkheimian moment, because it exposes the lack of a collective conscience as to how it should be received.[50] It is a true variation on the enigma of assisted conception.

REFERENCES

Anleu, SR, 'Reproductive autonomy: infertility, deviance and conceptive technology' in Kerry Peterson (ed), *Law and Medicine* (Melbourne, La Trobe University Press, 1994).
Brazier, M, 'Can you buy children?' (1999a) 11 *Child and Family Law Quarterly* 345.
Brazier, M, 'Regulating the reproduction business?' (1999b) 7 *Medical Law Review* 166.

[49] Hill (1965:1).
[50] For the template work which affords such an analysis see Erikson, 1966.

Brazier, M and Glover, N, 'Does medical law have a future?' in Peter Birks (ed), *Laws Futures* (Oxford, Hart Publishing, 2000).

British Medical Association, *Changing Conceptions of Motherhood. The Practice of Surrogacy in Britain* (London, BMA Publications, 1996).

Deech, R, 'Family law and genetics' (1998) 61 *Modern Law Review* 697.

Dickenson, D, *Property, Women and Politics* (Cambridge, Polity Press, 1997).

Dworkin, R, *A Matter of Principle* (Cambridge, Mass, Harvard University Press, 1985).

—— *Life's Dominion* (London, Harper Collins, 1993).

—— *Freedom's Law* (Oxford, Oxford University Press, 1996).

—— *Taking Rights Seriously* (London, Duckworth, 1997).

Erikson, K, *Wayward Puritans. A Study in the Sociology of Deviance* (Boston, Allyn & Bacon, 1966).

Freeman, M, 'Does surrogacy have a future after Brazier?' (1999) 7 *Medical Law Review* 1.

Gilligan, C, *In a Different Voice: Psychological Theory and Women's Development* (Cambridge, Mass, Harvard University Press, 1982).

Hale, B, *From the Test Tube to the Coffin: Choice and Regulation in Private Life* (London, Sweet & Maxwell, 1996).

Harris, J and Holm, S (eds), *The Future of Human Reproduction* (Oxford, Oxford University Press, 1998).

Hill, C, *Intellectual Origins of the English Revolution* (Oxford, Clarendon Press, 1965).

Illich, I, *Limits to Medicine* (London, Penguin, 1976).

Jacob, J, *Doctors and Rules: A Sociology of Professional Values*, 1st edn (London, Routledge, 1988).

Kennedy, I, *Treat Me Right: Essays in Medical Law and Ethics* (Oxford, Clarendon Press, 1991).

Knoppers, B and Le Bris, S, 'Recent advances in medically assisted conception: legal, ethical and social issues' (1991) 17 *American Journal of Law and Medicine* 329.

Koch, L, 'IVF—an irrational choice?' (1990) 3 *Issues in Reproductive Engineering* 235.

MacIntyre, A, *After Virtue: A Study in Moral Theory* (London, Duckworth, 1985).

Maclean, A, *The Elimination of Morality* (London, Routledge, 1993).

Mason, K, *Medico-Legal Aspects of Reproduction and Parenthood*, 2nd edn (Aldershot, Ashgate, 1998).

Mclean, S and Campbell, T, 'Sterilisation' in SAM McLean (ed), *Legal Issues in Medicine* (Aldershot, Gower, 1981).

Millns, S, *Between Domestication and Europeanisation: a Gendered Perspective on Reproductive (Human) Rights Law* (European University Institute Working Papers, RSC no 2001/8).

—— 'Reproducing Inequalities: Assisted Conception and the Challenge of Legal Pluralism' (2002) 24 *Journal of Social Welfare and Family Law* 19–36.

Morgan, D, 'Frameworks of analysis of feminisms' accounts of reproductive technology' in Sally Sheldon and Michael Thompson (eds), *Feminist Perspectives on Health Care Law* (London, Cavendish Publishing, 1998).

Noddings, N, *Caring: A Feminine Approach to Ethics and Education* (Berkeley, University of California Press, 1978).

Radin, MJ, *Contested Commodities: The Trouble with the Trade in Sex, Children, Bodily Parts, and Other Things* (Cambridge, Mass, Harvard University Press, 1996).

Robertson, JA, *Children of Choice: Freedom and the New Reproductive Technologies* (Princeton, New Jersey, Princeton University Press, 1994).

Singer, P and Wells, D, *The Reproduction Revolution. New Ways of Making Babies* (Oxford, Oxford University Press, 1984).

Smart, C, *Feminism and the Power of Law* (London, Routledge, 1990).

Warnock, M, *Report of the Committee of Inquiry into Human Fertilisation and Embryology*. Cmnd 9314 (London, HMSO, 1984).

6

Surrogacy and the Human Fertilisation and Embryology Act

MARTIN H JOHNSON

THE HUMAN FERTILISATION and Embryology Act 1990 (HFE Act) is concerned primarily with the generation, handling, storage and disposal of what the Act calls 'genetic material'. Thus, it regulates the processes of fertilisation *in vitro*, the development *in vitro* of embryos, what may and may not be done with them, how they should be treated, and what conditions apply to their use therapeutically or in research (discussed in Johnson, 1999). The Act was also used to 'tidy up' legislation on gamete donation (insemination mainly, but oocyte donation was also covered). This part of the Act also deals therefore with the transmission of 'genetic material', and so does fit within the general thrust of the Act. The Act implies a very genetic view of parenthood (discussed in Johnson, 1999).

In contrast, surrogacy is regulated only incidentally by the Act.[1] The distinctive focus of surrogacy is not on genetic parenthood but on gestational parenthood and its relationship to genetic and post-natal (sometimes called 'social') parenthood. So it is not really surprising that the issue of surrogacy is only marginal to the central thrust of the Act. Surrogacy is dealt with in section 30, in conjunction with the Surrogacy Arrangements Act 1985 (to which it refers and which it clarifies in section 36). It came into force only in 1994. The main reason for its inclusion within the HFE Act is because gamete or embryo 'donation' to the surrogate may occur in a licensed clinic–medically assisted surrogacy. Thus, in the clinic genetic material may be recovered *in vitro*, manipulated, stored and used in 'treatment' and so is covered by the provisions in the Act and its Code of Practice relating to these aspects. However, it is important to point out that involvement of the Act is not essential for surrogacy, and indeed many (perhaps most) surrogate pregnancies can involve private insemination (artificial or natural) of the surrogate with spermatozoa from the commissioning pair (Brazier, Campbell and Golombok, 1998).

In section 30, provision is made for the commissioning parents, who have a genetic interest in the child born of a surrogacy arrangement, to be made the legal parents through a parental order.[2] This removes the requirement to adopt

---

[1] See also the Parental Orders Regulations issued in 1994.
[2] In place of the surrogate mother and any father named on the birth certificate, whose parental rights are thereby extinguished.

the child, the only previous route to legal parenthood. It is important to note that section 30 of the Act includes the case of surrogacy through insemination, which may not involve licensed clinics. For an order to be made, the couple must apply to the courts within six months of the birth of the child. If granted, the order gives them sole parental responsibility. They must satisfy certain residence and age requirements, and, at the time of the application (and of the making of the order) the child's home must be with them, that is, the surrogate must have handed the child to them. Significantly, the order can only be made in favour of a married couple. This latter provision penalises non-married heterosexual couples, as well as homosexual couples of either gender, and single persons. It is unclear why this provision was included, and it may be susceptible to challenge.

In making its award, the court must be satisfied that no money or benefit (other than 'reasonable expenses') has been given to the surrogate other than that authorised by the court. A guardian *ad litem* is appointed to oversee the child's interests, but has no powers of investigation and so, some would argue, cannot be considered able to fulfil his/her function effectively. Critically, an award cannot be made without the informed consent of the surrogate (and any father) and she cannot give that consent less than six weeks after the birth of the child. Thus, over this six-week period the gestational and immediate post-natal birth mother is given priority as the legal parent, whether or not she has a genetic interest in the child.[3] In cases where the child is not genetically related to the surrogate, it is not clear why the birth mother should have a prior claim to that of a genetic parent and, indeed, this provision appears to run contrary to the genetic bias in the other provisions of the Act. Although in recent years we have gained a much greater appreciation of the consequences of gestational parenthood for the development of a range of traits,[4] that appreciation does not seem to be the basis for the prior claim of the birth mother implied in the wording of the Act.

This apparent anomaly may in fact simply reflect a deep unease at the dislocations between genetic, gestational and post-natal parenthood generated by surrogacy.[5] The generally disapproving and reluctant tone initiated in the Warnock Report and continued thereafter (eg BMA, 1990, 1996) seems to have led to grudging and incomplete legislation. There may have been, consciously or otherwise, a desire to discourage surrogacy by the *de facto* disadvantaging of those who pursue this route to parenthood (discussed in Brazier *et al*, 1998). This outcome is unfortunate, because surrogacy arrangements and procedures of different sorts continue to occur, although the scale of surrogacy is difficult to establish, as is its 'success' in the eyes of surrogates, commissioning parents and children. Its perceived 'unsavouriness' makes reliable data collection more

---

[3] As she would only in traditional surrogacy.

[4] See Johnson (1999) for discussion of different components of parenthood and the contributions made by each.

[5] See Lane, chapter 9, this volume.

difficult. High profile problematic individual cases suggest that the various parties to at least some surrogacy arrangements might benefit from some sort of coherent and humane regulatory strategy, but it is not clear how widespread the need for coherent regulation is. Likewise, if the intention of current legislation is to deter surrogacy, it is not clear whether introduction of a systematic regulatory framework might encourage more cases of surrogacy, and by how much.

What might a regulatory framework address? These issues are discussed at length in Brazier *et al* (1998), but include the potentially conflicting interests of the children to be born, of existing children of the surrogate and the commissioning parents, of the surrogate herself, of the commissioning parents, and of those involved in facilitating surrogacy. At a minimum, a framework of support for all those involved, aimed at minimising stigma and managing dispute, seems a desirable alternative to the present deficient legislation. However, such a framework would need to be drafted carefully given the current evident distaste for surrogacy, otherwise a harsh regulatory regime might be imposed that simply drove surrogacy arrangements underground or overseas, and so undermined rather than buttressed support for those involved. The parallels with the early days of IVF may be instructive. Then, IVF was perceived as being of practical use to few and generally undesirable ethically and socially. A sustained public debate over ten years changed public and parliamentary attitudes with the result that a more flexible and permissive legislation ensued eventually than would have occurred with hasty legislation. Perhaps concern about repressive legislation has led the Government essentially to ignore the recommendations by Brazier *et al* (1998)? However, public debate on the issue has been engaged only sporadically and often sensationally, and there is little reason to believe that public distaste for surrogacy has diminished or understanding of it increased.

If legislation is to be contemplated, is the HFE Act the appropriate place for it, and could the HFEA administer it? The HFEA itself does not think so, and submitted evidence to that effect to the Department of Health review of the laws regulating surrogacy (Brazier *et al*, 1998). First and foremost, the HFEA is concerned with infertility treatment in a medical context. Moreover, it seems barely able to handle expeditiously the issues raised in this remit. Many, perhaps most, surrogacy arrangements take place outside this setting and do not require the intervention of technology (although they might benefit from it). Second, the problematic issues involved in surrogacy are concerned not so much with conception itself but with its aftermath and the arrangements surrounding it. Surrogacy is dealing with real foetuses and babies more than eggs and spermatozoa, which are in a sense the easy bits. Reflecting this emphasis, the HFE Act talks only of 'taking account' of the (potential) child's interests in contrast to the Children Act (1989), in which the interests of the (real) child are paramount. Where a child is the subject of a dispute between surrogate and commissioning parents, should not its interests be paramount? This in fact has tended to be the outcome where disputes have reached the courts (summarised in Brazier *et al* 1998). It seems right that the HFEA should not be responsible for surrogacy.

A more suitable model might be one nearer to fostering or adoption (Callman, 1999), since the issues seem much closer, and the expertise more relevant.

The Brazier report also concluded that the HFEA was not the appropriate body to take responsibility for surrogacy, beyond those areas of technical intervention at conception. It did, however, conclude that there was a need for a coherent framework for surrogacy, not least as a 'risk minimisation' strategy. It proposed that a code of practice be developed by the Department of Health which placed the welfare of the child as *paramount*, at all stages of the surrogacy process. In particular, it recommended that any payments other than identifiable expenses should be banned. In doing so, ironically, it referred as a model to the ban on payments for gametes which at the time the HFEA had decided to impose, a decision that it subsequently reversed (Johnson, 2002). However, the review did not consider the role(s) of commercial surrogacy agencies (national and international) nor the law of contract in enforcing payment of surrogates or requiring surrogates to give up a child, since its brief excluded consideration of these matters. These issues would need to be considered in a coherent strategy for surrogacy. The subject thus remains incompletely considered and resting in limbo, no further action having been taken on the Brazier Report. This inertia contrasts strikingly with the approaches to infertility that are clearly associated with the HFEA's remit, such as research on embryos, preimplantation genetic diagnosis and embryo selection, stem cells, and cloning. The HFEA has been largely instrumental in setting the pace of public discussion on these issues, and seeing through decisions. In the absence of a comparable body to promote discussion on surrogacy, the subject is probably destined to languish. Perhaps another model from the history of the HFEA might be useful. During the period of public debate on issues to do with assisted reproductive technologies, the scientific and medical communities set up a voluntary licensing authority, which developed many of the procedures which were subsequently incorporated into the HFE Act. Is there a sufficiently interested body of clinicians and others to do the same for surrogacy? Until something like this happens, the legacy of distaste for surrogacy is likely to deter action to the detriment of all parties to at least some surrogacy arrangements.

REFERENCES

Brazier, M, Campbell, A and Golombok, S, *Surrogacy. Review for Health Ministers of Current Arrangements for Payments and Regulation. Report of the Review Team* Cm 4068 (London, HMSO, 1998).
British Medical Association, *Surrogacy: Ethical Considerations. Report of the Working Party on Human Infertility Services* (London, BMA Publications, 1990).
—— *Changing Conceptions of Motherhood. The practice of surrogacy in Britain* (London, BMA Publications, 1996).
Callman, J, 'Surrogacy—a case for normalization' (1999) 14 *Human Reproduction* 277.

Human Fertiliation and Embryology Act 1990 (London, HMSO, 1990).

Johnson, MH, 'A Biomedical Perspective on Parenthood' in A Bainham, SD Sclater and M Richards (eds), *What is a parent? A Socio-legal Analysis* (Oxford and Portland, Hart Publishing Ltd, 1999).

—— 'The art of regulation and the regulation of ART: the impact of regulationon research and clinical practice' (2002) 9 *Journal of Law and Medicine* 399–413.

Warnock, M, *Report of the Committee of Inquiry into Human Fertilisation and Embryology*. Cmnd 9314 (London, HMSO, 1984).

7

Clinical Aspects Of IVF Surrogacy in Britain

PETER R BRINSDEN

1. INTRODUCTION

THE EARLIEST MENTION of the use of surrogacy to help 'barren' women to have children is in the Old Testament of the Bible (Book of Genesis). Sara, at the age of 80, had been unable to bear Abraham a child and she suggested that Hegar, their maid, should bear their child conceived by Abraham. Abraham was then 90 years of age but their son Ishmail was born to Hegar as a result of this arrangement.[1]

Until the techniques of modern assisted conception became available, conceiving a child by 'natural surrogacy', as practised by Sara and Abraham, was the only means possible. When artificial insemination techniques became available, it became more acceptable to use this method than 'natural means'. Now that *in vitro* fertilisation (IVF) techniques are available, it is natural and reasonable that couples wishing to conceive children by surrogacy should do so using their own gametes, rather than by 'natural surrogacy', in which the egg of the host is used. Embryos can now be created with IVF using the sperm and eggs of the 'commissioning couple',[2] and these can then be transferred to the uterus of the host or surrogate mother, who carries and delivers a child that is genetically unrelated to her—a method known as 'IVF surrogacy' or 'gestational surrogacy'.

IVF surrogacy has been accepted in the United Kingdom since the late 1980s as a treatment option for infertile couples in whom the female partner is unable to carry a child. The earliest mention of IVF surrogacy in a regulatory context is in the *Report of the Committee of Enquiry into Human Fertilisation and Embryology* (HMSO (1984)) otherwise known as the Warnock Report, published in 1984. This recommended that 'treatment' involving any form of surrogacy should be made illegal. Before that time no regulations or guidelines had been issued. Fierce debate and controversy arose in 1985 when Kim Cotton gave birth to a child conceived within a 'natural surrogacy' arrangement, and the

---

[1] It is extraordinary that Sara was then able to bear her own child Isaac at the age of 90, also conceived by Abraham, who by then was 100 years of age.

[2] Otherwise known as the 'intended parents'.

Surrogacy Arrangements Act 1985 was rushed through the United Kingdom Parliament. This set out clear rules on surrogacy, which are dealt with in detail elsewhere in this volume. The British Medical Association (BMA) met at that time and passed a resolution that 'this meeting agrees that the principle of surrogate births in selected cases with careful controls' should be allowed (British Medical Association (1985)). However, in 1987, the BMA, after further deliberations, published a report stating that doctors should not be involved at all in surrogacy arrangements (British Medical Association (1987)). This decision was ratified at the 1987 Annual General Meeting. In 1989 the BMA established a working party that reported in 1990 stating that 'it would not be possible or desirable to seek to prevent all involvement of doctors in surrogacy arrangements, especially as the Government does not intend to make the practice illegal' (British Medical Association (1990)). The Report set out guidelines on the management of patients who have IVF surrogacy and made it clear that it was only after intensive investigation and counselling, and very much as a last resort since it was considered to be so controversial a treatment, that IVF surrogacy should be used as a treatment option to overcome infertility problems. The Human Fertilisation and Embryology Act 1990 (HFE Act) (HMSO (1990)) did not ban surrogacy. The most recent report of the BMA states that 'surrogacy is an acceptable option of last resort in cases where it is impossible or highly undesirable for medical reasons for the intended mother to carry a child herself' (British Medical Association (1996:59)).

Both IVF and natural surrogacy are banned in most European countries,[3] with the exception of Belgium and The Netherlands; indeed most countries worldwide ban it, although many do not have rules. The largest experience of both natural and IVF surrogacy is in the United States. Many states allow commercial surrogacy arrangements[4] and their early experience has been published (Utian, Goldfarb, Kiwi *et al* (1989)); (Marrs, Ringler, Stein, Vargyas and Stone (1993)).

Shortly after the passing of the Surrogacy Arrangements Act 1985 in the UK, Patrick Steptoe and Robert Edwards, the pioneers who were responsible for the birth of Louise Brown—the world's first 'test tube baby'—decided that they should treat their first patient by IVF surrogacy. They put a case up to the clinic's independent Ethics Committee which, after careful consideration and debate, approved the arrangement. This case was the first to go through IVF surrogacy in the United Kingdom, and the child was finally born in 1989. In 1990, after further discussion with the Ethics Committee, it was decided to proceed with a full IVF surrogacy programme. In 1991, the Committee issued their first guidelines on IVF surrogacy for patients treated at Bourn Hall. Every IVF surrogacy arrangement is now submitted to them for consideration, with written

---

[3] While natural surrogacy cannot, strictly speaking, be banned, it is in the sense that intended parents do not become legal parents.

[4] See Rao, chapter 2, this volume.

reports from the clinician and the counsellor,[5] and treatment only proceeds if approval is given. The Ethics Committee reviewed and reissued their guidelines in 1999 (see Appendix 1).

2. DEFINITION OF TERMS

There has always been some confusion over the use of the words 'surrogate' and 'host' as well as 'IVF surrogacy' and 'gestational surrogacy'. In this review 'IVF surrogacy', which is also known as 'full surrogacy' or 'gestational surrogacy', is defined as the treatment in which the gametes of the 'genetic couple', 'commissioning couple' or 'intended parents' are used to produce embryos by the process of *in vitro* fertilisation (IVF). These embryos are subsequently transferred to a woman who has agreed to act as a host for these embryos. In this case, the 'surrogate host' is therefore genetically unrelated to any child that may be born as a result of this arrangement.

'Natural surrogacy' or 'partial surrogacy' involves the insemination of the host with the semen of the husband of the 'genetic couple'. Any resulting child is genetically related to the male partner of the 'commissioning couple' but not the female partner.

3. INDICATIONS FOR TREATMENT

The principal indications for treatment of the genetic couples and the proportion of couples treated in each group treated at Bourn Hall are shown in Table 1 (Brinsden, Appleton, Murray, Hussein, Akagbosu and Marcus (2000)). Congenital absence of the uterus is the most obvious indication, with hysterectomy for uterine or cervical carcinoma or haemorrhage as the other main indications. Other women have suffered repeated miscarriage and were deemed to have little or no chance of carrying a child to term in future pregnancies. Repeated failure of treatment by *in vitro* fertilisation is another, but more controversial indication. It is used only for women who have not shown any signs of implanting normal embryos in an apparently otherwise normal uterus after at least eight IVF/embryo transfer cycles. IVF surrogacy has also been used where the female partner of the commissioning couple has a medical condition which would threaten her life were she to become pregnant: the principal conditions are severe cardiac and renal disease. In these cases, discussion is always held with the specialist looking after the medical problem and the Ethics Committee requires evidence that the female partner of the 'commissioning couple' will be able to look after any child adequately and that her life expectancy is reasonable. Women requesting IVF surrogacy purely for career or

---

[5] See Appleton, chapter 13, this volume.

Table 1. Indications for treatment by IVF-surrogacy

• Following hysterectomy	48%
• Congenital absence of the uterus	17%
• Repeated failure of IVF treatment	17%
• Recurrent miscarriage	13%
• Severe medical conditions incompatible with pregnancy	5%

social reasons are not considered for treatment, as presently we believe that surrogacy should be used only where there are medical indications.

4. RECRUITMENT AND MANAGEMENT OF THE GENETIC PARENTS

All of the 'genetic mothers' that have been treated at Bourn Hall Clinic in the last 13 years had been fully assessed by their referring consultants prior to being seen at the clinic. This assessment usually includes laparoscopy if there are congenital anomalies, but not if an hysterectomy has been performed. Evidence of ovarian function is obtained by taking a history and determining whether there are any cyclical premenstrual symptoms or symptoms of ovulation occurring on a regular basis. Ovulatory cycles can be confirmed by one or more estimations of serum follicle stimulating hormone (FSH) and luteinising hormone (LH), and appropriately timed progesterone (P) estimations. Basal temperature charts, if kept accurately, can also be helpful to women without a uterus in determining cyclicity.

The blood groups of the genetic parents are requested in case the host is rhesus negative, and both the genetic parents are tested for hepatitis B (HBV), hepatitis C (HCV) and human immunodeficiency virus (HIV) status. Ovarian ultrasound scanning is also helpful on some patients to confirm the presence of one or both ovaries, their position and evidence of follicular activity. Other investigations are carried out as necessary on an individual basis.

At the medical assessment, full details are given to the 'genetic parents' of the treatment, the implications of the treatment and likely chance of success. Couples are told that it is up to them to recruit their own host, since in the United Kingdom it is illegal for clinics to do so.[6] On completion of the medical assessment, provided the couple falls within the guidelines laid down by the Independent Ethics Committee at Bourn Hall Clinic, and that they comply with the Code of Practice of the Human Fertilisation and Embryology Authority (HFEA) (HFEA (2001)), particularly with regard to consideration of the welfare of any child born as the result of treatment, the couple are informed that the next stage is for them to find a suitable host for themselves.

---

[6] See Dodd, chapter 8, this volume.

A surrogate host may be a family member. In particular sisters have commonly been used for this treatment. Alternatively an arrangement can be made with other members of the family, a close friend or through an independent surrogacy support group in the UK known as COTS (Childlessness Overcome Through Surrogacy)[7] who have had many years of experience bringing together couples wishing to be involved in IVF surrogacy.

5. RECRUITMENT OF THE SURROGATE HOST

Only fit normal women under the age of about 40 years are allowed to act as hosts, because of the increasing likelihood of complications in pregnancies of women older than 40. Our own recommendations state that a host should have had at least one child and preferably have completed her family. The relationship of hosts to genetic mothers in our own series is shown in Table 2. Investigations for fertility are not usually necessary but all hosts and their partners are tested for HBV, HCV, and HIV before starting treatment. If the host is taking the oral contraceptive pill it may be discontinued one or two cycles before the replacement cycle and barrier methods of contraception recommended, or it may be continued up to the time of the start of the treatment cycle.

6. COUNSELLING AND SURROGACY[8]

The importance of in-depth counselling by a counsellor independent of the clinic to help to prepare all parties contemplating this last resort treatment cannot be overstated. The importance of 'getting it right' is emphasised to all couples, who are exhorted to bring into the open all matters of concern or potential

Table 2. Relationship of genetic mothers to their surrogate hosts in the
Bourn Hall series 1989–98

Relationship	Proportion	Number of cases
Related	37%	
−sister		9
−sister-in-law		5
−stepmother		1
Unrelated	63%	
−friend		4
−agency introduction		6
−other incentives		16

[7] Above, n 6.
[8] See chapters 12 and 13, this volume.

conflict well before starting treatment. Couples are told that they must be confident and comfortable with their decisions and have trust in each other, so that no one party is felt to be taking advantage of the other or to be exploiting the regulations laid down by Parliament or the guidelines issued by the Ethics Committee to Bourn Hall. Full consideration must be given to the welfare of any child who may be born as a result of this treatment and also the welfare of any existing children. The BMA in its 1990 report (British Medical Association (1990)) stated: 'the aggregate of foreseeable hazards should not be so great as to place unacceptable burdens on any of the parties—including the future child.'

Counselling of couples treated at Bourn Hall usually takes place in the home of the genetic couple and is done by an independent fertility counsellor. A counselling session may require several hours and frequently several visits. Follow-up counselling, often over many years, is also offered. The role of counselling in surrogacy is primarily to help couples to decide whether they have confidence in their actions and to be comfortable with their decisions, in particular both couples must be comfortable and open with each other. With the consent of all involved, the counsellor seeks permission to share information obtained from the counselling session with the Independent Ethics Committee who advise the clinic. Although there is no requirement under the HFE Act (1990) to refer cases of surrogacy to an independent Ethics Committee, the views and support of this group of people drawn from many disciplines, and with a lay majority, has been very valuable to the clinic staff and is generally appreciated by the patients themselves.

Failure of treatment has a profound effect on the commissioning couple and their families, as well as the host and her husband or partner and their children. Many of those who have not succeeded in surrogacy have, nevertheless, been grateful that they at least made an attempt at treatment and they feel that they are better able to adjust to their situation, knowing that they have explored all the possibilities and have made every possible effort. Counselling may continue for many years after the treatment, with support being available to either party of the original arrangement, or to the children themselves born of the treatment, should it be required.

7.   PATIENT MANAGEMENT

Management of the Genetic Mother

Following the work-up and Ethics Committee approval process, arrangements are made to start the IVF treatment cycle. Since most of the women requesting IVF surrogacy are normal with regard to ovarian function, the management of their IVF treatment cycles is straightforward. A standard ovarian follicular stimulation protocol with monitoring and oocyte recovery are used and have previously been described (Marcus, Brinsden, Macnamee, Rainsbury, Elder and

Edwards (1993); Macnamee and Brinsden (1999)). A standard luteal phase start down regulation protocol using an LH-RH analogue starting in the estimated mid-luteal phase of the 'cycle' is used, together with a standard follicular stimulation regime using recombinant FSH in our standard protocol (Macnamee and Brinsden (1999)), oocyte recovery is under sedation or general anaesthesia according to our standard practice (Brinsden (1999)). Occasionally in young women with congenital absence of the uterus and a very short vagina, a transabdominal ultrasound oocyte recovery is necessary.

   The Human Fertilisation and Embryology Act 1990 (HFE Act (1990)) states that donated sperm must undergo six months 'quarantine' with a repeat check of HIV status, before being used. This rule applies to IVF surrogacy as well. Therefore, the male partner of the commissioning couple is required either to store his sperm and undergo repeat HIV status checks six months later, before using it, or any embryos created with fresh sperm must be 'quarantined' for the six months. Normal practice at Bourn Hall is for the male partner to be encouraged to store sperm at least six months prior to his partner going through the stimulation and oocyte collection process. Any resulting embryos from the IVF process may be transferred 'fresh' to the host or frozen/thawed and transferred at a later date.

Management of the Surrogate Host

Only fit normal healthy young women with no serious medical or psychological problems are allowed to act as hosts. The Ethics Committee guideline states that they should be aged 39 years or less, but exceptions have been made. The host should generally have had at least one child and preferably have completed her family to reduce the chance of her wanting to retain the child. The guidelines also recommend that hosts should be married or in a stable relationship and that the husband or partner should be made fully aware during the counselling process of the implications of his partner acting as a surrogate host.

   The host is prepared for embryo transfer in a hormone controlled cycle (Sathanandan, Macnamee, Rainsbury, Wick, Brinsden and Edwards (1991); Marcus and Brinsden (1999)). This allows for greater control and flexibility of the host's cycle in order to try and synchronise it with that of the 'genetic mother'. The embryo transfer procedure is normally straightforward as the women will have had children before. A maximum of two embryos are transferred in order to reduce the chance of multiple pregnancy and any remaining embryos are frozen and may be used in subsequent attempts.

Pregnancy Management

The surrogate host will have a 30 to 35 per cent chance of achieving a pregnancy and approximately a 25 to 30 per cent chance of having a live child after each embryo transfer. The results of the treatment at Bourn Hall of one series of patients are shown in Table 3. The chance of miscarriage in our own series was relatively high and couples are counselled about the implications of this in detail before they start treatment. The strain on both couples of such a disappointing outcome is great and follow-up counselling and advice is provided if this happens.

If the pregnancy proceeds normally, then the host is managed and delivered in her local hospital. Both parties are encouraged to support each other during the pregnancy, attend antenatal appointments together and encouraged to be together at the time of the birth. Couples are encouraged to explain the arrangement to the team at the local hospital so that special arrangements can be made for the commissioning couple to be present at the birth and to receive the baby.

Until the Human Fertilisation and Embryology Act (1990), commissioning couples had to adopt their own child under the provisions of the Adoption Acts of 1976 and 1985. However, section 30 of the HFE Act 1990, allows for the parentage to be changed by the issue of 'parental orders', which has very much simplified the adoption process.

Table 3. Summary of results of treatment by IVF Surrogacy at Bourn Hall Clinic 1990–98

Treatment of genetic couples		
No patients started treatment	49	
Mean age at start (years)	32.9	Range = 22–40
Total stimulated cycles	80	Range = 1–5
Treatment of host surrogates		
No hosts started treatment	53	
No cycles to embryo transfer	87	Mean no. transfers/host = 1.6
Final outcomes		
Delivered or ongoing pregnancies per host transfer cycle	18/87	21%
Clinical pregnancies per surrogate host	31/53	58.5%
Delivered or ongoing pregnancies per surrogate host	18/53	34%
Clinical pregnancies per genetic couple	31/49	63%
Delivered or ongoing pregnancies per genetic couple	18/49	37%

Reproduced with permission of the Editor of the *British Medical Journal*

Results of Treatment

A summary of the results of the treatment of 49 commissioning couples at Bourn Hall Clinic is shown in Table 3.

8. COMPLICATIONS OF TREATMENT BY IVF SURROGACY

The majority of the problems that have arisen from surrogacy arrangements have been from 'natural surrogacy' arrangements. These have mainly been legal complications and have been associated with the rights of the commissioning couple as against those of the host. These have been well documented in the literature published on the subject (AFS (1986); ACOG (1990); Cohen and Friend (1987); Brazier, Golombok and Campbell (1998); Shuster (1991); Shuster (1992); Jones and Cohen (2001)). The majority of these problems have arisen in arrangements that were largely unsupervised and did not involve counselling. In IVF or gestational surrogacy arrangements, experienced clinicians and professional counsellors are involved and most units seek the advice of an independent Ethics Committee. In our own experience over the last 10 years, no serious ethical or legal problems have arisen, but a number of relatively minor issues have arisen which bear mention:

1. A few of the 'genetic mothers' have responded poorly or not at all to follicular stimulation and a few have produced poor quality oocytes which have failed to fertilise;
2. It has become apparent that normal fertile young hosts often tend to have unreasonably high expectations of success and some of the hosts who have failed to achieve a pregnancy have found it difficult to cope with that failure;
3. Some hosts who have miscarried pregnancies have again found it difficult to cope with the failure and often experience a profound sense of having let the genetic couple down. Similarly, the genetic couple have felt guilt because their host has gone through the trauma of miscarriage on their behalf.

Other ethical and legal issues arising from surrogacy treatment are discussed elsewhere in this volume.

9. CONCLUSION

Although very few infertile couples (less than one per cent in our own practice) need to resort to IVF surrogacy to help them to have a child, the subject has, nevertheless, provoked a lot of discussion over the past two decades. The major problems that have arisen from the practice of surrogacy have been from 'natural surrogacy' arrangements, with very few problems having been reported from IVF surrogacy. This is largely because professionals from the disciplines of medicine, ethics, law and counselling have all been involved with the treatment of these couples. Treatment by IVF surrogacy has largely been accepted as a reasonable treatment option in selected cases in the United Kingdom, but is still not accepted in most European countries and worldwide. In a recent survey (Jones and Cohen (2001)) only 12 countries out of 39 with regulations or guidelines on surrogacy permitted the practice of surrogacy.

Our own experience over the past 13 years has shown that this treatment does work and is relatively successful. Complications have been rare and of a minor nature. The indications for treatment are limited to a small group of women, mainly those without a uterus or with recurrent miscarriage. IVF surrogacy cases account for less than 1 per cent of patients treated at Bourn Hall. The treatment itself is very straightforward, involving only the normal process of *in vitro* fertilisation and embryo transfer. The complexity of the treatment is related to the selection, counselling and care of the host surrogate and the commissioning couple, to ensure that complications do not arise that might damage their relationship. At all times, the welfare of the child that may be born as a result of the treatment and also any existing children are the primary consideration and in-depth counselling, both in the short and the long term, must be provided.

The support and advice of an independent Ethics Committee is of inestimable value to the clinic providing the treatment and surely helps to prevent many of the complications that could arise from treatment. At Bourn Hall we believe that IVF surrogacy should be part of a comprehensive infertility treatment service and that this specialised treatment should be reserved for couples with no other opportunity of having their own genetic children.

BOURN HALL ETHICS COMMITTEE
GUIDELINES FOR SURROGACY

Introduction

Bourn Hall Ethics Committee is prepared to consider IVF surrogacy in cases where an embryo or embryos from the commissioning couple are transferred to the uterus of the host. The use of donor eggs or donor sperm and natural surrogacy may be considered in exceptional circumstances. They consider that surrogacy should only be undertaken as a last resort. The need to safeguard the welfare of any children born as a result of surrogacy arrangement will be a guiding principle.

The Committee considers that every case must be looked at by the Ethics Committee on its own merit, based on information provided by the Clinic.

Procedures

Following examination by a clinician, the prospective genetic parents and host and partner must be counselled by a professional counsellor. If the clinician and counsellor, who are not members of the Ethics Committee, are satisfied they will prepare a report, a copy of which must be submitted to each member of the Ethics Committee. The case will then be considered by the Ethics Committee in consultation with the clinician and counsellor. If they are satisfied that the case falls within the Guidelines and is acceptable, the Ethics Committee will make their recommendations to the Clinic. The genetic parents and host and her partner will be asked to take independent legal advice and encouraged to take out insurance.

Cases will not be considered if there is any doubt that the genetic couple will comply with the requirements for a parental order under section 30 of Human Fertilisation and Embryology Act 1990 or subsequent legislation.

Categories acceptable for treatment

1. Total or partial absence of the uterus either of congenital origin or after surgery.
2. Repeated miscarriage.
3. Multiple failure of infertility treatment. The clinicians must be satisfied that, there is no reasonable prospect of success in the future.

Motives considered unacceptable

1. Social reasons.
2. Prospective genetic parents with severe health problems. Clinicians and the Committee will need to be satisfied that the strain of bringing up a child might not damage the mother's health so seriously as to jeopardise the welfare of that child and the family.

Considerations which apply to all cases

1. The Clinic must not be involved in initiating or making arrangements between genetic and host couples.
2. The relationship between genetic couple and host must be carefully considered and avoid creating conflicting family relationships.
3. Independent counselling must be available to both genetic and host couples.
4. HIV, hepatitis B and hepatitis C antibody tests are required of both genetic and host couples.
5. The age of the genetic mother and of the host is important. In view of the HFEA Code of Practice, the Committee considers that 35 should be the maximum age of the genetic mother unless there are exceptional circumstances; however, the Committee will consider genetic mothers up to and including 38. The host should generally be below 40.
6. The principal motive of a prospective host should always be to help an infertile couple.
7. A prospective host should have had at least one child before becoming a surrogate.
8. The commissioning couple in a surrogacy arrangement should be married. The host should preferably be in a stable relationship. If the host is single then she should be adequately supported.

REFERENCES

American College of Obstetricians and Gynecologists' (ACOG) Committee on Ethics, *Ethical Issues in Surrogate Motherhood* (Washington DC, American College of Obstetricians and Gynecologists, 1990).

American Fertility Society (AFS) Ethics Committee, 'Ethical considerations in the New Reproductive Technologies' (1986) 46 (suppl) *Fertility and Sterility* 62.

Book of Genesis, *Holy Bible*. 16:1–15; 17:15–19; 21: 1–4.

Brazier, M, Golombok, S and Campbell, A, *Surrogacy: Review for Health Ministers of Current Arrangements for Payments and Regulation. Report of the Review Team* Cm 4068 (London, HMSO, 1998).

Brinsden, PR, 'Oocyte recovery and embryo transfer techniques for *in vitro* fertilization' in PR Brinsden (ed), *A Textbook of In Vitro Fertilization and Assisted Reproduction*, 2nd edn (Carnforth and New York, Parthenon Publishers, 1999).

—— Appleton, TC, Murray, E, Hussein, M, Akagbosu, F and Marcus, SF, 'Treatment by *in vitro* fertilisation with surrogacy: experience of one British centre' (2000) 320 *British Medical Journal* 924.

British Medical Association, *Annual Representative Meeting Report* (London, BMA Publications, 1985).

—— *Surrogate Motherhood. Report of the Board of Science and Education* (London, BMA Publications, 1987).

—— *Surrogacy: Ethical Considerations. Report of the Working Party on Human Infertility Services* (London, BMA Publications, 1990).

—— *Changing Conceptions of Motherhood. The Practice of Surrogacy in Britain* (London, BMA Publications, 1996).

Cohen, B and Friend, TL, 'Legal and ethical implications of surrogate mother contracts' (1987) 14 *Clinics in Perinatology* 281.

Human Fertilisation and Embryology Act 1990 (London, HMSO, 1990).

Human Fertilisation and Embryology Authority, *Code of Practice for Clinics Licensed by the Human Fertilisation and Embryology Authority* (London, Human Fertilisation and Embryology Authority, 2001).

Jones, HW and Cohen, J, 'IFFS surveillance 01' (2001) 76 Supplement 1 *Fertility and Sterility* 5.

Macnamee, MC and Brinsden, PR, 'Superovulation strategies in assisted conception' in PR Brinsden (ed), *A Textbook of In Vitro Fertilization and Assisted Reproduction*, 2nd edn (Carnforth and New York, Parthenon Publishers, 1999).

Marcus, SF, Brinsden, PR, Macnamee, MC, Rainsbury, PA, Elder, KT and Edwards, RG, 'Comparative trial between an ultrashort and long protocol of luteinising hormone-releasing hormone agonist for ovarian stimulation in in-vitro fertilization' (1993) 8 *Human Reproduction* 238.

—— and —— 'Oocyte Donation' in PR Brinsden (ed), *A Textbook of In Vitro Fertilization and Assisted Reproduction*, 2nd edn (Carnforth and New York, Parthenon Publishers, 1999).

Marrs, RP, Ringler, GE, Stein, AL, Vargyas, JM and Stone, BA, 'The use of surrogate gestational carriers for assisted reproductive technologies' (1993) 168 *American Journal of Obstetrics and Gynaecology* 1858.

Sathanandan, M, Macnamee, MC, Rainsbury, P, Wick, K, Brinsden, PR and Edwards, RG, 'Frozen-thawed embryo replacement in artificial and natural cycles; a prospective study' (1991) 5 *Human Reproduction* 1025.

Shuster, E, 'Non-genetic surrogacy: No cure but problems for infertility?' (1991) 6 *Human Reproduction* 1176.

—— 'When genes determine motherhood: Problems in gestational surrogacy' (1992) 7 *Human Reproduction* 1029.

Utian, WF, Goldfarb, JM, Kiwi, R, *et al*, 'Preliminary experience with in vitro fertilization-surrogate gestational pregnancy' (1989) 52 *Fertility and Sterility* 633.

Warnock, M, *Report of the Committee of Inquiry into Human Fertilisation and Embryology*. Cmnd 9314 (London, HMSO, 1984).

8

Surrogacy and the Law in Britain: Users' Perspectives

GENA DODD[1]

1. COTS AND SURROGACY SUPPORT IN THE UK

T HE MAIN FUNCTION of COTS (Childlessness Overcome Through
Surrogacy) is to put couples who cannot have children in touch with surrogates who can. COTS was launched in 1988 by two British women who had
personal experience of surrogacy. It now has over 750 members and achieved
437 surrogate births up to the end of 2002. It bears no resemblance to an
American-style agency; its prime objective is to pass on collective experience to
both potential surrogate mothers and would-be parents, thereby helping them
to understand the implications of surrogacy before they enter into an arrangement. It aims to help participants in surrogacy arrangements deal with any
problems that might arise, by providing practical advice on medical, legal and
interpersonal issues.

Essentially a voluntary, amateur organisation, COTS has a success rate of over
98 per cent. Failures—where the surrogate fails to hand over the baby to the
intended parents—are few and far between. However, as with most forms of
human activity, it is the failures that most interest tabloid journalists. In 1997, the
case of surrogate mother Karen Roche, who changed her mind about handing
over her baby because of stated doubts about the suitability of the Dutch commissioning parents ended up in the High Court with the, now requisite, media cir-
cus in tow. It was this case that led to Tessa Jowell, the then Health Minister in a
fairly newly elected Labour government, to order a review[2] of surrogacy with a
view to introducing legislation aimed at preventing future similar cases. COTS
was consulted in the course of the review but their views were largely ignored.
Ms Jowell moved on to pastures new and surrogacy fell out of the limelight.

There are fluctuations in both media and legal interest in surrogacy, but there
is always a need, which is not met by any regulatory framework, for the provision of information and support to those who become involved in surrogacy
arrangements. This chapter explores the role of COTS in meeting that need and
its view of surrogacy legislation.

---

[1] Gena Dodd is secretary of Childlessness Overcome Through Surrogacy.
[2] Brazier, M, Golombok, S and Campbell, A (1998).

2. SURROGACY LEGISLATION

Surrogacy in England and Wales is currently subject to a number of pieces of legislation. None of these, with the possible exception of the Human Fertilisation and Embryology Act 1990, are particularly suitable to deal with what is a fairly complex legal relationship. In order to understand the interface between the English law and surrogacy arrangements, it is necessary to appreciate that there are essentially two forms of surrogacy. COTS uses the terms 'straight surrogacy' and 'host surrogacy'. Straight surrogacy involves artificial insemination of the surrogate mother with sperm produced by the intended father, which can usually be achieved without the need for medical intervention. Host surrogacy, on the other hand, is a clinical procedure. It normally involves the collection of eggs from the intended mother or a donor and their *in vitro* fertilisation with the intended father's sperm (although donor sperm can also be used). This is followed by transfer of the fertilised eggs to the surrogate mother's womb.

Prior to the implementation of section 30 of the Human Fertilisation and Embryology Act 1990, the legal position regarding the parenthood of the child was that the surrogate mother was the legal mother and the only person with Parental Responsibility[3] (in accordance with The Children Act 1989).[4] The intended father was the putative father of the child. This was so with both forms of surrogacy—whether the surrogate mother was the host or genetic mother—and irrespective of the marital relationships of these parents (the surrogate mother and the intended father). The aim of section 30 of the Human Fertilisation and Embryology Act 1990 (HFE Act) was to simplify the process of transfer of Parental Responsibility from the surrogate and her partner to the intended parents of the child. It has, perhaps ironically and perhaps understandably, tended to muddy some already fairly muddy water. I will deal with that later in this chapter.   *HFE: simply process of Parental transfer*

3. CONTRACT BETWEEN THE SURROGATE MOTHER AND THE INTENDED PARENTS

In terms of basic principles, the law of England, Wales and the Channel Islands generally says that there can be no legally binding contract between those who wish to parent a surrogate child and the woman who offers her gestational

---

[3] Parental Responsibility encompasses all legal rights, duties, powers and responsibilities that a parent should have in respect of a child including the right to say where and with whom a child will live.

[4] Children Act 1989, chapter 41, part I, section 2 (HMSO, 1989). Available at http://www.hmso. gov.uk/acts/acts1989/Ukpga_19890041_en_1.htm

services.[5] One consequence of this is that the surrogate mother is the only person who has Parental Responsibility in respect of the child. So if a surrogate wants to take the money[6] and keep the baby, there is very little that the intended parents can do about it. One significant effect of the law therefore is to keep intended parents in a state of uncertainty and lack of control prior to the birth. Before the child is born there are no steps that they can take with a view to eventually securing their legal parenthood of that child.

Once the child is born, there are two steps that should be taken immediately. The first is the registration of the child's birth in accordance with the Birth and Deaths Registration Acts 1836 to 1947. While this would appear relatively straightforward, often it is not. COTS volunteers spend many hours each year dealing with queries about registration arising from apparently inconsistent advice from registrars. There is little confusion about whose name should go in the space marked 'name and maiden surname of mother' on the birth certificate; in the vast majority of cases, the surrogate mother's name goes there. However, confusion can occur when those registering the birth of a surrogate baby ask the registrar to advise whose name, if any, should go in the space marked 'name and surname of father'. Registrars' advice tends to vary between three recommendations. First, some recommend that as the surrogate mother is not married to the biological father of the child, no name should be entered. Alternatively, they might advise that as the surrogate has a husband[7] his name should be entered even though he is not the biological father of the child. A third option is the recommendation that as the sperm was provided by the intended father of the child, his name should be entered. Similarly inconsistent advice may be given by registrars when asked whose surname the baby should be registered under. Part of the reason for these inconsistencies lies in the fact that, locally, cases of registration of a surrogate birth are uncommon and might well be the only one a particular registrar has dealt with.

In view of the confusion surrounding registration, COTS' advice to its members is twofold. First, it is best to register the birth exactly as advised by the particular registrar on the understanding that he or she has been given all of the relevant information and has given advice on that basis. Secondly, what is entered on the original birth certificate is not important because that certificate will only be valid until a Parental Order or an Adoption Order is made in respect of the child and in favour of the intended parents whereupon a new one will be issued.

---

[5] Section 2 of the Surrogacy Arrangements Act 1985 makes it a criminal offence to make surrogacy arrangements on a commercial basis, and the Human Fertilisation and Embryology Act 1990 s 36 made surrogacy arrangements unenforceable in the courts—so that even if commissioning parents and surrogate mother decide to draw up a contract together, this cannot be legally enforced.

[6] Which is generally considered to be her 'reasonable expenses' involved in being pregnant with the child but which can run to figures in excess of £10,000.

[7] Very occasionally this advice is given to surrogate mothers who are not married but have a partner.

The second step which should be taken after the baby's birth is for the surrogate mother and the intended father of the child to enter into a Parental Responsibility Agreement in accordance with section 2(2) of The Children Act 1989. The effect of a Parental Responsibility Agreement is that the surrogate mother shares Parental Responsibility with the biological father of the child. This has two important implications. First, it places the biological father on a similar, almost equal, legal footing with the surrogate mother. Secondly, it means that the biological father can make important decisions about the care of the child, such as giving consent for emergency medical treatment to take place, without seeking the surrogate mother's permission to do so.

The procedure for making a Parental Responsibility Agreement is fairly straightforward. Standard forms can be obtained at any family proceedings court. When they have been completed by the applicant—the intended father—and the surrogate mother, the agreement can usually be entered into at the court office. Copies of the forms are retained by the intended father and the surrogate mother and a third copy is sent to the central registry.

If a surrogate mother does not wish to enter into a Parental Responsibility Agreement with the intended father of the child, it is open to him to apply to the court for a Parental Responsibility Order under section 4(1) of The Children Act 1989. A much more significant issue here is where and with whom the child is living. Broadly speaking, if the child has been handed over to the intended parents by the surrogate they will have a good chance of keeping it in the long term. On the other hand, if the surrogate does not hand over the child, there is really very little chance of it being taken from her and given to the intended parents against her will.

In addition to the Parental Responsibility Agreement, the intended parents or the intended father alone can apply for a Residence Order, under section 8 of the Children Act 1989, in respect of the child. Such an order simply determines where a child should live. However, Residence Orders are usually only made where there is some dispute about where and with whom a child should live and COTS would not advise intended parents to apply for such an order unless they felt that the surrogate might be going to try to remove the child from their care.

As soon as the child is six weeks old the final step of applying for a Parental Order under section 30 of the HFE Act 1990 should be made.[8] Applications can

---

[8] Section 30 of the Human Fertilisation and Embryology Act 1990 states:

30.—(1) The court may make an order providing for a child to be treated in law as the child of the parties to a marriage (referred to in this section as 'the husband' and 'the wife') if—(a) the child has been carried by a woman other than the wife as the result of the placing in her of an embryo or sperm and eggs or her artificial insemination, (b) the gametes of the husband or the wife, or both, were used to bring about the creation of the embryo, and (c) the conditions in subsections (2) to (7) below are satisfied. (2) The husband and the wife must apply for the order within six months of the birth of the child or, in the case of a child born before the coming into force of this Act, within six months of such coming into force. (3) At the time of the application and of the making of the order—(a) the child's home must be with the husband and the wife, and (b) the husband or the wife, of both of them, must be domiciled in a part of the United Kingdom or in the Channel Islands or the Isle of

only be made by married couples who are both at least 18 years of age and who are domiciled in England, Wales or the Channel Islands. The application must be made after the child is six weeks old and before he or she is six months old and the court can only make an order if the surrogate and her partner or husband have agreed with the arrangement and are fully and unequivocally in agreement with the making of such an order. As mentioned before, a Parental Order transfers Parental Responsibility for the child to the applicants. It also permanently extinguishes that of the surrogate and her husband. Although this piece of legislation was meant to simplify the process of transfer of Parental Responsibility for the child from the surrogate and her partner to the intended parents, it is clear that there remains much confusion about the exact interpretation of certain aspects of this provision.

Section 30 of the HFE Act 1990 was meant to be a relatively simple way for transferring all the rights, duties and responsibilities regarding the child from the surrogate to the intended parents. It is not always straightforward in practice. Intended parents need to obtain an application for a Parental Order from a court office. However, COTS has received many reports of Magistrates' Courts and some county courts telling applicants that they do not have the forms or they have never heard of the order sought. Perseverance may well be required to get beyond this point.

The court, on receiving the completed application, should appoint a Parental Order Reporter. He/she is an experienced officer who has spent many years working in the courts in connection with children's cases. He/she will almost certainly not be experienced in dealing with Parental Order applications. Furthermore, the reporter will have been used to working independently in the interests of children in need and to carrying out appropriate investigations in that regard. This experience does not interface well with the very specific and limited duties and responsibilities he/she has in connection with an application for a Parental Order. In fact, all the reporter is required to do is to check the application, see the surrogate and her husband or partner if he agreed to the arrangement and make sure that she or they agree to the making of an order. A secondary, and equally limited, function is to check that whatever has changed hands between the intended parents and the surrogate is consistent with the rather abstract concept of 'reasonable expenses', a matter dealt with below.

Man. (4) At the time of the making of the order both the husband and the wife must have attained the age of eighteen. (5) The court must be satisfied that both the father of the child (including a person who is the father by virtue of section 28 of this Act), where he is not the husband, and the woman who carried the child have freely, and with full understanding of what is involved, agreed unconditionally to the making of the order. (6) Subsection (5) above does not require the agreement of a person who cannot be found or is incapable of giving agreement and the agreement of the woman who carried the child is ineffective for the purposes of that subsection if given by her less than six weeks after the child's birth. (7) The court must be satisfied that no money or other benefit (other than for expenses reasonably incurred) has been given or received by the husband or the wife for or in consideration of—(a) the making of the order, (b) any agreement required by subsection (5) above, (c) the handing over of the child to the husband and the wife, or (d) the making of any arrangements with a view to the making of the order, unless authorised by the court.

Finally, the Parental Order Reporter should ask the court to set a date for a hearing at which he/she may give a short, factual, written or verbal report and at which the Parental Order should be made. In COTS' experience, several intended parents seeking Parental Orders have encountered unnecessary investigations, including the ordering of DNA tests on the baby, the intended father and the surrogate, irrelevant questioning and general inappropriate interference on the part of the Parental Order Reporter. Others have found themselves ordered to appoint a solicitor to represent them (an unnecessarily expensive requirement and an illegal order) and they and the surrogate being required to file statements in the proceedings. However, many Parental Order applications run comparatively smoothly and COTS continue to advise intended parents to follow this route rather than opt for the more longwinded adoption application in respect of the child.

If intended parents do not make a successful application for a Parental Order, they can still apply for an Adoption Order in respect of the child. If they are married, they can apply jointly but if they are not, only one of them can apply. When an application for an Adoption Order is made the court must inform the local authority social services department. They are required to visit the child in his or her proposed adoptive home over several months and to prepare a detailed report about the child, the applicants, the birth family and the placement. When this has been done, the court will appoint a Reporter whose main job is to see that the birth mother (the surrogate) and anyone else with Parental Responsibility for the child, agrees to the child being adopted by the applicants.

If the Reporter finds that anyone with Parental Responsibility does not agree to the adoption, he/she must inform the court who will appoint another official who will advise the court whether such a person or people are being reasonable or unreasonable in withholding their consent to the adoption. At the end of the day, in cases where there is a dispute, the court will decide what is best.

As noted above, one function of the Parental Order Reporter is to check that the surrogate has only been reimbursed for 'reasonable expenses'. Payment of surrogate mothers, or the provision of 'reasonable expenses', is a controversial topic. It is the view of some that the general public does not like the idea of women charging a fee for carrying a baby for someone else.[9] COTS view of this is that having a surrogate baby for someone else amounts to an extraordinary act of altruism. Beyond this, however, it is a procedure that may be fraught with dangers, problems and complications, both medical, social and psychological. While the development of problems is rare, it is potentially devastating for those involved. Consequently, COTS does not at present advocate payments in excess of £10,000 to surrogates. However, in cases where there will be loss of potential earnings as a result of the pregnancy, we take the view that women should be properly remunerated for the service they provide and the risks they take.

---

[9] For example, surrogacy has been referred to as 'the unnatural and unfortunate practice which has sickened so many decent and family-loving people' (see Morgan (1986)).

[handwritten: ensures child has one]

4. CONSEQUENCES OF SECTION 30 AND THE INFREQUENCY
OF SURROGACY

[handwritten: problems if the father doesn't become legal father]

Part of the purpose of section 30 appears to be to ensure that children have a 'father', even in cases where the arrangement fails and the surrogate mother decides to keep the baby. This seems to be the only way to make sense of the provision that the surrogate's husband or male partner, if he agreed with the surrogacy arrangement, is deemed to be the 'birth father' of the child. There are obvious benefits in ensuring that a child in contemporary society has an identified father. However, there are perhaps unforeseen, potential problems with this provision. One could occur if intended parents withdraw from the agreement and the surrogate mother's partner is obliged to become the father to a child he never intended to parent. It would also be possible for a surrogate mother's husband to have little to do with the surrogacy arrangement initially and yet prevent the making of a Parental Order in respect of the intended parents once the child is born, with or without the agreement of the surrogate mother.

One probable result of the lack of regulation of surrogacy in England and Wales has been to discourage the making of surrogacy arrangements—or at least, not encourage them. In these circumstances, those who wish to pursue this route to parenthood must probably be dedicated and persistent. Although the number of cases is increasing, nevertheless surrogacy is still rare. This means that procedures and applications to do with surrogacy occur very infrequently in any particular geographical area. As a consequence, many legal officials, including magistrates and judges, will find themselves dealing with surrogacy matters for the first time. Many other professionals (perhaps including doctors, midwives, social workers) to whom intended parents and surrogate mothers might turn for advice may be similarly confused.

In COTS' early days, this also applied to social services departments, particularly those based in hospitals. Faced with an unexpected and novel situation, practitioners could act in ways that appear outrageous. For example, social workers might threaten to take surrogate babies into care simply because they were surrogate babies. The grounds for this would be that simply being a surrogate child represented some risk of moral danger. This kind of act was only prevented when legal advisers explained that a child could not be removed from the care of its parent unless it was likely to suffer significant harm if it was not so removed. A similar unfamiliarity with the law,[10] its intentions and implementation, has more recently led the courts, and court appointees, to perform unnecessary actions.

[handwritten: NOT NORMAL]

---

[10] Specifically, s 30 of the HFE Act 1990.

and reforming

5. CONCLUSIONS

The laws that currently apply to surrogacy seem, in most cases, to do the job of protecting the rights of the child and the surrogate and facilitating the transfer of parenthood from the surrogate family to the intended family. However, it is clear from the above discussion that there is some confusion in interpretation of some aspects of the provision. This kind of confusion might arise for a number of reasons. As suggested before, it may result from a relative lack of experience with cases of surrogacy and thus unfamiliarity with requirements. It might also be a consequence of individuals being required to perform tasks that are inconsistent with their main training, knowledge and experience. Lastly, it is possible that it could arise from deliberate attempts to deter people from embarking upon surrogacy. Without research, we cannot say how real this possibility is.

What changes, if any, would COTS therefore like to see? Essentially it is the belief of COTS that the regulations and procedures which are at present in place are relatively effective. It is clear that greater uniformity should be achieved in relation to the registration of surrogate births. Similarly, it would be helpful if Parental Order Reporters and courts dealt with applications for Parental Orders in accordance with the Act. This is however more an issue of education and training of relevant professionals, rather than difficulties with the law. COTS are already in the process of communication with the Lord Chancellor and the Superintendent Registrar regarding the problems described herein. The failure in this country to introduce proper regulation (rather than piecemeal legislation) may have led to some confusion on the part of professionals and resultant inconsistent advice to users. However, the general view is that things should be left more or less as they are. This brings us back to the statement at the beginning of this chapter to the effect that 98 per cent of COTS surrogacies are successful. It is therefore hard to see how any tinkering with the law could improve on what must be seen as a very impressive record for an agency of such modest means.

REFERENCES

Brazier, M, Golombok, S and Campbell, A, *Surrogacy: Review for Health Ministers of Current Arrangements for Payments and Regulation. Report of the Review Team* Cm 4068 (London, HMSO, 1998).

Morgan, D, 'Who to Be or Not to Be: The Surrogacy Story' (1986) 49 *Modern Law Review* 358.

9

Ethical Issues in Surrogacy Arrangements

MELISSA LANE

1. INTRODUCTION

Paradoxes in the Significance of Surrogacy

UNLIKE MANY OF the so-called new reproductive technologies, the practice of surrogacy has been possible in certain 'low-tech' cultural forms for thousands of years.[1] The Hebrew Bible, for example, records the practice of a man having sex with a female servant, in order to procreate a child who will be socially viewed as the offspring of the man and his infertile wife. The advent of medicalised artificial insemination from the nineteenth century combined with certain social changes to produce culturally recognised practices of what we will call 'traditional' surrogacy in a number of countries in the 1980s, in which a man's sperm (usually that of the husband of a woman unable to conceive) was introduced (usually artificially) into a woman, who conceived and gestated a child with the intention of giving that child up to the genetic father and his partner, if any, at birth. The development of IVF then also made possible what we will call 'IVF' surrogacy, in which a 'birth mother' has an embryo created out of another woman's egg (and sperm from some man) implanted in her womb and carried to term, intending to give the child so conceived to the 'commissioning parent(s)' to adopt and raise.[2]

---

[1] In an effort to comply with ordinary usage (including the title of this volume) while also acknowledging that questions are raised by the conventional referent of the term 'surrogate mother', this chapter will use forms of 'surrogacy' as noun and adjective in the conventional way, except that it will refer to the woman carrying the baby in a 'surrogate' pregnancy as the 'birth mother' in contexts where it is clear that surrogacy and not ordinary adoption is at stake. While the term 'birth mother' is standard in adoption contexts in English, and so acknowledges the many similarities between surrogacy and adoption, the choice in this chapter to use 'commissioning parents' in place of something like 'adoptive parents' is meant to highlight the initiating role played by such persons in the establishment of a pregnancy in surrogacy, as contrasted with ordinary adoption. The 'commissioning parent(s)' are normally but not always the donors of the egg and/or sperm used to create the embryo, as they may instead choose to arrange for other egg and/or sperm (donated or purchased) to be used.

[2] A further distinction can be drawn between 'contract' surrogacy in which a formal contract for some consideration is involved, and 'gift' surrogacy where relatives, friends or acquaintances arrange surrogacy as a non-financial and non-contractual relationship among themselves.

It is striking that public concern about surrogacy predated the advent of IVF surrogacy, attaching instead to the prominent attempts to commercialise surrogacy arrangements by means of brokering agencies in Britain and America in the 1980s. At least four reasons explain why surrogacy became controversial when it did, despite the fact that it did not necessarily involve any of the new advanced reproductive technologies. First was the introduction of commercialisation itself. Second is the fact that like the new reproductive technologies, even traditional surrogacy involved the 'manipulation' and 'handling' of 'human gametes and embryos outside of the body', which 'raised the problem of moral responsibility and legal ownership' (Pfeffer (1987:95)). Alongside this issue of reproduction across traditional bodily boundaries, surrogacy also seems to have stirred inchoate anxiety about a third issue: reproduction across traditional social boundaries relevant to procreation. Unlike the donation of gametes (perhaps anonymously) where the birth mother intends to raise the child, surrogacy explicitly puts birth outside the boundary of the marriage or partnership, and allows a child to be intentionally procured from beyond that boundary (see, for example, Zipper and Sevenhuijsen (1987: 119)).

It is worth pausing over this third point to observe a striking contrast: there has been much less widespread and vehement public debate about practices of gamete donation than about practices of surrogacy (Glover (1989)). Medicalised practices of sperm donation in particular evolved within nineteenth- and twentieth-century common law regimes in the context of marital presumptions of legitimacy for all children born to a married wife, based on the presumption that such children should legally and socially count as the offspring of her husband. Even after abandoning the legal concept of legitimate and illegitimate birth in the Family Law Reform Act 1987 (section 1), for example, UK legislation still maintained in the Human Fertilisation and Embryology Act 1990 (HFE Act) that a child born within a marriage following the use of donor sperm is to be regarded as the child of the mother and her husband. The difficulty arising with surrogacy is that the marriage, if any, within which the child is born is that of the birth mother. While adoption or other court decisions can alter the list of those with parental responsibility for the child, the shift from a presumption of marital legitimacy to an acceptable intention to overturn such a presumption is one which may not be so easily resolved in the public mind as in the law courts.

The fourth element in the public reaction to surrogacy in the 1980s was concern with the nature and value of the intentions which surrogacy involves, and in particular uneasiness about the intentionality displayed by a woman who chooses to allow herself to be made pregnant for the specific purpose of giving up the child to others to raise. This view was graphically reported by the British Warnock Committee (which did not endorse it directly, although endorsing the same conclusion to which the view tends): 'in such an arrangement [of surrogacy] a woman deliberately allows herself to become pregnant with the intention of giving up the child to which she will give birth, and this is the wrong way to approach pregnancy' (Warnock (1985:45)).

It is helpful to compare surrogacy with a widely accepted practice to which it is in any case linked (by virtue of the legal requirements for the relinquishment of parental responsibility by some, and establishment of it for others): the practice of adoption. Here too genetic ties are intentionally severed, together with any claims they might entail, by the intentional appropriation of a child by a marriage or domestic partnership from which that child did not issue. In the case of adoption, the intentionality involved in the practice is typically denied any status until a certain period after the child is born. Even though a woman may decide to continue a pregnancy only on condition that she be able to give the child up for adoption, and even though an adoptive family may stand ready to receive the child as soon as they learn this during the pregnancy, and even though in some American states the adoptive family may pay for the birth mother's living and medical expenses, neither the woman's intention nor the adoptive family's is in any common law jurisdiction allowed to become legally binding until varying periods of time after the birth. This is often explained by appealing to the possibility that seeing the actual child may profoundly and unpredictably change the birth mother's views, and to the thought that her views as mother of that child once born should override both any prior intentions of her own and any claim on the part of potential adoptive others.

In light of these comparisons, one might parse traditional surrogacy as a peculiar combination of an unusual form of gamete donation and adoption. After the birth its structure becomes like that of ordinary adoption, in that a child is born and then relinquished to adopting parents. But the difficulties peculiar to surrogacy begin to manifest themselves in the question, which gamete should count as having been 'donated'? The aims of traditional surrogacy seem to require us to say that it is the egg that has been donated, although it remains in the 'donor' woman for fertilisation and gestation. For if one were to say, instead, that the sperm has been donated, the usual legal construction of donor insemination would suggest that the baby's parents were instead the birth mother and her partner, if any. But unlike the case of egg donation in which the donated gametes are handled outside the female body, and the egg donor is not construed as the mother, the combination of internal fertilisation and gestation in the case of surrogacy makes both proponents and opponents of the latter practice see it as something quite distinct from ordinary egg donation. What British surrogacy pioneer and proponent Kim Cotton stated (controversially) to hold for the subjective experience of birth mothers in surrogacy arrangements, can serve to illustrate the contrast between egg donation and surrogacy more generally:

> It is a strange phenomenon that a woman bearing a child from a donated egg convinces herself that she is the true mother as she gives birth to the child, whereas it is the exact opposite in host [here, 'IVF'] surrogacy, when the surrogate mother is

pregnant with a transferred embryo. After the birth she is just as positive she is not the true mother (Cotton (1992:135)).[3]

'IVF' surrogacy, in which both egg and sperm are provided by the intended adoptive parents, shares these fundamental features with 'traditional' surrogacy. As one observer defines surrogacy in a definition embracing both types: 'a surrogate agrees before she becomes pregnant that she will on the birth of the child she carries throughout her pregnancy, hand that child to the couple [sic][4] with whom she has made the surrogacy arrangement' (Morgan (1989:61)). Traditional surrogacy might appear to be like 'ordinary illegitimacy', in that a man inseminates a woman with whom he is not linked in marriage. IVF surrogacy goes further—being construed by most proponents and opponents at present so as to emphasise the role of the gestating woman as a 'mere carrier' of the baby who genetically as well as intentionally belongs elsewhere. What is true for a given baby in such arrangements is that this (particular) baby *could* not have been conceived without the genetic contribution of another woman and of a man who is not the birth mother's own partner; and that this (particular) baby *would* not have been conceived had not another person or persons commissioned its birth with the intent to parent the child so born.

So far we have defined surrogacy in relation to similar practices of gamete donation and adoption. Beyond its definition lie the social and cultural questions it raises. Perhaps the most difficult issue here is the way in which surrogacy disassociates elements which have usually been combined in our ideal of motherhood; it raises the possibility that a child may have more than one 'real' or 'natural' mother.[5] While the pill and other contraceptive technologies uncou-

---

[3] Kim Cotton, the first commercial birth mother in the UK who later served as a 'gift' birth mother for a second time, co-founded COTS (Childlessness Overcome Through Surrogacy), on which see Dodd, chapter 8, this volume. Cotton passionately advocated surrogacy in her two books on the subject, although she changed from defending the anonymous surrogacy arrangements she used in her first surrogate pregnancy (Cotton (1985)), to defending surrogacy in the context of friendly contact with the commissioning parents in her second surrogate pregnancy (Cotton and Winn (1985)). But when Cotton was interviewed by Fergal Keane on BBC Radio 4 on 12 October 1999, having resigned from COTS and retired from surrogacy, she admitted having 'cried buckets' when she left the hospital after giving birth to 'baby Cotton' in an anonymous surrogacy arrangement, which she now called 'barbaric', and commented generally about giving up a baby that 'you can do it, but at great cost to yourself' (a reference I owe to Shelley Day Sclater).

[4] Most discussions of surrogacy—including, but not limited to, those defences which seek to 'normalize' it—tacitly assume that the birth mother is commissioned by a couple, and most of those assume the couple involved is heterosexual. Analysts of the social significance and imagery of surrogacy should bear in mind that surrogacy arrangements can and have been commissioned by single men and gay and lesbian couples, and could in theory also be commissioned by single women.

[5] Techniques of chromosomal extraction and transfer between eggs now mean that there could theoretically be at least four distinct initial claimants to the title of 'mother' for a given child: the donor of the egg, the donor of the transferred chromosomes, the birth mother, and the commissioning or intended adoptive mother: this without consideration of the technique of combining different embryos into 'chimaeras' which can double the numbers of genetic donors (see generally Johnson (1999)). Should chromosomes become singly transferable or human cloning widespread, the number and gender of parental claimants could change still further. Meanwhile step-parent relations can also add indefinitely many further claims to the list.

pled sex and reproduction, and IVF can divorce conception from gestation, (surrogacy separates the mothering function of pregnancy (gestation and birth) from the mothering function of raising a child. So does adoption, of course, but in surrogacy the birth mother is not initially intended by anyone, including herself, ever to claim any right to mother the child after birth. Reproductive technologies have powerful symbolic meanings too—the very existence and use of such technologies can alter our common consciousness about how reproduction and motherhood function and what they mean. Thus the significance of surrogacy can only be fully appreciated in the light of a number of other social and cultural developments which have conditioned our very understanding of that significance.

Social Contexts Making Surrogacy 'Special'

A fundamental shift in social context has already been noted above: the transformation or abolition (in different jurisdictions) of the common law paradigm of 'legitimacy'. One might think that 'social legitimacy' has been supplanted straightforwardly by the claims of the 'genetic', as suggested by some commentators (eg Roberts (1995)), who also points out the racialised element of the genetic tie particularly in the United States, in light of the legal and social legacy of slavery). But the widespread legal and public acceptability of gamete donation as described earlier shows that the claims of the 'genetic' have still to be evaluated within particular social and intentional contexts. It is not that the claims of social legitimacy have given way unambiguously to the genetic, but rather, that they have been supplanted by a more multivalent and shifting set of claims arising from the nexus between 'the natural' and 'the intentional'.

In tandem with the proliferation of reproductive technologies goes a proliferation of discourses about the 'naturalness' of the resulting processes and products. This naturalness has at least three possible interpretations and contrasts, all relevant to the evaluation of surrogacy. 'The natural' can be linked to kinship and gift as contrasted with the contractual—for example, egg donation or familial surrogacy versus egg sales or contractual surrogacy. It can be linked to the complex and prolonged processes of physical maternity as contrasted with the one-off nature of physical paternity—for example, the birth mother who does the real work of mothering, exalted above the tenuous claims of the physical father. And it can be prioritised in its interpretation as 'the genetic' in a new twist that can come into conflict with earlier usage. For example, the claims of commissioning parents in IVF surrogacy, who are genetically the parents of the child, may be exalted above the claims of the birth mother. Controversies over the meanings of 'the natural' are inextricably b(attempts to use constructions of 'the natural' to identify a 'real child born of surrogacy, and go beyond this to help fashion our u of reproduction, kinship, and social order generally.

maybe mention

Two further contexts must be identified in order to appreciate the source and nature of the ethical controversies about surrogacy. One is a general concern about the market and the limits of commodification (see Blyth and Potter, chapter 15, this volume). The prominence of surrogacy in the 1980s resulted as noted above from a wave of surrogacy contracts and publicity-seeking brokers. Part of the public outcry was based specifically on the contractualisation of gestation for financial reward, even though sperm had long since been contractually available as commodity. The debate over what should be inalienable in the market (the useful concept of market-inalienability was introduced by Radin (1987); see also Radin (1996)) arose from the Right—which had always sought sharply to distinguish market from family relations—as well as from the Left's longstanding suspicion of the degrading and alienating effects of market relations.

There are two different ways in which surrogacy may be held to commodify reproduction. One charge is that it commodifies women's reproductive capacity, putting some women into the role of 'paid breeder' in a way which is 'incompatible with a society in which individuals are valued for themselves' (Capron and Radin (1988:62)). If widespread surrogacy arrangements were to make women into 'second-class citizens', they could be banned on grounds of sex discrimination (Sunstein (1993:288)). Some feminists have gone so far as to suggest surrogacy should be considered a form of prostitution, contractualising reproduction just as sexuality has long since been contractualised in the prostitution market (Dworkin (1983:182)); quoted and endorsed in Corea (1985b:39)). The other charge made by anti-commodificationists is that surrogacy commodifies children, in that the babies involved are 'paid for' and so 'sold' (Ketchum (1989)). This charge may be rebutted by the claim that the fee paid is for the woman's reproductive services rather than for the baby, and that the baby cannot be 'resold' or exchanged for money as would be the case were babies to be fully commodified. Nevertheless, anti-commodificationists urge that a baby resulting from surrogacy is treated as an 'object' in the course of the transaction, and that this is at least an element in if not a slippery slope towards the moral odium of a market in babies (Capron and Radin (1988:63)).

Feminist concerns about commodification form part but by no means the whole of the complex continuum of feminist responses to surrogacy—and feminism itself is the final social context to be introduced here. Some feminists, as just noted, have concentrated their ire on the 'capitalist' nature of surrogacy arrangements and their interference with 'natural' reproduction. Others have imagined and celebrated 'natural' reproduction (Zipper and Sevenhuijsen (1987:125)), rejecting the arrangements dominating all forms of reproduction in current developed societies as tools of a patriarchal regime bent on increasing its control over women's reproductive powers (Corea (1985a; 1985b)). The initial circumstances in which surrogacy came to prominence—in which fathers claimed rights over the children born of traditional surrogacy, paternal right overriding maternal right in both its genetic and gestational forms—reinforced this perception of its social purpose.[6]

In contrast with these anti-capitalist and radical-cultural feminists, other feminists who may be called 'choice' feminists argue that surrogacy could help transform gender relations by potentially empowering women to use their reproductive powers as they choose, and to receive such reward for them as capitalism might muster (Andrews (1988); Sistare (1988)). On this view, while existing surrogacy contracts might seem to disempower the surrogate, the possibility of using contract law to protect and to empower women, and by so empowering them to transform gender relations, should be celebrated and explored (Shalev (1989); Shevory (2000)). The relative prominence and strength of the radical feminist analysis of all social institutions as fundamentally shaped by patriarchy, has meant that the majority of feminists writing on the topic have opposed surrogacy, even though there are legitimate feminist interests and arguments which can be articulated on the other side.

2. ETHICAL DEBATES

Is (any form of) Surrogacy Moral?

The discussion of ethical issues in surrogacy in an international context necessarily abstracts from the particular features of a given surrogacy proposal or regime. Yet the difference between the approach in an American state where agencies are operative and most surrogates already have children and are married, and the regime in Israel—where birth mothers involved in surrogacy must be unmarried and of the same religion as the commissioning parents, and surrogacy agreements must be supervised by the state—is profound (see chapters by Rao, Schuz and Schenker, this volume). The focus in this chapter will be on jurisdictions where, whether or not surrogacy contracts are legally enforceable, there is a practice of arranging surrogacy between relative strangers as well as practices of arranging surrogacy between friends and relatives, but there is no state supervision of such arrangements (Israel being the only country in the world where such supervision exists).

Ethical issues arise on at least three levels. First comes the most general question as to whether surrogacy of any kind is moral or immoral. Next is the related but distinct question of whether surrogacy of any kind should be legal and, if so,

---

[6] Judge Harvey J Sorkow's trial court decision in the 'Baby M' case, where the surrogate mother Mary Beth Whitehead wished to retain custody and maternal rights to the child, has become the *locus classicus* of such a patriarchal judicial view. But it should be remembered that the most offensive aspects of his decision—which denied maternal rights and any claim in the baby to Whitehead, denigrating her social status compared with that of the commissioning father, and suggested *en passant* that her signing of the contract showed her to be maternally unworthy—were overturned by the New Jersey Supreme Court. See *In re Baby M* (1988) 109 N.J. 396 [537 A.2d 1227].

which kind and what form it should take. And finally, there are questions to do with the consequences of allowing some form of surrogacy to be practised.

Most arguments supporting the morality of surrogacy begin from some kind of fundamental liberty or fundamental right.[7] Arguments from liberty need not defend the morality of surrogacy as a practice, but rather operate at a higher level of abstraction, defending instead the morality of retaining the freedom to participate in surrogacy (in any of the roles it involves). However, since arguments that surrogacy is immoral often suggest that it should therefore be banned or restricted, the liberty-argument in its favour—that surrogacy is part of a fundamental freedom which people should enjoy—is an important defence against the immorality charge.

The interest invoked might be a general interest in liberty. But usually it is a certain kind of liberty that is advanced, and the choice colours the nature and implications of the defence of surrogacy. The two most common kinds of liberty invoked are freedom of contract, on the one hand, and reproductive freedom, on the other; as their implications are so different they will be discussed separately below. In each case, the argument put forward is denied by opponents of surrogacy who claim that rather than forming part of a fundamental and protected liberty-interest, surrogacy represents the unwarranted intrusion of individual liberty-claims into some area of other interest which deserves overriding protection.

Freedom of Contract

To argue that surrogacy is covered by the fundamental interest in freedom of contract is to assume what many of its detractors would deny: that gestational and birth arrangements can and should be (allowed to be) made contractually. Arguments for this assumption can begin from an economic perspective, such as that of Richard Posner, who suggests that surrogacy could be a partial remedy for the absence of a free market in baby-selling (Posner (1987)). More typically, they begin from a general liberal presumption favouring freedom of contract in the absence of significant harms caused by that practice, and an argument that no such harms are caused in the case of surrogacy. Note that surrogacy contracts need not involve payment of a significant fee; a private arrangement for peppercorn consideration would qualify, and one might argue that the general freedom to transact includes the freedom to make non-commercial arrangements of the same kind as any permitted contractual arrangement. The freedom to serve as a birth mother through surrogacy and the freedom to contract with such a birth mother on this view derive from a common source in freedom of contract.

---

[7] In American discourse fundamental liberties are normally represented as rights, and this formulation has influenced most discussions of surrogacy in the literature.

There are two major problems that the contract perspective must confront. First is the challenge that surrogacy contracts do not normally conform to central requirements of contract law. One way in which this challenge is often put is by suggesting it wrong to believe that a birth mother's consent to such a contract could be 'freely' given, in light of the peculiar nature of the process of pregnancy that will intervene between the original consent and the moment of giving up the baby. But the danger of such arguments is that they risk infantilising women, by refusing to hold them responsible or able to act freely in one aspect of their reproductive choices (Andrews (1988); Sistare (1988)). The legitimate concern about a lack of fit between surrogacy and contract is better captured, not by denying the potential voluntariness of consent to serve as a birth mother through surrogacy, but by challenging the eligibility of consent to serve as a legitimation for the practice at all. Just as we do not allow people to consent to sell themselves into slavery or to alienate other inalienable rights (though just which those are is open to question: McConnell (2000)), so it may be that consent should be rejected as a legitimating device for surrogacy.

Such rejection might rely on the grounds that surrogacy contracts will be intrinsically exploitative. This is a charge often made, though seldom worked out in detail. It might mean that although the exploited woman benefits at least financially (and so both parties benefit to some degree), the benefit to the commissioning party is so much greater that any payment will fail to do justice to the 'good' produced and then alienated by the birth mother.[8] Or the eligibility of consent might be rejected on still broader grounds, related to the notion that some contracts are simply unconscionable, or to the even more fundamental claim that some relationships shouldn't be contractualised at all (Anderson (1993:141–89); Radin (1987)). The thought here would be that giving up a birthed child is the kind of choice which one should not be allowed to make in advance, not because one could not make it freely, but because it is not the sort of choice that anyone should (be allowed to) make. In other words, the point would be not that surrogacy cannot be made to look enough like an ordinary contract, but that it would be wrong to try to make it look so. Arguments converge on this point from both Right and Left. Both agree that surrogacy commercialises and degrades what should be sacrosanct, the Right stressing the way that it violates the sanctity of the marriage bond while the Left stresses the additional exploitation of women which surrogacy constitutes in a regime of patriarchy or deep-rooted gender inequality.

The second and related major challenge to a contractualist justification of surrogacy is that treating surrogacy as a contract treads on ground which properly belongs to family law (Capron and Radin (1988)). Because surrogacy structurally and legally requires adoption, it appears difficult to rule out all the

---

[8] In the most thorough philosophical account of exploitation, however, Alan Wertheimer concludes that in cases where there is some (though unequal) benefit to both parties—including the case of surrogacy, which he considers explicitly—the charge of exploitation alone is insufficient to establish that the practice should be prohibited by law (see Wertheimer (1996:96–122, 296–309)).

[handwritten margin note: need scrutiny of court as child involved before binding]

concerns which family law normally considers—and in particular, concerns with the best interests or the welfare of the child—on the grounds that a prior contract has declared them irrelevant. Just as divorcing parties are not permitted to make their own prior contract legally binding in relation to arrangements for their children, so it seems plausible to argue that parties contracting to surrogacy should not be permitted to make their own prior contract legally binding in relation to child adoption without the scrutiny of the court. But if so, then the contract can at best be indicative of intentions, and surrogacy cannot rest its case in terms of freedom of contract alone. To put the point more generally, the fact that surrogacy involves the welfare of a 'third-party'—a child—makes it difficult to assimilate entirely under ordinary freedom of contract justifications. This is not to say that there may not be grounds for allowing surrogacy contracts of some form to be used, but only that those grounds cannot be constructed of the freestanding good of contract itself.[9]

[handwritten margin note: child so can't be contract]

Reproductive Freedom

A more promising route to a fundamental defence of surrogacy appears to be that of reproductive freedom: both the reproductive freedom of women to act as birth mothers through surrogacy and that of women or men to contract with surrogates. Here the freedom to contract is not the baseline interest, but rather is at best corollary of a fundamental interest in reproductive freedom and privacy, which should permit use to be made of whatever technology or process may safely realise that interest in the form of a child (Sistare (1988)). If a narrowly contractualist perspective must be embarrassed by some consideration of the child's interests, and an adoption-perspective has trouble giving weight to the intentionality of the commissioning parent(s), a reproductive-freedom perspective would treat the choice to procreate by or as a surrogate on a par with other decisions to procreate (Robertson (1994)). These should not in liberal societies require licensing or scrutiny in terms of the child's interests, even though the child's interests do become a concern of the state after birth if he or she is seriously endangered or if the parents divorce (Jackson (2002)).[10] Though the decisions to procreate by employing a birth mother as a surrogate, or by acting as a birth mother through surrogacy, should not on this argument be scrutinis-

---

[9] Contractarian defences of surrogacy typically address this point by weakening the standard of the child's interest which must be met. So Posner suggests that the relevant standard is only whether the child will be better off being born than not being born (Posner (1987)), while Stumpf suggests that a standard of 'adequate' concern for the child's interests (rather than the 'best interests' of the child) is appropriate (Stumpf (1986:206)).

[10] In fact this claim is compromised somewhat by the higher standards to which many users of assisted conception technologies are held compared with the absence of standards to which reproducers by 'normal' means are answerable. Commissioning parents and courts may also seek to hold surrogate pregnancies—although increasingly, in the United States, courts are seeking to hold ordinary pregnancies as well—to high standards of foetal welfare which risk invading the freedom and privacy of the birth mother.

able, the family law adoption concerns may nevertheless come into play after the child is born. Arguments for surrogacy from reproductive freedom will endorse at least 'gift' surrogacy, and may or may not also endorse contractual surrogacy as a corollary of the interest in reproductive freedom.

Insofar as a reproductive-freedom argument is used to justify contractual surrogacy, objectors might suggest that rights of reproductive privacy are already given up when contractual rights are invoked and sought. Objectors to the reproductive-freedom argument more generally might also suggest that there are compelling societal interests that block the subsumption of surrogacy under such general individual interests as reproductive freedom and privacy. For it is a commonplace of liberal argument that my liberty to swing my fist ends where your nose begins. If surrogacy causes substantial harms to those not participating in the agreement (or perhaps even to the contracting parties, on paternalist or general social welfare grounds), then reproductive freedom might be justifiably restricted. Concerns about the welfare of the children born as a result of surrogacy arrangements, either when they work and deprive children of contact with their birth mothers, or when they break down and children are wanted by all parties or by none, are an example of the kind of harms which might be raised here.

Morality and Public Policy

While some would affirm that there is an overriding moral case so compelling that surrogacy must be allowed whatever concerns it might raise (as in the case of freedom of conscience) others would argue equally strongly that it must be prohibited regardless of the benefits it might bring. However, most discussions presuppose that neither is the case.[11] Rather the morality of surrogacy is assessed in broadly consequentialist terms. The freedom to engage in a certain practice (a freedom which only some few individuals will exercise) is weighed up against the harms or potential harms to others and to society as a whole from allowing such practices to be freely pursued. Those harms may include the harms to 'others' (not party to the surrogate contract or arrangement) mentioned in the previous section, as well as (with due consideration to the problem of paternalism) harms to the parties themselves—for instance, the birth mother (if exploited) and the intended adoptive mother (if made marginal to the father's legal arrangements)—as well as the harms to some or all of these people and to others caused by court battles over parental identification (Rowland (1992:191–94)).

Harms to be considered may also include harms to society more generally, caused by the practice of surrogacy. For instance, one could argue that simply

---

[11] Absolutist moral arguments against surrogacy on, say, Qu'ranic or Catholic grounds, would not normally be considered compelling reasons, or even candidate reasons, for public policy decisions in a liberal and pluralist society.

legalising (or not criminalising) surrogacy, makes available certain choices, such that the option of not having to make such a choice is thereby foreclosed (Strathern (1992:37)). While the foreclosure of the choice not to choose, by the granting of a choice, is not normally counted as a weighty harm, it may be argued to be such on the grounds that surrogacy thus treats as a market choice relationships (kinship, and the gestation and birth of children) which have historically belonged to the realm of fate rather than choice (Strathern (1992:31–43)). Similarly, surrogacy has been held to undermine ideas of the unity and naturalness of motherhood; it has also been charged with symbolising, reinforcing, or realising the subordination of women to men and of the poor to the rich, by seeking to exploit and control the bodies of poorer women for the benefit of wealthy men and women. Just as it has been claimed that all women are harmed by the existence of pornography (MacKinnon (1989)), so it has been suggested that all women are harmed by the existence of surrogacy (Dworkin (1983)).

The multiplicity of harms which have been ascribed to surrogacy must be taken seriously whatever ethical and analytical framework one adopts; many of them require further investigation and evaluation. Still, it is difficult to evaluate such a mixed bag of consequences without recourse to a fundamental organising idea or paradigm, whether freedom of contract, reproductive freedom, or the idea of patriarchy. The moral evaluation of surrogacy depends, ultimately, on a fundamental choice between a liberal perspective—which prioritises freedom for distinct individuals in the choices they make, and a radical perspective—which questions the meaning of such individual freedom in light of the effects of various forms of social power and prioritises the control or elimination of such power. It is impossible to give conclusive grounds for the making of such a fundamental choice of paradigm in this brief chapter. Three points which tell against a wholesale adoption of the radical perspective—while acknowledging the important issues it raises—can nevertheless be made.

First, in assimilating surrogacy to other forms of patriarchal control of reproduction, it becomes less clear why surrogacy should be identified as particularly problematic: will patriarchy be undermined if it cannot practise surrogacy? The second point is the fact that surrogacy is widely attacked from the Right as well as the Left, and this suggests that there may be some anti-patriarchal transformative potential in the practice despite current patriarchal manifestations. This potential is rooted in the way that surrogacy makes evident the distinction between birthing and raising a child, so making both visible as distinct and valuable activities, and making the women involved in a surrogate pregnancy into collaborators in reproduction (Shevory (2000:51–55, 67–73); Sistare (1988)). And the third point against a wholesale adoption of the radical critique of surrogacy is its unproblematic derivation of individual ethics from systemic analyses.

Exemplifying the radical approach on this third point, Barbara Katz Rothman writes: 'We will have to lift our eyes from the choices of the individual woman, and focus on the control of the social system that structures her choices, which rewards some choices and punishes others, which distributes the rewards and punishments for reproductive choices along class and race lines' (Rothman (1982:33) quoted [but as Rothman (1984)] in Woliver (1995:357)). Feminist ethics certainly depends upon canny and cogent analysis of social systems that are structured and distorted by inequalities of gender, class, and race. And it may be the case, as Debra Satz has argued, that whatever the transformative possibilities of surrogacy (say) in another context, the structuring context of gender inequality in which it is practised today makes it objectionable on feminist grounds (Satz (1992)). But it is too hasty simply to equate social analysis with individual ethics. Ethical evaluation depends (at least) on moral principle, particular circumstances, individual life history (which shapes the particular demands of our own moral integrity) as well as on analysis of social systems. And even within a feminist analysis of patriarchy, it must be acknowledged that the desires and goals of particular women will manifest traces of patriarchal as well as feminist consciousness, and will be no less real and authentically theirs for that (Bartky (1990)). While, on any given issue, we may ultimately decide that an overall social prohibition or reconstruction of some practice is justified on feminist grounds, we must take care not to leap too quickly from judgments of ideal feminist life-styles to a condemnation of the will, desires, and choices of individual women.[12]

What Legal Form (if any) should Surrogacy Take?

If neither a global claim of reproductive integrity nor a global analysis of patriarchy is found to justify an absolute prohibition of surrogacy, one must then ask what attitude the law should take to different forms of surrogacy. While surrogacy of some kind may be supported by our interest in reproductive freedom, this leaves open the questions of the validity of contracts, and the disposition of rights, risks, and benefits among the parties involved in the contract, as well as the privacy of the parties in relation to a subsequent child's right to information.

In the Anglo-American world, it has been widely accepted that private surrogate relationships could not and should not be effectively prevented by the law, as the technology required is in fact do-it-yourself and it would be wrong to criminalise the birth of any child so conceived. There has also been a widespread preference for 'gift' over 'contract' surrogacy arrangements.[13] The primary legal

---

[12] A similar though stronger position has been put thus: 'In concrete events of life we have to accept will and longings as given. There is a difference between individual choices of women and political strategies of feminism. In our opinion it is a mistaken interpretation of the slogan "the personal is political" to deny women these choices and decisions and to develop a feminist morality about the rights and wrongs of life-styles. We have to develop concepts that do not subsume individual women under a supposed collectivity of women.' (Zipper and Sevenhuijsen (1987:126)).

[13] The ethical purity of 'gift' surrogacy can however be questioned, as family pressure can be as or more exigent and extortionate as market pressure, without the protection which contract might afford and with the real risk of the breakdown of such 'loving' relationships under the strain.

issues therefore include whether surrogacy contracts should be permissible, whether if permissible they should be enforceable, and whether if enforceable, the remedy for failure to comply with the contract should include 'specific performance'[14] or be limited to compensation only. In America, there is the additional issue of whether the enforceability of a surrogacy contract would violate any constitutional rights.

Arguments for enforceability stem from the general defence of freedom of contract considered above. It has been argued that to prohibit women from entering into binding surrogacy contracts is paternalistic and deprives them of their equal moral and rational status, treating pregnancy and childbirth as disabling of that status in a conventionally patriarchal way (Shalev (1989); Andrews (1988)). One might also adopt a general feminist argument in favour of rights, to suggest that enforceable contracts and the rights they provide might serve as a 'safety net' if and when the relationships involved in surrogacy go wrong (Waldron (1993)). While feminist ire has been concentrated on cases like that of Baby M, in which the lower-court judge held the surrogacy contract to be sufficient reason to take a baby away from a birth mother who had changed her mind about relinquishing the child, one should also be concerned about cases where the commissioning parent(s) might change his, her, or their mind, and the birth mother be left responsible for a child she never intended to keep (Stumpf (1986:202–4)).[15] The problem of moral risk that this raises will be discussed further below. If women are to enjoy the reproductive freedom of engaging in surrogacy, it may be in their interests to have the protection of an enforceable contract even where such a contract may in some cases turn out to be against their interests as later understood.

A principal argument on the other side—against the enforceability of surrogacy contracts—would seek to make them more comparable to ordinary adoptions. Just as the intention to give a child up for adoption cannot be formalised until after the baby is born, so it is argued should be the case for surrogacy; any prior contract to the contrary must not be treated as automatically enforceable. Some have argued that surrogate pregnancies should be treated identically to other pregnancies in terms of the rights and obligations of the pregnant woman, and be handled as ordinary adoption cases after birth (Capron and Radin

---

[14] 'Specific performance' means that a contracting party is ordered to perform precisely what he or she had contracted to do. Its rejection means that a singer who is ill, for example, will not be ordered to sing anyway, but rather to pay damages to the venue she lets down. In the case of surrogacy, 'specific performance' would require a birth mother who had contracted to do so, to hand over the child to the commissioning parents.

[15] Consider the tragic case in the US of *Stiver v Malahoff* , in which a child was born to Judy Stiver suffering microencephaly and a strep infection. The commissioning father, Alex Malahoff, first sued to prevent the hospital from treating the child and, when that failed, he refused to take the child or pay the surrogacy fee, instead successfully bringing a case to prove that the genetic father of the child was Judy Stiver's husband. The court gave (unwanted) custody to the Stivers, who had unsuccessfully counter-claimed that the child's disabilities were due to a virus in Malahoff's sperm, and who immediately institutionalised the child. The case is described in Tong (1995:56).

(1988); Annas (1988:52)). The difference between ordinary adoption and surrogacy however, in terms of the expectations and intentions of the commissioning parent(s), does deserve some moral consideration.[16] Here a willingness on the part of the state to play a greater role in evaluating surrogacy contracts could help to establish some middle ground between specific performance and unenforceability of contracts altogether, for example, by establishing presumptions which could be overridden in individual cases should compelling reasons to do so arise. This might discourage some commissioning parents and potential birth mothers from engaging in the practice, but would recognise the importance of evaluating contracts in specific circumstances and with reference to some standard for the interests of the child in disputed cases.

It seems that women have several interests—which means different women may attach primacy to different ones—all of which need to be protected: an interest in being treated as contracting equals; an interest in the protection which contract can afford; an interest in being in control of the experience and the crucial decisions affecting any pregnancy they may conceive, including the possibility of terminating that pregnancy; and an interest in retaining parental status in relation to any child they bear until after that child's birth. The typical public policy justification for thoroughgoing unenforceability, such as that adopted in the UK, does not take adequate account of the first two interests.[17] It makes it impossible for women to have their initial intentions in undertaking a pregnancy or in supplying genetic material to another woman for certain purposes, or contracting her to undertake a pregnancy, taken into account by a court. On the other hand, strict enforceability, including specific performance, is repugnant to ordinary personal service contracts (Tong (1995:57–59))—musicians who default on contracted performances are made to pay, not play—and even more repugnant in this case. One alternative would be to treat a surrogacy contract not as 'void from inception' but as nevertheless still 'voidable', to adopt R Alta Charo's description of certain court opinions on surrogacy in the United States (Charo (1988:94)). As Charo explains, this would give the courts discretion to determine whether the commissioning parents were manifestly unfit, and also to void the contract should the birth mother change her mind within a statutory time period, meaning that she would lose any contractually agreed fees but retain the rights and obligations of any birth mother in the absence of a contract. As described in chapter 3, courts have this power in Israel, and also have the further power to scrutinise contracts beforehand as part of a legislatively established scheme of regulation. But such a system requires a level of state intervention which Anglo-American jurisdictions might find alien, and a level of agreement about the goals of surrogacy and the moral restrictions

---

[16] Tong (1995:76) also argues that regulated fees should be permissible.

[17] Derek Morgan criticises the unenforceability of surrogacy contracts in the UK saying that the effect is to treat all parties 'as gamblers in a wagering contract, in which the bargaining chips will be moral pressure and financial inducement, the risks, emotional vulnerability, psychological distress, and familial uncertainty' (Morgan (1989:70)).

on their pursuit (attained in large part in Israel by religious discourse, as chapter 16 shows) that Anglo-American jurisdictions might find impossible or undesirable or both.

Moral Risks and the Social Imaginary

A surrogacy arrangement of any kind necessarily involves all parties in grave moral risks.[18] Given that the outcome of such an arrangement depends both on the actions and omissions of many individuals, and also on fate or chance, its outcome cannot be neatly predicted, nor the moral burdens involved neatly allocated. A birth mother may become ill from some antibody in the introduced sperm or an immune reaction which her body generates to it, or simply from the natural course of pregnancy which may result even in death. The moral responsibility of the commissioners in this case is not eliminated by the fact that the surrogate may have consented to the arrangement. Or disablement to the child may result, either from actions or omissions by the birth mother, or in the course of birth as a result of actions or omissions by another or by fate. The commissioners will not receive what they presumably intend, a healthy child. And of course there is the moral risk that each party may wish to default on its agreement with the other. Participation in a surrogacy arrangement makes incurring such moral risks inevitable, and they cannot be ignored in evaluating the morality of such participation. Moral evaluation cannot limit its own standard to the 'best-case scenario': it demands recognition of moral risks and the willingness to respond to them flexibly and adequately, if it is to consider approving of a practice at all. Justifications for surrogacy must attend to the consequences of the 'worst-case' possibilities and evaluate how harms so arising will be addressed if they are to count as full moral justifications at all.

There is also a less obvious and more general category of moral risk in surrogacy, from which many of the ethical problems about it flow. This is the moral risk of wishing to erase the consequences of certain actions and relationships from future consideration. It is not surrogacy *per se* that is morally objectionable, but the use of surrogacy with the intention of erasing and forgetting that use so far as possible; as though the relationship between commissioners and birth mother could conveniently be forgotten (or hidden) once its object had been achieved. The idea that surrogacy involves treating one person as a means to the ends of others gains force to the extent that efforts are made to keep the role of the birth mother strictly circumscribed, and her relation to the child nullified after that child's birth. While the means-end objection can be made in principled moral terms, it can also be given an experiential dimension: Heléna

---

[18] A moral risk is a risk of incurring moral duties or obligations, or more generally inhabiting a changed moral universe, as a result of one's actions or of one's involvement in the actions of someone else.

Ragoné has argued that it is the relationships with the commissioning parents that many birth mothers most value, and the severing or diminution of those relationships after the birth that hurts them most (Ragoné (1994), and chapter 14, this volume). The attempt to use, and then forget, surrogacy flows from a social imaginary in which it is 'natural' for children to have only one mother, and in which technology and the relationships it involves serve only to reproduce something as close to this 'natural' ideal as possible, in which any other contributions to reproduction must be minimised so that the 'natural' bonds can be achieved. It is in this context that harm can currently be done to surrogate mothers and their families, of the kind powerfully described by Elizabeth Kane: 'surrogate motherhood is nothing more than the transference of pain from one woman [an infertile commissioning mother] to another [a birth mother]' (quoted in Rowland (1992:189)).[19]

Ironically, divorce and the advent of 'open' adoption has already shown that legal systems and, to an increasing extent, public cultures can accommodate children with more than one maternal and paternal actor in their lives. What is paradoxical about surrogacy is the extent to which discomfort with it drives appeal to the most traditional of paradigms—marital privacy and all it entails—to understand and legitimate it, no matter that fewer and fewer couples marry and reproduce within that paradigm at all. Were we to transform our social imaginary to accept the fact that surrogacy makes families possible, but does so by creating other relationships which should be valued and acknowledged, surrogacy could be accepted as one way of forming families rather than as the embodiment of their dissolution. The Solomonic view of surrogacy—that only some people deserve to have parental status in relation to children born through it—reflects a conservative and constricting vision of what motherhood could come to mean. One moral imperative on those participating in surrogacy arrangements is to question those constraints and the false imagined neatness of the moral life from which they derive.[20]

REFERENCES

Anderson, E, *Value in Ethics and Economics* (Cambridge, Mass, Harvard University Press/The MIT Press, 1993).
Andrews, LB, 'Surrogate Motherhood: The Challenge for Feminists' in L Gostin (ed), *Surrogate Motherhood: Politics and Privacy* (Bloomington, Indiana University Press, 1988).

[19] Kane was reportedly the first commercial surrogate in the United States. After fulfilling a contractual obligation with her surrogate agency to speak out in favour of the practice, she became active in the [United States] National Coalition Against Surrogacy.

[20] I am most grateful to the editors, Rachel Cook and Shelley Day Sclater, as well as to Lucy Delap, Miranda Fricker, and Peter Lipton for their comments on previous versions of this chapter; to Emily Jackson and Rhona Schuz for helpful information; and to Ásta Sveinsdottir and the Harvard students who studied surrogacy and other dilemmas of feminism with me in spring 2002, for instructive and challenging discussions.

Annas, GJ, 'Fairy Tales Surrogate Mothers Tell' in L Gostin (ed), *Surrogate Motherhood: Politics and Privacy* (Bloomington, Indiana University Press, 1988).

Bartky, SL, *Femininity and Domination: Studies in the Phenomenology of Oppression* (London, Routledge, 1990).

Capron, AM and Radin, MJ, 'Choosing Family Law Over Contract Law as a Paradigm for Surrogate Motherhood' in L Gostin (ed), *Surrogate Motherhood: Politics and Privacy* (Bloomington, Indiana University Press, 1988).

Charo, RA, 'Legislative Approaches to Surrogate Motherhood' in L Gostin (ed), *Surrogate Motherhood: Politics and Privacy* (Bloomington, Indiana University Press, 1988).

Corea, G, *The Mother Machine: Reproductive Technologies from Artificial Insemination to Artificial Wombs* (New York, Harper and Row, 1985a).

—— 'The reproductive brothel' in G Corea, R Duelli Klein, J Hanmer, HB Holmes, B Hoskins, M Kishwar, J Raymond, R Rowland and R Steinbacher, *Man-Made Women: How New Reproductive Technologies Affect Women* (Melbourne, London, Sydney, Auckland, Johannesburg, Hutchinson, 1985b).

Cotton, K, *Second Time Around* (Barnet, self-published, printed by Dornoch Press Limited, 1992).

—— and Winn, D, *Baby Cotton: For Love and Money* (London, Dorling Kindersley, 1985).

Duelli Klein, R, 'What's "new" about the "new" reproductive technologies?' in G Corea, R Duelli Klein, J Hanmer, HB Holmes, B Hoskins, M Kishwar, J Raymond, R Rowland and R Steinbacher, *Man-Made Women: How New Reproductive Technologies Affect Women* (Melbourne, London, Sydney, Auckland, Johannesburg, Hutchinson, 1985).

Dworkin, A, *Right-Wing Women* (New York, Perigree Books, 1983).

Glover, J, *Fertility and the Family: The Glover Report on Reproductive Technologies to the European Commission* (London, Fourth Estate, 1989).

Jackson, E, 'Conception and the Irrelevance of the Welfare Principle' (2002) 65 *Modern Law Review* 176.

Johnson, MH, 'A Biomedical Perspective on Parenthood' in A Bainham, SD Sclater, and M Richards (eds), *What is a Parent? A Socio-Legal Analysis* (Oxford and Portland, Oregon, Hart Publishing Ltd, 1999).

Ketchum, SA, 'Selling Babies and Selling Bodies' (1989) 3 *Hypatia* 116.

MacKinnon, CA, *Toward a Feminist Theory of the State* (Cambridge, Mass, Harvard University Press, 1989).

McConnell, T, *Inalienable Rights: The Limits of Consent in Medicine and the Law* (Oxford, Oxford University Press, 2000).

Morgan, D, 'Surrogacy: an introductory essay' in R Lee and D Morgan (eds), *Birthrights: Law and Ethics at the Beginning of Life* (London, Routledge, 1989).

Pfeffer, N, 'Artificial Insemination, In-vitro Fertilization and the Stigma of Infertility' in M Stanworth (ed), *Reproductive Technologies: Gender, Motherhood and Medicine* (Cambridge, Polity Press, 1987).

Posner, R, 'The Ethics and Economics of Enforcing Contracts of Surrogate Motherhood' (1987) 5 *Journal of Contemporary Health Law and Policy* 21.

Radin, MJ, 'Market-Inalienability' (1987) 100 *Harvard Law Review* 1849.

—— *Contested Commodities: The Trouble with the Trade in Sex, Children, Bodily Parts, and Other Things* (Cambridge, Mass, Harvard University Press, 1996).

Ragoné, H, *Surrogate Motherhood: Conception in the Heart* (Boulder, Westview Press, 1994).

Roberts, DE, 'The Genetic Tie' (1995) 62 *University of Chicago Law Review* 209.

Robertson, JA, *Children of Choice: Freedom and the New Reproductive Technologies* (Princeton, Princeton University Press, 1994).

Rothman, BK, *In Labor: Women and Power in the Birthplace* (London, Junction Books, 1982).

Rowland, R, *Living Laboratories: Women and Reproductive Technology* (London, Lime Tree, 1992).

Satz, D, 'Markets in Women's Reproductive Labor' (1992) 2 *Philosophy and Public Affairs* 21.

Shalev, C, *Birth Power: The Case for Surrogacy* (New Haven and London, Yale University Press, 1989).

Shevory, TC, *Body/Politics: Studies in Reproduction, Production, and Reconstruction* (Westport and London, Praeger, 2000).

Sistare, CT, 'Reproductive Freedom and Women's Freedom: Surrogacy and Autonomy' (1988) 19 *The Philosophical Forum* 227.

Strathern, M, *Reproducing the Future: Essays on Anthropology, Kinship and the New Reproductive Technologies* (Manchester, Manchester University Press, 1992).

—— 'Surrogates and substitutes: new practices for old?' in J Good and I Velody (eds), *The Politics of Postmodernity* (Cambridge, Cambridge University Press, 1998).

Stumpf, AE, 'Redefining Mother: A Legal Matrix for New Reproductive Technologies' (1986) 96 *Yale Law Journal* 187.

Sunstein, CR, *The Partial Constitution* (Cambridge, Mass., Harvard University Press, 1993).

Tong, R, 'Feminist Perspectives and Gestational Motherhood: The Search for a Unified Legal Focus' in JC Callahan (ed), *Reproduction, Ethics, and the Law: Feminist Perspectives* (Bloomington and Indianapolis, Indiana University Press, 1995).

Waldron, J, 'When Justice Replaces Affection' in J Waldron, *Liberal Rights: Collected Papers 1981–1991* (Cambridge, Cambridge University Press, 1993).

Warnock, M, *A Question of Life: The Warnock Report on Human Fertilisation and Embryology* (Oxford, Basil Blackwell, 1985).

Wertheimer, A, *Exploitation* (Princeton, Princeton University Press, 1996).

Woliver, LR, 'Reproductive Technologies, Surrogacy Arrangements, and the Politics of Motherhood' in MA Fineman and I Karpin (eds), *Mothers in Law: Feminist Theory and the Legal Regulation of Motherhood* (New York, Columbia University Press, 1995).

Zipper, J and Sevenhuijsen, S, 'Surrogacy: Feminist Notions of Motherhood Reconsidered' in M Stanworth (ed), *Reproductive Technologies: Gender, Motherhood and Medicine* (Cambridge, Polity Press, 1987).

SECTION 2

Psychology and Culture

10

Psychological Assessment in 'Surrogate' Motherhood Relationships

ROBERT J EDELMANN

1. BACKGROUND

THE OPPORTUNITY TO become a parent has been described as one of the most important developmental milestones in a person's life (Heinecke (1995)). Hence, reproductive failure can be a particularly distressing experience. Infertility has been defined as the inability to achieve a successful pregnancy after 12 months of regular sexual intercourse without the use of contraception (Cook (1987); Valentine (1986)). According to a population-based study in the UK undertaken in the 1980s, at least one in six couples will require specialist help for an infertility problem at some time in their lives (Hull *et al*, (1985)). The indications are that infertility has increased among younger people. There are a variety of reasons for this including problems posed by sexually transmitted diseases, exposure to occupational hazards and environmental toxins and postponing child-bearing and hence increasing vulnerability to age-related biologic risk of infertility. As a result, the period for attempting conception has been condensed into a shorter time period and is likely to take longer (Aral and Cates (1983)). These factors, allied with the development of technology-intensive treatments and, in the UK, the decline in the availability of adoption as an alternative to infertility, have fuelled the demand for infertility related investigations and treatments (Taub (1988)).

While treatment options have increased so has the emotional investment and time required of couples seeking such treatment (van Balen, Verdurman, and Ketting (1997)). For example, Van den Akker (2001a) reports that her sample of 42 women recruited from three UK infertility clinics had known about their infertility for an average five years (ranging from 1 to 19 years). Of the treatments they had received, six had undergone GIFT (Gamete IntraFallopian Transfer), 17 IVF (*in vitro* fertilisation) and ICSI (intra-cytoplasmic sperm injection), six had received pharmacological treatment and eight had tried egg donation. In the case of couples seeking surrogacy arrangements most tend to be older, have known of their difficulty conceiving for many years and have undergone many prior investigations and treatment procedures. Blyth (1995) notes that his sample of 20 commissioning couples all recounted histories of significant gynaecological problems and/or unsuccessful attempts to start a family and experiences of repeatedly unsuccessful IVF attempts.

While some studies suggest that the longer the known period of infertility the more distress such couples will experience (O'Moore *et al* (1983)) other studies have not found such an effect (eg Connolly, Edelmann, and Cooke (1987)). One issue here may be that, for some couples, time leads to a resolution of their difficulties (either with successful conception or a decision to remain childless) while for others it may lead to an increasingly desperate search for a medical solution to their difficulties; in many instances surrogacy offers them a last chance of having a child of their own. Those seeking surrogacy arrangements may therefore be potentially more vulnerable psychologically. It is worth noting, however, that research tends to indicate that while the experience of infertility is undoubtedly distressing, those seeking treatment for infertility are generally well adjusted (Connolly *et al* (1992); Edelmann, Connolly, and Bartlett, (1994)).

A further additional stressor with regard to surrogacy relates to the difficulty of finding a compatible surrogate. Van den Akker (2000) reports that, of 29 women seeking surrogacy arrangements in the UK, eight had negotiated with two potential surrogates, three had negotiated with three and one had negotiated with four surrogates.

While surrogacy has increased in the past two decades, the incidence is impossible to estimate due to the many informal arrangements which take place (BMA (1996)). By the 1990s many hundreds of children were known to have been born through surrogacy arrangements in the USA (Bartels (1990)) while the numbers of live births from such arrangements in the UK were thought to exceed 100. Information from surrogacy agencies in the UK indicate that by 1998 up to 8,000 women had approached them in an attempt to have a child (van den Akker (1998a)). It is not known how many of these pursued their endeavours, nor indeed, how many actually proceeded to the successful conclusion of a wished for child.

The relationships involved in surrogacy arrangements vary considerably. In some cases the surrogate mother carries a baby who is biologically related to the commissioning parents, as a result of IVF using the commissioning woman's egg and her partner's spermatozoa. This has been termed gestational surrogacy (ASRM (1990)). In other cases, the child may be related genetically to the surrogate mother and not to the mother who adopts and brings up the child. This has been referred to as genetic surrogacy (ASRM (1990)). The success rates from surrogacy procedures are likely to be highly variable with good success rates from the technically more straightforward (insemination of surrogate with the commissioning male's semen) and lower rates from the technically more complex (any procedure involving IVF). The two arrangements raise comparable but also some differing psychological issues. The former procedure has to be undertaken medically and hence contact with mental health professionals is likely [see Brinsden, chapter 7, this volume] and counselling may be available [see chapters 12 and 13, this volume]. The latter procedure can be undertaken informally. This, allied with the genetic link of any resultant child with the surrogate may increase the potential for both attachment to occur and problems to arise which could have been aired had mental health professionals been involved.

2. SURROGACY: PSYCHOSOCIAL CONCERNS

It has been suggested that surrogate motherhood raises 'intense feelings of endangering the family and society, evoking adultery and incest taboos and raising legal concerns and theological objections' (Shiloh, Larom, and Ben-Rafael (1991)). Some have argued that women who do not require surrogacy for reasons of infertility may want access to it because of career demands, convenience or a simple fear of or distaste for pregnancy (Field (1988)). While there is no evidence that this has occurred there are legitimate concerns that such demands would serve to increase commercialisation and the commodification of pregnancy and childbirth. In a survey of over 5,000 women of reproductive age living in Canada, three-quarters disapproved of commercial surrogacy (Krishnan (1994)). A smaller survey of 400 randomly selected residents in the US also indicated that the majority disapproved of surrogate motherhood (Weiss (1992)). It is difficult to tell whether attitudes may have changed in the past decade or whether they are comparable across the Western world. The studies cited did not investigate the specific factors influencing such disapproval although Krishnan notes that those who were less educated, highly religious and with a low income were less likely to be liberal in their views. Religious and social assumptions no doubt play a part but one suspects that the issues are rather more complex than this with the media playing its role in fuelling negative attitudes by widely publicising the few problematic cases which have arisen (see below).

Although in both the media and scientific community in the Western world controversies surrounding surrogacy arrangements have raged for the past two decades, the notion of such arrangements is not new, having been documented from biblical times. In the *Book of Genesis* Abram's wife Sarai, who had no children, instructed her husband to sleep with her servant Hagar so that Sarai might have a family through such means. It could perhaps have served as a salutary lesson for more recent times to note that subsequently Sarai (the social mother) drove Hagar (the biological mother) and the resultant child Ishmael from Abram's house. There are also certain parallels between Hagar's position as a servant to Sarai with more contemporary arrangements. In modern times the surrogate tends to be a lower income mother while the intending parents are more usually reasonably well paid professionals (Edelmann (1994)).

The earliest reported contemporary surrogate mother case is generally agreed to have been in the USA in 1980 (Holder (1988)). In the UK the Surrogacy

Arrangements Act 1985 legalised surrogacy, provided it was non-commercial, although a subsequent act rendered any arrangements and contracts unenforceable in law (HFE Act (1990)).

The public profile of surrogacy has been highlighted in the UK by the case of Baby Cotton (Cotton and Winn (1985)) and in the US by the case of Baby M (eg Bartels *et al* 1990; Lichtendorf (1989)). A brief description of both cases serves to highlight some of the major difficulties which can occur.

The Case of Baby Cotton

Baby Cotton was born on 4 January 1985 to an American father whose semen had been used to artificially inseminate the baby's mother, Kim Cotton, whom he never met. The social services department in whose area Baby Cotton was born, obtained a place of safety order under the Children and Young Persons Act 1969. This prevented Kim Cotton from relinquishing the baby to the father as was originally intended; she left the hospital without the baby. The biological father then issued a summons in the Family Division of the High Court of Justice seeking an order to make the child a ward of court and that care and control of the child should be given to him and his wife. He also sought approval to take the child to the USA. Baby Cotton was secretly flown out of the country with his 'new' parents some five days after the birth. The judge found that the birth mother, Kim Cotton, had voluntarily relinquished her rights and that no one was better equipped to care for the child than the biological father and his wife.

The Case of Baby M

On the 27 March 1986, Mary Beth Whitehead, a mother of two, gave birth to a daughter (subsequently referred to as 'Baby M') conceived with sperm from William Stern, at which stage she had agreed to give the child to him for a fee of $10,000. Three days after the baby's birth Mary Beth Whitehead took the baby home from the hospital and gave her up to the Sterns. She then changed her mind and pleaded to have her baby back; fearful of what action Ms Whitehead might take, the Sterns agreed. Ms Whitehead then informed the Sterns she intended to keep the baby and, over the following three months, she and her husband went on the run with the baby until it was seized by the Florida police. In the judgment that followed, it was ruled that the surrogacy contract was valid and Mr Stern's wife, Dr Stern, was told she could legally adopt the child. On appeal the earlier verdict was overturned, it was ruled that the surrogacy contract was invalid and unenforceable and that the adoption of Baby M by Dr Stern was improperly granted. The court further held that the issue of custody was determined solely by the child's best interests and that these would best be served by Baby M remaining with the Sterns with the natural mother having visitation rights.

A psychologist had apparently raised concerns relating to Ms Whitehead's ambivalence about giving up the child prior to the surrogacy proceeding (Steinbock (1988)). The natural mother's three days of contact with the baby following her birth is also not usual in successful surrogacy cases. There were a number of other disturbing issues raised by the Baby M case which have been debated in numerous publications (eg Lichtendorf (1989); Steinbock (1988)). Apparently, at the request of the surrogate, no-one at the hospital was aware of the surrogacy arrangement. The involvement of the police and the lengthy custody battle served to fuel concerns of those opposed to surrogacy. However, as Steinbock notes, 'the case seems to have been mismanaged from start to finish and could serve as a manual of how not to arrange a surrogate birth' (p 45).

Such cases have highlighted psychosocial and ethical [see Lane, chapter 9, this volume] concerns in relation to surrogacy arrangements and their regulation, with arguments against focusing on a number of issues. First, there is a need to protect the potential surrogate from a choice she may later regret and conversely to avoid exploiting a surrogate who is undertaking a risk for financial gain. In such circumstances appropriate psychological assessment and counselling can play an important part in facilitating both decision making and the emergence of a healthy 'working' relationship between the surrogate and the intending parents. A further concern raised by the cases described is that children are not property to be bought and sold; attention needs to be paid to whether or not there are psychosocial consequences for a child born in this way. These issues are addressed in the following sections of this chapter.

3. THE ROLE OF PSYCHOLOGICAL ASSESSMENT

With regard to surrogacy arrangements what exactly is the role of the psychologist? With regard to infertility treatment in general McCartney and Downey (1993) suggest five possibilities: screening, helping patients with decision making, helping partners reach consensus, helping patients cope with the stresses of infertility treatments and management of depression in women undergoing infertility treatment.

McCartney and Downey (1993) refer to screening in relation to concerns about emotional stability of the potential parents involved, the appropriateness of seeking a pregnancy for such a couple and their ability to be parents. As the authors point out, however, it would be inappropriate for psychiatrists and psychologists to play the role of gatekeeper. After all, parents who conceive by natural means are not screened as to their suitability to be parents.

Rather than seeking to screen couples or surrogates, a far more appropriate role for the mental health professional is to seek to facilitate patients' decision making, so that, in reality, both patients and surrogates screen themselves. In other words, rather than the mental health profession telling the intending parents that they should not consider parenthood or the surrogate that she should not consider playing such a role, the ideal would be for mental health professional to encourage the party or parties concerned to come to such a realisation themselves. It would then be a very unusual case where any other direct preventative action would be required. An additional concern in the context of surrogacy is that it is not just the separate views of the intending parents and the surrogate and her partner which need to be considered but also the interaction and relationship between the parties concerned. Effective assessment must then consider both congruent and incongruent views of all parties concerned.

One central aim of a psychological assessment should be to inform the provision of counselling. Again both the commissioning couple and the surrogate and her family should be considered in this regard. As noted previously, the involvement of mental health professionals is most likely in relation to gestational surrogacy. However, organisations such as COTS (Childlessness Overcome Through Surrogacy (see Dodd, chapter 8, this volume)) in the UK have recognised the need for counselling to be available and have taken steps to facilitate this.

4. PSYCHOLOGICAL ASSESSMENT: QUESTIONS TO ADDRESS

Psychologists and other mental health professionals are asked to screen and counsel both couples seeking surrogacy arrangements and women volunteering to be surrogate mothers, particularly in the US (Franks (1981); Slovenko (1985)). In the US selection procedures are more stringent than is the case in other countries partly because the practice is more regulated and commercial (Ragoné (1994)). In the UK 'screening' does not occur and arrangements are often based on trust between people who start as complete strangers (van den Akker (1999)). In the case of gestational surrogacy clinics usually require a psychological assessment but, as noted previously, this is more to inform decision making and counselling need than to specifically 'screen' the parties concerned. In this context, given that we know very little at present about the consequences of surrogacy, the most important role of assessment is to anticipate what the reactions and responses might be (Harrison, 1990). The main aims are to judge whether problems will occur in the relationship between donor couple and host and to judge whether the host will feel able to part with the child after the birth (Edelmann (1995)).

5. ASSESSING THE SURROGATE

The first issue to consider is the adjustment of the potential surrogate mother: Does she have any clinical problems such as depression or anxiety? Does she exhibit a stable personality profile? The limited research examining the psychological profile of surrogates tends to suggest that they are well-adjusted (Franks (1981); Hanafin (1987)). In both studies the Minnesota Multiphasic Personality Inventory (MMPI) was administered to small samples of surrogates, both studies finding that the profiles were unremarkable with little deviation from the norm. Although these findings reflect anecdotal reports from the UK, administration of standard psychometric measures to assess for psychopathology allows for comparison with normative data and hence should be an essential starting point.

The second issue to consider relates to the surrogate's motivation. Why is the woman considering acting as a surrogate? For example, is it to make up for previous childbearing losses (eg elective abortion)? Is there pressure from others? Is there a financial incentive and financial need? There is limited research in the UK into the issue of what motivates a woman to act as a surrogate. That which exists indicates that altruism is reported to be a prime motivating factor for most women and many perceive surrogate motherhood as a way of obtaining a sense of value and achievement (Blyth (1994); Edelmann (1994)). Few refer to money as a prime motivating factor, and indeed most surrogates themselves think that it should not be (Blyth (1994)). While reimbursement for the discomfort, inconvenience, risk and costs incurred is expected, clearly if the financial issues were high on the list of motivating factors for a surrogate, from a psychological perspective this would give rise to concerns. Financial worries may lead to desperate and ill thought through actions which may later be regretted.

A very few surrogates see surrogacy as a way of dealing with feelings of guilt or anxiety about past actions such as the loss of a child or their own placement for adoption (Parker (1983)). Steadman and McCloskey (1987) rightly raise a note of caution about such women acting as surrogates. Having not come to terms with one's own past losses, engendering a further loss (when the child is handed to the intended parents) may actually serve to reinforce the surrogate's distress rather than relieve them of it.

From a psychological perspective a surrogate who has a close family network, with children of her own, who knows someone with infertility problems and, as a result, has been motivated to help for altruistic reasons may be best placed to act in such a capacity.

In this context, the third issue to consider is the surrogate's relationship with her family and friends. How does the woman's spouse feel? Has she informed parents and friends and will they be supportive? As it is likely that she will have children herself what will she tell them and how? Surrogate mothers report being aware of the ambivalence and potential hostility that other people might have towards surrogacy. They also tend to receive less familial and social support than non-surrogate mothers (Fischer and Gillman (1991)). Hence, the question of when and whether to tell other people is not necessarily a straightforward matter. Most surrogates choose to inform their children if they consider them old enough to understand (Blyth (1994); Edelmann (1994)). In this context Schwartz (1991) suggests that the children and spouses of surrogates could benefit from an exploration of their feelings and that continued counselling would be appropriate as the pregnancy progresses both to raise issues and address concerns. It has been suggested that surrogate arrangements might engender anxieties in the surrogate's own children (Holder (1988)) although there are no data pertaining to this possibility. However, in order to gauge the extent to which the surrogate has thought through important and potentially difficult issues, any assessment should raise with her the question of what she will tell her children about her pregnancy and the subsequent 'loss' of their 'brother' or 'sister' (Edelmann (2000)).

The fourth issue to consider in the assessment of the surrogate mother is her previous experience of pregnancy and childbirth. Are her expectations about childbirth realistic? Were the births of her children relatively straightforward? Given that most surrogates have children of their own (Blyth (1994); Edelmann (1994); Franks (1981); Parker (1983)) it is not surprising that most express a general awareness about the negative as well as the positive aspects of pregnancy. It is clearly important to gauge during a psychological assessment whether the relative balance of such factors is realistic.

Fifthly, a key concern in surrogacy is the successful separation of the surrogate mother from the child. It may be more difficult for her to separate from a child which is genetically related to her than one which is not. Psychological assessment should explore what gives the woman confidence in her ability to separate from the child. Has she thought about how she will feel and react? Given the issues and concerns raised on both sides of the Atlantic (Lichtendorf (1989)) about surrogate mothers relinquishing the baby it is perhaps not surprising that the question of separating from the child is a central issue. Some commissioning couples are naturally concerned that it might be emotionally difficult for the surrogate to relinquish the baby (Van den Akker (2000)). Blyth (1994) notes that the surrogate mothers he interviewed spoke of their sorrow and distress about parting with the child. However, these emotions were mixed with a sense of happiness for the commissioning couple and a sense of satisfaction for the part they had played. Interestingly Fischer and Gillman (1991) report that surrogate mothers exhibited less of an attachment to the foetus than a comparable group of non-surrogate mothers. They also note that a common explanation in response to the question of how the current surrogate pregnancy differed from previous pregnancies was that knowing the baby was not hers and considering it the intended parent's baby from the very beginning of the process made the surrogate mother feel differently towards it. Any psychological assessment should focus on the degree of realism the surrogate expresses about her role and her recognition of the difficulties she might well face. A potential surrogate who foresees few if any difficulties is unlikely to be prepared for the task which lies ahead of her.

6. THE RELATIONSHIP BETWEEN THE INTENDED PARENTS AND
SURROGATE MOTHER

While some surrogate arrangements are between friends or family members, the majority of surrogacy arrangements involve individuals who are total strangers at the outset. Many surrogates and intended parents regard the surrogacy arrangement as a business arrangement which will terminate once the baby has been delivered to the intended couple (Blyth (1994)). A central part of any assessment should be to examine the congruence or otherwise of the views and wishes expressed by the parties involved, as well as the extent to which such views are likely to be fixed or flexible.

Key issues include: Do the donor couple and host share similar views on important matters? Do both parties have the same view about tests such as amniocentesis? If there was evidence of handicap and therapeutic abortion was suggested would both parties have the same view? From a psychological perspective it is not the specific views of the respective parties which are important; the central issue is that the parties concerned have discussed and agreed upon the options available to them given the various circumstances which might arise. It is of interest to note that of her 29 intended parents, approximately a third of whom were in the early stages of the surrogacy arrangement and half of whom had the baby living with them, Van den Akker (2000) reports that only four expected that there would be some difficulties during the surrogacy process. Thirteen of the intended parents were using the surrogate's egg so that the resultant child would be genetically related to her. Although problems are the exception rather than the rule the few which do arise tend to involve genetic surrogacy. This is in part due to the fact that the parties concerned can proceed without the involvement of any psychological assessment or support but also as the genetic link may give rise to a greater sense of attachment for the surrogate.

A second important issue relates to the question of the contact both parties expect during pregnancy and after the birth of a child. Do they expect the same amount and style of contact? Blyth (1995) notes in his sample of 20 commissioning parents comprising nine couples, a commissioning mother and a commissioning father, who between them had had nine children following surrogacy arrangements, that it was generally agreed with the surrogate mother that the commissioning mother would be present at the birth of the child. Unfortunately in four cases the arrangements did not materialise due to late complications in the pregnancy. While it is assumed that it is psychologically beneficial for the intended mother to be present there is no data to indicate whether or not this is the case.

While some commissioning couples and surrogates prefer to have no contact after the baby has been born, many make arrangements for continuing contact including exchange of photographs, letters, cards, telephone calls and visits. Unfortunately there is no available data to indicate whether or not it is psychologically beneficial for the intended parents, surrogate or the resultant child for couples and surrogate to retain contact. Clearly, the central issue is that the parties concerned discuss and agree on the type of contact acceptable to all involved. It may be inevitable that, in some instances, the parties concerned may subsequently change their minds which may the give rise to difficulties. Ongoing support from a counsellor may be helpful in such instances but is unlikely to be generally available.

Van den Akker (2000) reports that of her sample of 29 commissioning women almost half expected to have a 'committed relationship' with the surrogate mother and to get on well with each other. As Blyth (1995) points out, however, despite positive intentions, such continuing contact could be problematic. Although there is a paucity of research evidence in relation to this, one might suppose that the surrogate mother would be constantly reminded about the child she has given up and the commissioning parents may fear interference in the upbringing of 'their' child. Steadman and McCloskey (1987) note that there may be occasions when the surrogate and the commissioning couple have developed a strong personal relationship prior to the baby's birth but that the latter then terminate the relationship abruptly after delivery. As they further note, such issues and concerns strengthen the argument in favour of mandatory counselling for the surrogate mother before, during, and after the pregnancy to help them navigate the difficult passage they have to traverse.

7. ASSESSING THE COMMISSIONING COUPLE

When assessing the intended parents a key question is their motivation. Do either of them have children from a previous relationship and do they both wish to have children? It has been argued that childlessness makes couples feel like 'second-class' citizens and that this drives the desire of many to become parents (Miall (1987)). A more intrinsic motive is their desire to continue the family's genetic line (Schwartz (1990)). Others have noted the desire to have a biological connection between the child and one of the prospective parents rather than to adopt an unrelated child (Kane (1988)). As Schwartz also notes, however, other possible and somewhat more questionable motives for seeking surrogacy arrangements relate to possible health risks assumed to be associated with childbirth or merely for convenience. Such possibilities raise concerns about the commodification of childbirth and the exploitation of women, especially poor women. Blyth (1995) reports that, of his sample of intended parents, none fell into either of these categories; indeed, it is unlikely that such instances will arise, other than rarely. However, it is important that such matters are gauged during the assessment.

It is also important that the couple themselves have discussed and agree on various issues relating both to their desire to have children and also the involvement of a third party. As Saltzer (1986) notes: 'A wife who is uncomfortable with the idea but agrees to surrogate parenting because her husband is opposed to adoption or insists on his own genetic input is setting herself up for future problems' (p 227). Pursuing a particular option to please one's partner, even if opposed to it oneself, may inevitably result in future resentment and possible marital conflict. As Saltzer (1986) additionally notes, those who seem to be using this procedure to cement a failing marriage or a couple who search endlessly for the 'perfect' surrogate should also be viewed with caution.

The second issue for the commissioning couple is the degree of support or hostility they may receive from others. What are the feelings of friends, parents and other relatives? The psychological literature is replete with studies noting the importance of social support with regard to emotional well-being; conversely, withdrawal of that support can impact negatively on those concerned.

Finally, psychometric assessment is useful to gain an impression of the extent to which both parties will be strong enough to withstand the stress of surrogacy and the strength of the commissioning couple's relationship.

8. ASSESSMENT: WHAT ABOUT THE CHILDREN?

The little available research evaluating the impact of being a child conceived via the new reproductive technologies suggest few, if any, psychological problems. Studies have found no major differences between children conceived by such means and those conceived naturally with regard to emotions, behaviour, the presence of psychological disorders or the children's perceptions of the quality of family relationships (Golombok *et al* (1995, 1996); Golombok *et al* (2001)). Indeed, some research assessing parents tends to suggest that quality of parenting in families conceived by assisted conception is superior to parenting in families with a naturally conceived child (Golombok *et al* (1993)). Intriguingly, in one study, Golombok and her colleagues also report greater psychological well-being among mothers and fathers in families where there was no genetic link between the mother and the child when compared with those where there was a genetic link (Golombok *et al* (1999)). These studies involved families created by donor insemination, egg donation or *in vitro* fertilisation; no studies to date have specifically assessed children born to surrogate mothers.

Although Steadman and McCloskey (1987) have suggested that, in relation to surrogacy, 'the feelings of inadequacy that usually accompany infertility may be magnified and may have seriously deleterious effects on the development of the child from infancy onward' (p 548) there are no data to substantiate such a view. Indeed, the research findings noted earlier tend to suggest a very positive outlook in terms of child development.

There are limited data relating to the question of whether parents are likely to inform children born of surrogate parents about their origin. Van den Akker (2001a) reports that of a group of adoptive parents, over 80 per cent of whom were subfertile, 65.5 per cent reported that they would tell a child its origin if it were conceived via a surrogacy arrangement, 59.6 per cent would inform their family but only 42.5 per cent would inform friends. This compares with 59 per cent who would tell their child its origins if it were conceived via Donor Insemination (DI) and 77.8 per cent who would tell their child if they were conceived via IVF. In a further study with a small group of 42 women attending infertility clinics 42.9 per cent reported that they would tell a child its origins if it were conceived via a surrogacy arrangement (21.4 per cent were unsure and 35.7 per cent would not tell) 50 per cent would tell their family (16.7 per cent were unsure and 33.3 per cent would not tell), while only 33.3 per cent would tell their friends (26.2 per cent were unsure and 40.5 per cent would not tell). This compares with 40.5 per cent who would tell their child its origin if it had been conceived via donor insemination and 71.4 per cent would tell if their child was conceived via IVF (Van den Akker (2001b)).

In relation to these figures it needs to be borne in mind that there is frequently a discrepancy between what people report they will do and what they do in reality. For example, although two-thirds may think they will tell their child its origins if born via DI, in reality, most do not do so (Owens, Edelmann, and Humphrey (1993)). Thus, while there may be greater openness with regard to surrogacy the 65 per cent reported above as those who felt they would tell their child its origins is likely to be an over-estimate. There is no research to indicate the percentage of parents of children born via a surrogate who actually do inform their children.

Research in relation to children born as a result of DI and IVF suggests that in the former case parents are likely to keep their child ignorant of its origin while they are much less likely to do so in the latter instance (Golombok *et al* (1995); McWhinnie (1995); Edelmann (1989, 1990)). When male infertility becomes an issue, secrecy seems to be preferred. Such secrecy seems to be less prevalent in the case of female infertility and in most cases involving surrogacy arrangements. Indeed, in a small sample of infertile women (N=29) recruited via COTS and who were or had been actively engaged in surrogate arrangements, all but one said they would tell their child of his/her origins. However, only ten said they would tell their child its origins if they had had to use donor sperm or donor eggs (Van den Akker (2000)), suggesting that concern may be related to the lack of a genetic link with both parents rather than a question of male versus female infertility. In a further comparable sample of 20 women also recruited via COTS and actively involved in surrogacy arrangements, all believed that the child should be told the full truth about his or her genetic origins (Blyth (1995)), a commitment shared with the surrogate mothers (Blyth (1994)).

If secrecy is preferred there is inevitably the possibility that this might be harmful to the child. As Menning (1981) comments, family secrets are among the most pernicious and destructive forces in the family. Certainly with regard to adoption, the benefits of disclosure have been noted (Howe, Feast, and Cosner (2000)). However, if the decision is to tell the child, there are no hard and fast rules about how they should be informed, when and with what message. Appropriate counselling can clearly help in this regard both to discuss the many issues involved and to facilitate parental decision-making.

10. COUNSELLING NEEDS

The importance attached to psychological support and counselling for involuntarily childless couples has increased in the past two decades. Certainly with regard to surrogacy, organisations such as COTS are to be applauded for their efforts (see Dodd, chapter 8, this volume). However, there has been little by way of systematic appraisal of need, and issues such as who might require additional assistance and what form it should take are important in planning services. At the very least counselling should address the issues which have been raised in preceding sections of this chapter. Particular questions which should be explored include the motivation of the surrogate, the anticipated future relationship between commissioning couple and surrogate and the views of the parties' wider family network and what they intend to tell the hoped for child. As noted, the ideal would be for assessment to inform counselling provision and for all parties concerned to be provided with such support.

The specific aim of counselling is not to limit psychological disturbance. As noted, studies tend to suggest that infertile couples are generally well adjusted (Connolly *et al* (1992); Edelmann (1994)) and counselling in relation to reproductive technologies does not further reduce general anxiety (Connolly *et al* (1993)). Counselling can, however, help to ease specific anxieties, facilitate decision-making in the hope that issues can be resolved at an early stage before difficulties have a chance to arise.

11. CONCLUDING COMMENTS

As Van den Akker (1998b) recently noted, surrogate motherhood is a 'hot topic' for discussion in the media, the medical and scientific community and in government. While there are very evident psychological issues that need to be addressed in relation to surrogacy, research is still limited and much 'evidence' is anecdotal or drawn from evaluations of psychological issues in relation to other reproductive technologies. However, as this chapter has illustrated there are a number of psychological issues which can usefully be addressed in the assessment of both commissioning couple and surrogate and which could be used to inform counselling provision. It is possible that the latter could not only help couples and surrogates through the difficult process of decision making but also help in the prevention of later possible difficulties. Little is known about either the impact of surrogacy on the parties concerned or the circumstances under which problems might arise. Research is required to address both these issues in order to inform future psychological practice relating to both assessment and counselling. Finally, it is perhaps surprising that there is such a complete lack of research in a key area of concern, that is, possible consequences for the child. While the process itself is receiving more attention from social scientists, the children have been sadly neglected. Without such research it is impossible to tell what is best for the child in terms of the various issues relating to information provision. Perhaps the central question for the coming decade should be 'what about the children?' (Edelmann (2000)).

REFERENCES

American Society for Reproductive Medicine (ASRM), 'Surrogate gestational mothers: Women who gestate a genetically unrelated embryo' (1990) 53 *Fertility and Sterility* [Suppl 2] 64–67.

Aral, SD and Cates, W, 'The increasing concern with infertility: Why now?' (1983) 78 *Journal of the American Medical Association* 2327–331.

Bartels, DM, ' Surrogacy arrangements: an overview' in DN Bartels, P Preister, DE Vawter and AI Capaln (eds), *Beyond Baby M* (Clifton, New Jersey, Humana Press, 1990).

Blyth, E, 'I wanted to be interesting. I wanted to be able to say "I've done something interesting with my life": Interviews with surrogate mothers in Britain' (1994) 12 *Journal of Reproductive and Infant Psychology* 189–98.

—— 'Not a primrose path: commissioning parents' experiences of surrogacy arrangements in Britain' (1995) 13 *Journal of Reproductive and Infant Psychology* 185–96.

British Medical Association, *Changing Conceptions Of Motherhood. The Practice Of Surrogacy In Britain* (BMA Publications, London, 1996).

Connolly, KJ, Edelmann, RJ, Bartlett, H, Cooke, ID, Lenton, E and Pike, S, 'An evaluation of counselling for couples undergoing treatment for in-vitro fertilization' (1993) 8 *Human Reproduction* 1332–38.

—— —— and Cooke, ID, 'Distress and marital problems associated with infertility' (1987) 5 *Journal of Reproductive and Infant Psychology* 49–57.

—— —— —— and Robson, J, 'The impact of infertility on psychological functioning' (1992) 36 *Journal of Psychosomatic Research* 459–68.

Cook, EP, 'Characteristics of the biopsychosocial crisis of infertility' (1987) 65 *Journal of Counselling and Development* 465–70.

Cotton, K and Winn, D, *Baby Cotton: For Love and Money* (London, Dorling Kindersley, 1985).

Edelmann, RJ, 'Psychological aspects of artificial insemination by donor' (1989) 10 *Journal of Psychosomatic Obstetrics and Gynaecology* 3.

—— 'Emotional aspects of in vitro fertilization procedures: A review' (1990) 8 *Journal of Reproductive and Infant Psychology* 161–73.

—— 'Psychological evaluation for "surrogate" motherhood arrangements' (1994) *The British Psychological Society, Abstracts* 49.

—— 'Surrogacy: The psychological issues' (1995) *The British Psychological Society, Abstracts* 118.

—— 'What about the children? Issues for commissioning couple and host in surrogacy arrangements' Abstracts of papers presented at the 2000 Annual Conference of the Society of Reproductive and Infant Psychology (2000) 18 *Journal of Reproductive and Infant Psychology* 257.

—— Connolly, KJ and Bartlett, H, 'Coping strategies and psychological adjustment in couples presenting for IVF' (1994) 28 *Journal of Psychosomatic Research* 355–64.

Field, MA, *Surrogate Motherhood* (Cambridge, Mass, Harvard University Press, 1988).

Fischer, S and Gillman, I, 'Surrogate motherhood: attachment, attitudes and social support' (1991) 54 *Psychiatry* 13–40.

Franks, DD, 'Psychiatric evaluation of women in a surrogate mother program' (1981) 138 *American Journal of Psychiatry* 1378–79.

Golombok, S, Brewaeys, A, Cook, R, Giavazzi, MT, Guerra, D, Mantovani, A, Van Hall, E, Crosignani, PG. and Dexeus, S, 'The European study of assisted reproduction families: family functioning and child development' (1996) 11 *Human Reproduction* 2324–31.

Golombok, S, Cook, R, Bish. A and Murray, C, 'Quality of parenting in families created by the new reproductive technologies: a brief report of preliminary findings' (1993) 14 *Journal of Psychosomatic Obstetrics and Gynaecology* S17–S22.

Golombok, S, Cook, R, Bish, A and Murray, C, 'Families created by the new reproductive technologies: quality of parenting and social and emotional development of the children' (1995) 66 *Child Development* 285–98.

Golombok, S, MacCallam, F and Goodman, E, 'The "test-tube" generation: parent-child relationships and the psychological well-being of in vitro fertilization children at adolescence' (2001) 72 *Child Development* 599–608.

Golombok, S, Murray, C, Brinsden, C and Abdalla, H, 'Social versus biological parenting: family functioning and the socioemotional development of children conceived by egg or sperm donation' (1999) 40 *Journal of Child Psychology & Psychiatry & Related Disciplines* 519–27.

Hanafin, H, *Surrogate parenting: Reassessing human bonding.* Paper presented at the American Psychological Association Convention, New York, 1987.

Harrison, M, 'Psychological ramifications of "surrogate" motherhood' in NL Stotland (ed), *Psychiatric Aspects of Reproductive Technology* (Washington DC, American Psychiatric Press, 1990).

Heinicke, CM, 'Determinants in the transition to parenting' in N Bornstein (ed), *Handbook of Parenting: Volume 3. Status and Social Conditions of Parenting* (NJ, Erlbaum, 1995).

Holder, AR, 'Surrogate motherhood and the best interests of children' (1988) 16 *Law, Medicine & Health Care* 51–56.

Howe, D, Feast, J. & Cosner, D. *Adoption, Search and Reunion. Long-term Experience of Adopted Adults* (The Children's Society, London, 2000).

Hull, MGR, Glazener, CMA, Kelly, NJ, Conway, DI, Foster, PA, Hinton, RA Coulson, C, Lambert, PA, Watt, EM and Desai, KM, 'Population study of causes, treatment, and outcome of infertility' (1985) 291 *British Medical Journal* 1693–97.

Human Fertilisation and Embryology Act 1990 (London, HMSO, 1990).

Kane, E, *Birth mother: The story of America's first legal surrogate mother* (New York, Harcourt Brace Janovich, 1988).

Krishnan, V, 'Attitudes toward surrogate motherhood in Canada' (1994) 15 *Health Care for Women International* 333–57.

Lichtendorf, SS, 'Divided Loyalties. Ongoing reactions to Baby M' in J Offerman-Zuckerberg (ed), *Gender in Transition. A new Frontier* (New York, Plenum Medical Book Company, 1989).

McCartney, CF and Downey, J, 'New reproductive technologies' in A Stoudemire and BS Fogel (eds), *Medical—Psychiatric Practice Volume 2* (Washington DC, American Psychiatric Association, 1993).

McWhinnie, A, 'A study of parenting of IVF and DI children' (1995) 14 *Medicine Law* 501–08.

Menning, BE, 'Donor insemination. The psychological issues' (1981) 18 *Contemporary Obstetrics and Gynaecology* 155–72.

Miall, CE, 'The stigma of adoptive parent status' (1987) 36 *Family Relations* 36, 34–39.

O'Moore, AM, O'Moore, RR, Harrison, RF, Murphy, G and Caruthers, ME, Psychosomatic aspects of idiopathic infertility: effects of treatment with autogenic training' (1983) 21 *Journal of Psychosomatic Research* 145–51.

Owens, DJ, Edelmann, RJ and Humphrey, ME, 'Male infertility and donor insemination: couples' decisions, reactions and counselling needs' (1993) 8 *Human Reproduction* 880–85.

Parker, PJ, 'Motivations of surrogate mothers: initial findings' (1983) 140 *American Journal of Psychiatry and Law* 117.

Ragoné, H, *Surrogate Motherhood: Conceptions in the Heart* (Boulder, Westview Press, 1994).

Saltzer, LP *Infertility. How Couples Cope* (Boston: Mass, GK Hall & Co, 1986).

—— ' Surrogate motherhood and family psychology/therapy' (1990) 18 *The American Journal of Family Therapy* 385–92.

Schwartz, LL *Alternatives to Infertility. Is Surrogacy the Answer?* (New York, Brunner/Mazel, 1991).

Shiloh, S, Larom, S and Ben-Rafael, Z, 'The meaning of treatments for infertility: Cognitive determinants and structure' (1991) 21 *Journal of Applied Social Psychology* 855–74.

Slovenko, R, 'Obstetric science and the developing role of the psychiatrist in surrogate motherhood' (1985) 13 *Journal of Psychiatry and Law* 487–518.

Steadman, JH and McCloskey, GT 'The prospect of surrogate mothering: clinical concerns' (1987) 32 *Canadian Journal of Psychiatry* 545–50.

Steinbock, B, 'Surrogate motherhood as prenatal adoption' (1988) 16 *Law, Medicine & Health Care* 44–50.

Taub, M, 'Surrogacy: a preferred treatment for infertility?' (1988) 16 *Law, Medicine & Health Care* 89–95.

Valentine, DP 'Psychological impact of infertility: identifying issues and needs' (1986) 11 *Social Work in Health Care* 61–69.

van Balen, F, Verdurmen, J and Ketting, E, 'Choices and motivations of infertile couples' (1997) 31 *Patient Education and Counselling* 19–27.

Van den Akker, OAB, 'The function and responsibilities of organisations dealing with surrogate motherhood in the UK' (1998a) 1 *Human Fertility* 10–13.

—— 'Surrogate motherhood: demystifying the controversies' (1998b) 6 *British Journal of Midwifery* 768–70.

—— 'Organisational selection and assessment of women entering a surrogacy arrangement in the UK' (1999) 14 *Human Reproduction* 262–66.

—— 'The importance of a genetic link in mothers commissioning a surrogate baby in the UK' (2000) 15 *Human Reproduction* 1849–55.

—— 'The acceptable face of parenthood' (2001a) 3 *Psychology, Evolution & Gender* 1–17.

—— 'Adoption in the age of reproductive technology' (2001b) 19 *Journal of Reproductive and Infant Psychology* 147–59.

Weiss, G, 'Public attitudes about surrogate motherhood' (1992) 6 *Michigan Sociological Review* 15–27.

11

Surrogacy Arrangements in the USA: What Relationships Do They Spawn?

1. INTRODUCTION

PUBLIC AWARENESS OF surrogate motherhood has increased sharply in the past two decades, and there has been recognition that the child born of a surrogacy arrangement is only one figure whose rights may be enhanced or at risk in a complex situation. This chapter explores the manifold and often tangled relationships that surrogacy spawns, relationships that involve the rights of the surrogate mother, her partner, her children, her wider family, as well as those of the intended parents. It also examines the intertwined longer-term connections that may result from the original agreement. Surrogacy generates many moral, ethical, social, psychological and legal questions that, over the years, have surfaced and that do not admit of easy solutions.

Surrogate motherhood clearly has generated a multitude of political positions and court cases, as well as inter- and intra-familial stresses. Some of the tensions reflect moral positions[1] or cultural and religious beliefs;[2] others reflect ideas about parenthood and 'family' values[3] and positions on parental responsibility, women's rights or fathers' rights. One highly debatable issue is the applicability of adoption laws to the child's placement, for the biological father need not adopt the child to be considered the father, although his wife should adopt (in some states in the USA *must* adopt) in order to make her legally the child's mother. Another critical issue, raised by Lamb (1993) is whether the end can justify the means, no matter how much the infertile couple's situation is deserving of sympathy. A third question concerns whether the commissioning parents can legitimately reject the child, for example, if their circumstances change or if the child is born with unexpected disabilities. Problems of a different sort may occur when state law requires that the name of the surrogate—the birth mother—be placed on the birth certificate, whether or not she is the genetic

---

[1] See Lane, chapter 9, this volume.
[2] See Schenker, chapter 16, this volume.
[3] See Teman, chapter 17, this volume.

mother (Lavoie (2001)).[4] In the case of gay and lesbian parents, the possibility of complications is even more manifest (Lilith (2001)).

2. WHAT IS SURROGATE MOTHERHOOD?

The term 'surrogate motherhood' incorporates at least two dimensions. The surrogacy aspect refers to the involvement of a third person, a female, in the reproductive process (Schwartz (2000)).[5] An egg donor may be anonymous, as sperm donors usually are, or may be a friend or relative of the recipient, in which case their relationship may be strengthened by the 'gift' or threatened by it.[6] The motherhood aspect is something else: 'What makes a woman a mother—genetic contribution, gestation, or the intent with which the woman contributed her reproductive function?' (Coleman (1996)). The question is limited here to the sphere of alternative reproductive technology, but could and should go beyond conception and gestation to ask what makes a mother in the child's eyes as he or she develops, which could include a 'social' mother—someone with no bio-logical connection to the child, such as a foster mother or an adoptive mother.[7]

Where donated eggs are used, in a situation that parallels donor insemination, it is rare for legal contests to ensue. But if the egg donor is known, the situation can be more complicated and there have been cases of conflict between relatives or friends about who is a given child's 'real' mother. Surrogacy clearly can spawn a variety of relationships. At one extreme, it is possible for the woman serving as gestational surrogate to develop an attachment to the child growing in her womb, even if she makes a conscious effort not to allow this. This can lead to a reluctance to surrender the baby to its biological parents, or to demands for visitation as has occurred in some of the well-publicised problem cases.[8] At the other extreme, a husband and wife, unable to conceive naturally or with the aid of other assisted reproductive techniques, pay to have the egg and sperm of anonymous donors mixed and fertilised in a petri dish, and then hire a woman to serve as gestational surrogate.

---

[4] Lavoie, D, Surrogates redefine term 'mother' (2 September 2001). *The Philadelphia Inquirer*, A 10. In some states, this means that the genetic parents must go to court to adopt their own child, and even then may not succeed in eradicating the original birth certificate.

[5] A fourth person may be involved in some cases—a sperm donor.

[6] On the gift relationship, see Ragoné, chapter 14, this volume.

[7] American Academy of Pediatrics. Ethical issues in surrogate motherhood (July 1992). 9*AAP News*. <www.aap.org.policy/178.html> and Schwartz (1993).

[8] *Johnson v Calvert* [1993] 851 P.2d 776. The Calverts contracted with Anna Johnson that she would carry an embryo created *in vitro* by them, for a fee, and that she would relinquish all rights to the resulting child. Under California's Uniform Parentage Act, both women could claim mater-nal status—one for the genetic contribution and the other for carrying and delivering the baby. When problems arose, the California Supreme Court ultimately ruled in the Calverts' favour, inas-much as their goal was procreation, not egg donation. For a fuller discussion of the issues, see Place (1994). In the 'Baby M' case, Mary Beth Whitehead retrieved the newborn from the commissioning parents, kept her for several weeks, and ultimately was declared, by the New Jersey appellate court, the legal mother with visitation rights. [*In re Baby M*, 537 A.2d 1227 (N. J. 1988)].

The case of *Buzzanca* is a well-known example of this type of surrogacy arrangement. There, complications arose because the intended parents decided to divorce after the process was initiated. With no genetic ties to the child, they thought that they could walk away from the surrogacy contract. Indeed, the court decided initially that the intended parents were not the child's legal parents—there were no biological or genetic ties to the child, and it ruled that the intended father had no financial obligations to the child. Subsequently, however, an appellate judge ruled that the intended father did have responsibilities to the child and that he could not avoid contributing to her support. In addition, the court took the view that his former wife, the intended mother, was the child's legal mother, even though she had supplied neither egg nor womb.[9] The crucial issue turned out to be the intended parents' intent to create the child, without which she would never have existed.

3. WHO ARE THE SURROGATE MOTHERS?

In brief, surrogate mothers are women who, for varying motives, are willing, perhaps even anxious, to gestate a fertilised egg, give birth, and then to surrender the baby to the person(s) who arranged for this to happen. They become involved in what one psychologist calls 'a bizarre situation' in which the woman has limited information, and experiences physical and psychological evaluations and stresses beyond those normally associated with pregnancy, and all to carry a baby whom she will surrender to someone else forever (Kanefield (1999)). Kanefield found that these are psychologically stable women whose personality allows them to compartmentalise their role and enables them to deny attachment to the baby growing within them. Similarly, Aigen (1996) reports on 200 potential surrogates who applied to The Surrogate Mother Program of New York over a three-year period and who were screened in three 90-minute interviews. Those who were accepted for the programme perceived surrogacy as a positive emotional experience, had high frustration tolerance and 'ego strength', had had positive and enjoyable prior pregnancies, enjoyed positive relationships with their children, and had a supportive home environment.

Motivations

As Overvold (1988) put it, some women find pregnancy 'spiritually intoxicating'. Indeed, some women enjoy the pregnancy more than they do child-rearing.[10] Altruism, the ability to do a 'good deed' for someone else's benefit, is

---

[9] *Buzzanca v Buzzanca (In re marriage of Buzzanca)* (1998). 72 *California Reporter* 2d 280, 293 (Ct. App.).
[10] See Fischer and Gillman (1991); Schuker (1987).

another motive, whether the 'someone else' is a relative, a friend, or a stranger.[11] This may be a healthy and positive motive, or may stem from a desire to do something 'praise-worthy', or to gain a sense of worthiness herself.[12] 'Some surrogate mothers are also motivated by a wish to repair a previous experience, such as an abortion or relinquishment of a baby for adoption, and now fantasise a reparative controlled placement' (Schuker (1987)).[13]

For many women, being a surrogate mother might be a means of 'earning' a substantial sum of money, usually about $10,000 over and above their medical and other pregnancy-related costs. This money cannot, however, be regarded as *payment* for the child, because buying and selling babies is against the law in every state, but might be regarded as compensation for the salary the woman might otherwise have been able to earn in more traditional employment. Those who 'regard their surrogate pregnancy as a job usually have in the past had easy, uncomplicated pregnancies' (Kanefield (1999:9)). 'Giving birth is something surrogates as a group view as a considerable skill' (Ragoné (1994:72)). Some of them simply regard their action as a means of satisfying both their altruistic urges and providing funds for some special family need or even an extravagance.

Effects On Their Relationships

Women who act as surrogate mothers have usually successfully borne at least one child previously. Their husbands, or possibly their partners, must agree in the contract to the procedure and to the limitations it places on their interaction with their partners. (The legal obligation is not as clear with partners of unmarried surrogates.) Responsibilities are placed on the man's shoulders as the woman's pregnancy progresses, both in terms of her physical condition and her ability to carry out her usual chores in the household (Schwartz (1991)). There is, therefore, a direct impact on the husband/partner and on their relationship, so that his motives for agreeing to the surrogacy arrangement should be explored by the commissioning parties and the intermediary agency or attorney.[14] The

---

[11] See Ragoné, chapter 14, this volume.
[12] See Kanefield (1999) and Schwartz (1991).
[13] See also Appleton, chapter 13, this volume.
[14] An extensive search of the professional literature and web sites failed to reveal any studies focused on the significant partner or husband of the prospective surrogate mother. On one web site (www.borenlaw.com/ surrogacy/app.asp) there are a few basic questions for prospective surrogate mothers about the name, occupation, and income of the husband or boyfriend. On another site (www.fertility-docs.com/surrogates_faq.phtml) an interpretation of California law is given: 'If gestational surrogate is married, her husband must be made a party to a properly drawn gestational surrogacy agreement. Sperm must have been provided to a licensed physician and surgeon.' In a sample contract included in Ragoné (1994), there is a clause stating that the surrogate's husband or partner shall be tested for venereal disease, and that he must sign the contract. Elsewhere she states that many surrogates view the money they are paid as a reward to their husbands who are obligated to abstain from sexual intercourse with them from the time insemination begins until a pregnancy has been confirmed, or longer (Ragoné. 1996).

woman usually must also agree to certain limitations on her own activities, such as not drinking, smoking, or taking non-prescription drugs; not to terminate the pregnancy; and not to indulge in any acts that might threaten the well-being of the foetus. A surrogate mother will usually agree 'by written contract, to gestate a child on behalf of its intended parent or parents and to relinquish the child and all rights and responsibilities as a mother upon birth of the child' (Hurwitz (2000:128)).

Ragoné (1994) looked at several established surrogacy programmes and found internal and external guidelines designed to reduce public criticism and to protect the parties involved. Among the guidelines was one stating that women on public assistance should not be accepted as surrogates (presumably to try to avoid charges of exploitation of poor women by wealthier ones); another was to permit only heterosexual married couples to apply for the services of a surrogate. Internal guidelines included the psychological evaluation of potential surrogates, extensive physical examinations, attendance at semi-monthly or monthly support group meetings for those accepted as surrogates, and encouragement to terminate the relationship between the surrogate and the potential parents after the child is born (except where agreement had been reached to have an 'open' or continuing relationship). Psychological evaluation would attempt to ascertain the prospective surrogate's mental health status, her motives for becoming a surrogate, the likelihood of her bonding with the baby *in utero*, and the probability of the surrogate being able to surrender the child after birth.[15]

Some surrogacy agencies require that the commissioning parents be willing to have an 'open' relationship with the surrogate mother, and that she be encouraged to have empathy for their infertility as well as be praised for the 'gift' she is making to them to resolve that plight. The commissioning parents may intend to maintain a relationship with the woman even after birth, but might come to see her as an intruder in their family after some months, or feel anxiety that the continuing contact might encourage her to try to 'reclaim' the baby. In most cases, unless the agreement between the commissioning parents and the surrogate specifies otherwise, the latter is helped to recognise that the relationship between her and the parents will be terminated after the baby's birth and safe delivery to his/her new home. That a strong bond between them often develops during the pregnancy is very evident in Teman's work (see chapter 17, this volume).

4. WHO IS INVOLVED IN A SURROGACY ARRANGEMENT?

Depending upon the type of surrogacy arrangement involved, there are at least three, and possibly as many as five, people directly involved. There are at minimum the commissioning couple, who may or may not be supplying gamete

[15] On issues of psychological assessment and counselling, see chapters 10, 12 and 13, this volume.

and/or egg, and the surrogate mother who may supply the egg and/or carry the couple's fertilised egg.

Roberts (1998)[16] found that closeness between the surrogate and commissioning mothers was an important element in the success of the arrangement for all concerned. Indeed, one surrogate mother said that she had 'sympathy pains' for the commissioning mother because the latter was not having the physical experience, including labour pains, that she considered necessary preparation for having the baby. Modern technology tries to enhance the experience by synchronising the hormonal cycles of the two women, allowing the commissioning couple to see the baby's image via ultrasound, having both women attend childbirth education classes, and other interactions, including being present at the delivery of the baby. Seeing the baby's ultrasound image, according to the surrogates interviewed by Roberts, gave all the parties involved an opportunity to share in the excitement, and the commissioning parents the opportunity to begin bonding with their baby. Given that the surrogate mother often sees herself as giving a very special 'gift' to the commissioning parents, she usually welcomes this opportunity to help them share the experience. Indeed, the intermediary working with them will usually encourage this.

Surrogate Mother as Supplier of Egg and Carrier

In the typical situation, there is a heterosexual couple who want a child but the wife is infertile. They arrange, usually through an agency or an attorney specialising in surrogacy arrangements,[17] with a woman to supply an egg, to be fertilised by the partner's sperm, with the resulting embryo to be gestated by the surrogate mother. The couple will meet with the woman, continue to see her throughout the pregnancy, and may be present at the time of delivery. A strong relationship is established over the period of about a year. The couple may meet the surrogate's partner. After delivery, there may be continuation of the relationship, with exchange of photos or letters, possibly even visits. Ragoné (1994) has explored these possibilities in her study of surrogacy programmes.

In some cases, the surrogate experiences a grief reaction lasting for up to five months after delivery, aggravated by loss of contact with 'the couple' (Verny (1994:81)). Verny described the variety of surrogacy arrangements possible, and the many questions that arise therefrom. He based these largely on the research of others as well as his own concerns about the impact of the baby's surrender on the surrogate's own children, her relationship with her husband, refusal to accept the baby by the commissioning couple for whatever reason, and the

---

[16] See also Teman, chapter 17, this volume.
[17] Some such agencies in the USA have readily accessible websites. See for example, www.borenlaw.com/surrogacy/app.asp, www.fertilitydocs.com/surrogates.phtml, www.givf.com/hostv.cfm, and www.surrogatemothers.com/

effects on the child and his/her relationships with parents of knowing that money had played a role in his/her creation. As he pointed out, if it is the surrogate's egg that is being carried, she usually has one or more children who are half-sibling to the child. Giving away the baby can 'trigger latent fears of abandonment which are present in all children. It can also lead to other reactions as it did in the boy who said to his mother: "Why don't you give away my sister and keep the baby?" ' (Verny (1994:82)).[18]

Extended Family and Friends of the Surrogate Mother

If the surrogate has living parents and she has told them of her action, how do they feel about this 'grandchild' leaving their lives? Further research is clearly needed. Some surrogate mothers do *not* tell their parents so that they do not begin to care about the foetus or to perceive themselves as grandparents (Fischer and Gillman (1991)).[19] Other biological relatives of the infant, such as aunts, uncles, and cousins, will also usually be excluded from the child's life, unless the surrogate mother and the intended parents are themselves related.

If the surrogate (and genetic) mother is a relative or friend of the intended parents, it will be far more difficult to exclude her from the child's life after birth. When such a plan is first broached, the people involved need to explore how their collaborative effort may affect their future relationship.[20] Further, counselling is appropriate to consider any unresolved family issues that may surface during the attempts to attain pregnancy, during it, or afterwards (Tarnoff (1996)). Preventing the rupture of family (or friendly) relationships may well be more important than pursuing the surrogacy arrangement. There are simply not enough solid research data to provide guidance on these crucial issues.

5. SURROGATE MOTHERS FOR NON-TRADITIONAL INTENDED PARENTS

Gay and lesbian couples have been permitted by a few states to adopt a child to raise together, although only Vermont permits a civil union of homosexual couples. Gay couples who employ a surrogate to enable them to have their 'own' child can find it difficult to escape media attention. Public reaction to gay and

[18] Among the many issues requiring further research are the children's feelings about their mother's pregnancy; whether they develop some kind of attachment to the baby as it grows *in utero*; whether they are afraid that they, too, may be given away or abandoned. Their concerns and feelings may be considered if there is a support group for the pregnant surrogate mothers, but no studies were found that bear on this issue.

[19] If the surrogate arrangement is within the family, however, this may not be possible (Fischer and Gillman (1991)).

[20] AM Braverman (1996). Intrafamilial gestational carrier situations. (The American Surrogacy Center, Inc., Marietta, GA). http://www.surrogacy.com/psychres/article/intafam.html

lesbian families tends to be mixed, although such data as exist regarding these arrangements indicate that children are not likely to be disadvantaged by them. One such study included children conceived by donor insemination in 55 families headed by lesbian parents as well as 25 headed by heterosexual parents. Chan, Raboy, and Patterson (1998:455) found that 'neither specific modes of conception, nor parental sexual orientation were good predictors of children's developmental status. Parental well-being and relationship quality were, however, significantly related to children's adjustment.' Those who are opposed to homosexuality call for more stringent provisions that would make these arrangements unlawful, while those who focus on the quality of parenting that might be provided for a child created in this way, and who see homosexuals as entitled to enjoy the pleasures of parenthood, applaud the scientific advances that make it possible.

Importantly for gay and lesbian families, most states recognise the biologically-connected individual as the child's legal parent. The partner typically has few, if any, rights regarding the child if the couple decides to discontinue their relationship. In one case, the biological mother carried the foetus as a favour to her former lesbian partner who was unable to become pregnant herself, and gave her the baby after birth. The non-biological care-taking mother, however, found that she had no legal status regarding medical care or other decisions for the child, and sought such rights. At that point, the biological mother regained custody of the child, then two-years old. The judge ultimately ruled in favour of the initial care-taking mother, declaring her an 'equitable parent' with the biological mother as she had, in fact, already created a family bond with the child. The biological mother was awarded legal and physical custody, *but* both women were to share equally in decisions regarding the child's upbringing and were to have equal time with the child.[21] A somewhat more complicated situation arises if the fertilised egg of one partner is implanted into the womb of the other partner, with the result that the child actually has *two* mothers under the laws of several states (Lilith (2001)). There is generally space for only *one* mother's name on a birth certificate. Thoughtful judges, in states where the law permits, tend to focus on what action would be in the child's 'best interests'. In those states where a same-sexed partner is permitted to become an adoptive parent, consideration is typically given in determining visitation, custody, and decision-making to the length of time the partner was involved with the child after his or her birth and in what role(s) (Crawford (1999)).[22]

[21] Anon. Lesbian named 'equitable parent' of two-year-old. (13 May 1996). *Missouri Lawyers' Weekly*. [Retrieved 30 August 2001 from the World Wide Web: <http://www.leighjoy.com/lesbian_named_equitable_parent.htm>.]

[22] Several permutations of laws are discussed here, including some that involve assisted reproductive technology and surrogate motherhood.

6. WHAT ABOUT THE FATHERS?

There are also legal questions that arise if the father does not fulfil his part of the contract (ie accepting custody of the child) because the infant is born with a disability, or because multiple children are born and he will only accept one of the infants (Moran (2001)).[23] In one case discussed by Nowakokski (1990) the surrogate mother was delivered of twins, a girl and a boy, but the biological father would only accept the girl, planning to place the boy in an adoptive home. The surrogate mother, very upset by this, sued for custody of both children. By the time the children were six weeks old, she and her husband were awarded custody of them; her husband promptly adopted them; and the biological father was not awarded visitation rights.

If the father refuses custody and the biological/ surrogate mother also refuses to accept custody, there is obviously more of a problem with no simple solution. The answers to the questions that arise vary from state to state and from focus on the contract to focus on the child's best interests. As a presentation of a proposed 'Assisted Reproductive Technologies Model Act' points out, traditional law, and specifically adoption law, are not readily applicable to these and other collaborative reproduction situations (Jaeger (1999)).

7. BEFORE AND AFTER THE BIRTH OF THE CHILD

The primary reason for clarifying legal parentage before the birth of the child is to provide a secure and safe home for the child from the moment of birth, including signaling who has authority to make medical treatment decisions for the newborn if needed. Clearly defining legal parentage is also important to clarify the relationship between the child, donors, gestators and intended rearing parents. . . . Clarity in custody rights will also send a positive message to the child that he is secure within his family and third parties will not later have grounds to disturb familial relationships by seeking him out. (Jaegar (1999) p 17).

In the Beginning

Sperm donors have long been anonymous figures. They are supposed to furnish true medical histories, be tested themselves for a variety of possible physical conditions, and remain unknown to recipients of their sperm or any resulting children. Screening appears to be satisfactory in most cases, although occasionally there is a need to find the donor because of a health problem that appears in

---

[23] In one case, the original commissioning parents refused to accept twins, but notified the surrogate later than was permitted in the contract. She refused to abort one foetus, and another couple subsequently welcomed the twins. See Schwartz (1991).

the child. In one case, at least two employees of a sperm bank were aware that a donor's sister and mother suffered from kidney disease, a fact that was not revealed to the recipient parents until two years after the insemination (Bauman (2001)).

In the case of egg donors who do not serve as gestational surrogates, most of the agencies found on the World Wide Web indicate that psychological as well as physical screening (including genetic, pelvic, infectious disease testing) is required. The psychological screening has been described above.[24] Jaegar (1999) lists a number of reasons for making a psycho-educational consultation mandatory for all donors, with the results of the mental health expert's recommendation made available to the recipient couple and any referring physician. Among the items to be explored in such a consultation are: psychological side effects of hormonal preparations and protocols, possibility of multiple pregnancy and the psychological risks associated with them, disclosure to others and the resulting child of the donor/surrogate's role, potential coercion by the commissioning couple, and 'the parameters of the donor or carrier's role with the recipient individual, intended rearing parent(s), and the potential child' (Jaegar (1999:25)).

If a family member is either egg donor and/or gestational surrogate, then counselling is strongly recommended both before the alternative procedures are undertaken and while the effort is in progress to explore both possible unresolved family issues and potential sources of conflict about such matters as how many cycles will be undertaken, selective reduction in the event of a multiple pregnancy, therapeutic abortion, who will be present at the birth, and the ways in which the collaborative reproduction effort will affect relationships among the parties (Tarnoff (1997)). As Braverman (1996) has pointed out, any changes in a person's status or experiences affect his or her relationships with others.

Disclosure of Origins

The commissioning parents are often torn, both before and after the child's birth, about what to tell the child of his/her origins. Any secret involving a gestational surrogate mother would clearly be more difficult to keep than the less involved sperm or egg donation. Shapiro, Shapiro, and Paret (2001) have discussed the pros and cons of openness and secrecy, including the possible impact of either decision on the child and on the parent–child relationship. The parental view may stem from the non-biological parent's view of his/her infertility and how this may affect the parent–child relationship rather than from the process itself.

Trying to keep a gestational surrogacy a secret would be difficult when so many among their friends and family may know the story. Ragoné (1994) found

---

[24] See, eg www.surrogatemothers.com, www.fertility-docs.com/surrogates_faq.phtml, and www.donoregg1.com/donor_who.cfm .

that some surrogate mother programmes would not accept prospective parent couples who preferred a 'closed' arrangement. This is very similar to situations where adoptive parents do not tell a child of the adoption, only to reveal it on a deathbed, or to have someone else reveal it decades later, sometimes with catastrophic emotional reactions on the part of the adoptee.[25] In the view of some mental health professionals, keeping donor insemination a secret would be psychologically and socially harmful to the within-family relationships, as well as ethically unacceptable.[26]

A study of those who became parents via donor insemination (DI), in vitro fertilisation (IVF), or adoption in terms of their reasons for disclosure of a child's origins (or non-disclosure), the effects of non-disclosure on the parents and on the parent-child relationship, and stress levels of parents who had or had not told others about their arrangements is one of the few that might provide clues to handling the surrogacy disclosure question (Cook, Golombok, Bish, & Murray (1995)). Mothers were interviewed and asked whether or not they planned to tell the child about his or her origins, whether or not they had told family or friends of the child's origins, and if their answer was 'not', what were their reasons for not telling. In addition, standardised tests were administered to discriminate between clinical and non-clinical groups, to measure parental stress, and to assess children's behavioural and emotional problems. There were significant differences among the groups, with most of the DI mothers planning not to tell the child of his or her origins, although about half had told a family member (but not necessarily friends), and most of the adoptive mothers having already told the child or planning to tell the child of their origins. IVF mothers were in the middle. The reasons given for secrecy by the DI mothers included protection of the child; protection of the father, both from rejection by the child and from others' knowledge of his infertility; lack of availability of genetic information about the donor; and difficulties in telling family members—mostly, again to protect the father, but also to protect the child from being regarded as a 'test-tube baby'. Adoptive parents typically do not have these concerns, but some of the IVF parents did.

In a study of the socio-emotional development of children born of combined donor-biological effort, no differences were found with respect to quality of parenting or socio-emotional development of the child between those parents who had told a family member of the conception using a gamete donor and those who had not (Golombok, Murray, Brinsden and Abdalla (1999)). With respect to children born to surrogate mothers, there was concern expressed by others that the child would be perceived as a commodity, available for money paid, rather than for the creative miracle that he or she was (Verny (1994)). 'What will a child feel knowing money has played a role in his/her existence?' (Verny (1994:52)).

---

[25] Author's case notes.
[26] Landau (1998); McGee, Brakman, and Gurmankin (2001).

Since donor insemination is usually anonymous, in contrast to the obvious contribution of the gestational surrogate mother, the studies cited are not totally analogous to the problems of disclosure in the latter case. Moreover, female infertility or gynaecological problems, for which the diagnostic procedures can be both invasive and embarrassing (Cook (1987)) are not usually viewed today as being as threatening to the female's *persona* as they were a few decades ago when motherhood was seen as a woman's primary, perhaps only role (other than wife) (Zucker (1999)). Today she has more options, such as having a career, although this may vary with race or ethnic culture (Gerrity (2001)).[27] The man's infertility problems may affect his self-perception of virility and even self-esteem, although this is not universally true (Greil (1997)).[28] The male is expected to make his name in his field of endeavour rather than as a father. Nevertheless, the difficulties of what to tell the child, and when and how to tell the child, as well as who else should know of the surrogacy arrangement can cause concern to those who become parents via this route. There are some support groups of surrogate parents that can be helpful about questions of disclosure, but therapists should also be aware of disclosure being a potential source of stress to the individual parent as well as to the parent–child relationship.

8. EXTRA-FAMILIAL ATTACHMENTS

The question of sibling association rights, another potentially challenging factor in contested surrogacy situations, was explored with respect to foster care and adoption by Patton and Latz (1994). In one case cited by Patton and Latz, the parents had testified that their children would be psychologically harmed if separated, and the court 'ruled that all evidence concerning sibling bonding . . . was inadmissible' (1994:749).[29] As Patton and Latz pointed out, interest groups in the mid–1980s and early 1990s focused on the rights of extended family members (aunts, uncles, grandparents) to maintain contact with minor relatives after the latter had been removed from their parents, but there were few similar groups acting on behalf of siblings:

> Courts and legislatures, without much analysis, have usually determined that siblings' associational rights are of less value than parent/child rights and have made those decisions without fully considering the contrary medical, *psychological*, and sociological data (Patton and Latz (1994:751)) italics added).

---

[27] As Gerrity notes, there have been relatively few studies of ethnically diverse populations.

[28] This review of more than 100 research studies around the world reveals considerable diversity in size and source of samples, comparison groups, measures used, and core findings. Most studies focused on women, although some included couples; few were longitudinal. Very few examined the impact of fertility on the marital relationship other than, perhaps, the stress on the sexual relationship during periods of medical treatment. Where men have admitted concerns about their feelings of virility, it has been anecdotal or occasionally in a clinical setting. See also Mahlstedt (1985).

[29] The reasoning was not given in the notes.

The impact of not seeing, holding, or interacting with the half-sibling born of a surrogacy arrangement will vary with the age and developmental level of the surrogate mother's children. Harrison (1990) commented on these potential negative effects—depression, sadness, confusion, fear of being abandoned themselves, but had no data on whether they were given psychological counselling to help them understand and deal with the 'sibling' who never came home. A committee that deals with ethical issues for the Conservative Jewish movement has expressed concern for the potential psychological harm that exists for these older children when the newborn goes to a different home.[30]

Considering the child placed away from the biological mother, whether as the result of adoption or surrogacy, there is a question whether that child has a right to be aware of and to become acquainted with biological half- or full siblings. Patton and Latz (1994) asserted that 'Since children cannot vote or donate to political campaigns, legislatures have historically refused to seriously determine their specific rights or respond adequately to their individual needs' (p 768). On the other hand:

> Two apparently contradictory historical developments have occurred simultaneously in family law. One involves a gradually growing emphasis on privacy and individual rights; the other, a gradual increase in the involvement of the legal system in the internal functioning of families (Mintz (1992:635–36)).

Some groups in recent years have encouraged adoptees to search on the Internet for their biological families (often without regard for whether they *want* to be found), and may do the same with the children of surrogate mothers, arguing about the alleged 'superiority' of biological ties over any others. Again, there is considerable potential for negative outcomes for relationships both within the family enhanced via surrogacy and between them and the surrogate and her family, although there seems to be little useful research on this issue.

9. THE MARITAL RELATIONSHIP

There are two sets of marital relationships that can be enhanced or weakened by a surrogacy situation. One is the relationship between the woman serving as surrogate mother, genetic or gestational, and her partner or husband; the other is the relationship between the couple seeking to have a child via a surrogate mother.

In the first case, there are obviously restrictions placed on the woman in the surrogacy contract that can detract from her normal interaction with her partner. The principal potential source of friction may be the requirement that they abstain from sexual relations while the attempt to impregnate her successfully

---

[30] Committee on Jewish Law and Standards. A Jewish response to the use of a surrogate. (1999) 8 (2) *JTS Magazine*.

for the contracting parents goes on, and perhaps for some months afterwards. As noted earlier, his expectations of and motives for agreeing to his partner becoming a surrogate mother should be explored by a psychological consultant prior to any contract between the couples.

Infertility can divide a couple or bring them closer depending on the two people involved, the strength of the motivation of each partner to become a parent, the stress resulting from the frustration of being infertile as well as the ongoing medical tests to determine the source(s) of the problem, and the decisions to be made about how to overcome the problem.[31] For the couple undergoing the tests and varied procedures, besides the anxiety generated by these measures, there is often a feeling of having lost control of their lives and their future as a potential family:

> Because the surrogacy arrangement is often initiated to relieve the suffering of infertility, the marital bond might even be more consolidated by the spouses' shared commitment to the birth and upbringing of a child (Lamb (1993) p 404).

On the other hand, it is also possible that one commissioning partner pushes for surrogacy more than the other, perhaps to carry on the family's genetic line, with the spouse being made to feel inadequate and secondary. Deep unspoken feelings of resentment could result, leading to a strain on the marital relationship. Should a divorce occur at some later date, this motive could lead to a bitter custody battle, no matter how good a parent the non-biological parent has been (Coleman (1996)).[32]

10. THE PSYCHOLOGIST'S ROLE

In a legitimate service involved with surrogate motherhood, there is, or should be, as previously noted, psychological screening of women who offer themselves as possible surrogate mothers. As Harrison (1990) pointed out, 'Many surrogacy contracts include a provision that the surrogate mother not form any emotional attachment to the child' (p 100). To many people, such a stipulation appears to be beyond the woman's voluntary control, and hence an inappropriate demand or even expectation. On the other hand, apparently most of the women who serve successfully as surrogate mothers are able to resist attachment, to see their role as being an 'incubator' or caretaker for another couple's child. They may be able to do this because they idealise the man or the couple whose child they are carrying, because they feel they are giving a child a good

[31] See Edelmann and Connolly (2000) and Zucker (1999).
[32] *McDonald v McDonald* 608 N.Y.S. 2d 477 (N.Y. App.Div., 1994). In this case, the husband's sperm had been mixed with a female donor's eggs, but implanted in the wife's uterus for the pregnancy. When he sued for divorce soon after the birth of twin girls, he sought to retain sole custody on the grounds that he was the only genetic and legal parent. He lost. The court ruled that a woman who carries a foetus that is the result of an egg donation, with the intention of raising the resulting child as her own, *is* the child's mother.

chance at life (often a reparative motive), or because they care more about the fee being paid than the child for whom it is paid (no matter what language is used to describe the payment).[33]

A prospective surrogate mother who is married or who has a partner should also bring in her partner for evaluation as *his* support during the pregnancy and after delivery will be critical, as noted above, to a successful outcome of the arrangement. It might also be appropriate for psychological evaluators to raise the question of how the prospective surrogate mother will explain her role to her own children, and how she expects them to react when she ultimately delivers and surrenders the newborn. Is her perspective realistic? Is she prepared to have them receive psychological counselling if they become confused, depressed, or stressed by what she is doing? Obviously, answers to these questions rest in part on the age(s) of her child(ren).

The surrogate programmes studied by Ragoné (1994) indicated that they did not request that prospective parents have a psychological examination, but it might be helpful to such couples if they did. Psychologists should evaluate the prospective parents in terms of *their* motives, commitment, and the effects of infertility on their marital relationship. Relatively few couples seek counselling or therapy as they progress through months or years of infertility testing and treatment, so that therapy to reduce the effects of that stress might well be appropriate even as they consider becoming involved in a surrogacy arrangement. A counsellor might explore with them what relationship, if any, they anticipate having with the surrogate mother, both during the pregnancy and after the child's birth, what they expect of the child, and how they plan to explain the child's origins to him or her at a future time.

Lantos (1990) cited a number of situations involving new reproductive technologies where the psychologist's 'loyalty' might be divided between the best interests of the parties, the clinic, the potential child, and even institutional or social policies. This may become more of a challenge if the psychologist or psychiatrist is called as an expert witness in the event of a custody conflict (Harrison (1990)) or is questioned by the media. Psychologists working in this area would do well, as a group, to establish guidelines for responding in potentially conflicting situations.[34]

11. SURROGACY AND RELATIONSHIPS: CONCLUSIONS

It is apparent that surrogate motherhood is not a simple matter. The would-be parents have had to confront infertility with the many attendant physical and psychological stresses it can bring. They have had to determine their next step: to remain childless, to serve as foster parents, to try to adopt, or to try the

---

[33] Aigen (1996). See also Ragoné (chapter 14, this volume).
[34] This has not been done to date for reasons unknown to the author.

surrogacy route to starting a family. If they choose surrogacy, it is clear that they should locate a legitimate agency or intermediary to minimise risks in the arrangement.

Choice of a surrogate poses many questions in terms of what characteristics the intended parents are seeking in that person; their expectations if, for example, the insemination produces a multiple pregnancy, and their feelings about whether the relationship with the surrogate mother should or should not continue in the longer term. The necessary presence of a contract has the potential to de-humanise both the arrangement and the baby if the payment of money to the surrogate implies more a purchase of 'property' rather than an exchange of 'gifts' between the parties. Once the child is born, many questions arise about his/her relations with the surrogate mother and her family, as well as how to explain such relationships to the child as he or she asks questions about origins. Questions may arise within the surrogate's family also, and there is a need to try to anticipate what explanations will be made and their likely effect on the people involved.[35]

Surrogate programmes have something unique and highly desirable to offer. It is clear that those who seek to become involved with them need to be aware in advance of the negative as well as positive outcomes that may occur, of the options in relationships, and of the questions that may arise in the indeterminate future.

REFERENCES

Aigen, BP, *Motivations of surrogate mothers: parenthood, altruism and self-actualization (a three year study)* (Marietta, GA, The American Surrogacy Center, Inc, 1996). <http://www.surrogacy.com/psychres/article/ motivat.html>

American Academy of Pediatrics, 'Ethical issues in surrogate motherhood' (1992) 9(7) *AAP News* <www.aap.org.policy/178.html>

Braverman, AM, *Intrafamilial gestational carrier situations* (Marietta, GA, The American Surrogacy Center, Inc, 1996). http://www.surrogacy.com/psychres/article/ intrafam.html

Bauman, JH, 'Discovering donors: Legal rights to access information about anonymous sperm donors given to children of artificial insemination' (2001) 31 *Golden Gate University Law Review* 193.

Buzzanca v Buzzanca (In re Marriage of Buzzanca), 72 Cal. Rptr. 2d 280, 293 (Ct. App. 1998).

Chan, RW, Raboy, B and Patterson, CJ, 'Psychosocial adjustment among children conceived via donor insemination by lesbian and heterosexual mothers' (1999) 69 *Child Development* 443.

Coleman, M, 'Gestation, intent, and the seed: defining motherhood in the era of assisted human reproduction' (1996) 17 *Cardozo Law Review* 497.

[35] Unfortunately, there is a dearth of good research about all of these issues, leaving many questions unanswered.

Committee on Jewish Law and Standards, 'A Jewish response to the use of a surrogate' (1999) 8(z) *JTS Magazine*.

Cook, EP, 'Characteristics of the biopsychosocial crisis of infertility' (1987) 65 *Journal of Counselling and Development* 465.

Cook, R, Golombok, S, Bish, A and Murray, C, 'Disclosure of donor insemination: Parental attitudes' (1995) 65 *American Journal of Orthopsychiatry* 549.

Crawford, JM, 'Co-parent adoptions by same-sex couples: From loophole to law' (1999) 80 *Families in Society* 271.

Edelmann, RJ and Connolly, KJ, 'Gender differences in response to infertility and infertility investigations: real or illusory' (2000) 5 *British Journal of Health Psychology* 365.

Fischer, S and Gillman, I, 'Surrogate motherhood: Attachment, attitudes and social support' (1991) 54 *Psychiatry* 13.

Gerrity, DA, 'A biopsychosocial theory of infertility' (2001) 9 *Family Journal* 151.

Golombok, S, Murray, C, Brinsden, P and Abdalla, H, 'Social versus biological parenting: family functioning and the socioemotional development of children conceived by egg or sperm donation' (1999) 40 *Journal of Child Psychology and Psychiatry & Related Disciplines* 519.

Greil, AL, 'Infertility and psychological distress: A critical review of the literature' (1997) 45 *Social Sciences & Medicine* 1679.

Harrison, M, 'Psychological ramifications of 'surrogate' motherhood' in NL Stotland (ed), *Psychiatric Aspects of Reproductive Technology* (Washington DC, American Psychiatric Press, 1990), 97–112.

Hurwitz, I, 'Collaborative reproduction: finding the child in the maze of legal motherhood' (2000) 33 *Connecticut Law Review* 127.

Jaeger, AS, *Assisted Reproductive Technologies Model Act* (Family Law Section, American Bar Association, Assisted Reproduction and Genetic Technologies Committee, 1999).

Kanefield, L, 'The reparative motive in surrogate mothers' (1999) 2 *Adoption Quarterly* 5.

Katers, LM, 'Arguing the 'obvious' in Wisconsin: why state regulation of assisted reproductive technology has not come to pass, and how it should' (2000) *Wisconsin Law Review* 441.

Lamb, SR, 'The ethics of surrogacy: a framework for legal analysis' (1993) 31 *Family and Conciliation Courts Review* 401.

Landau, R, 'Secrecy, anonymity, and deception in donor insemination: a genetic, psychosocial and ethical critique' (1998) 28 *Social Work in Health Care* 75.

Lantos, JD, 'Second-generation ethical issues in the new reproductive technologies: divided loyalties, indications, and the research agenda' in NL Stotland (ed), *Psychiatric Aspects of Reproductive Technology* (Washington DC, American Psychiatric Press, 1990) 87–96.

Lavoie, D, 'Surrogates redefine term "mother" ' (2001) 2 September *The Philadelphia Inquirer* A10.

Lilith, R, 'The G.I.F.T. of two biological and legal mothers' (2001) 9 *American University Journal of Gender, Social Policy & Law* 207.

Mahlstedt, MM, 'The psychological component of infertility' (1985) 43 *Fertility and Sterility* 335.

McGee, G, Brakman, S-V and Gurmankin, AD, 'Disclosure to children conceived with donor gametes should not be optional' (2001) 16 *Human Reproduction* 2033.

Mintz, S, 'Children, families and the State: American family law in historical perspective' (1992) 69 *Denver Law Review* 635.

Moran, M-B, 'New parents found for surrogate's twins' (2001) 14 August *The Philadelphia Inquirer* A9.

Nowakoski, P, 'How could I let them separate my twins?' (1990) July *Redbook* 38.

Overvold, AZ, *Surrogate Parenting* (New York, Pharos Books, 1988).

Patton, WW and Latz, S, 'Severing Hansel from Gretel: an analysis of siblings' association rights' (1994) 48 *University of Miami Law Review* 745.

Place, JM, 'Gestational surrogacy and the meaning of "mother": Johnson v Calvert, 851 P.2d 776 (Cal. 1993)' (1994) 17 *Harvard Journal of Law & Public Policy* 807.

Ragoné, H, *Surrogate Motherhood: Conception in the Heart* (Boulder, Westview Press, 1994).

—- 'Chasing the blood tie: surrogate mothers, adoptive mothers and fathers' (1996) 23 *American Ethnologist* 352.

Roberts, EFS, ' "Native" narratives of connectedness: Surrogate motherhood and technology' in R. Davis-Floyd and J Dumit (eds), *Cyborg Babies: From Techno-sex to Techno-tots* (New York, Routledge, 1998).

Schuker, E, 'Psychological effects of the new reproductive technologies' (1987) 13 *Women & Health* 141.

Schwartz, LL, *Alternatives to Infertility: Is Surrogacy the Answer?* (New York, Brunner/Mazel, 1991).

—— 'What *is* a family? A contemporary view' (1993) 15 *Contemporary Family Therapy* 429.

—— 'Surrogacy: Third leg of the reproductive triangle' in FW Kaslow (ed), *Handbook of Couples and Family Forensics: A Sourcebook for Mental Health and Legal Professionals* (New York, John Wiley, 2000) 42–61.

Shapiro, VB, Shapiro, JR and Paret, IH, *Complex Adoption and Assisted Reproductive Technology: A Developmental Approach to Clinical Practice* (New York, The Guilford Press, 2001).

Tarnoff, S, 'All in the family: using a family member as surrogate' (Marietta, GA, The American Surrogacy Center, Inc, 1996) <http://www.surrogacy.com/psychres/article/allfamily.html>.

Verny, TR, 'The stork in the lab: biological, psychological, ethical, social and legal aspects of third party conceptions' (1994) 9 *Pre- and Perinatal Psychology Journal* 57.

Zucker, AN, 'The psychological impact of reproductive difficulties on women's lives' (1999) 40 *Sex Roles* 767.

12

Safety in the Multitude of Counsellors:[1] *Do we Need Counselling in Surrogacy?*

RACHEL COOK[2]

1. INTRODUCTION

WHILE MOST CLINICIANS propose that medical reasons are necessary in order for surrogacy to be considered as a 'treatment',[3] we should not be distracted by this into thinking that surrogacy is a just another medical problem. It is a paradox of infertility that treatment might be effective and yet the outcome is not the desired one—for example, a woman's fallopian tubes might be successfully unblocked and yet she does not become pregnant. In IVF surrogacy, pregnancy may be successfully achieved, yet the surrogate mother decides to keep the child. In the end, whether or not the treatment is a medical success is not the key issue—if infertility treatment treats anything, it 'treats' the psychological or social problems that arise when we desire a child, but cannot have one.

In Western societies this may be not widely acknowledged. We tend to view infertility (or the unfulfilled desire for a child) as a problem located in the body and requiring medical treatment. Yet the problem of infertility is not mainly located in the body. It is in the mind—in our thoughts, feelings and desires. And it is in the social world, that prescribes parenthood as normal and stigmatises childlessness (Miall (1985, 1986); Martin-Matthews and Matthews (1986)). The body is therefore treated in order to solve the problems in the mind and in the social world. Surrogacy is seen here as a possible 'last resort' solution to these problems.

These multiple 'locations' of infertility point to the insufficiency of the medical model and the need for a biopsychosocial perspective,[4] an approach which recognises the importance of emotional and social aspects of the patient as well

---

[1] The title is derived from *The Holy Bible*, Proverbs xi.14: 'In the multitude of counsellors there is safety'.

[2] I am grateful to Shelley Day Sclater for her very helpful comments on this chapter.

[3] A recent American study shows however that around 20% of infertility clinic directors are in favour of surrogacy for non-medical reasons (Stern, Cramer, Garrod and Green (2002)).

[4] A model proposed by Engel (1977).

as the physical. One way in which this recognition might be achieved in practice is via counselling skills and counselling expertise.[5] The use and process of counselling in surrogacy, the typical issues that arise, and the tensions between assessment and counselling are addressed by Appleton in chapter 13. This chapter considers the ways in which counselling is linked with some types of infertility treatment in the UK, why infertility patients who use surrogacy as a route to parenthood might need counselling, and whether counselling is effective. In view of the absence of research into counselling in surrogacy, some key issues are addressed by borrowing where necessary from literature on more general infertility counselling.

2. THE PRESCRIPTION FOR COUNSELLING IN INFERTILITY

We should first distinguish between counselling skills, which are skills that might be used by any health professional who comes into contact with surrogacy participants, and counselling as an interpersonal process undertaken with a qualified person to provide support and the opportunity to change.[6] Counselling is therefore not just patient-centred care (Strauss and Boivin (2001)).

Counselling and communication skills may be useful in many health contexts, but in some medical conditions there is perceived to be a particular need for the involvement of trained counsellors (Davis and Fallowfield (1991a)). It is highly unusual however in health care for this perceived need to be reflected in regulations (Glover, Abel and Gannon (1998)). In Britain, as a result of the Human Fertilisation and Embryology Act (HFE Act) 1990, counselling must be offered to those who undergo infertility treatment in licensed centres. The Act requires that people considering using assisted methods of conception are given 'a suitable opportunity to receive proper counselling about the implications of the proposed steps.'[7] Thus people who plan to use IVF surrogacy at a clinic licensed by the HFEA must be offered such counselling before engaging in any medical procedures. The report of the King's Fund Centre Counselling Committee (1991) points out that this requirement for counselling is reinforced by the need

---

[5] The term counselling has many meanings, ranging from the general—attentive listening, helping—to the more specialist and specific psychotherapeutic relationship between a professionally qualified counsellor and patient. In the latter case it may not be easy to distinguish from psychotherapy (eg Patterson (1986)).

[6] In medical care, it makes sense to distinguish between the use of counselling skills by health professionals such as doctors and nurses, where counselling is only one part of the relationship, and the specialism of counselling, where counselling is the main activity (Nelson-Jones (1983); Davis and Fallowfield (1991b:26)). Just as it can be difficult to define what counselling is, so it is difficult to identify what constitutes a 'qualified' counsellor. However, the HFEA recommended minimum qualifications for infertility counselling are a qualification in social work, accreditation by the British Association for Counselling, or Chartered Psychologist status (but not necessarily a qualification in counselling psychology).

[7] Section 13(6) of the Human Fertilisation and Embryology Act 1990 (HMSO).

to take account of the 'welfare' of any child who may be born, and other children who might be affected by the birth. The rationale behind the Act's requirement is not made explicit; however the King's Fund Report states:

> Counselling is available because of the *stressful and complex situation* created by the
> issues surrounding infertility and for *the long term consequences for the couple and
> for the child conceived in this way*; it is not made available because of any particular
> failure of the patient to cope, or because of the presence of abnormal reactions to
> infertility or the desire for a child (3.4, p 11, my emphasis).[8]

As well as a requirement that counselling be offered, the kinds of counselling
which should be available have been identified. The HFEA Code of Practice
1990 identifies three types of counselling which should be available:

a. *Implications counselling*: this aims to enable the person concerned to
   understand the implications of the proposed course of action for him or
   herself, for his or her family and for any children born as a result;
b. *support counselling*: this aims to give emotional support at times of particular stress, eg when there is a failure to achieve a pregnancy;
c. *therapeutic counselling*: this aims to help people cope with the consequences of infertility and treatment, and to help them to resolve the problems which these may cause. It includes helping people to adjust their
   expectations and to accept their situation (1990, 6.4: 6.i)

The report of the King's Fund Counselling Committee added a further type to
these three—information counselling—which constitutes the provision of
information (and clearly must underlie implications counselling). It also noted
that therapeutic counselling might constitute more 'sustained help' aimed at
adjusting to 'particular life circumstances'.[9]

Clearly the provision of some of these specified types of counselling requires
a trained counsellor; other kinds might be provided by doctors, nurses, friends
and family. The King's Fund Committee proposes that information counselling
'may be provided by any suitable member of the infertility team'[10] who need not
have formal training or a qualification in counselling. Implications counselling
however is deemed to require a team member who has training in infertility
counselling skills (a trained infertility counsellor).[11] Support counselling 'may
be provided by the range of professionals working in the infertility team' and
also friends, family and support groups. The kind of person suitable to provide
therapeutic counselling is not described, but implied to be a person who is a
trained counsellor. The counsellor, besides having counselling skills, will need a
thorough knowledge of the procedures involved in surrogacy including its legal

---

[8] This is an interesting statement for several reasons, not least because many of the long-term
consequences for the couple and the child were unknown at the time (and still are to a great extent).
[9] Reading between the lines, this means help to adjust to childlessness.
[10] Section 2.9, p 5. The Report does not say how suitability is determined.
[11] Recommendation 8, p 6.

aspects (see Appleton, chapter 13, this volume). Read (1995, p 5) argues that without this understanding, counsellors might find it difficult to deal with clients' anxieties, and clients would be likely to lose faith in the counsellor. The qualifications and training of counsellors in practice, however, have not really been examined. They might be nurses, social workers, psychologists or counsellors (see eg Shaw (1991)).

While the BMA suggests that counselling should be integral to the surrogacy process, it is not actually its use but its availability which is seen as the key (Bartlam and McLeod (2000)) and, just as licensed centres should not be obliged to counsel everyone, so everyone should not be obliged to take up the offer (Read (1995)). Therefore, although the recommendation is that there be at least one counsellor employed in a clinic, there is likely to be considerable variation between clinics in the extent to which counselling is available. The extent to which counselling is seen as primary (an end in itself) or secondary (a means to an end of getting through the treatment and its accompanying psychological problems) is also likely to vary. Some clinics may adopt a very 'medical' perspective while others might take a more holistic approach.

There is however an 'official' recognition that counselling is required in infertility and, by extension, surrogacy. Indeed, the British Medical Association sees counselling as an integral part of surrogacy arrangements and states:

> The BMA strongly recommends that people considering surrogacy be actively encouraged to take advantage of counselling in order to satisfy themselves that they have fully considered the issues and their implications (British Medical Association (1996:54)).

Despite this view, counselling is only built into surrogacy arrangements that occur in a clinical context. While support agencies such as COTS might encourage participants to seek counselling, there are no regulations or social structures which ensure this occurs when surrogacy is arranged outside medical provision. We might infer from this that being seen to provide counselling is more important than its actual provision, or its uptake.

The types of counselling which have been identified seem to reflect three concerns or issues: first, that there are often difficult decisions to be made, with far-reaching implications[12]; secondly, that infertility is potentially distressing, and patients may need support; and third, that treatment is likely to fail, and counselling is therefore required to support those whom medicine cannot help. Davis and Fallowfield (1991a:19) argue that in the same way that we need specialists as well as generalists in health care, so there is a need for specialist counsellors 'to work with people on more complex and long term difficulties.' In the next section we look at whether there is any support in the literature for the notion of a 'need' for counselling.

---

[12] It is worth noting that much research which has examined the implications of reproductive technologies, for example, in terms of the psychological well-being of parents and the physical, social and emotional development of the children, has demonstrated very positive outcomes.

3. IS COUNSELLING NEEDED?

Is there any evidence to support the notion that infertility patients, particularly those undergoing surrogacy, need counselling? Following the concerns raised above, there might well be a case for counselling if there is evidence that infertility causes distress or psychological problems, if traditional medical care does not appear to provide sufficient emotional support, and if the nature of surrogacy is such that there is a particular need for counselling in these circumstances.

Is Infertility Distressing?

While infertility is portrayed as a medical problem, it is generally accepted as being associated with psychological distress (see eg Domar, Zuttermeister and Friedman (1993); Bartlam and MacLeod (2000)). There are numerous reports in the literature documenting stress, depression and anxiety among those with a diagnosis of infertility or those undergoing infertility treatment. In addition, problems with self-esteem, marital and sexual difficulties, blame and guilt, stigmatisation, loss and role failure have been reported to be associated with the experience of infertility (eg Nachtigall, Becker and Wozny (1992)). Infertility has also been described as a chronic stressor (e.g Newton, Sherrard and Glavac (1999)). For example, Lukse and Vacc (1999) report grief and depression in women before, during and after infertility treatment (IVF or medication which induces ovulation). It is these kinds of reported experience that lead to the notion that counselling is required for infertility. Much research presents negative images that emphasise threats and vulnerability rather than advantages and strengths.

There is something of a discrepancy between these images and the reality, however. The empirical psychological literature on the consequences of infertility provides a much cloudier picture, with little indication of clearly discernible, common negative reactions (from large rigorous studies). This reflects the interesting contrast perceptible from the 'two kinds' of literature on the psychological consequences of infertility, as noted by Dunkel-Schetter and Lobel (1991). Anecdotal and descriptive studies suggest that psychological symptoms are a common, perhaps inevitable, consequence of infertility, whereas empirical literature using standardised measures of distress generally finds no strong, consistent evidence of psychological problems.[13] As they put it,

> . . . currently available, methodologically rigorous research suggests that the majority of people with infertility do not experience clinically significant emotional reactions, loss of self-esteem, or adverse marital and sexual consequences (Dunkel-Schetter and Lobel (1991:50).

---

[13] Reasons for this discrepancy are discussed in detail by Dunkel-Schetter and Lobel (1991) and not reiterated here.

They argue that the most likely reason for this discrepancy is that there is considerable variability in psychological responses to infertility.

Another way of viewing the distress of infertility patients is to compare it with that of patients with other medical conditions where counselling is received. Thus infertile people can have similar levels of psychological symptoms to cancer patients (eg Domar, Zuttermeister and Friedman (1993)). On the basis of this, Domar *et al* argue that 'standard psychosocial interventions for serious medical illness should also be applied in infertility treatment' (p 45).

It is reasonable, therefore, to ask as Reading (1991) does, whether infertility is 'sufficiently distressing' to warrant the provision of some kind of psychological intervention. For a proportion of individuals, in some circumstances, it is (eg Freeman, Boxer, Rickels, Tureck and Mastroianni (1985)). We might also ask further whether it is infertility or its treatment that leads to a need for counselling, and whether medicine has a responsibility to provide it.

Emotional Support in Traditional Medical Care

The representation of infertility as a medical problem gives credibility and legitimacy to the claim for counselling. However, Kentenich (2001) notes the *danger* of reducing the problem to a medical issue and thereby failing to address the emotional aspects of infertility. He notes also that counselling in infertility is different from that in relation to other reproductive health problems for a number of reasons. He argues that it is not really a medical problem; that there are additional ethical issues involved because treatment aims to produce a new person who cannot be involved in decision-making; that repeated treatments, involving inevitable failures, are often required; and diagnostic procedures and interventions affect the marital and sexual relationship.

Davis and Fallowfield note that despite advances in medical care, many people remain dissatisfied with their interactions with health care professionals. While there has been increasing awareness among those responsible for medical education that doctors must take account of the psychosocial aspects of illness, and that medical students must receive training in communications skills, emotional care of the patient may be ignored (Davis and Fallowfield (1991a)). This matters, if only because patients' psychological well-being may impact upon their physical health. The 'expert model' described by Cunningham and Davis (1985), which is prevalent in health care, encourages clinicians to be seen by themselves and their patients as experts. This means they tend to focus on the diagnostic process, ignore 'silly' questions or irrelevant anxieties of the patient, and neglect the patient's (the non-expert's) point of view (Davis and Fallowfield (1991a)). Doctors and other health professionals do not necessarily behave in this way because they are uncaring, but they may appear uncaring to the patient.

Thus, infertility patients may feel that their emotional needs are not catered for by health care systems (Schmidt (1999)). Several commentators argue that provision of emotional care and psychological counselling should occur in tandem with the medical care of infertile people (eg Place, Laruelle, Kennof, Revelard and Englert (2002); Stotland (2002)). That is, all those involved in their care, including general practitioners, should have counselling skills that enable the provision of emotional support, since infertility involves 'the most heartfelt hopes and profound disappointments' (Stotland (2002:13)). This is important for reasons of humanity, apart from anything else (such as failure rate). One further problem with seeing infertility as a medical problem is that any kind of care for the infertile person or couple may cease once treatment has been unsuccessful. Yet a study following up women four to nine years after unsuccessful IVF treatment, found that those who had failed subsequently to have a family[14] continued to be distressed, dissatisfied and depressed. Thus we also find strong arguments for the continued provision of counselling after treatment has ended (Bryson, Sykes and Traub (2000); Kee, Jung and Lee (2000); Place *et al* (2002)).

There are, however, many other experiences in life which are recognised as being stressful yet for which counselling is neither recommended nor prescribed. What is there to suggest that infertility or surrogacy are different to other kinds of stressors?

Is Surrogacy Special?

There are a number of ways in which surrogacy might be seen as different from other conditions. Two are considered here: the suggestion that surrogacy is particularly emotionally challenging and the problem that patients may otherwise lack access to social support.

It has been noted in this volume and elsewhere that surrogacy is a potential emotional minefield. Appleton (chapter 13) notes major problems that might arise: the surrogate fails to become pregnant, the child is withheld by the surrogate, the child is born with a disability, and so on. In addition, the process is a lengthy one that involves many unusual and unpredictable events. From a psychological point of view, these are exactly the kinds of events likely to be stressful. Events which are outside our previous experiences, and which are unexpected, tend to be more stressful than those with which we are familiar (and therefore we know the demand they are likely to place on us and have already developed coping strategies for) and which we can predict (and therefore can engage in at least some anticipatory coping). All surrogacy participants, not just the intending parents, are facing considerable uncertainty. The stress may go beyond this too, for example, to intending grandparents. Participation in surrogacy is therefore emotionally and cognitively demanding.

---

[14] Thirty-one percent of the sample had either conceived spontaneously or adopted a child (Bryson, Sykes and Traub (2000)).

However, it is the social aspects of surrogacy—dealing with new and uncommon relationships—that may make it particularly challenging, even when it works. The psychological experience of surrogacy is profoundly influenced by its social context. It has been noted elsewhere that we have much more variation in family structure and routes to parenthood than is generally recognised (British Medical Association (1996)) and it has been convincingly argued that, from a psychological point of view, surrogacy does not seem to pose greater problems than those which society tolerates for conventional and assisted reproduction and parenting (Stratton (1990)). Much of what is psychologically difficult about surrogacy is a consequence of our social construction of family relationships and notions of how mothers and fathers 'ought to' behave.[15] Thus the key tasks in counselling relate to the management of social relationships and we might argue that surrogacy therefore goes a step beyond other infertility treatments in the challenges that it creates for those who take this route to parenthood. Participants may therefore *benefit* from help in facilitating their decision-making in a complex and demanding situation (eg see Reading (1991); Edelmann, chapter 10, this volume)) whether or not they *need* it.

While surrogacy is inextricably concerned with social relationships, those involved may experience stigma as a result of their infertility and so their access to social support may be limited (Dunkel-Schetter and Stanton (1991)). Thus we could argue that a key role for the counsellor in surrogacy is to provide this social support. Research in other areas of health care suggests better adaptation and psychological well-being where there is good social support.[16]

Patients tend to use partners and family for social support but this may not be a useful strategy in the long term. Surrogacy participants may experience social victimisation, and the negative social reactions (avoidance, rejection, jokes about sexual ability and so on) may add a further stress to the experience (Gonzalez (2000)). Family and friends may lack knowledge of surrogacy and therefore try to be supportive but say or do things that the patient doesn't find helpful. Support givers may also feel excessive demands placed upon them and be frustrated at having to provide support over a long period of time (Abbey, Andrews and Halman (1991)). In addition, spouses provide most support, and while they are likely to provide the best social support they are also the 'best' source of conflict (Abbey *et al* (1991)). A crucial role for the counsellor may therefore be to provide long-term social support for surrogacy participants.

A final reason for seeing infertility and surrogacy as especially deserving of counselling provision is the risk of failure. Infertility treatment is often ineffective and surrogacy is seen as a 'last resort'. The promotion of counselling as an essential component of care for infertility could be seen as an acknowledgement that, for many, medical treatment will fail and therefore some other provision

[15] As described by Appleton, these parental prescriptions can be set aside for us by children, whose notions of good parental behaviour may be different from those of adults.
[16] For example, cancer patients' adaptation is affected by social support, eg Bloom (1982).

is important. It is clearly not only infertility itself but also the issues associated with treatment which provide the argument for the provision of counselling. Reading (1991), for example, refers to the 'double-edged sword' of new medical treatments for infertility which are similar to surrogacy in offering 'the promise of success, but also (perpetuating) the struggle' (p 185). Thus, counselling should not be seen as a panacea, even if it is effective in relieving individual psychological distress, since it cannot alter the social context in which infertility and surrogacy are constituted as problematic.

These three aspects of the nature of surrogacy—that infertility is distressing, traditional medicine is uncaring and surrogacy is special—provide us with justification for the offer of counselling. Let us turn therefore to look at the way in which counselling is used.

4. THE USE OF COUNSELLING

Consistent with the BMA view, counselling is often a requirement for those undergoing IVF surrogacy (eg see Brinsden, chapter 7, this volume). Appleton (chapter 13, this volume) presents us with evidence that patients use counselling and also that some continue to do so long after the specific procedures have been completed, suggesting that it is valued by patients. However, there has tended to be an assumption that counselling is useful and little systematic evaluation of counselling for surrogacy. For example, Lukse and Vacc (1999) argue that participation in counselling should be offered 'for preventive and remedial purposes' (p 250). They propose that counsellors should, in addition to providing patients with the opportunity to explore their feelings, offer 'instruction on new adaptive behaviors for coping' with infertility and its treatment and teach 'more assertive communication styles.' They argue that 'on the basis of these findings . . . it is evident that the inclusion of counseling in infertility programs could benefit all participants involved and result in increased satisfaction with infertility treatment procedures' (p 250), yet this does not appear to be a logical conclusion. The common assumption that infertility patients will benefit from counselling makes it hard to judge the extent to which patients use and value counselling, or the extent to which it is effective, whatever its aim. In view of the absence of research into surrogacy counselling, this section considers its potential usefulness by drawing upon research into use of counselling in infertility clinics.

Although we lack evidence from surrogacy participants, we do have evidence from studies of infertility patients which shows that a proportion want counselling (eg Shaw, Johnston and Shaw (1988)). We also have some evidence that individuals or couples see counselling as an appropriate way of dealing with their distress (whether or not the distress is clinically or statistically significant). For example, in opinion surveys varying proportions of patients agree that counselling should be available, or ask for counselling, or take up offers of it (eg Daniluk (1988); Shaw *et al* (1988); Paulson, Haarmann, Salerno and Asmar

(1988); Baram, Tourtelot, Meuchler and Huang (1988)). Consistent with this, a small qualitative study of the experiences of 26 intended parents in surrogacy arrangements found that some couples believed counselling during the process of pregnancy would have helped them (Kleinpeter (2002)). It appears therefore that counselling is generally viewed positively by patients. However, in considering the implications of this finding, we must bear in mind two things. First, that counselling is invariably perceived positively by those who receive it and this kind of self-report cannot tell us much about effectiveness. Second, all intended parents, not just those intending parenthood through surrogacy, might feel the benefit of counselling. Neither necessarily imply that counselling is needed or should be provided.

It is interesting to note therefore that the proportion of those who take up counselling is much smaller than the proportion of those who say they would use it if it were available (eg see Pook, Röhrle, Tuschen-Caffier and Krause (2001))—only around 20 per cent of patients accept counselling (eg Boivin (1997)). There are a number of reasons proposed for this low uptake.[17] First, it may be because most patients are not distressed enough to feel the need of it (eg Boivin, Scanlan and Walker (1999); Pook *et al* (2001)). Thus, for example, they may obtain sufficient information from the nurse and enough social support from their spouse.

Secondly, patients may be concerned about the cost of counselling,[18] particularly if a clinic counsellor felt that referral for therapeutic counselling was necessary. Much regulated infertility treatment provision in the UK remains in the private sector and patients may be worried that counselling will be an additional cost, or will take up too much time. There is variation in the way that counselling is paid for in clinics: in some it is included in the cost of treatment. In others a first session is included (Bartlam and McLeod (2000)). Some clinics require patients to pay separately for all counselling. This could have fundamental implications for both the availability of counselling in practice (not just theory) and the counselling process.[19]

Thirdly, patients may misunderstand the purpose of counselling and the extent to which the counsellor is independent from the infertility team.[20] They may worry about being assessed by the counsellor and anxious that s/he will discover mental health problems that may make them ineligible for treatment. Or they may feel their problems are not great enough. Another misperception that they might have is that counselling is a dumping ground for those who have failed

---

[17]   There is some anecdotal evidence for these, but no systematic research indicating how widespread such views are.

[18]   Although the King's Fund Report proposed that it be presented as an integral part of treatment.

[19]   For example, a patient may want more in-depth counselling but be unable to afford it.

[20]   It is not uncommon for patients to misunderstand the purpose of counselling or for there to be a mismatch between patient and therapist expectations, eg see Michie, Marteau and Bobrow (1997); Benbenishty and Schul (1987). This may have implications for the success of counselling and psychotherapy.

treatment and patients may (reasonably) want to avoid seeing themselves in this position. A fourth reason why uptake of counselling is low is that couples may also prefer to depend upon social support from one another. Infertility is very personal and involves intimate aspects of the self, including the sexual, and many patients perceive infertility as a private matter (Menning (1980)). Infertility patients tend to use spouse and family for social support in preference to more formal sources of support (Boivin *et al* (1999)).[21] In addition, while social support from partners is associated with reduced emotional distress, social support outside the family is not always beneficial (McEwan, Costello and Taylor (1987)).

Generally therefore uptake of counselling is low. This is consistent with the evidence showing that there is considerable variation in the extent of distress experienced by people with fertility problems. Indeed, Boivin *et al* (1999) have found that the main reason for not taking up infertility counselling varied according to level of distress. Less distressed patients felt no need for counselling whereas more distressed patients had the kind of practical concerns outlined above—so they may have recognised the need for counselling, but did not obtain it, as a result of practical barriers.

These findings are hard to evaluate in relation to surrogacy, since in some surrogacy arrangements, counselling may be a required part of treatment. But low uptake may indicate that counselling is not what many patients want or need (eg Pook *et al* (2001)).

5. THE EFFECTIVENESS OF COUNSELLING

More than ten years ago, Shaw (1991) noted that the provision of counselling for people undergoing infertility treatment was a relative innovation[22] and therefore there was very little research examining the effectiveness of counselling or evaluating specific techniques or approaches. Ten years later, infertility counselling is clearly incorporated into the provision of regulated infertility treatment as a result of the HFE Act and HFEA Code of Practice, yet with respect to research into effectiveness the position has not greatly improved.

If we are examining the effectiveness of counselling, its purpose and strategies need to be clear. Is the aim to support people while they undergo the rigours of treatment, or to deal with feelings of loss when treatment fails? The answers may of course vary.[23] There is not much evidence that infertility-specific

---

[21] We should note the corollary to this is reduced access to social support for infertility patients, although one good social support relationship may well be sufficient to act as a stress buffer (eg see Cohen and Wills (1985)).

[22] A brief history of the development of infertility counselling in the UK can be found in Blyth and Hunt (1995).

[23] Note that historically, a therapist in an infertility clinic would have been there to uncover the unconscious conflicts in the woman which prevented conception, thereby enabling pregnancy. With the demise of the notion of a major role of psychogenesis in infertility, counselling is now focused on, in various ways, stress reduction (eg Read (1995)).

models of counselling are well-developed in the UK, with some counsellors advocating or describing the use of approaches which do not generally enjoy empirical support (eg stage models of grief/loss).[24] There are however some proposals from the literature about what might be appropriate in terms of strategies for infertility counselling. For example, Lukse and Vacc (1999) and also Newton *et al* (1999) propose various kinds of useful interventions such as cognitive restructuring.

It is hard to draw firm conclusions about the usefulness of infertility counselling in general, or surrogacy counselling in particular, without knowing whether such strategies are effective. There are a small number of studies of counselling which demonstrate no benefit. One randomised controlled trial (RCT) examined the adjustment of patients who received information about problems associated with infertility and coping strategies, versus those who did not. Contrary to expectations, patients who did not receive the information were better adjusted (Takefman, Brender, Boivin and Tulandi (1990)).[25] More specifically, Connolly, Edelmann, Bartlett, Cooke, Lenton and Pike (1993) compared distress in IVF patients who had three counselling sessions (or nothing) and found no greater reduction of distress in the counselled group. A further RCT, which evaluated the effect of a professionally-led support group, found no benefit (Steward, Boydell, McCarthy, Swerdlyk, Redmond and Cohrs (1992)).

There are few studies suggesting psychological benefit from counselling of infertility patients.[26] Two studies enabling patients' coping strategies found increased well-being, but it is interesting to note that those which show an effect are quite specifically concerned with coping (Tuschen-Caffier, Florin, Krause and Pook (1999); McQueeney, Stanton and Sigmon (1997)). Most recently, Terzioglu (2001) carried out a controlled study of the effects of counselling, including the provision of written information, for patients undergoing assisted reproductive techniques, which had positive results. The counselled group had significantly lower anxiety and depression, and significantly higher life satisfaction and pregnancy rates.

Thus there does not seem to be much evidence that counselling is effective in infertility. But we cannot conclude that counselling is ineffective—there is simply not enough research to draw this conclusion.

---

[24] These kinds of models appear still to be used by some counsellors and it has been noted elsewhere in other medical contexts that the use of this kind of model can potentially lead to difficulties, eg if using the model in a prescriptive way (Hale (1996)).

[25] A possible explanation for this is that the study did not take account of patients' coping strategies, and while some patients prefer to receive information, others find information receipt distressing. This draws our attention to the inadequacies of standard interventions, where patients might require more individual responses to their needs.

[26] There are a couple suggesting increased fertility, but these are not considered here.

6. BARRIERS TO COUNSELLING EFFECTIVENESS IN SURROGACY

The way that infertility counselling is currently offered may present a specific barrier to effectiveness. One of the significant problems in infertility counselling which also applies to surrogacy is the issue of confidentiality, especially when the counsellor is part of a multidisciplinary team—which issues must be kept confidential and which must be disclosed? There is an obvious ambiguity in the role of the counsellor at present and the extent of their independence is in question (eg see Bartlam and McLeod (2000); Bond (2000) and Appleton, chapter 13, this volume). This ambiguity can be seen in the clinics, where some counsellors are involved in the screening of patients (Bartlam and McLeod (2000)), and also in recommendations and regulations, such as those of the King's Fund Counselling Committee. For example, the committee believed that gamete donors should undergo psychological assessment of their suitability, and yet made a recommendation that '*Counselling* of donors should take place in order to assess their psychological suitability' (Recommendation 30, p 15).[27] Why this ambiguity has developed is less clear.

This ambiguity is a particular issue where counselling is required in IVF surrogacy. It seems paramount that if we believe it important that those undergoing regulated infertility treatment require some kind of psychological evaluation before being accepted for treatment, then this should be undertaken by a psychologist.[28] If we believe that patients should receive independent counselling then this should be provided by a counsellor. The two provisions should be separate. If they are not, we maintain a situation where patients (and indeed staff) may not be clear about the purpose of counselling, with the consequence that they may not take up the offer of counselling or, if they do, may be reluctant to disclose personal information to a counsellor. Williams and Irving (2002) draw attention to the singular nature of the 'universe of discourse' which counselling represents: a special place where patients can disclose very personal information (which would normally occur within a marital or parental relationship) and social norms can be contravened. Access to this safe 'universe' may be particularly beneficial for surrogacy participants whose access to other sources of social support may be limited. If patients retain anxiety that disclosure may not be safe—information might be shared with other staff in the clinic—the real benefit of counselling is diminished, thus compromising effectiveness.

---

[27] My emphasis. This suggests that the counsellor needs skills in psychological assessment, if their training does not already provide these. It is quite possible to be a chartered psychologist, for example, and not have skills in the kind of psychological assessment that seems to be required here.
[28] See Schwartz (chapter 11, this volume). Note however that Leiblum (2000) suggests that psychological evaluations 'are often viewed as perfunctory' and their stated purpose (to screen patients for psychological health) is at variance with their actual (tacit) function, which is 'to identify and discourage the ones who might cause trouble legally or have difficulty complying with the medical protocols' (p 80).

An issue which follows from this is whether, in surrogacy, there should be one counsellor who sees all those involved and therefore has a valuable overview of the arrangement and the relationships and interactions therein. Alternatively, models from other countries such as New Zealand (see Daniels, chapter 4, this volume) and Israel (see Schuz, chapter 3, this volume) might be deemed more appropriate, where each family group has their own counsellor. Both scenarios have advantages and there is not an international consensus upon the most appropriate model.

7. DO WE NEED COUNSELLING IN SURROGACY?

This brief discussion draws to our attention a number of issues. It seems that while some people who undergo infertility treatment want counselling, the proportion may be relatively small. This may be for practical reasons discussed above but might also be because many patients do not need counselling. The problems which are feared to make surrogacy stressful and complex (such as failure to hand over the baby to the intended parents) do not often occur (eg see Appleton, chapter 13 and Dodd, chapter 8, this volume; MacCallum and Golombok (2002)). Counselling may therefore not be the vital component of care it was once thought to be.

While figures on uptake suggest that most patients do not need counselling, some may have psychological problems and might benefit from some kind of intervention. Should this be counselling? Uptake may be low because counselling fails to supply what patients need. Boivin (1997) argues that the strong recommendations for counselling that we see in clinical literature do not fit well with uptake rates and therefore other ways of providing interventions for infertility patients, or other kinds of interventions, should be developed (Boivin *et al* (1999)). For example, techniques teaching coping strategies, as well as established techniques such as cognitive behaviour therapy, might be more appropriate for patients who are distressed (eg see Reading (1991); Hunt and Monach (1997)).

If we look at the provision of counselling we might also argue that counselling is not seen to be necessary. While those who participate in IVF surrogacy are seen to require counselling, partial surrogacy participants escape this requirement. Much of what has been discussed has been in the context of provision of counselling in an infertility clinic and therefore cannot apply to those who arrange surrogacy outside a medical setting. Many of these will have access to social support via a self-help group. The importance of this kind of support may be more helpful than that which a counsellor can provide and should not be ignored (see Dodd, chapter 8, this volume). It can provide confirmation that surrogacy, while unusual, is not pathological,[29] and participants might use the

---

[29]   ACCESS in Australia ask infertile people to tell their personal stories in public, to demonstrate the normality of the infertile (see Kirkman (2001)).

narratives of others to make sense of their own experience (eg see Kirkman (2001)).

8. CONCLUSIONS

The continued provision of counselling in the absence of evidence for its effectiveness might lead to the suspicion that it has some purpose other than to enable informed decision-making and alleviate distress. It is noted elsewhere that infertility, although presented as a medical problem with psychological consequences, is most importantly a social problem. Therefore counselling may be used in a particular way. Our society values fertility and the traditional family. One consequence of this is that we develop social structures to support these values, and we can see counselling in infertility as part of this. We might argue that, from this perspective, it does not matter whether it works, because what matters is that it is offered.

At present we can conclude that there may be barriers to counselling within the present system which could be removed, thereby creating an environment in which those who want counselling can get it. In order to improve the effectiveness of provision we urgently need to examine patients' perceptions and expectations of what is provided as well as evaluate counselling effectiveness.

In the history of infertility counselling there has tended to be an assumption about the effectiveness of counselling. Yet decisions about the kind of care and interventions that might be provided should, where possible, be based on research evidence rather than on the opinions of experts or untested assumptions about what is likely to be useful (eg see MacDonald (1998); Goss and Rose (2002)). Although there is fairly unanimous agreement within the literature that counselling is appropriate in surrogacy, there are no studies of its effectiveness. Counsellors from some perspectives (eg psychodynamic) might argue that use of established scientific techniques such as RCTs to evaluate counselling effectiveness is inappropriate. Evaluation may require a range of techniques therefore, such as qualitative methods and phenomenological approaches (eg MacLeod, Craufurd and Booth (2002)). Without this research, however, we cannot say whether surrogacy participants will indeed find safety in the multitude of counsellors.

REFERENCES

Abbey, A, Andrews, FM and Halman, LJ, 'The importance of social relationships for infertile couples' well-being' in AL Stanton and C Dunkel-Schetter (eds), *Infertility. Perspectives from Stress and Coping Research* (New York, Plenum Press, 1991).
Baram, D, Tourtelot, E, Meuchler, E and Huang, K, 'Psychosocial adjustment following unsuccessful in vitro fertilization' (1988) 9 *Journal of Psychosomatic Obstetrics and Gynaecology* 181.

Bartlam, B and McLeod, J, 'Infertility counselling: the ISSUE experience of setting up a telephone counselling service' (2000) 41 *Patient Education and Counselling* 313.

Benbenishty, R and Schul, Y, 'Client-therapist congruence of expectations over the course of therapy' (1987) 26 *British Journal of Clinical Psychology* 17.

Bloom, J, 'Social support, accommodation to stress and adjustment to breast cancer' (1982) 16 *Social Science and Medicine* 1329.

Blyth, E and Hunt, J, 'A history of infertility counselling in the United Kingdom' in SE Jennings (ed), *Infertility Counselling* (Oxford, Blackwell Science, 1995).

Boivin, J, 'Is there too much emphasis on psychosocial counselling for infertile patients?' (1997) 14 *Journal of Assisted Reproduction and Genetics* 184.

Boivin, J, Scanlan, LC and Walker, SM, 'Why are infertile patients not using psychosocial counselling?' (1999) 14 *Human Reproduction* 1384.

Bond, T, 'Issues of confidentiality in fertility counselling' (2000) 3 *Human Fertility* 259.

British Medical Association, *Changing Conceptions of Motherhood. The Practice of Surrogacy in Britain* (London, BMA Publications, 1996).

Bryson, CA, Sykes, DH and Traub, AI, 'In vitro fertilization: a long-term follow-up after treatment failure' (2000) 3 *Human Fertility* 214.

Cohen, S and Wills, TA, 'Stress, social support and the buffering hypothesis' (1985) 98 *Psychological Bulletin* 310.

Connolly, KJ, Edelmann, RJ, Bartlett, H, Cooke, ID, Lenton, E and Pike, S, 'An evaluation of counselling for couples undergoing treatment for in-vitro fertilization' (1993) 8 *Human Reproduction* 1332.

Cunningham, C and Davis, H, *Working with Parents: Frameworks for Collaboration* (Milton Keynes, Open University Press, 1985).

Daniluk, JC, 'Infertility: Intrapersonal and interpersonal impact' (1988) 49 *Fertility & Sterility* 982.

Davis, H and Fallowfield, L, 'Counselling and Communication in Health Care: The Current Situation' in H Davis and L Fallowfield (eds), *Counselling and Communication in Health Care* (Chichester, John Wiley and Sons, 1991a).

Davis, H and Fallowfield, L, 'Counselling Theory' in H Davis and L Fallowfield (eds), *Counselling and Communication in Health Care* (Chichester, John Wiley and Sons, 1991b).

Domar, AD, Zuttermeister, PC and Friedman, R, 'The psychological impact of infertility: a comparison with patients with other medical conditions' (1993) 14 *Journal of Psychosomatic Obstetrics and Gynaecology* 45.

Dunkel-Schetter, C and Lobel, M, 'Psychological reactions to infertility' in AL Stanton and C Dunkel-Schetter (eds), *Infertility. Perspectives from Stress and Coping Research* (New York, Plenum Press, 1991).

Dunkel-Schetter, C and Stanton, AL 'Psychological adjustment to infertility: future directions in research and application' in AL Stanton and C Dunkel-Schetter (eds), *Infertility. Perspectives from Stress and Coping Research* (New York, Plenum Press, 1991).

Engel, GL, 'The need for a new medical model: a challenge for biomedicine' (1977) 196 *Science* 129.

Freeman, EW, Boxer, AS, Rickels, K, Tureck, R and Mastroianni, L, 'Psychological evaluation and support in a program of in vitro fertilisation and embryo transfer' (1985) 43 *Fertility & Sterility* 48.

Glover, L, Abel, PD and Gannon, K, 'Male subfertility: is pregnancy the only issue?' (1998) 316 *British Medical Journal* 1405.

Gonzalez, LO, 'Infertility as a transformational process: a framework for psychothera-peutic support of infertile women' (2000) 21 *Issues in Mental Health Nursing* 619.

Goss, S and Rose, S, 'Evidence based practice: a guide for counsellors and psychothera-pists' (2002) 2 *Counselling and Psychotherapy Research* 147.

Hale, G, 'The social construction of grief' in N Cooper, C Stevenson and G Hale (eds), *Integrating Perspectives on Health* (Buckingham, Open University Press, 1996).

Human Fertilisation and Embryology Authority, *Code of Practice* (London, HFEA, 1993).

Hunt, J and Monach, J, 'Beyond the bereavement model: the significance of depression for infertility counselling' (1997) 12 *Human Reproduction* 188.

Jennings, SE, (ed), *Infertility Counselling* (Oxford, Blackwell Science, 1995).

Kee, BS, Jung, BJ and Lee, SH, 'A study on psychological strain in IVF patients' (2000) 17 *Journal of Assisted Reproduction and Genetics* 445.

Kentenich, H, 'Introduction' Section 1 in J Boivin, TC Appleton, P Baetens, J Baron, J Bitzer, E Corrigan, KR Daniels, J Darwish, D Guerra-Diaz, M Hammar, A McWhinnie, B Strauss, P Thorn, T Wischmann, H Kentenich and European Society of Human Reproduction and Embryology, 'Guidelines for counselling in infertility: Outline version' (2001) 16 *Human Reproduction* 1301 (full text also at http://www.eshre.com).

King's Fund Centre Counselling Committee, *Counselling for Regulated Infertility Treatments* (London, King's Fund Centre, 1991).

Kirkman, M, 'Thinking of something to say: public and private narratives of infertility' (2001) 22 *Health Care for Women International* 523.

Kleinpeter, CB, 'A model of parents' experiences with surrogacy arrangements' (2002) 77 *Fertility and Sterility* S14.

Leiblum, SR, 'Some thoughts and comments about screening candidates for third-party assisted reproduction: the clinician's dilemma' (2000) 15 *Sexual and Relationship Therapy* 79.

Lukse, MP and Vacc, NA, 'Grief, depression, and coping in women undergoing infertil-ity treatment' (1999) 93 *Obstetrics & Gynaecology* 245.

MacCallum, F and Golombok, S, 'Outcomes for families created through surrogacy' (2002) paper presented at ESHRE conference, Vienna, July 2002.

MacDonald, G, 'Promoting evidence based practice in child protection' (1998) 3 *Clinical Child Psychology and Psychiatry* 71.

MacLeod, R, Craufurd, D and Booth, K, 'Patients' Perceptions of What Makes Genetic Counselling Effective: An Interpretative Phenomenological Analysis' (2002) 7 *Journal of Health Psychology* 145.

Martin-Matthews, A and Matthews, R, 'Beyond the mechanics of infertility: perspec-tives on the social psychology of infertility and involuntary childlessness' (1986) 35 *Family Relations* 479.

McEwan, KL, Costello, CG and Taylor, PJ, 'Adjustment to infertility' (1987) 96 *Journal of Abnormal Psychology* 108.

McQueeney, DA, Stanton, AL and Sigmon, S, 'Efficacy of emotion-focused and problem-focused group therapies for women with fertility problems' (1997) 20 *Journal of Behavioural Medicine* 313.

Miall, CE, 'Perceptions of informal sanctioning and the stigma of involuntary childless-ness' (1985) 6 *Deviant Behaviour* 383.

Miall, CE, 'The stigma of involuntary childlessness' (1986) 33 *Social Problems* 268.

Menning, BE, 'The emotional needs of infertile couples' (1980) 34 *Fertility and Sterility* 313.

Michie, S, Marteau, TM and Bobrow, M, 'Genetic counselling: the psychological impact of meeting patients' expectations' (1997) 34 *Journal of Medical Genetics* 237.

Nachtigall, RD, Becker, G and Wozny, M, 'The effects of gender-specific diagnosis on men's and women's response to infertility' (1992) 57 *Fertility & Sterility* 113.

Nelson-Jones, R, *Practical Counselling Skills* (New York, Holt, Rinehart and Winston, 1983).

Newton, CR, Sherrard, W and Glavac, I, 'The Fertility Problem Inventory: measuring perceived infertility-related stress' (1999) 72 *Fertility & Sterility* 54.

Paulson, JD, Haarmann, BS, Salerno, RL and Asmar, P, 'An investigation of the relationship between emotional maladjustment and infertility' (1988) 49 *Fertility & Sterility* 258.

Patterson, C, *Theories of Counselling and Psychotherapy* (New York, Harper & Row, 1986).

Place, I, Laruelle, C, Kennof, B, Revelard, P and Englert, Y, 'Quel soutien les couples en traitement de FIV attendent-ils de l'equipe soignante? Enquete et pistes de reflexion' (2002) 30 *Gynécologie Obstétrique et Fertilité* 224.

Pook, M, Röhrle, B, Tuschen-Caffier, B and Krause, W, 'Why do infertile males use psychological couple counselling?' (2001) 42 *Patient Education and Counselling* 239.

Read, J, *Counselling for Fertility Problems* (London, Sage Publications, 1995).

Reading, AE, 'Psychological intervention and infertility' in AL Stanton and C Dunkel-Schetter (eds), *Infertility. Perspectives from Stress and Coping Research* (New York, Plenum Press, 1991).

Schmidt, L, 'Infertile couples' assessment of infertility treatment' (1999) 78 *Acta Obstetrica Gynecologica Scandinavica* 559.

Shaw, P, 'Infertility Counselling' in H Davis, and L Fallowfield (eds), *Counselling and Communication in Health Care* (Chichester, John Wiley and Sons, 1991).

Shaw, P, Johnston, M and Shaw, R, 'Counselling needs, emotional and relationship problems in couples awaiting IVF' (1988) 9 *Journal of Psychosomatic Obstetrics and Gynaecology* 171.

Stern, JE, Cramer, CP, Garrod, A and Green, RM, 'Attitudes on access to services at assisted reproductive technology clinics: comparisons of clinic policy' (2002) 77 *Fertility and Sterility* 537.

Steward, DE, Boydell, KM, McCarthy, K, Swerdlyk, S, Redmond, C and Cohrs, W, 'A prospective study of the effectiveness of brief professionally-led support groups for infertility patients' (1992) 22 *International Journal of Psychiatric Medicine* 173.

Stotland, NL, 'Psychiatric issues related to infertility, reproductive technologies, and abortion' (2002) 29 *Primary Care* 13.

Stratton, P, 'Does surrogacy raise major psychological problems?' (1990) *Bulletin of the Society for Reproductive and Infant Psychology* 11.

Strauss, B and Boivin, J, 'Counselling within infertility' Section 2:1 in J Boivin, TC Appleton, P Baetens, J Baron, J Bitzer, E Corrigan, KR Daniels, J Darwish, D Guerra-Diaz, M Hammar, A McWhinnie, B Strauss, P Thorn, T Wischmann, H Kentenich and European Society of Human Reproduction and Embryology, 'Guidelines for counselling in infertility: Outline version' (2001) 16 *Human Reproduction* 1301 (full text also at http://www.eshre.com).

Takefman, JE, Brender, W, Boivin, J and Tulandi, T, 'Sexual and emotional adjustment of couples undergoing infertility investigation and the effectiveness of preparatory information' (1990) 11 *Journal of Psychosomatic Obstetrics and Gynaecology* 275.

Terzioglu, F, 'Investigation into effectiveness of counseling on assisted reproductive techniques in Turkey' (2001) 22 *Journal of Psychosomatic Obstetrics and Gynaecology* 133.

Tuschen-Caffier, B, Florin, I, Krause, W and Pook, M, 'Cognitive behavioral therapy for idiopathic infertile couples' (1999) 68 *Psychotherapy and Psychosomatics* 15.

Williams, DI And Irving, JA, 'Universes of discourse: implications for counselling and psychotherapy' (2002) 30 *British Journal of Guidance and Counselling* 207.

13

Emotional Aspects of Surrogacy: A Case for Effective Counselling and Support

TIM APPLETON

1. INTRODUCTION[1]

FOR SOME COUPLES surrogacy may be the only hope. But it has been described as an 'emotional minefield' and a 'last resort' form of treatment for infertility. The UK Parliament provided for surrogacy in the Human Fertilisation and Embryology Act 1990 (HFE Act) but it remains an area that needs a considerable amount of heart searching and planning by all who are considering it—the emotional tangles can be difficult. Many clinics in the UK remain uncomfortable with surrogacy. Others feel it best to leave this treatment to those with a wide experience of surrogacy. Everybody needs to understand it and be comfortable with it before they should proceed with it. The British Medical Association[2] provided a useful and wise warning: 'The aggregate of foreseeable hazards should not be so great as to place unacceptable burdens on any of the parties, including the child.'

2. COUNSELLING EXPERIENCE

This chapter is based on the author's experience gained in counselling over 140 cases of surrogacy which have proceeded through all stages of evaluation—clinical, counselling, ethical (or review) committee. I shall use the term 'host' or 'surrogate' to refer to the surrogate and 'genetic couple' to refer to the commissioning couple. Not all those cases have necessarily resulted in treatment being commenced. All but three were by IVF (host) surrogacy where the surrogate was, or would be, carrying an embryo that had no genetic relationship to her—three required insemination of the donor because there was a genetic reason why it would have been dangerous to use the eggs from the genetic couple.

---

[1] In this chapter the term 'genetic couple' and 'commissioning couple' are used synonymously.

[2] British Medical Association—Report on Surrogacy (1990). The British Medical Association was originally opposed to surrogacy on ethical grounds. In its 1990 report it suggested that it was both ethical and legal and drew up comprehensive guidelines.

Tables 1–6 summarise the experience gained during counselling. The marital status of the hosts and genetic couples is shown in Table 2—most (88.4 per cent) of the genetic couples were married and others were in stable relationships. The marital status of the hosts was much more varied with only 53.1 per cent married and 14.3 per cent living together in a stable relationship.

The indications for surrogacy (Table 3) for more than half the half of the cases were lack of a lack of uterus in the genetic woman—42.6 per cent because of hysterectomy, 9.5 per cent congenital absence of the uterus and 2.4 per cent 'blind' uterus. The distress that such indications promote is very severe and the relief that surrogacy might enable that couple to have a child was very high.

The range of issues that needed to be addressed in counselling was extensive and sometimes occurred after the birth of a child (see Table 4). This points to the need for the availability of counselling to be continuing and suggests that counsellors should make a commitment for long-term availability.

The majority of cases were from three clinics—but 11 other clinics (who treated the occasional case of surrogacy) also referred patients for counselling:

Table 1. Relationships

	(n)	(%)
Mother	1	0.7
Stepmother	2	1.4
Daughter	3	2.1
Cousin	1	0.7
Niece	1	0.7
Sister in law	15	10.5
Sister	20	14.0
Friend	28	19.6
Initially unknown	72	50.3
Total	143	100.0

Table 2. Marital status

	H (n)	H (%)	G (n)	G (%)
Widowed	3	2.0	0	0
Separated	5	3.4	0	0
Stable living apart	3	2.0	0	0
Stable living together	21	14.3	17	11.6
Divorced	11	7.5	0	0
Single	26	17.7	0	0
Married	78	53.1	130	88.4
Total	147	100.0	147	100.0

Table 3. Indications

	(n)	(%)
Growth hormone deficiency	1	0.6
Blind uterus	4	2.4
RKH syndrome	1	0.6
Repeated fetal death	1	0.6
Repeated ectopic pregnancy	2	1.2
Repeated miscarriage	13	7.7
Repeated failure assisted reproductive technology	44	26.0
Congenital absence of uterus	16	9.5
Pregnancy contraindication	15	8.9
Hysterectomy	72	42.6
Total	169	100.0

14 couples sought counselling before contacting a clinic or seeking a host. Half of the cases involved a relationship where the host and the genetic couple were initially 'unknown'—all but ten were as a result of introduction from the support group COTS (Childlessness Overcome Through Surrogacy), one through the Surrogate Parenting Centre (an organisation based in central England which no longer exists), and eight as a result of potential surrogates contacting me directly. The parties took varying periods of time to get to know and trust each other—this period of time varied considerably but was never less than four months and was frequently as long as 18 months.

Clinics within the UK have different criteria for considering surrogacy—some do not consider surrogacy appropriate where persistent failure of fertility treatment is a suggested indication. Others have found that the 'uterine component' is often the reason for failure and surrogacy has been successful. In general the success rate of surrogacy is among the highest for fertility treatments—not surprising when the majority of cases are from women with no functional uterus who are still comparatively young.

Counselling has, with exception of two cases, always been within the home environment, usually in the home of the commissioning couple with all parties present—this has included cases with a European dimension (Table 6). Although a home study report is not required for a change in parentage under section 30 of the HFE Act[3] 1990, many guardians *ad litem*, whose task it is to report to the courts, have reported that their task has been easier when the

---

[3] The Human Fertilisation and Embryology Act 1990 received the Royal Assent in November 1990. Most aspects of the Act were implemented in August 1991 but it took several years before s 30 came into effect.

Table 4. Particular Issues encountered

Host withdrew—relationship breakdown	10
–failure too difficult	10
–moved abroad	1
–marriage breakdown (H[4])	1
–changed mind (host/and or couple)	6
Changed from IVF to DIY insemination	5
Death of genetic mother	1
Spontaneous pregnancy in genetic mother before treatment	3
Withdrawal over financial reasons	3
Foetal deaths/miscarriages	>30
Neonatal death	1
Abnormalities resulting in TOP	2
Marriage breakdown (G[5])	2
Host felt lack of support from genetic couple	2
Sense of vulnerability	
–host exerting pressure or making demands	1
–genetic mother exerting pressure	2

Table 5. Reasons for rejections

	(n)
Too many hazards	11
Welfare of the child	3
Age of genetic couple too high—high risk of abnormalities	20
Legal difficulties (change in parentage or adoption)	5
Medical risks in parenting	2
No proper indication	5
Host had no children	1
Total	47

Table 6. Cases with European Dimension

German	3
France	1
Iceland	1
Netherlands	2
Denmark	1
Italy	4
Total	12

[4] H = Host couple
[5] G = Genetic couple

counselling has been in the home. Several magistrates' clerks and one magistrate have expressed similar views. With the permission of the genetic couple and the host a report is presented to the clinic for their consideration or review by an independent committee. Some of the reasons why ethics committees or clinics have rejected cases are illustrated in Table 5 and it is quite clear that patients who have been rejected by one clinic have been accepted by another. The basis on which such decisions are made vary considerably between clinics: this is particularly true of the clinician's view of the point at which the risks of abnormalities due to maternal age becomes too great. It is the clinic and/or committee which makes the decision to accept or reject a case, but the decision should be based on advice from counsellors or psychologists. This frees the counsellor to provide further support whether the case continues, is rejected, results in the desired outcome, or fails. Counselling should strive to reach a conclusion with which the various parties can live, and which can enable them to move forward in their lives.

Counselling is a process that is intended to help all concerned identify and cope with the many issues they will have to face. At the same time, counsellors are also asked to make an assessment on whether the case should proceed. All clinics will use one or more counsellors to help them decide on whether to accept a surrogacy case—some reasons for rejections shown in Table 6. This dual role can present a dilemma for counsellors. Assessment doesn't always fit comfortably with counselling yet, at the same time, it is necessary to consider whether the parties concerned have the emotional stability and strengths to undertake such a complex tangle of emotional relationships. Surrogacy presents so many emotional, ethical and legal questions that counsellors asked to counsel in surrogacy should work alongside those with existing experience.

Many people consider that handing over the child would be the greatest difficulty/hazard but, in fact, it is rare. Of the 125 cases seen by the author, only one suggested that the host might find it difficult to part with the children (twin pregnancy) and, when the children were born, everything proceeded as planned. Comparatively high success rates in treatment have been reported by Brinsden, Appleton, Murray, Hussein, Akagbosu and Marcus (2000); and see Brinsden, chapter 7, this volume. But failure in treatment is always a deep disappointment in any fertility treatment—it is further heightened in surrogacy and is potentiated when the relationship is between members of the family or between friends of long standing—the strain in relationships has, in two cases known to the author, divided the families concerned. Failure is an obvious disappointment for the commissioning couple, but it can also be very difficult for the surrogate and her family. Whereas a host who was 'initially unknown' can express sorrow and walk away, a friend or relation cannot, and the guilt, in what she may perceive as failing her friend/sister, can be very real and long lasting. She may not have experienced reproductive 'failure' before –now it is thrust upon her and her family.

3. ISSUES DISCUSSED DURING COUNSELLING

There is now considerable research evidence that patients benefit from the provision of written information in addition to verbal communication (eg see Ley (1988)) and, similarly, issues to be discussed in counselling should be reinforced by the provision of supportive written material (eg Appleton (2001); Lenton (1995)). Such information may be particularly invaluable for couples considering surrogacy. They may take many months, and more commonly several years, before they are successful and it is easy to forget what was discussed such a long time ago. At the initial counselling the details may seem remote, and it is only when they become a reality that they become important again and easily forgotten. Typical issues that need to be addressed will include: the relationship of trust which must operate between all parties; attitudes of family, especially any future grandparents and other close relatives, as well as friends; support from others, such as the family doctor; the legal situation; handing the child to the commissioning couple; registration of the birth; provision and recording of expenses; possible failure of treatment.

In addition, some issues require particular attention: the potential effects of surrogacy on others; motivations; the possibility of abnormalities or other difficulties during pregnancy; and the issue of telling the child. All those involved need to be aware of the potential effect of surrogacy on their own lives, but must also consider the view of families, friends and work colleagues. The surrogate will eventually be obviously pregnant, but after the birth where is the child? Has there been a stillbirth, or a miscarriage? The genetic mother also now has a child but there has been no sign of a pregnancy. Where did the baby come from? All of those involved in surrogacy will need to consider how to deal with these kinds of questions that others are likely to raise and they will also need to feel able to be honest with those relations, friends and colleagues who need to know. Counselling has to help people to be open and honest about their actions and the consequences of those actions for themselves, existing children and any which come about as a result of surrogacy. There will need to be a level of honesty with family friends and neighbours. That is not always an easy thing to do but two comments by patients made during counselling are worth repeating: 'You only have to tell the truth once!', and 'the truth can be very disarming!'

Motives for surrogacy are also an important issue. Most hosts say they enjoy being pregnant: some even that they enjoy giving birth. Many have experienced the pain of childlessness in friends or family and want to share their joy in having a family with others—many also donate eggs. In a survey of 20 hosts I asked the question 'How many children do you have and how many pregnancies have you had?' In 40 per cent there were more pregnancies than births—all had had termination of pregnancy(ies) as teenagers. I believe that, consciously or unconsciously, the need to be involved with surrogacy can sometimes be compensation for some unhappy earlier event, and that wanting to do something special for someone else might help put things right. But occasionally motives are not so overtly emotional. In three cases the host withdrew after a frank discussion over the question of expenses—an indication that their motive was a financial one.

Inevitably with pregnancy comes the possibility of complications during the pregnancy, or postnatal depression, and the possibility of abnormalities being detected in the foetus. All parties need to have addressed the question of abnormalities and how they might react if it does occur—they need to be prepared.

After the birth, the surrogate mother may or may not continue in contact with the family. Those within the family will usually keep close contact. Some of the 'initially unknown' (see Table 1) maintain contact while others drift apart. Alongside this decision comes the issue of telling the child about its origins. The child has the right, at age 18, to have an original birth certificate and therefore know who their birth mother was. All couples counselled by the author have been positive in wanting to tell the child about the miracle that made it possible for them to be there. One boy of four, when asked if he knew who gave birth to him, replied very simply 'Aunty Mary of course, mummy's tummy was broken and couldn't make babies.' Aunty Mary was clearly Aunty Mary and Mummy was the genetic mother—what could be simpler? His face told the story. Later on more difficult questions would be asked, but this would take place on the foundation of this simple happy story.

Counselling is made available for as long as any of the parties need it, including future children, and I have always stressed that they must all feel free to talk on the phone as treatment progresses or, for that matter, ceases. Few weeks go by without several calls from those involved in surrogacy. Having a booklet which we have previously used together by the phone helps me as a counsellor—help can often be given again by referring to the relevant page.

4. CHILDREN

In the UK we are bound by regulations and by law to take the 'welfare of the child' into account.[6] In surrogacy this means considering the welfare of any existing children of the genetic or the host couple, as well as any children resulting from the surrogacy. It is important that counselling[7] takes this into account and considers how, for example, the children of the host mother, will react.[8]

The reaction from most of the children of the host mother was very supportive. One girl of four said: 'You are so kind mummy, now you can do it for everyone who doesn't have children!' A seven-year-old boy made it quite clear that it was OK provided his mother promised not to keep the baby—he was the

---

[6] The Guidelines of the Human Fertilisation and Embryology Authority require clinics to take into account the welfare of any existing or future children.

[7] Ethics committees should also take this into account.

[8] In the series of cases upon which this chapter is based, only two host mothers were single and without children (see also Table 2).

youngest in the family and certainly didn't want to share his toys. One 11-year-old girl couldn't understand how IVF surrogacy could work. I prepared a simple story with illustrations for her: she asked to consider this on her own and, after reading this account, said she now understood and 'yes it was fine.' But another three-year-old boy (with a three-month-old sister) was quite adamant: 'You don't give away babies—that is wrong!' Clearly that case could not go ahead until that matter had been resolved. Many couples have gained comfort and strength from the natural way that their children responded to the pregnancy. On several occasions either the host or the genetic couple have rung to tell me how much the children had helped by simple but understanding remarks: 'I felt your baby move today'—'Julie's baby is kicking again mummy.'

5. COMPLEX ISSUES AND MANY EMOTIONS

The complexity of the issues and uncertainties which need to be addressed have been discussed in this chapter and are illustrated in the summary Tables 1–6. Surrogacy puts human nature under pressure because it creates uncertainties in relationships—those uncertainties go far wider than the commissioning mother and father who are desperately seeking a child. It raises fundamental questions about how other people's lives are going to be affected by a surrogacy arrangement. There is a wide variation in the levels of counselling and support in any fertility treatment and in particular surrogacy.[9] There are also some fundamental differences in both the levels of counselling offered in surrogacy and decisions made by some clinics and ethics committees. There is however clear research evidence that infertility counselling can be effective, for example, in improving life satisfaction and reducing anxiety and depression (eg Terzioglu (2001)). While this kind of evidence is not yet available from research on surrogacy in the UK, the complexity of issues involved indicates that, aside from the requirements of legislation,[10] the provision of suitable counselling to those involved in surrogacy is a compassionate and humane response.

Mr Justice Latey,[11] in passing judgment in an early surrogacy case in the Family Division of the High Court, pointed to the emotional complexities of surrogacy arrangements when he said:

One cannot sit in these courts and hear the multitude of professionals and others without knowing well the depth of longing in couples, devoted to each other, who cannot have a child through no fault of their own. But before they go down that path they should know fully, what it may entail. It is no primrose path.

[9] For example, see Jennings (1995); Van den Akker (1998, 1999).
[10] For example, the HFEA Code of Practice requires that those involved in treatment which uses donated gametes (as surrogacy, technically, does) must have an opportunity to receive counselling.
[11] Re: Adoption Application AA212/86 (Adoption Payment) [1987] 2 FLR 291

REFERENCES

Appleton, T, 'Surrogacy' (2001) 11 *Current Obstetrics and Gynaecology* 256.

Brinsden, PR, Appleton, TC, Murray, E, Hussein, M, Akagbosu, F and Marcus, SF, 'Treatment by *in vitro* fertilisation with surrogacy: experience of one British centre' (2000) 320 *British Medical Journal* 924.

British Medical Association, *Report on Surrogacy* (London, BMA, 1990).

—— *Changing Conceptions of Motherhood* (London, BMA, 1996).

Jennings, SE (ed), *Infertility Counselling* (Oxford, Blackwell Science, 1995).

Lenton, EA, 'Who should give fertility counselling?' in SE Jennings (ed), *Infertility Counselling* (Oxford, Blackwell Science, 1995).

Ley, P, *Communicating with Patients: Improving Communication, Satisfaction and Compliance* (London, Croom Helm, 1988).

Terzioglu, F, 'Investigation into effectiveness of counseling on assisted reproductive techniques in Turkey' (2001) 22 *Journal of Psychosomatic Obstetrics and Gynaecology* 133.

Van den Akker, OBA, 'The function and responsibilities of organisations dealing with surrogate motherhood in the UK' (1998) 1 *Human Fertility* 10.

—— 'Organisational selection and assessment of women entering a surrogacy arrangement in the UK' (1999) 14 *Human Reproduction* 262.

14

The Gift of Life: Surrogate Motherhood, Gamete Donation and Constructions of Altruism[1]

HELÉNA RAGONÉ

Blessed are those who can give without remembering, and take without forgetting.

Princess Elizabeth Asquith Bibesco

IN THE ANTHROPOLOGICAL literature, one of the first systematic and comparative studies on the cultural significance of gift giving was Mauss's *The Gift*. As Mauss so eloquently said:

> Things have values which are emotional as well as material; indeed in some cases the values are entirely emotional (Mauss (1967:63)).

Mauss's assessment of gifts is not dissimilar to that of Levi Strauss who has also written:

> Goods are not only economic commodities but vehicles and instruments for realities of another order: influence, power, sympathy, status, emotion . . . (Levi Strauss (1965:262)).

In American culture, a culture in which commercialisation penetrates nearly all domains, one cannot help but be struck by the widely varied uses to which the 'gift of life' theme has been applied. The cultural significance of the gift theme resides in its ability to provide both a literal and a symbolic counterpoint to the increasing commodification of modern life. While many anthropologists have studied the significance of the gift, it is interesting that the gift for the most part remains understudied in industrial capitalist society (Carrier (1990)). Traditionally, in American culture, the gift's application has been confined (almost entirely) to the arenas of blood donation and organ donation where it has been 'lavishly applied' (Fox and Swazey (1992:44)). The inclusion of organ donation and blood donation under the rubric of 'gift' may be an attempt by

[1] This chapter was originally published in *Transformative Motherhood: On Giving and Getting in a Consumer Culture* (1999) Linda Layne (ed), New York: New York University Press and is reproduced here by kind permission of the publisher.

210   *Heléna Ragoné*

participants and by society to retard, at least symbolically, the trend towards the commodification of life.[2]

My own interest in the cultural resonance of the gift of life theme came about somewhat circuitously as I was conducting research on surrogate motherhood. During the course of that research, I discovered that surrogate mothers often conceptualise the child/children they are producing for commissioning couples as a 'gift of life' and/or as 'gifts'. This they do in spite of the fact that they are compensated for their reproductive act.

In 'traditional surrogacy', or 'artificial insemination surrogacy', the surrogate contributes an ovum and is artificially inseminated with the sperm of the commissioning father. In such cases both surrogates and commissioning couples routinely refer to the children born of these arrangements as gifts. This practice can be understood as related to EuroAmerican kinship ideology, in particular its emphasis upon the importance of biogenetic relatedness. Perhaps not surprisingly, I have also discovered that with gestational surrogacy, where the surrogate gestates the couple's embryos, noticeably less 'gifting language' is utilised to describe these children, an issue that I will address in greater depth in a later section of this chapter.

The gift of life theme, when applied to traditional surrogate motherhood, reveals the ways in which issues such as work, indebtedness, pricelessness, family, and kinship are being reconfigured. In this chapter, I would like to explore the multivariant meanings attaching to the gift theme in the context of traditional surrogacy, gestational surrogacy and gamete (ova and sperm) donation. I would also like to explore how the gift of life theme serves as powerful reinforcement for EuroAmerican kinship ideology and speaks (at least in the context of traditional surrogacy) to the inviolability of the blood tie.

1. METHODS

When I began my research on surrogate motherhood in 1988, gestational surrogacy was a relatively uncommon procedure (the first such case occurred in

---

[2] However, it is important to bear in mind that in spite of the heavy symbolic load associated with the gift of life 35% of all blood donors in the United States were paid for their donation until 1964, and this practice which attracts 'alcoholics and other unfortunates who return frequently to blood banks' (Titmuss (1971:114)). Remuneration is a critically important issue since many blood donors are aware that 'they will be deprived of money if they answer yes to questions about jaundice, malaria, and other infectious diseases' (Titmuss (1971:114)). It is clear that the practice has affected the safety of our blood supply; and experts have concluded that blood received from non-commercial banks is categorically safer than blood obtained from commercial banks (Titmuss (1971:152)). Profit also permeates the field of organ donation and it has resulted in the argument that a donor's family is entitled to compensation (for their loss, act of generosity, and because all the other parties involved benefit, eg, the recipient, transplantation teams, hospitals, and so on) a position to which I have expressed strong opposition (Ragoné (1996b)).

1987). Surrogate mother arrangements required that the surrogate contribute an ovum to the creation of the child and be inseminated with the intending father's semen. However, during the six-year period that followed, the practice of gestational surrogacy increased in the United States at a rather remarkable rate, from less than five per cent of all surrogate arrangements to approximately 50 per cent as of 1994 (Ragoné (1994; 1998)). In gestational surrogacy, the surrogate does not contribute an ovum, but instead 'gestates' a couple's embryo(s); for this reason, gestational surrogates in general tend to begin the process with different concerns and expectations than traditional surrogates. But not all gestational surrogate arrangements involve the couple's embryos; numerous cases involve the use of donor ova and the intending father's semen. The question is why couples who use donor ova pursue gestational surrogacy when traditional surrogacy can provide them with the same degree of biogenetic linkage/relatedness to the child and has a higher likelihood of success. It also costs significantly less. Typically two reasons are cited by the largest surrogate mother programme, which is now also the largest ovum donation programme in the United States, with over 300 screened donors on file. The primary reason is consumer choice, specifically that couples who choose the donor ova/gestational surrogacy route rather than traditional surrogacy have a significantly greater number of ovum donors to choose from than they have traditional surrogates. But of equal importance is that when commissioning couples choose donor ova/gestational surrogacy they are severing the surrogates' genetic link to and/or claim to the child, whereas with traditional surrogacy the adoptive mother must emphasise the importance of nurturance and social parenthood, while the surrogate de-emphasises her biogenetic tie to the child (Ragoné (1994; 1996a)).

This chapter draws on my research on 'traditional' surrogacy conducted from 1988 to 1994, which involved interviews with 28 surrogates and 17 individual members of contracting couples as well as interviews with programme directors and programme staff. I also engaged in participant observation of numerous programme activities such as staff meetings and intake interviews at three 'open' surrogate programmes, that is, programmes in which surrogates and couples meet in person and select each other, then interact closely throughout the pregnancy.

Likewise, my more recent research on gestational surrogacy has involved observation of numerous consultations between programme staff, intending couples, and prospective surrogate mothers in addition to formal interviews with twenty-six gestational surrogates, five ovum donors, and twelve individuals who had enlisted the services of gestational surrogates. Some of these individuals are/were clients at the largest surrogate mother and ovum donation programme in the world. I also intentionally included couples who had advertised for and screened their own gestational surrogates rather than contracting with a programme in order to compare their experiences against those of couples enrolled in programmes.

In my research on both 'traditional' and 'gestational' surrogacy I have attempted, whenever possible, to select individuals from the various phases of the gestational surrogacy and ovum donation process, for example, individuals who have not yet been matched, who are newly matched and who are attempting 'to get pregnant', who have confirmed pregnancies, who have recently given birth, as well as individuals for whom several years have elapsed since the birth of their child in order to assess what, if any, shifts individuals might experience as they go through the process.

2. REMUNERATING THE GIFT

Thus far, the image of surrogate mothers has been shaped principally by media, legal, and scholarly portrayals of surrogates either as motivated principally by monetary gain or as unwitting, altruistic victims of the patriarchy. This tendency to cast surrogates' motivations into either/or, often antagonistic categories may reveal a great deal more about EuroAmerican culture than it does about surrogacy itself.

Surrogates readily acknowledge that remuneration was one of their initial considerations, although they consistently deny that it was their primary motivation (and nearly all surrogates state—repeatedly—that the importance of remuneration decreased over time).[3] When questioned about remuneration, surrogates consistently protest that no one would become a surrogate for the money alone because, they reason, it simply 'isn't enough'. Many surrogate programme directors report that surrogates telephone their programmes unaware that payment is involved, a phenomenon that would seem to reinforce surrogates' claims that remuneration is not their primary motivation. As Jan Sutton, founder and spokeswoman for a group of surrogates in favour of surrogacy, stated in her testimony before an information-gathering committee to the California state legislature, 'My organisation and its members would all still be surrogates if no payment were involved,' a sentiment not unrepresentative of those expressed by the many surrogates I have interviewed over the years.[4] Interestingly enough, after Sutton had informed the committee of that fact, several members of the panel who had previously voiced their opposition to surrogacy in its commercial form began to express praise for Sutton, indicating that her testimony had altered their opinion of surrogacy. In direct response to her testimony, the committee began instead to discuss a proposal to ban commercial surrogacy but to allow for the practice of non-commercial surrogacy (in which a surrogate is barred from receiving financial compensation, although the

---

[3] The version frequently put forth by surrogate mother programmes is that the importance of money decreases as the pregnancy progresses.

[4] Since 1988 I have formally interviewed 30 traditional surrogates and 25 gestational surrogates, and I have also had countless informal conversations with surrogates.

physicians and lawyers involved are allowed their usual compensation for services rendered, as in organ donation). This perceptual shift on the part of committee members can be understood to result from an overriding cultural imperative that motherhood, reproduction and family be squarely situated in a non-commercial sphere, a position which also explains why these same committee members saw no inconsistency in permitting 'professionals,' ie physicians and attorneys, to receive compensation for services rendered.

The following are typical surrogate responses to questions about how payment influenced their decision to become a surrogate:

> *It sounded so interesting and fun. The money wasn't enough to be pregnant for nine months*

and:

> *I'm not doing it for the money. Take the money. That wouldn't stop me. It wouldn't stop the majority.*

and again:

> *What's $10,000 bucks? You can't even buy a car . . . . Money wasn't important. I possibly would have done it just for expenses, especially for the people I did it for. My father would have given me the money not to do it.*

Surrogates' devaluation of payment as insufficient to compensate for 'nine months of pregnancy' can be understood to fulfil two functions. It is, of course, representative of the cultural belief that children are 'priceless' (Zelizer (1985)) and in this sense, surrogates are merely reiterating a widely-held belief when they devalue the remuneration they receive. But their devaluation also serves as evidence that the perfect gift is one that is priceless, one that transcends 'material expression and economic worth' and that renders the material immaterial (Carrier (1990:23)).[5]

Interestingly enough, when the largest surrogate mother programme changed its newspaper advertisements from 'Help an Infertile Couple' to 'Give the Gift of Life,' the new formula attracted the type of woman the programme wished to attract and the programme received a considerably larger volume of response from suitable prospective surrogates.[6] The advertisement struck a chord with surrogates because it acknowledged that their act is one that cannot be compensated for monetarily; instead, it cast surrogacy in a poignant and life-affirming

---

[5] This tendency to de-emphasise remuneration has also been found among Norwegian teenage baby-sitters (known as *passepike*, or girls who 'look after' children). Marianne Gullestad reports that even though remuneration is important to these girls, they share in a cultural ideology that devalues the importance of payment for such a service. For this reason, when asked, the girls say that 'they do not look after children for the sake of money, but because they are fond of children (*er glad I barn*)' (Gullestad (1992:119)).

[6] The programme had changed its advertising copy due to the fact that the newspaper refused to print an advertisement that explicitly sought a woman to serve as a surrogate. This policy has since changed.

light, more clearly locating it in the gift economy. The above example reveals the highly gendered nature of the gift, falling as it does unequivocally within the female domain be it surrogates, and ovum donors, but interestingly enough not with sperm donors.

Surrogates' dismissal of the importance of remuneration also serves an underlying function, as reflected in the following quotes. Here, a surrogate who had earlier dismissed the importance of money, offers a more revealing account of her decision to become a surrogate mother:

> *I wanted to do the ultimate thing for somebody, to give them the ultimate gift. Nobody can beat that, nobody can do anything nicer for them.*

Another surrogate, who also used the word 'ultimate', discussed her feelings about surrogacy in a similar way:

> *It's a gift of love. I have always been a really giving person, and it's the ultimate way to give. I've always had babies so easily. It's the ultimate gift of love.*

Another surrogate echoed the gift theme:

> *They [the couple] consider it [the baby] a gift and I consider it a gift.*

And here, a surrogate who initially opposed AI surrogacy explained her decision in this way:

> *I wasn't using those eggs every month and I realized they didn't mean as much to me as I thought they did. It was like giving an extra gift to the couple, one extra part of me.*

We can surmise that when this surrogate used the word 'extra' to describe the gift, she did so as a means to underscore the extraordinary nature of the gift. Another surrogate critiqued the very notion of associating the child with a dollar value when she said: 'You can't put a price on a baby's life.'

The gift formulation holds particular appeal for surrogates because it reinforces the idea that having a child for someone is an act that cannot be compensated; the gift of life narrative is further enhanced by some surrogates to embrace the near-sacrifice of their own lives in child birth.[7] Thus, when surrogates define the children they are reproducing for couples as 'gifts', they are tacitly suggesting that no amount of money would ever provide sufficient compensation. Distributive justice (Swartz (1967)) cannot be attained in the traditional surrogacy arrangement. The child as a gift clearly approaches the highest ideals of gift giving since it fulfils the criteria for the perfect gift.

For EuroAmericans it is 'gift relations' rather than economic exchanges that characterise the family (Carrier (1990:2)). Thus, when surrogates minimise or dismiss the importance of money, they are on the one hand reiterating cultural

---

[7] Surrogates frequently discuss their feelings concerning difficult pregnancies and deliveries in terms that suggest 'heroic suffering' and 'heroism' (Ragoné (1994; 1996a)).

beliefs about the pricelessness of children, and they are on the other hand suggesting that the exchange of a child for money is not a relationship of reciprocity but of kinship.

With traditional surrogacy, as with adoption (Modell (1999)) the relationship is one of indebtedness. Even though surrogates are discouraged from thinking of their relationship to the couple as a permanent one, surrogates recognise that they are creating a state of enduring solidarity between themselves and their couples. This belief complicates the severing of that relationship once the child has been born even though the surrogate knows in advance that the surrogate–couple relationship is structured to be impermanent.

Surrogates' framing of the equation as one in which a gift is given thus serves as a reminder to their couples that one of the symbolic functions of money, namely, the 'removal of the personal element from human relationships through its indifferent and objective nature' (Simmel (1978:297)), may be insufficient to erase certain relationships, and that the relational element may continue to surface despite the monetary exchange.

Of all the surrogates' motivations, remuneration is the most problematic. On a symbolic level, of course, remuneration detracts from the idealised cultural image of women/mothers as selfless, nurturant and altruistic, an image that surrogates do not wish to lose; in addition, if surrogates were to acknowledge the money as a fair and equal exchange or sufficient compensation for their reproductive work, they would lose the sense that theirs is a gift that cannot be compensated for monetarily.

In Britain, where commercial surrogacy was outlawed in 1985 with the passage of the Surrogacy Arrangements Bill (Wolfram (1987:189)) the situation has been framed in moral terms:

> *The symbol of the 'pure' surrogate who creates a child for love was pitted against the symbol of the 'wicked' surrogate who prostitutes her maternity* (Cannell (1990:683)).

The idea of 'pure' versus 'wicked' surrogacy and, correspondingly, good versus bad surrogates, is predicated on the belief that altruism precludes remuneration. The overwhelming acceptance of the idea of unpaid or non-commercial surrogacy (both in the United States and abroad) can be attributed to the fact that it 'duplicates maternity in culturally the most self-less manner' (Strathern (1991:31)). But perhaps even more important, the rejection of paid or commercial surrogacy may also result from a cultural resistance to conflating the symbolic value of the family with the world of work to which it has long been held in opposition. Drawing together those two spheres is the agency of the surrogate who bridges them through her reproductive work. In the *Baby M* case, for example, the most 'decisive issue' was one of 'payment to the surrogate' (Hull (1990b:155)). As David Schneider so succinctly described the equation, 'what is done is done for love, not for money. And it is love, of course, that money can't buy' (Schneider (1968:45)).

This truth is reflected in one father's remarks about his surrogate:

I realize now that what Jane [the surrogate] gave was a part of herself; that's fairly profound.

Thus, the child serves as a point of connection between the surrogate and the father in the same way that it does between the wife and husband. When Swartz pointed out in 1967 that 'the gift imposes an identity upon the giver as well as the receiver' (Swartz (1967:2)) he could not have envisioned the literalisation of this idea through surrogacy. By acknowledging that the surrogate child is a gift, the couple accepts a permanent state of indebtedness to their surrogate. The quote cited above, in which the father refers to the surrogate giving part of herself, also reflects the enduring quality of the blood tie, a relationship that can never be severed in American kinship ideology. This is because, as Schneider noted, blood is 'culturally defined as being an objective fact of nature' (Schneider (1968:24)). It is therefore impossible for a person to have an ex-blood relative, eg, an ex-mother, ex-father, or ex-sibling. In addition to the fact that blood is understood to be 'a shared bodily substance', there is also the 'connection between ideas of blood . . . and ideas of genes' (Strathern and Franklin (1993:20)). Fathers cannot help but acknowledge this connection and comment upon it, and neither can surrogates and adoptive mothers.

Because all gift giving creates a degree of gratitude, when couples bestow additional gifts upon their surrogates (as they do from the moment the pregnancy is confirmed, to the moment the child is born and even after), they, like their surrogate, enter into a gift economy. Gifts are given with such regularity and predictability by couples to their surrogates (and to her children as well) that such acts have become encouraged by surrogate programmes. However, the actual birth of the child and the surrogate's relinquishment of the child to the couple is viewed by all participants as the embodiment of the penultimate act of giving/gifting. It is therefore of interest that couples routinely bestow upon their surrogates gifts of jewellery that prominently feature the child's birthstone. Much as in the case of pregnancy loss explored by Layne (2000) the gift of such jewellery simultaneously symbolises the 'preciousness' of the child and the enduring relationship between mother and child even in the face of a lifelong physical separation (see also Wozniak (1999)). Worn on the surrogate's body, the jewellery symbolises and validates the special intimate bodily connection between surrogate and child and represents an acknowledgement that gifts such as vacations are mere tokens of appreciation and cannot repay the extraordinary generosity of the surrogate. In this way, gifts of precious and semi-precious stones stress the permanent connection that prevails between surrogates and child and bespeak the inviolability of the blood tie in EuroAmerican kinship ideology.

Of critical importance for surrogates is their ability to describe the child as a gift, a description that serves as validation for their reproductive work. But perhaps of even greater importance, the gift formulation acknowledges their unique contribution toward the creation of a family, an act that cannot (and in the view of many participants, should not) be reduced to mere commodification. This perspective also prevails in the world of adoption, where language utilised by participants emphasises the 'gift, giving, and generosity' and ultimately softens the idea that adoption creates a 'market for babies' (Modell (1999)).

But surrogates and couples also recognise, at least tacitly, that true distributive justice cannot be achieved since such justice is only possible in pure economic exchanges. It does not occur in social exchanges that involve relationships (Swartz (1967:8)), and certainly not in those that involve the gift of life. As Fox and Swazey pointed out in their research on organ donation, it is not unusual for organ recipients to feel a 'sense of obligation' due to the extraordinary nature of the gift proffered. Like an organ, a child is a gift exchange that is 'inherently unreciprocal' since it does not have a 'physical or symbolic equivalent' (Fox and Swazey (1992:40)).

3. COMMODIFYING GESTATIONAL SURROGACY

The children produced through traditional surrogacy arrangements tend to be viewed by all parties through the gift lens, a formulation that explicitly rests upon the shared acknowledgement that what the surrogate gives is literally a part of herself.[8] However, a shift has occurred as gestational surrogacy supersedes traditional (which involves either the implantation of the couple's embryos or donor ova and husband's/partner's semen into a gestational surrogate), specifically, this gift rhetoric is notably underused. One probable explanation is the influence of the hegemonic biogenetic model of kinship. The explicit articulation of relatedness reveals the tendency on the part of commissioning couples to view themselves as 'ending up with exactly the same child that they would have ended up if it were not for the wife/woman's inability to carry a pregnancy to term,' as one resident psychologist explained to me.

Her assessment demonstrates that with gestational surrogacy there is a tendency, perhaps a logical one, for couples to place less emphasis upon the role and/or contribution of their surrogate and more emphasis on the outcome. Because she does not contribute an ovum, or a 'piece of herself,' the surrogate's role is increasingly seen by some participants as that of 'vessel' or 'vehicle',[9] as reflected in couples' language. For example, one 36-year -old father offered the following assessment concerning the role of his gestational surrogate and her relationship to him, his wife, and the child:

---

[8] Interestingly enough, in other contexts, all parties intentionally de-emphasise this contribution (Ragoné (1994, 1996a)).

[9] Tentatively, I would suggest that this appears to be especially true when couples have located their gestational surrogate independently rather than through a programme since they do not receive any guidance about appropriate behaviour.

*I don't think about it much. She was **an oven** . . . . she doesn't see herself as the mother. We don't see her as the mother and that's the way it is* [emphasis added].[10]

With gestational surrogacy, commissioning couples place less emphasis on the children as gifts and greater emphasis on the processural component of reproduction than do AI couples. When I discussed my theory about the absence of gift rhetoric with the director of the largest surrogate mother programme, she confirmed my observations. She had observed, for example, that IVF (gestational) surrogacy couples, are in her experience, 'more difficult' and 'less kind at the birth and soon after the birth' to their surrogates. Typically, for example, surrogates want their own children to see and/or hold the child/children shortly after they are born. This practice is intended to provide the surrogate's children (and the surrogates themselves) with closure, and it is encouraged by the programme and its psychologists. And here again, this director observed that the only time 'I have had couples run out of a hospital (with the baby) is IVF couples. AI couples will stay around for ten days (after the birth of the child and her/his discharge from the hospital).' AI couples, on the other hand, the director noted, 'want the (surrogate's) children to hold the babies.' By way of explanation, many IVF couples say that they do not want anyone holding their children because they fear contagion or 'germs'. But the director's observations were that these couples appear to feel that a surrogate's children 'have the right' to hold their infants and they 'almost behave like a stranger situation.'

Even when the pregnancy produces a multiple birth, a fairly common phenomenon, a situation that might be expected to produce a heightened sense of gratitude in couples, the director had observed that they are actually less 'kind' to their surrogate than when a 'singleton' (one child) is born. The centre's contract states that for every additional child couples must pay an additional $3,000 and, according to the director's assessment, a new pattern is emerging in which couples who have twins or triplets tend to give their surrogates smaller gifts. Couples frequently propose to give expensive gifts to their surrogate but very few IVF couples who receive multiple children keep this promise, and it appears (at least initially) that surrogates who give birth to singletons receive more gifts. How do we account for this behaviour? The programme director's theory is that because a multiple birth means that a couple's family is complete and will no longer require the surrogate's services (or the programme's services), such couples therefore 'don't care what we think of them either,' often flouting programme directives concerning appropriate behaviour toward their surrogate.

---

[10] When this husband's wife telephoned me one year later (for information unrelated to our interview) she apologised for the way her husband had spoken of their surrogate, assuring me that he no longer felt that way although she did not provide specific details of this, glossing over his comments and seeming embarrassed by them.

4. OVUM DONATION: WHERE HAVE ALL THE GIFTS GONE?

My interest in gamete donation was generated by the intersection of ovum donation with gestational surrogacy. The largest surrogate mother programme is also the world's largest ovum donation programme. Intending couples who are unable to produce their own embryos have the option of choosing from over 300 screened ovum donors at the surrogate programme. It should be noted that what constitutes relatedness in one context and appears to be consistent with EuroAmerican kinship ideology is, however, inconsistent in other contexts, most notably with gamete donation.

Interestingly, gamete donation programmes/clinics/banks intentionally seek to separate gametes from their donors in ways that bear a striking similarity to adoption practices. Like adoption, gamete donation (both ovum or sperm donation) 'arose out of market concerns; an imbalance between supply and demand, a scarcity of the desired product . . .' (Modell (1999:6)), and it was the routinisation and naturalisation of IVF that resulted in an increased demand for ova. Intense competition among infertility clinics and the prospect of enormous profits coupled with weak regulatory policies (Reame (1998:1)) has created a volatile environment. Although a great deal has been written about the practice of inflating their 'success rates', at infertility clinics little has been written about the common practice of advertising for ova donors in college newspapers. Acting on the questionable assumption that women in college possess the genetic potential to produce more intelligent children, clinics seek ova from a cohort known to be in need of financial compensation by using financial incentives (just as sperm banks do). It is interesting to note that while gamete donation programmes/banks only accept donations from individuals who are either currently enrolled in college (or who are college graduates) no such emphasis exists in the field of blood or organ donation. In an attempt to recruit college-aged women, advertisements for ova donors have changed their rates from a $2,500 payment for one cycle to a single, larger sum of $10,000 (for 3–4 cycles), a sum of money that is more attractive. These advertisements do not indicate, however, the number of cycles involved in the larger payment, intending to draw in candidates through the appeal of a lump sum payment. Ovum 'donation' then, like sperm 'donation' is explicitly predicated on a remunerative model, it may appear to be outside the province of gifting, but it is not.

The idea of altruism in the context of gamete donation, in particular ovum donation provides a particularly interesting and vital link to an understanding of the complexity of the gift. As we will see gift rhetoric is not only contextually dependent, it is also highly gendered.

5. GENDERING THE GIFT

Gender in the world of assisted conception is a crucial, if curiously understudied variable, particularly with respect to men and gamete donation. For example, studies on sperm donation have revealed that: 71 per cent of sperm donors are motivated by the following factors: remuneration (Schover, Rothman and Collins (1992)), a desire to assess their own fertility (Handelsman, Dunn, Conway, Boylan and Jansen (1985); Daniels (1989)), altruism (Handelsman *et al* (1985); Daniels (1989); Schover *et al* (1992)) and, interestingly enough, outcomes, ie donors are interested in knowing whether children were born from their donation (Handelsman *et al* (1985); Daniels (1989); Mahlstedt and Probasco (1991); Purdie, Peek, Adair, Graham and Fisher (1994); Schover *et al* (1992)). Before a donor is accepted his semen is assessed for motility, sperm count, and so on which allows a donor to assess his fertility. These test results are different from those that inform donors about the actual number of births that have occurred as a result of their act of donation. Given a cultural model that equates good mother with nurturance and altruism, ovum donors are less likely than sperm donors to acknowledge the importance of remuneration. The dictates of this cultural model are mirrored by sperm banks and ovum donation programme staff. Clinicians, for example, are 'highly influential' in 'creating the overall atmosphere . . . in which donors and recipients experience gamete donation,' (Haimes (1993:1518)) as revealed in a study conducted by the University of Southern California's oocyte donation programme. The clinicians Sauer and Paulson reveal that as part of the screening process for prospective ovum donors the USC programme insists that the 'primary reason for participation . . . [be] a desire to help an infertile woman have a baby' (Sauer and Paulson (1992a:727)). In spite of this policy, which is intended to screen out women who express financial incentive, 76 per cent of the women who had completed 'at least one aspiration stated that compensation was important for their continued participation' (Sauer and Paulson (1992a:727; 1992b)).

Why then are women who express some financial motivation turned away in spite of the fact that approved donors, once accepted, subsequently reveal that remuneration is important to them? And why are sperm donors, who routinely state the importance of financial compensation, accepted? Sauer and Paulson's conclusion was that 'oocyte donors represent a rather unique group of individuals. . . . very different from men donating to our sperm bank' (Sauer and Paulson (1992a:726)), a conclusion that is questionable in view of the fact that 76 per cent of that programme's screened and accepted ovum donors appear to value compensation as do 71 per cent of all sperm donors. Such assessments regrettably conflate commonly accepted, essentialist notions about gender, selectively reinforcing ideas of 'altruism' and 'gifting' only as they pertain to women.

The irony of programmes using financial incentive to attract ovum donors and then requiring them to de-emphasise its importance reveals a deep-seated ambivalence in EuroAmerican culture about commercialising, commodifying, and fragmenting both the body and the family. And ovum donors are the first to reflect this ambivalence. As one 28-year-old ovum donor's unsolicited explanation illustrates, 'Whatever money I acquired I would use in some way to better my children's life.' Another ovum donor felt that her donation needed an explanation, 'I got brownie points somewhere.' As these remarks reveal, it is not uncommon for ovum donors to indirectly apologise for or somehow excuse their having accepted compensation for their reproductive work. Responses such as these hearken back to the script-like quality responses I received from traditional surrogates to de-emphasise the remunerative component and to foreground ideas consistent with feminine/maternal behaviour, such as altruism, caring, and sharing (Ragoné (1994; 1996a)); such responses can be understood to reflect the tension between market driven forces that set the price on how much an infertility clinic can compensate a donor for her ova and the altruistic component of donors' acts. One 24-year-old donor provided a fairly explicit synopsis of this cultural tension when she said:

> *I was worried what people would think of me. A close friend made a snide comment about me selling off parts of myself. It made me feel like it was a trashy kind of thing to do. What kind of women would do it? Then it became, 'I am the kind of women who would do this!'*

Specifically, when programmes insist upon anonymity, ie minimal or no contact between ovum donor and intending couple, they tend to reinforce the idea that gamete donation is a quid pro quo exchange, ie donors receive payment and couples receive gametes. But although psychological studies indicate that the anonymous model is not ideal, most programmes respond to the wishes of their paying clients (Baran and Pannor (1989)). As the director of the world's largest sperm bank informed me, in spite of his own psychological staff informing him of the importance of abolishing anonymity and moving the bank into a more interactive and open model, there are currently no plans to implement this since he reasoned it is not what his clients wanted. The belief that children's psychological response is healthier when they are informed of their birth origins, that secrecy in the family should be discouraged, and that infertile individuals must come to terms with their infertility are the primary reasons that psychologists recommend more interactive open models be implemented for donation.

Anonymous models of donation appear to have produced negative consequences for some donors as revealed by a 28-year-old ovum donor whose first donation (facilitated by a private physician) was completely anonymous. She described her experience as an emotionally difficult one:

> *It made me feel like a prostitute. It was disgusting. I left there crying. In the end, I said, 'I will never do this again.' It was a horrible experience.*

However, she went on to donate two additional times in a programme that encouraged open communication between ova donors and recipient couples/individuals. One of the psychologists at the programme she chose described the donor's decision to donate again in an open programme as one that 'help[ed] her to heal.' In this case, participating in an open donation programme appears to have accorded the donor a greater degree of agency and to have placed her act of donation into the gift economy.

The decision of many clinics to retain the anonymity model in spite of evidence that it is not necessarily in the best interest of donors or children has produced an untenable situation for many ovum donors since they are required, on the one hand, to view their donation as altruistic, an aspect of the gift model, but on the other hand, because they will never have contact with the couples or women who receive their ova the relationship resembles an economic arrangement. The previously quoted donor who reported feeling that she had 'prostituted' herself, and the other who felt that she was 'selling body parts', were expressing feelings remarkably similar to those expressed to me by surrogates participating in anonymous programmes, namely that the process served to produce feelings of fragmentation of self.

Anonymity facilitates the denial of the genetic component of donation for both donors and recipients and permits recipient couples to deny their infertility. The following quote by a 32-year-old, however, reveals the confusion facilitated by an anonymous model that seeks to ignore issues of relatedness:

> I thought 'wow, my eggs are going to be a child.' I don't consider it my child. It is in a way my child. It was a weird feeling. Donating eggs is much different than being face to face with what you donated. I don't think of them as related to me.

Although this donor later added, 'It's a good feeling helping someone have a baby,' it is not uncommon for ovum donors to ignore the link between ova and children. This conceptual gap is the by-product of both anonymity and commodification.[11]

One 33-year-old ovum donor explained her view of the separation between her ova and the potential child in this way, creating a self and other distinction based on that which is inside the body and that which is outside the body:

> It [the baby] really isn't mine even though they [the ova] are mine. Once it's not **in** me, I don't consider it mine (emphasis added).

Her statement echoes the perception embraced by most gestational surrogates, specifically, that the children are not theirs because they do not have any 'genetic' connection to the children they produce. The difference, however, between gestational surrogates and ovum donors is that ovum donors are in fact genetically linked to these children, whereas gestational surrogates are not.[12]

---

[11] Even in anonymous programmes, it is not unusual for donors to inquire about the outcomes of their donation. Some programmes do inform donors as to whether or not their donation resulted in children. Some also provide information about the gender of the child, while others will not.

[12] Fathers, it should be noted, who have participated in traditional surrogacy also tend to downplay the significance of their genetic relationship to the child by foregoing the paternity test (Ragoné (1994; 1996a)).

But what is of fundamental importance is that various versions as to what does or does not constitute relatedness in EuroAmerican kinship ideology co-exist and their co-existence has a great deal to do with the fragmentation and commodification of the body, as illustrated by the following quote by 28-year-old donor mentioned earlier who analogised her donation experience to that of prostitutes. Placing her gift in context, she added the following:

> *I compare it [ovum donation] to donating blood, platelets or bone marrow. You aren't* **giving** *life, but you are* **saving** *life* (emphasis added).

Her statement can be understood as an attempt to reconceptualise her act of donation and to provide a more finely textured, albeit unclear, theory about life, ie 'giving life' we are informed cannot be understood as the equivalent of 'saving life', a distinction which reveals the deep-seated ambivalence some ovum donors experience. One psychologist who routinely screens ovum donors informed me that ovum donors often equate their donation with blood, organ and bone marrow transplantations, an analogy that is intended to include their act of donation in the gift economy. One particularly astute 24- year-old donor described her experience of trying to separate herself from her ova and the potential child in the following way:

> *I was concerned I would have an emotional attachment to the baby. I was concerned down the road if I was the biological mother. If the child wanted to meet you . . . it would be cruel not to. It is something I don't think about a lot. Keeping up that line in my mind I knew that the one thing I had to do was keep an emotional distance in myself . . . I knew I had [to] for my own sanity, I had to do it. I had to draw the line in the sand because I cannot risk an emotional attachment.*

The attempt at emotional distancing and the figurative act of 'drawing a line in the sand' to separate herself from the child(ren) a donation might produce represents both an explicit acknowledgement of the biogenetic tie and an attempt to deny that connection. In another study that examines the experiences of recipient couples at the Center for Reproductive Medicine and Infertility at Cornell University Medical College, Applegarth *et al* (1995:576) inform us that 90 per cent of couples in their programme use anonymous donation while another 9.7 per cent use 'known' donation, eg biological sister donation. The authors concluded that only a 'small percentage', 10 per cent of husbands and 26 per cent of wives, 'expressed the desire to meet their ovum donor' (Applegarth *et al* (1995:577)), but the fact that more than one-quarter of the women wanted to meet their donors seems significant, especially in a programme where such meetings are in all likelihood discouraged. It is also impossible to ascertain whether the following remarks attributed to several recipient women are typical. According to Applegarth *et al.*, recipients offer thanks for their ovum donation in the following order: to 'God', 'the wonders of modern medical miracles', and 'fantastic technology'. Only one of the recipients had expressed thanks to her donor (Applegarth *et al* (1995:580)).

The attempt by programmes and clinicians to argue that anonymity is an acceptable strategy may be understood as an attempt to privilege the desires of paying clients, ie the recipient couple, a practice that has a long history in the annals of sperm donation. It is disconcerting that, due to the anonymity model, individuals who are able to have children through gamete donation do not feel the same sense of indebtedness to their donors as do those who participate in traditional surrogacy. As we have seen, the practice of anonymity in both ovum donation programmes and sperm banks contributes to the further fragmentation of reproduction and the body, a fragmentation that is inextricably connected to the desire to maintain the commodification model.

6. CONCLUSION

An exploration of the gift in the context of surrogate motherhood and gamete donation illuminates the many and contradictory tensions that the commodification of life produces, from a resistance to conflating the symbolic value of family with work, on the one hand, to a desire to justify and even embrace the commodification of life, on the other. With surrogacy, as with gamete donation, the enduring power of EuroAmerican kinship ideology continues to surface in spite of concerted attempts to obscure it. As one surrogate programme director stated, in the course of discussing the New Jersey Supreme Court's ruling that surrogacy represents a form of baby selling in the *Baby M* case, 'How can a father buy his own child? He can't!'

Whether it is used in surrogate motherhood or gamete donation, gift exchange is, as Malinowski noted, 'one of the main instruments of social organisation' (Malinowski (1922:167)). It sheds light on the quality and value of human relationships (Titmuss (1971:13)), and the multivariant forms that the gift of life takes will undoubtedly continue to puzzle and in some respects confound us, as technology continues to raise previously unimaginable questions.

REFERENCES

Applegarth, L, Goldberg, N, Cholst, I, McGoff, N, Fantini, D, Zeller, N, Black, A, and Rosenwaks, Z, 'Families Created Through Ovum Donation: A Preliminary Investigation of Obstetrical Outcome and Psychosocial Adjustment' (1995) 12 *Journal of Assisted Reproduction and Genetics* 574.
Baran, A and Pannor, R, *Lethal Secrets: The Psychology of Donor Insemination* (New York, Amistad Press, 1989).
Cannell, F, 'Concepts of Parenthood: The Warnock Report, the Gillick and Modern Debates' (1990) 17 *American Ethnologist* 667.
Carrier, J, 'Gifts in a World of Commodities: The Ideology of the Perfect Gift in American Society' (1990) 29 *Social Analysis* 19.
Daniels, KR, 'Semen Donors: Their Motivations and Attitudes to Their Offspring' (1989) 7 *Journal of Reproductive & Infant Psychology* 121.

Fox, R and Swazey, J, *Spare Parts: Organ Replacement in American Society* (New York and Oxford, Oxford University Press, 1992).

Gullestad, M, *The Art of Social Relations* (Oslo, Norway, Scandinavian Press, 1992).

Haimes, E, 'Do Clinicians Benefit from Gamete Donor Anonymity?' (1993) 8 *Human Reproduction* 1518.

Handelsman, DJ, Dunn, SM, Conway, AJ, Boylan, LM and Jansen, RPS, 'Psychological and Attitudinal Profiles in Donors for Artificial Insemination' (1985) 43 *Fertililty and Sterility* 95.

Hull, R, 'Gestational surrogacy and surrogate motherhood' in R Hull (ed), *Ethical Issues in the New Reproductive Technologies* (Belmont, CA, Wadsworth Publishers, 1990) 150–55.

Layne, L, 'Baby Things as Fetishes? Memorial Goods, Simulacra, and the "Realness" Problem of Pregnancy Loss' in H Ragoné and F Winddance Twine (eds), *Ideologies and Technologies of Motherhood: Race, Class, Sexuality, and Nationalism* (New York and London, Routledge, 2000).

Levi-Strauss, C, 'The Principle of Reciprocity' in LA Coser and B Rosenberg (eds), *Sociological Theory* (New York, Macmillan, 1965).

Mahlstedt, PP and Probasco, KA, 'Sperm Donors: Their Attitudes Toward Providing Medical and Psychological Information for Recipient Couples and Donor Offspring' (1991) 56 *Fertility and Sterility* 747.

Malinowski, B, *Argonauts of the Western Pacific* (London, Routledge, 1922).

Mauss, M, *The Gift: Forms and Functions of Exchange in Archaic Societies* (New York and London, Norton and Company, 1967).

Modell, J, 'Freely Given: Open Adoption and the Rhetoric of the Gift' in L Layne (ed), *Transformative Motherhood: On Giving and Getting in a Consumer Culture* (New York, New York University Press, 1999).

Purdie, A, Peek, J, Adair, V, Graham, F and Fisher, R, 'Attitudes of Parents of Young Children to Sperm Donation—Implications for Donor Recruitment' (1994) 9 *Human Reproduction* 1355.

Ragoné, H, *Surrogate Motherhood: Conception in the Heart* (Boulder, Westview Press, 1994).

—— 'Chasing the blood tie: surrogate mothers, adoptive mothers, and fathers' (1996a) 23 *American Ethnologist* 352.

—— 'Book Review of Life and Death Under High Technology Medicine. Ian Robinson' (1996b) 2 *Man* 378.

—— 'Incontestable Motivations' in S Franklin and H Ragoné (eds), *Reproducing Reproduction: Kinship, Power, and Technological Innovation* (Philadelphia, University of Pennsylvania Press, 1998).

Reame, N, *Unintended Consequences: What America Should do About Assisted Reproduction. A Health Policy Report to the American Academy of Nursing and Institute of Medicine* (Washington, DC, 1998).

Sauer, M and Paulson, R, 'Oocyte Donors: A Demographic Analysis of Women at the University of Southern California' (1992a) 7 *Human Reproduction* 776.

—— 'Understanding the Current Status of Oocyte Donation in the United States: What's Really Going On Out There?' (1992b) 58 *Fertility and Sterility* 16.

Schneider, D, *American Kinship: A Cultural Account* (Englewood Cliffs, NJ, Prentice Hall, 1968).

Schover, LR, Rothman, SA and Collins, RI, 'The Personality and Motivation of Semen Donors: A Comparison with Oocyte Donors' (1992) 7 *Human Reproduction* 575.

Simmel, G, *The Philosophy of Money* (London, Routledge and Kegan Paul, 1978).

Strathern, M, 'The Pursuit of Certainty: Investigating Kinship in the Late Twentieth Century' (1991). Distinguished lecture presented at the annual meeting of the American Anthropological Association, Chicago.

Strathern, M and Franklin, S, 'Kinship and the New Genetic Technologies: An Assessment of Existing Anthropological Research. Brussels: European Commission'. (1993) Report commissioned for the Commission of the European Communities Medical Division [DGXIT] Human Genome Analysis Programme.

Swartz, B, 'The Social Psychology of the Gift' (1967) 73 *The American Journal of Sociology* 1.

Titmuss, R, *The Gift Relationship: From Human Blood to Social Policy* (New York, Pantheon Books, 1971).

Wolfram, S, *In-Laws and Outlaws: Kinship and Marriage in England* (Beckenham, England, Croom Helm, 1987).

Wozniak, D, 'Gifts and Burdens: The Social and Familial Context of Foster Mothering' in L Layne (ed), *Transformative Motherhood: On Giving and Getting in a Consumer Culture* (New York, New York University Press, 1999).

Zelizer, V, *Pricing the Priceless Child* (New York, Basic Books, 1985).

15

Paying for it? Surrogacy, Market Forces and Assisted Conception

ERIC BLYTH AND CLAIRE POTTER

1. INTRODUCTION

If an infertile couple can buy an egg, and rent a womb, why should they not buy the finished product?

(Brazier (1999:345))

T HE QUESTION OF whether or not a surrogate mother should be paid a fee for her services, beyond expenses, has been described as one of the most controversial aspects of the surrogacy debate (Rae (1994)). In this chapter we provide a critical analysis of the role of commercialisation in surrogacy arrangements, contextualising this within the wider debate concerning the remuneration of gamete and embryo donors. Although we write primarily from a UK perspective, we have drawn on wider policy and legislative developments and, in conclusion, we consider what other jurisdictions that have yet to consider legislation and/or regulation governing surrogacy might learn from the UK experience.

2. SURROGACY ARRANGEMENTS IN THE UK: THE 'REASONABLE EXPENSES' MODEL

We start our consideration of surrogacy in the UK with the report of the Warnock Committee, established by the Government in 1982 to undertake an inquiry into embryo research and the provision of assisted conception services and to make recommendations for policy and regulation. Despite lack of information about the prevalence of surrogacy, the Committee was concerned about the possibility of its practice—and, in particular, commercial surrogacy—which presented it with 'some of the most difficult problems we encountered' (DHSS (1984:46)). Indeed, the Committee's distaste for commercial surrogacy (especially 'for convenience') led it to conflate commercial and non-commercial surrogacy and to recommend a complete ban on surrogacy *per se*. However, two members of the Committee dissociated themselves from their peers, and produced a separate *Expression of Dissent* believing surrogacy to be a 'last resort' that should be available but subject to 'stringent' control.[1]

The intended government consultation on the Committee's proposals for regulation and legislation was overtaken by events (at least as far as surrogacy was concerned) when in 1985 it was revealed that a British woman, Kim Cotton, had contracted to become a surrogate mother for an American agency (Cotton and Winn (1985)). In an effort to proscribe the apparent excesses of commercialism, the Government (with all party support) speedily passed the Surrogacy Arrangements Act 1985, under which certain commercial activities connected with a surrogacy agreement were criminalised, although neither surrogacy itself nor commercial surrogacy *per se* were prohibited (see Blyth (1993)). Thus, legislation failed to provide any clear lead for policy makers or legislators—or indeed anyone who might be contemplating involvement in a surrogacy arrangement. For example, Freeman (1986) noted that the payment to a surrogate mother for maintaining a diary of her pregnancy was not considered an infringement of the Surrogacy Arrangements Act.

Further restriction on financial agreements between a surrogate mother and commissioning parent(s) was left to the Human Fertilisation and Embryology Act 1990 (hereafter 'the 1990 Act'), although this did not specifically prohibit financial transactions between a surrogate mother and commissioning parent(s) either. Such limits as exist are governed by section 30 of the 1990 Act that introduced new procedures for the legal transfer of parental responsibility for a child born as a result of a surrogacy arrangement from the child's birth mother to the commissioning parents by means of a Parental Order. One of several conditions that must be met before a Parental Order may be granted is that the court considering the case must be satisfied that 'no money or other benefit (other than for expenses reasonably incurred)' has been paid to the surrogate mother 'unless authorised by the court.'

These restrictions owe much to pre-existing UK adoption legislation, upon which the proposals for Parental Orders were based, and were designed to prevent the development of trade in children via a surrogacy arrangement. Blyth (1993) outlines the particular circumstances under which section 30 of the 1990 Act became a late addition to the legislation, noting that not only had such proposals received no mention in the Warnock Report, neither had they emerged in the subsequent government consultation paper (DHSS (1986)), nor in the White Paper (DHSS (1987)), nor the Bill that was introduced to Parliament in late 1989. A key consequence was that the Parental Order requirements received little detailed debate in Parliament itself and none outside Parliament. Once Parliament had legislated, the Government realised its proposals were 'considerably more complex than they first appeared' (Sackville (1994)) and they did not take effect until 1 November 1994, several years after implementation of the main provisions of the 1990 Act.

---

[1] For a more detailed critical review of the Warnock Committee's consideration of surrogacy arrangements see Freeman (1989).

Blyth (1993) anticipated that the introduction of section 30,

> may exercise an important symbolic impact on the acceptability of surrogacy as a form of family creation. With hindsight it may come to be seen as the acceptable face of surrogacy (p 258).

While it is not possible to isolate the impact of section 30 *per se*, the team appointed by the Government to review surrogacy arrangements considered that 'the existence of surrogacy is now accepted' (Brazier, Campbell, and Golombok, (1998:4.5)). In the meantime, medicalised versions of surrogacy had become subject to the full panoply of the Human Fertilisation and Embryology Authority's regulatory system (HFEA (1993a));[2] the British Medical Association had acknowledged surrogacy as a 'reproductive option of last resort', publishing ethical and practice guidance for health and other professionals (BMA (1996)); an increasing number of licensed centres were providing treatment involving a surrogacy arrangement (Balen and Hayden (1998)); treatment involving a surrogacy arrangement had received NHS funding (Foxcroft (1997)), and the number of children known to have born in the UK as a result of a surrogacy arrangement continued to increase (COTS (2001)).

Of particular importance for our discussion, the regulatory framework appears to have done little to stem the development of commercial surrogacy. In particular, the Brazier review team failed to identify any instance of a court refusing to grant a Parental Order, despite finding evidence of a wide range of payments made to surrogate mothers. Brazier and her colleagues concluded that 'in many cases a component of the amount paid to the surrogate mother is a direct payment for services rendered rather than the reimbursement of actual expenses' (Brazier *et al* (1998) para 5.3, p 43).

Of 34 Parental Order applications about which the review team obtained information, details about the payment made to the surrogate mother were available in 32 cases. Seven received payment up to £999 (including three surrogate mothers who were paid nothing); 15 received between £1,000 and £4,999; nine received between £5,000 and £9,999, and one received £12,000. The mean payment was £3,468 (Figure 1).

More comprehensive information about payment in UK surrogacy arrangements is provided by a membership survey undertaken by Childlessness Overcome Through Surrogacy—a non-commercial surrogacy organisation (COTS (undated)). From a total of 251 known surrogacy arrangements completed between 1988 and 1999, COTS obtained 188 responses. The payments made are detailed in Table 1 below. What is especially interesting about these is the high frequency of similar levels of payment: £10,000 (68); £8,000 (24); £6,500 (19); £7,000 (14); £6,000 (10); £12,000 (8); £15,000 (6), suggesting further evidence of 'payment for services', rather than simply remuneration of actual

---

[2] See Johnson, chapter 6, this volume.

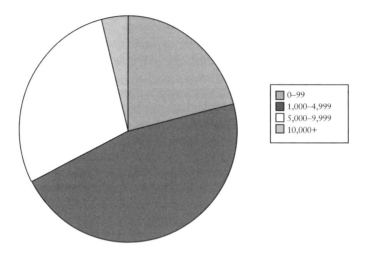

Figure 1. **Payment made to surrogate mothers in section 30 Applications (Brazier** *et al* **(1998))**

expenses. Indeed, COTS itself characterises the payment as 'compensation'— for the risk to the surrogate mother and for putting her life and her family's lives 'on hold', rather than merely reimbursement of expenses or payment for services rendered.

That Parental Orders are being granted notwithstanding evidence of payment exceeding reimbursement of expenses actually incurred suggests that courts are applying very liberal definitions of 'reasonableness' and/or 'expenses'. Alternatively, given the limited options if a court refuses to grant a Parental Order, some courts may simply be disregarding apparent excesses and routinely 'authorising' such payments. Indeed, in 1996, a court considering a Parental Order application gave retrospective authorisation to the payment of over £8,000 to a surrogate mother in respect of a child she had carried on behalf of commissioning parents (*Re Q* [1996]).[3] Whatever may be influencing courts' decision-making, it can hardly be claimed that the 'reasonable expenses' model adequately describes contemporary surrogacy practice in the UK.

3. COMMERCIAL SURROGACY

The explicit rejection of commercial surrogacy by the Warnock committee and the UK Government has been endorsed in a number of other jurisdictions, for

[3] The ruling in *Re Q* (Re Q (Parental Order) [1996] 1 FLR 369) mirrored the decision of Latey J in *Re An Adoption Application (Re An Adoption Application [Surrogacy]* 1987 2 All ER 826) in providing retrospective authorisation to the payment made to a surrogate mother and the granting of an adoption order in favour of commissioning parents.

Table 1. Payment made to surrogate mothers in 188 surrogacy arrangements 1988–99
(COTS (undated))

Amount (£)	Number	Amount (£)	Number	Amount (£)	Number
0	2	4000	7	7000	14
2000	1	5000	2	7500	3
3000	2	6000	10	8000	24
3500	5	6500	19	8500	2
3600	1	6900	1	8600	1

Amount (£)	Number	Amount (£)	Number
9000	2	13000	1
10000	68	14000	2
10500	3	15000	6
11000	2	16000	1
12000	8	20000	1

example in Europe, Denmark, France, and The Netherlands prohibit any form of payment, while Austria, Germany, and Sweden proscribe any form of surrogacy (Brazier *et al* (1998)). However, surrogacy has its advocates and is practised in certain parts of the world. Commercial agencies—providing a total pre- to post-natal medical, nursing, scientific, psychological and legal package—are primarily located in the USA although they operate in an international market via the Internet. A trawl of internet sites undertaken for the purposes of this chapter revealed a range of fees charged from US$22,000 to over US$65,000;[4] Caldwell (2001) notes that current 'fees' payable to the surrogate mother range between US$10,000–$30,000.

The debate concerning commercial surrogacy has tended to focus on the key issues of autonomy, dignity and exploitation. In our discussion below we consider these issues from the perspective of the surrogate mother, commissioning parents and the child born as a result of a surrogacy arrangement. Finally we discuss some pragmatic considerations regarding the sanction or prohibition of commercial surrogacy.

The Kantian injunction that people should be treated as ends in themselves not as a means to someone else's end has been used in respect of both the surrogate mother and the child born of a commercial surrogacy arrangement (see Lane, chapter 9, this volume). It is rehearsed in numerous assertions of the inherent tension between personal dignity and the commodification of women's bodies and their reproductive functions. For example:

[4] See, eg, East Coast Assisted Parenting (www.russiansurrogacy.com); Fertility Institutes (www.fertility-docs.com); Center for Surrogate Parenting (www.creatingfamilies.com)

the woman's dignity requires that her body should not become a mere instrument for use by others in their own interest, that procreation must not become the object of a commercial transaction (Council of Europe (1989:29)).[5]

Proponents of commercial surrogacy have attempted to counter this position, asserting a woman's right to make an informed choice whether or not to become a commercial surrogate mother, and arguing that preventing her from engaging in whatever activities she chooses—including commercial surrogacy—is an infringement of her dignity, autonomy and her civil liberties. Shalev (1989) even uses this argument to justify not only the establishment of a legally binding pre-conceptual contract, but also to enforce a surrogate mother's obligation to relinquish her child to the commissioning parents should she change her mind. She claims that the refusal to enforce contracts invalidates women as capable of acting as rational and moral agents able to think through and make decisions for themselves.

Opponents argue that the woman's ability to make an informed choice is absent in commercial surrogacy (eg Overall (1987); Shanley (1993); Royal Commission on New Reproductive Technologies (1993); Brazier *et al* (1998)). First, a woman cannot foresee all potential risks involved with her pregnancy and second, at the time the agreement is made, it is impossible for a woman to predict how she will feel about fulfilling the terms of the agreement after the child is born. However, McLachlan and Swales (2001) question the validity of such arguments on the grounds that many risks in life are unforeseeable and risk-taking is accepted as a normal part of our everyday existence.

A further consideration is the extent to which a woman may be at risk of exploitation if she enters into a commercial surrogacy arrangement as a result of economic necessity. For Shanley (1993) commercial surrogacy allows economically secure men to purchase women's procreative labour and custodial rights. Such exploitation might be increased by socio-economic differences between surrogate mothers and commissioning parents. Tong (1997), for example, cites feminist argument that the surrogate mother's 'free' choice is in reality the product of economic coercion and that:

> most surrogate mothers, like most prostitutes, are much poorer than the people to whom they sell their services. Unable to get a decent job, a woman may be driven to sell her body if it is the only thing she has that anyone seems to value enough to buy. But to say that a woman 'chooses' to do this, claim feminist opponents of surrogacy, is to say that when a woman is forced to choose between being poor and being exploited, she may choose being exploited as the lesser of two evils (Tong (1997:200–01)).

---

[5] Similar sentiments are articulated in the European Convention for the Protection of Human Rights and Dignity of the Human Being with Regard to the Application of Biology and Medicine (Council of Europe (1996)), and in the reports of the Warnock Committee (DHSS (1984)), the New York State Task Force on Life and the Law (1988), the Glover Committee (1989), the Royal Commission on New Reproductive Technologies (1993) and the Nuffield Council on Bioethics (1995).

However, the force of socio-economic differentials between a surrogate mother and commissioning parents may be overplayed. While available evidence suggests that many—probably most—surrogate mothers would not have entered into the arrangement in the absence of financial benefit, Ragoné's (1994) American study showed that most surrogate mothers were educated and middle class, and none of the surrogate mothers in Blyth's (1994) UK study appeared to be in dire financial circumstances. Further, it may be argued that surrogacy provides a source of income enabling the surrogate mother to remain at home and care for other children or carry out other employment, and indeed may be preferable to any low paid job that may be less rewarding and more exploitative. If poverty is the problem then action should be targeted at poverty eradication rather than the means that some women choose simply to survive or to extricate themselves from poverty. Wertheimer (1996) suggests that:

> If a woman can reasonably regard surrogacy as improving her overall welfare given that society has unjustly limited her options, it is arguable that it would be adding insult to injury to deny her that opportunity (p 11).

It may be argued that not to compensate a surrogate mother for the discomfort and risks of pregnancy and childbirth and the inconvenience experienced by her family is itself exploitative (COTS, undated) and risks reinforcing stereotypical notions of women's work as 'unpaid non economic acts of love and nurturing' (Shanley (1993:623)). Dickenson (1997) suggests that donation involves financial costs which may not be reimbursed; therefore, women in the UK pay to donate eggs and, because most treatment takes place in the private sector, others benefit financially. Even Brazier *et al* (1998) observe that:

> payment for their services does not make people into mere means; on the contrary lack of payment (as in slavery or breadline wages) may be much more exploitative (p 35).

Another possibility is that commissioning parents could be exploited by the surrogate mother. Commissioning parents often pay a high price and are obliged to trust that the surrogate mother will not renege on the deal once she has been paid (Blyth (1994)).

We are not convinced that the arguments against commercial surrogacy so far adduced are sufficiently compelling to demonstrate that its practice is inherently contrary to human dignity. Where critics appear to be on surer ground, in our view, is where commercial surrogacy is alleged to represent the commodification of children.

4. SURROGACY AS THE COMMODIFICATION OF CHILDREN

Anderson (1993) provides a blunt critique of commercial surrogacy as a 'degrading traffic in children' (p 186). The New York State Task Force on Life and the Law (1988) extended the implications of commercial surrogacy beyond the individual progeny of a commercial surrogacy arrangement:

> The exchange of money for possession or control of children . . . threatens to erode the way that society thinks about and values children, and by extension all human life (New York State Task Force on Life and the Law (1988:76)).

However, apart from the issue of whether under a surrogacy arrangement a genetic father—as an intending parent—can be considered as purchasing his 'own' child, there has been considerable debate about what is being bought and sold under a commercial surrogacy agreement. Given the universal condemnation of practices that treat others as objects that may be bought and sold as intrinsically and deeply abhorrent, advocates of commercial surrogacy have had to challenge the assertion that it is analogous with buying and selling a child.

We are not convinced that commissioning parents are merely paying the surrogate mother for 'services rendered', ie to conceive, carry and give birth to the baby, and compensating her for the risks, discomfort and inconvenience of pregnancy and childbirth and/or for loss of income from her regular employment (eg Kornegay (1990); COTS (undated)). Commissioning parents want something more tangible than merely the knowledge that the surrogate mother has conceived and given birth. Indeed, recourse to legal action by commissioning parents when the surrogate mother has refused to relinquish the child provides clear illustration that what commissioning parents consider they are paying for is custody of the child.[6]

McLachlan and Swales (2000) provide the most elaborate claim yet that commercial surrogacy is not buying and selling children. Somewhat disingenuously, they note that, while commissioning parents may expect to receive something other than the knowledge that a baby has been carried and 'might even imagine that they have purchased a particular baby . . . what they have paid for is not necessarily the same as what they think they have paid for' (p 6). Thus, while they assert that the participants themselves may not know what is being sold and purchased, McLachlan and Swales claim to do so. In addition to purchasing the surrogate mother's services for carrying the child, the commissioning parents should also be considered as 'buying from the surrogate mother her refraining from pursuing her claim for the legal custody and parenthood of the child in addition to her physical surrendering of it' (p 11).

This seems the most comprehensive case made yet for the sale and purchase of a 'complete package'. Yet is this concept sufficiently distant from that of trafficking in children? Anderson (2000) is clear that it is not: 'If this isn't literally selling a child, it is selling a child out' (p 21). We are inclined to agree. Decisions about child custody are customarily—and rightly in our view—determined on the basis of judgments of what is in the child's best interests (however difficult these might be to make in practice). Such decisions should not be influenced by one party's potential claim to custody being bought off.

---

[6] See, eg, the case of *Baby M* (Re *Baby M* (1988) 537, A.2d 1227 (N.J. 1988)) in the USA and, in the UK, *A v C* [1985] FLR 445–61.

However, McLachlan and Swales have a further hand to play. They cite van Nierkerk and van Zyl (1995):

> Market norms do not in any way have to exclude the norms of parental love. Treating something as a commodity need not mean treating it **merely** or **only** as a commodity (p 168—emphasis in original),

arguing that paying a high price for something can mean that it is more valued and cared for.

It may also be argued that a child born following a surrogacy arrangement, for which her/his birth mother was financially compensated, could experience certain unique advantages. They would know that they were much wanted and that their creation was a conscious and joyous achievement and not unplanned or the result of a regretted sexual encounter. They would also know that their birth mother had been compensated rather than exploited (COTS (undated)). In the absence of empirical evidence about the experiences of people born as a result of a surrogacy arrangement, such outcomes remain speculative—although possible. Equally possible, though, knowledge of being conceived under such circumstances could generate feelings of having been bought and sold and of having to prove one was worth the expense.

Although we know comparatively little about the experiences of those born as a result of assisted conception, some people who have been conceived following 'donor' assisted conception[7] have certainly experienced the impact of commodification. For example, Suzanne Rubin (1983), who was born following donor insemination, poignantly asks:

> How do I reconcile my sense of integrity with knowing that my father sold what was the essence of my life for $25 to a total stranger . . . What kind of man sells himself and his child so cheaply and so easily? (Rubin:214).

And it would appear a moot point whether someone will feel better or worse about himself or herself knowing that $30,000 rather than $25 had changed hands in order to achieve their conception.

This brings us to consideration of whether payment in a surrogacy arrangement is any less acceptable than payment to sperm, egg or embryo donors. As we have indicated already, on the one hand there are a number of explicit injunctions to the effect that: 'the human body and its parts shall not, as such, give rise to financial gain' (Council of Europe (1996) Article 21, Chapter VII).

Nevertheless, payment for 'donation' of gametes and embryos has—and remains—the norm in assisted conception in many countries and attempts to develop internationally accepted protocols have singularly failed to deliver in respect of either payment to 'donors' or of surrogacy itself. For example, the International Federation of Fertility Societies, an association of 50 professional

[7] Daniels (1998) convincingly challenges the unqualified use of terminology such as 'donor' and 'donation' since, in practice, very few 'donors' actually 'donate' their gametes or embryos without some measure of financial gain or reward in kind.

associations (personal communication) has developed an *International Consensus on Assisted Procreation*. This document was initially drawn up in 1995 and further revised in 1998 and 2001. However, the closest this document comes to addressing issues of commercialism is a statement on payment to oocyte (egg) donors, where it states:

> There should be no compensation to . . . donors for providing the oocytes. However, this does not exclude the reimbursment [*sic*] for expenses, time and risk which are associated with the donation.

The document makes no explicit reference to surrogacy whatever nor to the payment of sperm donors (International Federation of Fertility Societies (IFFS) (1998)). However, IFFS acceptance of the legitimacy of paying an egg donor for her time and the risk involved would certainly provide some endorsement for those seeking to validate the remuneration of surrogate mothers, even though we anticipate that quantification of risk and its appropriate remuneration would be problematic.

In the UK remuneration of gamete and embryo donors may only be author-ised by the Human Fertilisation and Embryology Authority (HFEA) (Human Fertilisation and Embryology Act 1990 section 12(e)). When the HFEA was first set up, it was customary practice to make a small payment to donors and, although the Authority stated its intention to phase out payment to donors as a matter of 'principle' (HFEA (1993b); Johnson (1997)) it allowed centres that were already making payment to donors to continue to do so—to a maximum of £15. In November 1998 following a consultation ostensibly to determine the best way of achieving the termination of payment (HFEA (1998a)), the Authority decided on a total policy reversal (HFEA (1998b)). The explanation of this decision by the chairman of the HFEA, showed that ethical values had been trumped by practical considerations:

> It has become clear from the responses to the recent consultation that the removal of payment in the present climate would seriously jeopardise the supply of sperm donors. . . . We therefore feel it is important that the supply of safe, cryopreserved sperm in the UK remains adequate and do not feel that £15 payment is so wrong that we were pre-pared to threaten the entire service (Deech (1998)).

At the same time the Authority directed that centres established since 1991, that had hitherto been prevented from making any payment at all, would also be allowed to pay donors up to £15. The HFEA also authorised 'egg sharing'—an arrangement in which a woman undergoing assisted conception treatment who agrees to donate some of her eggs for the treatment of another woman is provided with free or subsidised treatment (HFEA (1998c)) although, not long before, it had described egg sharing as an 'unacceptable' practice (HFEA, undated) that should also be 'phased out' (Johnson (1997)). Although the HFEA professed continuing commitment to the withdrawal of payment, it gave no indication how it intended to pursue this—and has subsequently remained silent on the issue.

The Brazier review team evidently considered their recommendations on surrogacy to be totally in keeping with the HFEA's stated intentions to withdraw payment to donors (Brazier *et al* (1998) para 4.37, p 39; para 5.10, p 45). The successful implementation of both the HFEA's stated intentions and the Brazier team's recommendations would have secured the removal of financial incentive across the board in third party assisted conception. The HFEA's unanticipated *volte face* has done little to cement the Brazier review team's recommendations—which may, in part, account for the subsequent lack of progress on the Government's stated intention to undertake further consultation on these.

Although it may be argued that there is a qualitative difference between commercial surrogacy and the donation of sperm, eggs or embryos (since donors do not give birth to a child they will then relinquish) we do not accept that this difference is so great as to render the payment (over and above expenses) of gamete or embryo donors acceptable and that of surrogate mothers unacceptable. For us the issue of commodification of the child remains an insurmountable objection to direct financial reward over and above legitimate expenses.

5. DEVELOPING A 'GENUINE EXPENSES' MODEL

If surrogacy is not to be banned altogether (and very few seem to think that a complete ban is either justifiable or practical) a distinction needs to be made between a commercial, profit-oriented, model of surrogacy and that seeking to avoid or minimise exploitation through reimbursement of 'reasonable expenses'. The Brazier review team recommended a rigorously prescribed and monitored scheme of reimbursement to the birth mother that should cover only 'genuine expenses associated with the pregnancy' (Brazier *et al* (1998) para 5.24, p 47) to prevent surrogacy being undertaken for financial benefit. Brazier *et al* proposed two sets of limitations on payment of expenses. First, they itemised the type of expenses they considered 'genuine'. These included loss of 'actual' earnings, but considered that reimbursement should be 'minimal, and . . . represent no more than the difference between the surrogate mother's usual earnings and state benefits' (Brazier *et al* (1998) para 5.26, p 48). Significantly, Brazier *et al* rejected reimbursement of 'lost' potential earnings. Other 'allowable expenses' identified by Brazier *et al* were: maternity clothing; healthy food; domestic help; counselling fees; legal fees; life and disability insurance; travel to and from hospital/clinic; telephone and postal expenses; overnight accommodation; child care to attend hospital/clinic; medical expenses; ovulation and pregnancy tests; insemination and IVF costs; medicines and vitamins (Brazier *et al* (1998) para 5.25, p 48).

The second strand of Brazier *et al*'s more restrictive approach to 'genuine expenses' was to demand documentary evidence, both of actual lost earnings and other expenses that had been incurred.

In response to the Brazier team's recommendations, COTS (undated) proposed a 'compensatory' payment model that would take account of the inconvenience, discomfort and physical and psychological risks associated with the pregnancy and birth: 'the surrogate mother should be compensated for at least two years out of her and her family's lives, as all of the family's lives are basically on hold' (p 12).

6. CONCLUSION—IMPLICATIONS FOR POLICY

Several key policy questions remain at the end of our review of commercial surrogacy arrangements. First, the somewhat localised issue of where now for surrogacy in the UK? Secondly, what lessons might other countries learn from the UK experience? And thirdly, what future does surrogacy have within a world economy and globalised markets? Discussion of these questions cannot, of course, take place in a vacuum. We consider this is best located within a context that highlights the tension between expedience and ethics.

Some commentators (eg McLachlan and Swales (2000); COTS (undated)) have observed that a potential outcome of prohibiting commercial surrogacy is that it will be driven underground and/or that potential participants will seek such services in countries where it is permitted; in either case increasing the risks of potential exploitation of all parties. Given that the services of surrogate mothers will continue to be bought and sold, McLachlan and Swales (2000) question whether it is better that their services are:

> bought and sold on the open or the black market. . . . if the 'commodification' of babies and surrogate mothers were undesirable, then how much more so, one might think, would be their **illegal** commodification' (p 14—our emphasis).

In the UK the development of an extensive underground surrogacy market would appear unlikely and the costs of overseas surrogacy are likely to deter all but the wealthiest and/or most determined of the involuntarily childless (Troup and Thompson (2000); Lee and Morgan (2001)).

With commercial agencies being closer at hand, both the New York State Task Force on Life and the Law and the Canadian Royal Commission on New Reproductive Technologies had to face an increased likelihood of recourse to commercial surrogacy, but both firmly set out their unwillingness to accommodate the 'pragmatic' option:

> The difficulty of discouraging a practice does not dictate social acceptance and assistance. Society has not legalized the purchase and sale of babies to establish a better marketplace for that activity despite the fact that both the children and commissioning parents might be better protected. The laws against baby selling embody fundamental societal values and doubtlessly minimize the practice even if they do not eliminate it (New York State Task Force on Life and the Law (1988:126)).

> Given that Canadians could go to other countries, particularly the United States, to seek arrangements not permitted in this country, we believe that such a step [prohibition of commercial surrogacy] is needed on the part of the international community to

prevent the exploitation of women and the commodification of children. Adopting a domestic policy would be the first step toward this goal; encouraging other countries to adopt similar measures would reinforce and extend it (Royal Commission on New Reproductive Technologies (1993:692)).

Our view about the position of surrogacy within the UK has to take account of the government response to the report of the Brazier review team—a review that it commissioned itself. Five years after Brazier *et al* reported, there has been no action on the initial proposal to undertake a further round of consultation on their recommendations. At the time of writing, government preoccupations for health care are far removed from surrogacy arrangements. Therefore, it seems safe to assume no government action in the foreseeable future and to anticipate continuation of the current 'policy vacuum' criticised by Brazier *et al* that has permitted surrogacy arrangements to develop in a 'haphazard fashion' (Brazier *et al* (1998) p i). In consequence, we do not hold up the UK experience as a model for others to follow.

As our critique of commercial surrogacy has indicated, we do not endorse a commercial surrogacy market (nor, indeed, a commercial market in assisted conception more generally). Neither, while we can understand the moral principles on which certain jurisdictions have sought to ban surrogacy altogether, do we consider that such a policy is sustainable within the context of globalisation and 'reproductive tourism'. We conclude from this, since surrogacy will continue with or without state regulation, that the most responsible policy option is a regulatory system ensuring that the interests of all participants are safeguarded that incorporates a workable 'reasonable expenses' scheme that is sufficiently comprehensive to discourage recourse to the commercial market. Subject to further refinement, the basic framework to enable such a scheme to develop exists in the UK in the recommendations of Brazier *et al*. The more recent Israeli model of state-supervised surrogacy permitting payment of expenses and 'reasonable compensation' might also offer a lead to other countries seeking to establish a system for effectively managing surrogacy arrangements within an acceptable moral framework (see Schuz, chapter 3 in this volume). However, the Law of Agreements for the Carrying of Fetuses was only implemented in March 1996, this is of too recent origin for its impact yet to be properly evaluated (Benshushan and Schenker (1997); Teman (2001)).

Surrogacy is likely to remain very much a last resort for involuntarily childless people rather than an arrangement primarily made for purposes of convenience. Society should not discourage the opportunity of parenthood to people finding themselves in this position where another woman has offered to assist them by means of a surrogacy arrangement, so long as this does not result in the commodification of the child. For this reason, surrogacy should not be left to the whims of the commercial market and we must accept the responsibility and necessity of state intervention to protect the interests of all participants and of society as a whole.

REFERENCES

Anderson, E, *Value in Ethics and Economics* (Cambridge, Mass, Harvard University Press/The MIT Press, 1993).

Anderson, E, 'Why commercial surrogate motherhood unethically commodifies women and children: Reply to McLachlan and Swales' (2000) 8 *Health Care Analysis* 19.

Balen, A and Hayden, C, 'British Fertility Society survey of all licensed clinics that perform surrogacy in the UK' (1998) 1 *Human Fertility* 6.

Benshushan, A, and Schenker, JG, 'Legitimising Surrogacy in Israel' (1997) 12 *Human Reproduction* 1832.

Blyth, E, 'Section 30: the acceptable face of surrogacy?' (1993) 4 *Journal of Social Welfare and Family Law* 248.

—— 'I wanted to be interesting. I wanted to be able to say "I've done something interesting with my life": Interviews with surrogate mothers in Britain' (1994) 12 *Journal of Reproductive and Infant Psychology* 189.

Brazier, M, 'Can you buy children?' (1999) 11 *Child and Family Law Quarterly* 345.

Brazier, M, Campbell, A and Golombok, S, *Surrogacy. Review for Health Ministers of Current Arrangements for Payments and Regulation. Report of the Review Team*, Cm 4068 (London, HMSO, 1998).

British Medical Association, *Changing Conceptions of Motherhood. The Practice of Surrogacy in Britain* (London, BMA Publications, 1996).

Caldwell, R, 'I never wanted to keep them' *Globe and Mail*, 24 March 2001, http://www.globeandmail.com/gam/Arts/20010324/SALIFE4.html

COTS, *Report: AGM 13* (Lairg, COTS, 2001).

—— *Surrogacy. A Workable Solution. In Response to the Review Team's Report* (Lairg, COTS, undated).

Cotton, K and Winn, D, *Baby Cotton: For Love and Money* (London, Dorling Kindersley, 1985).

Council of Europe, *Human Artificial Procreation* (Strasbourg, Council of Europe, 1989).

—— *Convention for the Protection of Human Rights and Dignity of the Human Being with Regard to the Application of Biology and Medicine* (Strasbourg, Council of Europe, 1996).

Daniels, KR, 'The semen providers' in KR Daniels and E Haimes (eds), *Donor Insemination: International Social Science Perspectives* (Cambridge, Cambridge University Press, 1998).

Deech, R, *Payments for egg and sperm donors*, unpublished letter, 9 December (London, Human Fertilisation and Embryology Authority, 1998).

Department of Health and Social Security, *Report of the Committee of Inquiry into Human Fertilisation and Embryology* (The Warnock Report) Cmnd 9414 (London, DHSS, 1984).

—— *Legislation on Human Infertility Services and Embryo Research*. Cm 46 (London, HMSO, 1986).

—— *Human Fertilisation and Embryology: A Framework for Legislation*, Cm 259 (London, HMSO, 1987).

Dickenson, DL, 'Procuring gametes for research and therapy: the argument for unisex altruism—a response to Donald Evans' (1997) 23 *Journal of Medical Ethics* 93.

Foxcroft, L, 'Surrogacy—Warnock and After' (1997) 2 *Medical Law International* 337.

Freeman, M, 'After Warnock—Whither the Law?' (1986) 39 *Current Legal Problems* 33.

—— 'Is Surrogacy Exploitative?' in S McLean (ed), *Legal Issues in Human Reproduction* (Aldershot, Gower, 1989).

Glover, J, *Fertility and the Family: The Glover Report on Reproduction Technologies to the European Commission* (London, Fourth Estates, 1989).

Human Fertilisation and Embryology Authority, *Code of Practice* (London, HFEA, 1993a).

—— *Second Annual Report* (London, HFEA, 1993b).

—— *Consultation on the Implementation of Withdrawal of Payments to Donors* (London, HFEA, 1998a).

—— *HFEA minutes of meeting, November,* (1998b) www.hfea.gov.uk

—— *Paid Egg Sharing to be Regulated, not Banned* (press release) 10 December (London, HFEA, 1998c).

—— *Working Group on the Effects of Removing Payment to Donors Policy Statement on Payment for Gametes* (London, HFEA, undated).

International Federation of Fertility Societies, *International Consensus on Assisted Procreation* (Montpellier, IFFS, 1995).

Johnson, MHC, 'Payments to gamete donors: position of the Human Fertilisation and Embryology Authority' (1997) 12 *Human Reproduction* 1839.

Kornegay, RJ, 'Is Commercial Surrogacy Baby Selling?' (1990) 7 *Journal of Applied Philosophy* 45.

Lee, R and Morgan, D, *Human Fertilisation and Embryology—Regulating the Reproductive Revolution* (London, Blackstone Press, 2001).

McLachlan, HV and Swales, JK, 'Babies, Child Bearers and Commodification: Anderson, Brazier *et al* and the Political Economy of Commercial Surrogate Motherhood' (2000) 8 *Health Care Analysis* 1.

—— 'Exploitation and Commercial Surrogate Motherhood' (2001) 7 *Human Reproduction and Genetic Ethics* 8.

The New York State Task Force on Life and the Law (1988) *Surrogate Parenting: Analysis and Recommendations for Public Policy* (New York, The New York State Task Force on Life and the Law, 1988).

Nuffield Council on Bioethics, *Human Tissue: Ethical and Legal Issues* (London, Nuffield Council on Bioethics, 1995).

Overall, C, *Ethics and Human Reproduction: a Feminist Analysis* (London, Allen and Unwin, 1987).

Rae, SB, *The Ethics of Commercial Surrogate Motherhood: Brave New Families?* (London, Praeger, 1994).

Ragoné, H, *Surrogate Motherhood: Conception in the Heart* (Boulder, Westview Press, 1994).

Royal Commission on New Reproductive Technologies, *Proceed with Care: Final Report of the Royal Commission on New Reproductive Technologies* (Ottawa, Minister of Government Services, 1993).

Rubin, S, 'Reproductive Options 1: A Spermdonor Baby Grows Up' in J Zimmerman (ed), *The Technological Woman: Interfacing with Tomorrow* (New York, Praeger, 1983).

Sackville, T, *Official Report*, House of Commons, 26 October 1994, col 974.

Shalev, C, *Birth Power: The Case for Surrogacy* (New Haven and London, Yale University Press, 1989).

Shanley, ML, 'Surrogate Mothering and Women's Freedom: A Critique of Contracts for Human Reproduction' (1993) Spring, *Signs* 618.

Teman, E, 'Technological Fragmentation as Women's Empowerment: Surrogate Motherhood in Israel' (2001) 31 *Women's Studies Quarterly* 11.

Tong, R, *Feminist Approaches to Bioethics* (Boulder, Colorado, Westview Press, 1997).

Troup, J and Thompson, P, 'Gay Dads' Baby No 3' *The Sun*, 1 June 2000, 1.

van Niekerk, A and van Zyl, L, 'Commercial Surrogacy and the Commodification of Children: An Ethical Perspective' (1995) 8 *Medicine and Law* 163.

Wertheimer, A, *Exploitation* (Princeton, Princeton University Press, 1996).

16

Legitimising Surrogacy in Israel: Religious Perspectives

JOSEPH SCHENKER

1. INTRODUCTION

USING SURROGACY TO overcome childlessness is not a recent concept. Its first example was mentioned in the Bible (Genesis 16) 'Sarai said to Abram: Behold now, the Lord has prevented me from bearing children; Go to my maid, Hagar, it may be we shall obtain children from her. And Hagar bore Abram a son, Ishmael.' In another biblical example (Genesis 30) Rachel, who was childless, used her slave girl Bilha to bear a child for Jacob. This type of surrogacy was probably practised for centuries by peoples in different civilisations.

The only type of surrogacy that is legally sanctioned in Israel[1] is full (gestational) surrogacy, where the intended parents provide the gametes. Fertilisation is performed *in vitro* or by gamete intra-fallopian transfer (GIFT) or zygote intra-fallopian transfer (ZIFT). The pre-embryo is implanted in the uterus of the birth—or surrogate—mother. The resulting child is relinquished to the intended parents after legal adoption.

It is important for practitioners in the field of reproductive medicine to understand attitudes towards reproduction that derive from different religions. Religion deals with affairs that are regarded as extraordinary, and as such has a unique significance in all human cultures. It is often difficult to dissociate the influence of distinctly religious factors from other cultural conditions affecting women's reproductive health. Religious groups, however, still exert influence on the civil authorities in matters of reproduction. They have been active in pressing their bioethical positions on the public arena in pluralistic societies. Developments in reproductive medicine raise new ethical questions for the different religions that do not always have clear answers.

Israel is a multicultural society. In July 2001 its multi-ethnic population was estimated to be almost six million, of which Jewish people account for some 80 per cent,[2] 14.6 per cent are Muslim,[3] 2.1 per cent Christian, and 1.6 per cent

---

[1] See Schuz, chapter 3, this volume.

[2] Europe/America-born: 32.15%; Israel-born: 20.85%; Africa-born: 14.65%; Asia-born: 12.6%.

[3] The largest religious minority in Israel is Muslim. The majority adhere to the Sunni. The term Sunnah is used by Muslims to identify the majority group of Islam , known fully as people of sunnah and of community. The Sunnites belonging to the Shafi'i School.

Druze. Other faiths account for the remaining 1.6 per cent. In addition, according to a recent Palestinian census, 2.8 million Palestinians live in the West Bank, Gaza, and East Jerusalem—territory captured by Israel from Jordan in the 1967 Six-Day War. The 45,000 Christians that live there today make up about 1.8 per cent of the population.

The growth in the Jewish population is primarily accounted for by immigration. In the last 10 years, for example, one million Jews came from Russia. The Jewish population is diverse. Immigrants differed in skin colour and culture and brought with them languages and customs from a variety of countries. The two main religious groupings are formed by those who follow the Ashkenazi rite (Jews from central and eastern Europe and Diaspora) and those who follow the Sephardim and Oriental rite (Jews from the Mediterranean and from the Middle and Far East). Thus there are traditionally two chief rabbis in Israel, one Ashkenazi and one Sefardi. Religious Jewry in Israel constitutes a significant section of the population and has a strong political power. There is also, however, a strong movement that seeks to prevent religious bodies from dominating national life or from interfering with individual freedom of conscience. Disputes occasionally arise over differences of interpretation concerning the role of religious authority as distinct from the role of state authority.

Large Muslim communities also live in the towns. Like all other religious communities, Muslims in Israel enjoy considerable autonomy in dealing with matters of marriage and divorce and have separate religious courts. The state helps to maintain their customs and religious institutions. Among the Muslims about 45,000 are Bedouin; about three-quarters of these live in the Negev, and the rest live in Galilee. Today, Israel's Druze community numbers about 80,000, living in 17 villages in the Galilee, Golan and Carmel areas. The Druze were granted a nationality status distinct from the Arabic-speaking population, and are expected to serve in the Israeli army.[4]

2. JEWISH LAW IN ISRAEL

When Israel's independence was proclaimed in 1948, English ceased to be the predominant legal language and was immediately replaced by Hebrew. The law was henceforth made by the democratic authorities of the autonomous state which, in spite of an Arab minority, became Jewish in conception, way of thinking, and purpose. The rabbinate and the various functions of the rabbi in modern Israel differ fundamentally from their counterparts in any other part of the Jewish world, whether ancient or modern. A number of factors have contributed toward this unique state of affairs. In the first place there is the law of

---

[4] Since 1957 the Druze have been given official recognition in Israel as a separate religious community. In 1962 the Knesset set up official Druze communal courts. The spiritual leadership of the community is in the hands of its sheiks from the various centers of Druze population.

the State of Israel which establishes the halakhah as state law in all matters affecting personal status, which includes marriage, divorce, and legitimacy, and affords the rabbinical courts the status of civil courts of law within that wide sphere.

Jewish law continues to be applied by the rabbinical courts within their jurisdiction in matters of personal status. The jurisdiction of the rabbinical courts was defined in a Knesset law of 1953 which, save for one or two changes, entailed no substantial departure from the situation in the British Mandate period (1920–48). It gave the rabbinical courts exclusive jurisdiction in matters of marriage and divorce where they are naturally dealt with in accordance with Jewish law. In matters of personal status concerning Jewish parties the general courts are also required to decide according to Jewish law, except when law of the state makes express provision on the matter. The law of adoption in 1960 was excluded from the definition of matters of personal status. It is in this context that the law governing surrogate motherhood took shape.[5]

3. RELIGIOUS ETHICS

Religion, being concerned with affairs that are regarded as extraordinary and as having unique importance in life, is an intrinsic aspect of the culture of all societies. It is such an integral part of the texture of many cultures that it is not always easily isolated for separate analysis. In complex cultures distinctively religious institutions and values can have a more independent existence and their influence on reproductive health may be more specific. The role of theology in bioethics is foremost to clarify, for the different religious communities, the perceived attitudes toward these developments. At least three factors determine the influence of religious viewpoints: the size of the relevant community, the authority of the current viewpoints within the community, and the unanimity and diversity of opinion in the relevant community. The weight and authority of specific religious viewpoints will influence the number of adherents who draw on these views in considering public policy issues.

At one extreme are communities that emphasise the importance of individual judgments. These include religious communities such as the Baptists and the Evangelicals. At the other extreme are traditions with centralised teaching authorities, such as the Roman Catholic Church. In between are communities that formulate general policies at organised centralised meetings but that see these policies as reflections of current thinking rather than as authoritative teachings. These include the decisions of the General Convention of the Episcopalian Church, the General Assembly of the Presbyterian Church, and the General Conference of the United Methodist Church. Also in between are communities that emphasise the authority of leading religious scholars, while

---

[5] See Schuz, chapter 3, this volume.

recognising that these scholars may disagree. These include the Muslim community and the Jewish community.

The final factor to consider is the diversity of opinion in the relevant community. The greater the diversity of opinion, the less constrained individual infertile couples will feel when confronting choices about particular treatment decisions and the less the community in question will be able to influence public policy decisions.

4. THE STRUCTURE OF JEWISH LAW

A strict association between faith and practical ruling characterises the Jewish religion. Jewish law has two divisions, written and oral. The foundation of the written law and the origin of authority are the Torah, the first five books of the Scripture. It is an expression of God's revelation, reaching and guiding humanity. The Torah is viewed as a single unit, a divine text that includes moral values as well as practical laws. The oral laws interpret, expand, and elucidate the written Torah and regulate new rules and customs. Its authority is derived from the written Torah. The dominant parts of the oral law are as follows:

Mishnah. Numerous scholars compiled an early textbook systematically over a few centuries. Its final form was established early in the third century. The Mishnah includes early traditional and original interpretations of the written Torah, ancient regulations that are not written in the Torah, and post-Bible regulations.

Talmud. For approximately three centuries after the final compilation of the Mishnah, the great interpreters studied the six orders to the Mishnah and wrote a monumental composition called Talmud.

Post-Talmudic codes. After the compilation of the Talmud, an enormous amount of Talmudic knowledge was essential for efficient ruling. These post-Talmudic codes came to the world with the intention of assisting access to the laws, regulations, and customs of the Talmudic Halakha. Different scholars[6] until the sixteenth century summarised and reviewed the Halahic conclusions of the Talmud in the post-Talmudic Codes.

Responsa. The various attitudes of rabbinical scholars about the way religion should be applied in the changing world is analysed and discussed with regard to the legal codes, and written opinion is given by qualified authorities to questions about aspects of Jewish law. Responsa is the term usually confined to written replies given to questions on all aspects of Jewish law by authorities from the time of the later Geonim to the present day. About 1,000 volumes, containing more than half a million separate Responsa have appeared in print.

---

[6] Among the scholars were Rashi (l040–1105), Rabbi Moshe Ben Nachman (1195–1270), and Rabbi Menahem Ben Shalom Hameiri (1249–1316).

The application of new technology according to Jewish law is based on the following principles: The Mishnah emphasises that only prohibitive, strict decisions require juridical substantiation while permissibility or leniency needs no supportive precedent. The absence of a prohibitive substantiation is to be equated with halakhic permissibility. This implies that any technological innovation is permissible unless there is a halakhic reason for prohibiting it.

In order to be sure that there is no halakhic prohibition against a new procedure, an accepted halakhic authority must be consulted. Jewish law differentiates between the authority to abrogate a temporary prohibition and the authority to determine permanent permissibility. Faced with uncertainty or insufficient information, one is entitled to be strict with one-self; no special authority is needed for prohibition by the individual. On the other hand, in order to establish permissibility, there must be unequivocal information. When there is no clear precedent in halvah'ha to decide the issue at hand, one must be thoroughly versed in all galactic sources before definitely confirming that no galactic reason for prohibition exists. There are well-known galactic rules for deciding controversial issues. If, for example, there is a doubt in a matter prohibited by the Torah, the ruling is prohibitive; if the doubt is related to a rabbinical ruling the decision is usually permissive.

5. CHRISTIANITY

Christianity is centred on Jesus Christ as the supreme revelation of God and as lord of his followers and is based on his teachings. Christianity comprises three principal divisions: the Roman Catholic Church, Protestant churches, and Orthodox Catholic churches. It is particularly characterised by its universality and the missionary activity which results from its attempts to extend this doctrine to all humanity. The most striking development in the evolution of Christianity from its Jewish origin was the transition from a national religion (of the Jewish nation) to a universal religion. At the heart of Christianity are issues of sexuality, marriage, and parenthood. The intervention of the church in the field of reproduction is inspired by the love it feels for humans, helping them to recognise and respect their rights and duties. The Old Testament and the New Testament form the scriptures that are sacred to Christians. The Old Testament emphasises the idea of an agreement between God and his people and contains a record of Jewish history to show how faithfully this agreement was observed. The New Testament contains promises made by God to humanity, as shown in the teaching and experiences of Christ and his followers.

6. ROMAN CATHOLICISM

Roman Catholics base their beliefs on both the Bible and the traditions of their church. The traditions come from the declarations of church councils and popes. They also come from short statements called creeds and from dogma. The Roman Catholic Church recognises in marriage and its indissoluble unity the only setting worth of truly responsible procreation. The church abides by principles used to guide believers. The first principle is related to the protection of the human being from its very beginning, which is conception; the right to life is fundamental. The second principle is that procreation is inseparable from the psycho-emotional relationship of the parents. However, from the moral point of view, a child must be the fruit of the marriage. The fidelity of the spouses involves acknowledgement that they become a father and a mother only through each other; the child is a living image of the parents' love, the permanent sign of their conjugal union. Procreation is not performed by a physician; the physician may be in the position to help the parents achieve conception but is not the one who is the 'baby maker'. The third principle is related to the personal norm of human integrity and dignity, and it should be taken into consideration in medical decisions, especially in the field of infertility.

7. THE EASTERN ORTHODOX CHURCH

The Eastern Orthodox Church was formally formed in 1054 when a split between the eastern and western churches occurred. The Eastern Orthodox religion consists of several independents and self-governing denominations and some that are not self-governing. The four principal self-governing denominations are Constantinople, Turkey; Alexandria, Egypt; Antioch (Damascus), Syria and Jerusalem. Others in order of size are the churches of Russia, Romania, Serbia, Greece, and Bulgaria. Georgia, and Cyprus. Eastern Orthodox congregations also are located in Western Europe, North America, Central Africa, and the Far East, but they are not fully self-governing. Marriage is one of the seven major sacraments. The church permits divorce and allows divorced persons to remarry, but the first marriage is the greatest in the eyes of God.

8. PROTESTANTISM

Protestantism resulted chiefly from the Reformation, a religious and political movement that began in Europe in 1517. At its base was protest against the bureaucracy and policies of the Roman Catholic Church. The result was the formation of several Protestant denominations. Protestants disagree with other Christians about the relationship between humanity and God. As a result, certain of their beliefs differ from those of other Christians, specifically ones related to the nature of faith and grace and the authority of the Bible. Most Protestants believe that the Bible should be the only authority of their religion. Protestantism is most widely practised in Europe and North America. A Protestant religion is the state religion in a number of nations, including Denmark, Norway and

Sweden. Protestantism has strongly influenced the cultural, political, and social history of these and other countries. The Baptist, Methodist, Lutheran, Mormon, Presbyterian, Episcopal, United Church of Christ, Christian Science, Jehovah's Witness, and Mennonite religions have liberal attitudes towards infertility treatments.

The Anglican Church

Before the Reformation the Church of England separated from the Roman Catholic Church. Anglicanism became the state religion of England and spread as British colonists settled in North and South America, Africa, and Asia. It is the official faith of the United Kingdom. Anglicans live in the ancient faith of the Christian church as expressed in the Apostles and Nicene creeds. They base their religion on scripture, tradition, and reason. They follow the Book of Common Prayer, which is the basis for doctrine and discipline as well as for worship, but they acknowledge the right of national churches to revise the Book according to their needs. Anglicans often view themselves as a bridge between Roman Catholics and Protestants.

9. ISLAM

Islam was founded by the Prophet Muhammad (ac700–632) born in Mecca. In middle life an inner conviction dawned on him that he was the prophet chosen by Allah to convey eternal messages to the Arabs. There are two broad subdivisions of Islam—Shia and Sunnis. Shia originally referred to the partisans (Shiva) of Ali and over the centuries developed its own body of law. This differed in minor ways (inheritance and the status of women) from that of the majority of Sunnis. Sharia law is the heart of the Islamic religion, defining the path in which God wishes humans to walk. It deals not only with matters of religious ritual but also regulates every aspect of political, social, and private life. The main roots from which it is derived are the Quran and the Hadith, the tradition of the Prophet Muhammad. According to orthodox Muslims, the law is founded in divine revelation, and since revelation ended with the death of Muhammad, the Sharia is immortal.

There are two sources of Sharia in Islam, primary and secondary. The four primary sources include, first, the holy Quran, the word of God; secondly, the Sunna, the customs and authentic tradition and sayings of the Prophet Muhammad, collected by specialists in Hadith (tradition); thirdly, Igmaah, the consensus of the community of believers, who, according to a saying of the Irophen, would not agree on any error; finally, Kias (analogy). This is the intelligent reasoning with which to rule on events the Quran and Sunna do not mention, by matching against similar or equivalent events ruled on.

Good Muslims resort to secondary sources of Sharia for matters not dealt with in the primary sources. The Sharia is not rigid and leaves room to adapt to emerging situations in different times and places. It can accommodate different honest opinions, as long as they do not conflict with the spirit of its primary sources and are directed to the benefit of humanity. Muslim modernists however have proclaimed the right of every qualified person to examine the sources of the Sharia. The result is that in most Muslim countries today, the Sharia laws are restricted and dominate only personal affairs.

Even in personal matters, a great deal of attention is now given to ways of adapting Islamic law to modern life. The progressive attitudes of some religious leaders are revealed not only in familiar law but also with respect to other matters, especially those having to do with medical developments in the field of reproduction. Muslims will want to be assured that modern medicine is also acceptable according to Sharia Islamic norms.

Islamic medical ethics is based on Egyptian Fatawa—the legal responses provided by religious scholars on request from lay persons or government authorities. Its main characteristics include a constant attempt to base modem medical treatments in the classic sources of Islamic law; the idea that the problems raised derive directly from the commandments and prohibitions of Islamic law; and when Islamic law and state law on certain medical ethics are contra indicatory, the Fatawa is issued to mediate. Islamic medical ethics is often inseparable from social and political issues.

The Druze Religion

The Druze religion is secret. Founded in Cairo by al-Hakim in the tenth century, the faith spread in the Middle East through a preacher called al-Darazi who gave it his name. After the death of its founder the sect was persecuted. The moral system of the Druze religion consists of seven principles: love truth, take care of one another, renounce all other religions, avoid the demon and all wrongdoers, accept divine unity in humanity, accept all al-Hakim's acts in total accordance to al-Hakim's will. The Druze follow a life style of isolation where no conversion is allowed, neither out of, nor into, the religion. When Druze live among people of other religions, they try to blend in, in order to protect their religion. Druze have earlier been reported to practice polygamy. But there is no evidence of such practise today. Marriage outside the faith is forbidden.

The Status of Women

Both biblical and Talmudic literatures depict varying attitudes towards women, not always favourable. References made to women's social, legal or religious status, written almost exclusively by men, reflect personal experiences, as well as recognition of the biological and functional differences between the sexes.

A major difference between the roles of men and women in Jewish religious life concerns the performance of the commandments. The woman is commanded to observe all the prohibitions just as is a man. She differs from the man, however, in that she is not always required to perform those positive precepts, which are to be performed at a specific time.

Christianity did not bring revolutionary social change to the position of women, but it made possible a new position in the family and congregation. In Judaism of the period of the early church, women were held in very low esteem, and this was the basis for Jewish divorce practices that put women practically at men's complete disposal. With the prohibition of divorce, Jesus himself did away with this low estimation of women. Paul substitutes even the Jewish view of the patriarchal position of man with a new spiritual interpretation of marriage: 'There is neither male nor female; for you are all one in Christ Jesus.'

This created a change in the position of women in the congregation: in the synagogue the women were inactive participants in the worship service and sat veiled on the women's side, usually separated from the rest by an opaque lattice. In the Christian congregation, however, women appeared as members with full rights. Besides the higher status of women in family and congregation, a lower estimation is constantly present in radical asceticism because women carry 'the stain of Eve'. Women were considered authors of sin, sexual depravation, sources of impunity, of sexual passions, of perdition for men, like in paradise. Probably one of the reasons why women were inconceivable as priests was their characteristic of being the origin of sin.

The general attitude towards women reflected in the Hadith is positive. The Hadith elaborates on the Quran's teaching regarding the spiritual equality of women and men. The nature of women as reflected in the Hadith spans the whole spectrum from the saintly to the evil and unclean. The Hadith gives unquestionable evidence that the Hijab, which implies not only the face veil but also the sum of practices connected with the seclusion of women, was legislatively made obligatory for the wives of the Prophet. It also contains much evidence of women's visibility as well as full participation in communal matters in the early Islamic period. Later generations of pious scholars changed these patterns considerably; rather, they sanctioned such changes as occurred within Islam under foreign influence. Through the centuries, traditionalist commentators on the Quran emphasised restrictive norms with the distinct purpose of legitimising the newly restricted status of women in Islam. The result was that restrictions increased with the progression of time.

Marriage

Marriage is a combination of a religious and legal act between a man and a woman. The couple commit themselves to their mutual duties and creates between them a binding religious relationship that also affects others. From a practical perspective marriage is a mitzvah (religious duty) and considered to be among the most useful means of preventing sexual sins. It is also the proper way to fulfil God's command to be fruitful and multiply. The duty to marry and procreate is independent of social status or religious position.

The Christian understanding of marriage has been strongly influenced by the Old Testament view of marriage as an institution primarily concerned with the founding and procuring of a family, rather than sustaining the individual happiness of the marriage partners. Until the Reformation, the patriarchal family structure not only had been preserved but also had been defended from all attacks by sectarian groups. In spite of this, a transformation occurred from the early days of Christianity. Marriage as an institution experienced a growth of individualism and spiritualism, and these eventually led to the demise of traditional patriarchy. Christianity has contributed to a spiritualisation of marriage and family life, to a personal deepening of the relations between marriage partners and between parents and children, as well as between heads of households and domestic servants in large families, in contrast to patriarchal Jewish family life.

The Quran explicitly encourages marriage, even the marriage of slaves: 'And marry those among you who are single and those who are fit among your male slaves and your female slaves; if they are needy, Allah will make them free from want of His Grace.' The Quranic divorce laws that stipulated the obligatory Niddah (a waiting period of about three months after the final pronouncement of the divorce formula) ameliorate a woman's position; time for reflection is mandated, and the woman must be treated fairly if the man ultimately resolves to divorce her. These laws, although they improve women's status, do not establish political, social, or economic equality of the sexes, since men are considered a degree above women.

Sexual Practices

Sex is part of human life. The Jewish approach to sex has always been free, healthy, and lacking frustration, and Jewish law recognises sexual desire. Complete abstinence by a married couple is not condoned. Each married partner has conjugal duties toward the other. The wife has conjugal rights based on Mitzvat Onah, which is one of the three elementary duties of the husband: supporting his wife with food, clothing, and conjugation.

In the early times of Christianity the church fathers in Rome articulated principles for sexual intercourse. The objective of sexual intercourse in married couples was almost exclusively procreation. Pleasure was excluded as evil and unworthy of a Christian.

Similarly, Islam links marital sex to procreation and family formation. The Quran restricts sexual intercourse to that of the penis in the vagina, because this is the route for procreation and continuation of humankind. A husband may enjoy his wife's body in any way except anal intercourse. Oral sex was not mentioned in the primary source of Sharia. However secondary sources of Sharia indicate that it is disliked but not forbidden.

Reproduction

Jewish attitudes toward infertility can be discerned from the fact that the first command from God to Adam was, 'Be fruitful and multiply.' This is expressed in the Talmudic saying from the second century, 'Any man who has no children is considered as dead man.' This attitude arises from the Bible itself and refers to the words of Rachel, who was barren: 'Give me children or else I die.' A rabbinic disagreement in the Mishnah deals with the number of children required to fulfil the divine command of procreation. The Shammai School claimed that two sons were sufficient and referred to Moses with his two sons as a proper model. The Hillel school insisted that one son and one daughter are essential. Their view was based on God's creation of the rib, with Adam and Eve as the first humans. As in most cases, Talmudic preference is in accord with the Hillel School. Although a man who accomplishes the basic command of procreation is not committed by the Torah to continue to procreate he is obligated to be married and not live in celibacy. Along these lines, the Mishnah raises an interesting question: Does the demand to procreate rest equally on men and women, or is it an exclusive obligation of men, while women who bear all of the risk of childbearing bear no responsibility? According to Jewish law, an infertile couple should undergo diagnosis and treatment as a single unit. However, the medical treatment is different for men and women. From a strictly religious point of view, one should first examine the woman. If a pathologic condition is not found, the man is examined.

The preferred method of seminal fluid analysis is the post-coital test, which examines motile sperm in a mucus sample collected from the woman's vagina several hours after coitus. If the results are inconclusive or abnormal after repeated attempts, the ejaculate should be collected after coitus interruptus with a special condom. Examination of the semen for an infertility evaluation is not included in the prohibition against spilling one's seed. If other methods are not possible for mechanical or psychological reasons, some rabbis permit collection of an ejaculate obtained by means of masturbation.

The halakhot (religious laws) surrounding a woman's menstrual cycle form the basic backdrop for this discussion because they govern the normal sexual life of a religiously committed Jewish couple. Understanding their basic concepts is indispensable to professionals providing fertility therapy to an observant couple. A menstruating woman is called Niddah in the Bible and in the Talmudic and post-Talmudic literature. As long as she is within the status of Niddah, sexual contact with her is forbidden. The laws concerning Niddah are some of the most fundamental principles of the halakhic system, and the historical development of the relevant tracts through the centuries is also extremely complicated.

Christianity, like other religions, is characterised by great diversity of sects. It is difficult to find common elements, other than origin and the acceptance of common sacred writings and symbols, among all Christian sects. There is, however, a core of common principles within the early Christian movement, the Western medieval church, and the modern Roman Catholic and major Protestant churches. But in so far as a core of European Christian principles exists, its relations to fertility are largely indirect and cannot easily be formulated. Christianity intensifies some types of group cohesion; it exerts a moral force tending towards the stability of marriage and other social relations, and it heightens the evaluation of children as immortal souls received by parents in sacred trust. All these factors are conducive to high fertility, but they are influences common to many religions rather than characteristics peculiar to Christianity.

According to Roman Catholic instruction the suffering of spouses who cannot have children or who are afraid of bringing a handicapped child into the world is a suffering that everyone must understand. The desire for a child is natural: it expresses the vocation to fatherhood and motherhood inscribed in conjugal love. This desire can be even stronger if the couple is affected by sterility.

Nevertheless, marriage does not confer upon the spouses the right to have a child, but only the right to perform those natural acts, which are *per se* ordered to procreation. A true and proper right to a child would be contrary to the child's dignity and nature. The child is not an object to which one has a right, nor can s/he be considered as an object of ownership. For this reason, the child has the right, as already mentioned, to be the fruit of the specific act of the conjugal love of her/his parents; and he also has the right to be respected as a person from the moment of conception. The community of believers is called to shed light upon and support the suffering of those who are unable to fulfil their legitimate aspiration to marriage, and is a living testimony of the mutual giving of the parents.

Couples with infertility problems must not forget that even when procreation is not possible, conjugal life does not for this reason lose its value. Physical sterility in fact can be for spouses the occasion for other important services to the life of the humanity; for example, adoption, various forms of educational work, and assistance to other families and to disadvantaged children.

Islam gives strong and unequivocal emphasis to high fertility, and social structures universally support high fertility.

Assisted Reproduction

There are three basic principles in the Jewish religion which, with certain restrictions, favour the permissibility of fertility treatment: First, the command-ment 'Be fruitful and multiply'; secondly, the mitzvah of loving kindness (Gmilut Hasadim); and, thirdly, family integrity. The first commandment in the Torah is based on the verse 'Be fruitful and multiply and replenish the earth.' In halakhic literature the fulfilment of this command is considered of greatest importance because the fulfilment of all other commandments depends on it. Despite the importance of this commandment, Halakhah does not permit indis-criminate multiplication of genetic offspring. On the contrary, a system of laws and marital restrictions (laws of incest) limiting sexual activity to a closed fam-ily framework emphasises not only the dissemination of biological genes, but also the equally important transmission of cultural and moral traditions from generation to generation.

Obviously, a childless couple is within the category of personal suffering and according to the commandment of loving kindness there exists a clear obliga-tion to assist them in every permissible way, as long as no one else is thereby harmed. Domestic peace and the integrity of the family are extremely important in Jewish law.

There is near unanimity of opinion that therapeutic insemination with hus-band's sperm (AIH) is permissible if no other method will allow the wife to become pregnant. However, certain qualifications do exist. First, the couple must have attempted conception for a reasonable period of time (5 to 10 years) and medical proof must exist of the absolute necessity for AIH. Second, accord-ing to many authorities, insemination may not be performed while the woman is in Niddah.

Most rabbis allow sperm to be obtained from the husband both for analysis and insemination, but opinions differ about the best method of procuring it. Masturbation should be avoided if at all possible, and coitus interruptus and the use of a special condom are preferred. Therapeutic insemination with donor sperm (AID) is accepted by part of the Jewish population in Israel. According to the regulations of the Ministry of Health, it is allowed under special regulations. AID is not morally accepted by all infertile couples or their physicians, however, and is unacceptable to most rabbinical authorities. Rabbis have been discussing the principles involved in AID for many centuries. The discussions are based on ancient sources in the Talmud and codes of Jewish law that from the fifth cen-tury mention procreation without intercourse.

Experts agree that AID using the semen of a Jewish donor is forbidden. It is the severity of the prohibition that is debatable. The question is whether AID constitutes adultery, which is strictly forbidden by the Torah, or whether the injunction stems from the source—primarily the legal complications of the birth of a AID offspring—as most experts hold. Some rabbinical authorities permit

AID if the donor is a non-Jew. This eliminates some of the legal complications related to the personal status of the offspring. If the donor is a gentile, the child is pagan (blemished); if the child is a girl, she is forbidden to marry a Cohen (priest). Jewish law prohibits AID for a variety of reasons: incest, lack of genealogy, and problems related to inheritance. In addition, donors and the physicians who use the semen are violating the severe prohibition against masturbation. Many rabbinical scholars consider a child conceived through AID as having the status of Mamzer (bastard) which severely limits the offspring's prospects of marriage and implies a severe functional handicap from a social point of view. Other rabbis believe the offspring to be legitimate.

The various aspects of the 'test tube baby' are of considerable interest. The basic fact that allows IVF-ET to be considered in the rabbinical literature at all is that the oocyte and the sperm originate from the wife and husband based on the commandment of procreation stated in the Bible. What are some of the delineating factors that would nevertheless withhold Jewish law from allowing IVF-ET? Some individual rabbis take a strict position and suggest that legal and biologic ties be severed with the removal of the egg. The fact that the host environment is sustained by means of medical intervention could change the biologic and legal status of the child. The majority Jewish religious point of view, however, formulated by the chief rabbis of Israel, one of the Ashkenazi sectors (European origin) and one of the Sephardim sector (Oriental origin), supports both IVF and ET. Jews living outside Israel are generally subjected to the laws of the country in which they live, except when they wish or are required obeying the Jewish traditional personal-status regulations. In such cases, local rabbinical authorities apply rules applicable in the Stale of Israel when such exist and are recognised.

Jewish law places limits on semen collection, management of menstrual problems, and homologous and heterologous insemination. These factors are considered when IVF-ET is undertaken. As mentioned, the collection of semen can present problems because of the prohibition against masturbation and seed wasting. However, for fertility analysis, many rabbinical authorities permit the collection of semen by means of coitus interruptus or by the use of a condom with a perforation. If a condom is used, it must be of the type that will not damage sperm vitality. Using either natural cycles or induced cycles to prepare a woman for oocyte retrieval may interfere with the Niddah state. Despite these concerns, thousands of Jewish children have been born as a result of IVF procedures in Israel, many of them to very religious couples.

The main issue with regard to egg or embryo donation is whether the oocyte donor or the recipient should be considered the mother. Jewish law says that the mother determines the religious status of the child. Contrary to the Talmudic interpretation, the father of a child resulting from AID is the sperm donor. Thus there is a divisible partnership-ownership of the egg and the environment in which the embryo is conceived. The child is related to the one who finished its formation, the one who gave birth. A judgment in the Mishnah states that if a person starts an action but does not complete it and another person comes along and completes it, the one who completes the action is considered to have done it all. Only the offspring of a Jewish mother is regarded as a Jew. For purposes of lineage, the recipient woman rather than the ovum donor is the mother, although the latter is certainly the genetic parent. If the recipient is Jewish, then the child is Jewish.

Cryopreservation of pre-embryos is routinely practised in IVF programmes. Because it stops the development and growth of the embryo, cryopreservation raises the basic question of whether it cancels all rights of the pre-embryo's father. As far as the mother is concerned the problem is simple, since the embryo is transferred into her uterus later and will renew the mother-embryo relationship.

As for the father, whose main function is to fertilise the oocyte to form the pre-embryo, the period of freezing may sever his relationship with the child. Freezing the sperm and pre-embryo is permitted in Judaism only when all measures are taken to ensure that the father's identity will not be lost. The Jewish religion does not forbid gestational carriage or surrogacy. If surrogacy is practised, the infant should be placed in the custody of the producer of the sperm. From the religious point of view, the child belongs to the man who gave the sperm and the woman who gave birth.

The Vatican statement on assisted reproduction is very clear: assisted reproduction is not accepted. In 1956, Pope Pius XII declared that attempts at artificial human fecundation *in vitro* must be rejected as immoral and absolutely unlawful. The Church argues that IVF involves disregard for human life and separates human procreation from sexual intercourse. The Vatican's instruction on respect for human life made an important contribution to discussion on the practice of new reproductive technologies. It was issued by the Congregation for the Doctrine of the Faith in February 1987, signed by Cardinal Joseph Ratzniger, and approved by Pope John Paul II. The document is a response to inquiries from Episcopal conferences and individual bishops about the interventions into human reproduction. The key value in the instructions is respect for the dignity of the human person. The criteria for evaluating these interventions are the respect defence, and promotion of a human being and his or her primary and fundamental right to life and dignity as a person who is endowed with a spiritual soul and with moral responsibility.

Fertilisation is licit when it is the result of a conjugal act, that is, sexual intercourse between husband and wife. From the moral point of view, procreation is deprived of its proper perfection when it is not desired as a result of the conjugal act, that is, the specific act of the spouses' union. The instruction is quite clear in its judgment on reproductive technology. Although augmented by modern concepts of human dignity and moral rights, this position relies heavily on the traditional natural-law analysis that intercourse has two inseparable dimensions: procreative and unitive. There can be absolutely no separation of any dimension of any aspect of reproduction. Consequently, the instruction prohibits IVF-ET, surrogate motherhood, and cryopreservation of embryos. It also rejects AIH and IVF on the grounds that they involve a separation between 'the goods and meanings of marriage.' Separation of these two dimensions means that procreation thus achieved is 'deprived of its proper perfection' and is therefore 'not in conformity with the dignity of the person.' A child must be conceived through an act of love and, indeed, of sexual intercourse.

Within marriage AIH cannot be accepted except for situations in which the procedure is not a substitute for the conjugal act but facilitates it so that the act attains its natural purpose. Gamete intrafallopian transfer (GIFT) is acceptable because sperm can be removed from the vagina after a normal sexual act and implanted into the fallopian tube, where fertilisation occurs.

Heterologous artificial fertilisation is contrary to the unity of marriage, to the dignity of the spouses, to the vocation proper to parents, and to a child's right to be conceived and brought into the world in and from marriage. As mentioned, this method of conception also violates the rights of the child, compromises his or her parental origins, and can interfere with the development of personal identity. This position eliminates any use of donor semen whether for artificial insemination or for IVF. Furthermore, artificial fertilisation of a woman who is unmarried or a widow, whoever the donor may be, cannot be morally justified. The practice of ovum donation is prohibited on the same basis as sperm donation.

The Eastern Orthodox Church supports medical and surgical treatment of infertility. However, IVF and other assisted reproductive technologies are absolutely rejected, and the Church opposes gamete donation, especially AID, on the basis that it is an adulterous act.

The Baptist, Methodist, Lutheran, Mormon, Presbyterian, Episcopal, United Church of Christ, Christian Science, Jehovah's Witness, and Mennonite religions have liberal attitudes toward infertility treatments. All denominations except Christian Science accept IVF with the spouse's gametes and no embryo wastage. Christian Science poses no objection to AIH but opposes IVF because of use of drugs and surgical procedures. All of these religions oppose IVF with donated gametes and all oppose the practice of surrogacy. Assisted reproductive technology was developed in Great Britain and Australia. The Anglican Church is liberal on the use of IVF.

Islamic law strictly condemns the practice of AID on the grounds that it is adulterous. It enhances the risk for inadvertent brother-sister marriage and violates the legal system of inheritance. The procedure also entails the lie of registering the offspring of a man who is not the real father and therefore leads to confusion of lines of genealogy, the purity of which is of prime importance in Islam. If a man's infertility is beyond cure, it should be accepted. Artificial reproduction was not mentioned in the primary sources of Sharia; however, these same sources affirmed the importance of marriage, family formation, and procreation. When procreation fails, Islam encourages treatment, especially because adoption is not an acceptable solution. Thus attempts to cure infertility are not only permissible but also a duty. The Quran, as well as the Old Testament, states emphatically that to have progeny is a great blessing from God. The pursuit of a remedy for infertility is therefore legitimate and should not be considered a rebellion against a fate decreed by God.

The procedure of IVF-ET is acceptable, but it can be performed if it involves only the husband and wife. The fusion of sperm and egg, a step beyond the sex act, should take place only within a legal marriage. Since marriage is a contract between wife and husband, during their marriage no third party can intrude into the marital functions of sex and procreation. A third party is not acceptable, whether providing egg, sperm, embryo, or uterus. If a marriage has come to an end through divorce or death of the husband, artificial reproduction cannot be performed on the woman even with sperm cells from her former husband. Oocyte donation presents many medical, ethical and legal questions. Ovum donation is similar to sperm donation in that it involves intervention of a third party other than the husband and wife and thus is not permitted. Donation of embryos is also prohibited. It was suggested that oocyte donation can be prac-tised between the wives of a Moslem husband. Frozen pre-embryos are the property of the couple alone and may be transferred to the woman in a succes-sive cycle. For women with absent or abnormal uteri and intact ovaries, use of a surrogate gestational carrier is forbidden. The proposal that surrogacy could be practised between the wives of a Moslem husband was recently forbidden.

10. CONCLUSIONS

The Israeli legislation on surrogacy is partly based on the Jewish Law, Halakha. There are three basic principles that, with certain restrictions, favour the accept-ability of the practice of surrogacy: First, the commandment 'Be fruitful and multiply.' Secondly, the mitzvah of loving kindness (G'miluth hasadim). In cases of personal suffering a Jew is duty-bound to practise the mitzvah of G'miluth hasadim which originates in the verse 'Love thy neighbour as thyself' (Leviticus 19:8). A childless couple will fall within this category and there exists a clear obligation to assist them in every permissible way, as long as no one else is thereby harmed. Thirdly, family integrity—domestic peace and the integrity of the family—are extremely important in Jewish law. On the other hand, Jewish Halakha also presents some problems for surrogacy, which are only par-tially resolved. The principal problems are mamzerut and the risk of a brother and sister marrying in the future, which would amount to incest.

There is a fundamental distinction between paternity and maternity in surro-gacy. While paternity is based on the genetic and only on the genetic function, maternity normally has two aspects—a genetic one of providing the oocyte and the physiological function of gestation and parturition. The employment of new reproductive technologies in full surrogacy has made it possible to divide these two functions between two women. As Teman (chapter 17, this volume) shows, surrogate mothers and intended mothers, as well as health professionals, engage in a range of practices whose effect is to transfer 'maternity' from the surrogate to the intended mother. And, as Schuz (chapter 3, this volume) shows, Israeli surrogacy law includes provisions that are intended to address these anomalies of parentage and status that inevitably arise. Crucially, it can be seen that issues of religious faith and cultural heritage cannot be separated from the law, the practice or the experience of surrogacy. In this context, law remains something of a clumsy tool for regulating personal relationships.

17

'Knowing' the Surrogate Body in Israel

ELLY TEMAN

1. INTRODUCTION

SURROGATE MOTHERHOOD IS an anomaly that disrupts familiar conceptions of motherhood, kinship and family (Macklin (1991)). In contractual surrogacy, a woman makes a preconception agreement to waive her parental rights in exchange for a paid fee (Farquhar (1996)), a practice that calls some of the most basic structures of society into question. Social relations created in surrogacy deviate from the traditional model of marriage which centres sexual relations and fertility issues around two members of a heterosexual couple. Moreover, surrogacy defies mainstream assumptions that identify pregnancy with the birth mother's commitment to the project of subsequent lifelong social mothering of the children to whom she has given birth (Farquhar (1996)).

As such, surrogacy threatens dominant Western ideologies that presume an indissoluble mother-child bond (Gailey (2000); Farquhar (1996)). Surrogacy has been theorised as bringing about the gradual 'deconstruction of motherhood' (Stanworth (1987)) separating the perceived unity of the maternal role into genetic, birth, adoptive, surrogate and other maternities (Sandelowski (1990)). To this point, conservative voices express concern over the fragmentation, lack of connection, and loss of maternal wholeness, and treat surrogacy as a deviance that must be censured (Farquhar (1996)).

Because surrogacy does not comfortably fit the cohesive and consistent system of conceptual categories of Western cultures, cultures are challenged to develop ways of dealing with its anomalous connotations (Davis-Floyd (1990)). Colligan (2001:3) reminds us that 'anomaly is not simply a problem of classification but an embodied status that must be worked out in everyday social situations.' In the following, I wish to call attention to the negotiation tactics that dealing with classificatory contradictions can engender in women who participate in surrogacy agreements and the techno-medical professionals that accompany them through the process.[1]

---

[1] As of the writing of this paper, there have been 38 gestational surrogacy births in Israel, and over a hundred contracts have been approved. Data for this article were obtained from 19 in-depth, open interviews conducted between March 1998 and December 2000 with nine surrogate mothers

How do surrogates and intended mothers accommodate and resist the anomalous connotations of this reproductive strategy? How do they assess and negotiate their own positions in Israeli society through surrogacy? I will argue that
throughout the surrogacy process, surrogates and intended mothers, together
with doctors, nurses and ultrasound technicians, collectively generate alter-
ations in received scripts about the maternal nature of pregnant bodies and the
non-maternal makeup of infertile bodies.

I shall engage the concept of 'authoritative knowledge' in order to shed light
on these questions. This concept refers to the way that 'knowledge is produced,
displayed, resisted and challenged in interactions' (Davis-Floyd and Sargent
(1997:21)). In their comprehensive edited volume on childbirth and authoritative knowledge, Davis-Floyd and Sargent (1997) bring together ethnographic
research on childbirth in 16 countries. They show that, while techno-medical
'ways of knowing' increasingly dominate obstetrics worldwide, indigenous
models of authoritative knowledge still exist and interactional co-operation and
accommodation between biomedicine and other ethno-obstetrical systems are
possible.

2. SURROGACY IN ISRAEL AS A CULTURAL ANOMALY

The classificatory challenges that surrogacy raises make Israel into a particularly interesting place to study surrogacy. Israel is a pronatalist society whose
Jewish-Israeli population will try anything in order to have a child (Kahn
(1997)). This cultural 'cult of fertility' (Baslington (1996)) among Israeli
women has been described as a social pressure to reproduce that 'borders on
obsessiveness and irrationality' (Shalev (1998)). Israel's pronatalist impulse has
made it into one of the leading countries in the world in the research and development of new reproductive technologies. This small country currently holds
the highest number of fertility clinics per capita in the world—and Israel's
national health insurance funds IVF treatments for up to two live births for
childless couples and for women who want to become single mothers (Shalev
(1998); Kahn (1997)). The option of not becoming a mother is virtually
non-existent in Israel, while solutions such as international adoption are still
considered to be secondary options when genetic parenthood is possible.

The Israeli surrogacy law of 1996 made Israel the first and only country in the
world where all surrogacy contracts are publicly legislated by a government-

and 10 intended mothers. All of the women interviewed were Jewish, Israeli citizens currently resid-
ing in Israel and between the ages of 28 and 42. Geographically, they spanned the entire country, and
ethnically, they were from diverse heritage bases including Ashkenazi (Jews of European descent),
Georgian, Kurdish, Moroccan, Iraqi, and Tunisian. The names of all of the women interviewed
have been changed. Most of the interviews were conducted in the women's homes and lasted
between one-and-a-half to six hours. They were recorded and transcribed verbatim, then translated
from Hebrew to English.

appointed commission (Kahn (1997:171)).[2] According to the law, an approval committee was nominated by the government health minister to screen all potential surrogacy agreements in Israel. In its aim to 'cope with the conceptual threat' (Davis-Floyd (1990)) that surrogacy presents, the surrogacy law removes the practice from everyday life, limiting its availability and subduing its boundary-threatening connotations. The practice is not officially encouraged and is strictly limited in scope to adult Israeli citizens. It is offered only as a last resort to couples wherein the female partner has no womb, has been repeatedly unsuccessful with other reproductive strategies, or who is at a severe health risk in pregnancy. While the law itself can be interpreted as a framework through which the state officially recognizes surrogacy's anomalous connotations and aims to deal with them, this is not the concern of this chapter. This chapter uses ethnographic research to address the way that surrogates, intended mothers, and health professionals attempt to solve the anomaly of surrogacy in practice, engaging intuitive, technological and medical knowledge systems in the process.

3. THE BODY THAT 'KNOWS': INTUITIVE KNOWLEDGE

In their exploration of intuition as authoritative knowledge among American midwives, Davis-Floyd and Davis (1997) claim that American midwives use intuition as a tool for 'knowing' the pregnant body in childbirth. While trained in the intricacies of technomedical birth, the midwives made decisions during labour based on their 'inner knowing', even when it opposed external, medicalised signs. In surrogacy, intuitive knowledge of the pregnancy was employed by both surrogates and intended mothers as a source of authoritative knowledge concerning the pregnancy. By constructing a situation in which the intended mother 'knows' the pregnant body inhabited by the surrogate, intended mothers were able to claim maternity while surrogates were able to disconnect emotionally from the pregnancy.

By intuitive or indigenous knowledge of the body, I refer to the internal, 'gut' feelings and instinctive responses of the individual that arise as a result of listening to their own internal, embodied voices. It is 'the act of or faculty of knowing or sensing without the use of rational processes; immediate cognition' (*American Heritage Dictionary* (1993), cited by Davis-Floyd and Davis (1997:317)). Often, intended mothers began their narratives with a determined statement linking their bodies with maternity through such intuitive knowledge. Leah, an intended mother, claimed:

> I always knew that I would have my own (child). I knew right here (she makes a fist and hits it against her stomach). That is what got me through all of those years of IVF after IVF. I always knew.

[2] See Schuz, chapter 3, this volume.

For Leah, and other intended mothers like her, this inner knowledge carried them through up to 25 IVF attempts[3] and countless other fertility treatments over periods of up to 17 years or more. Instincts and gut feelings also accompanied their choice of a surrogate. In their search for 'the right surrogate,' they primarily relied on their bodily and emotional instincts as indicators of compatibility. These signs were privileged over measurable data insisted upon by the approval committee, such as psychological, physical and social aptitude tests.[4] Sarit, an intended mother, let her body indicate to her when she had met the 'right' woman:

> When you meet the right woman, you feel it in your stomach, and you know it is the right thing . . . that this (woman) is what best suits me. We had immediate chemistry.

Surrogates emerged as strong believers in intuitive knowledge as well. Narrative accounts of both women's first encounters with one another reverberated with a vocabulary of 'chemistry', 'immediate connections' and 'clicks', used to define the internal physical trigger that these women felt upon meeting one another for the first time. Two thirds of the surrogates and intended mothers interviewed described instances of immediately recognising one another at first sight even though they were strangers, assuming that cosmic intervention had caused their meeting.

Constructing one another as the 'right surrogate' for the 'right couple', surrogates and intended mothers were able to decommodify and re-naturalise the surrogacy process even before the commercial contract was signed. The concept of the 'right' partner in the process served to minimise the randomness of the relationship in favour of a cosmically ordained nature, imposing a certain natural and moral imperative on the surrogacy process as a whole.[5] For intended mothers, it served as a reassuring sign that they were meant to have a child; while for surrogates, it constituted a sign that God and nature had meant for them to become surrogates.

Both women drew upon their intuitive connection in order to define motherhood as a product of 'internal knowing', allowing them to attach their own meanings to the pregnancy. Surrogates were thus able to credit their intended mother with 'knowing' the pregnancy instead of them, which emerged as a strategy for dismissing any expectations for their own emotional attachment to the pregnancy. While awaiting confirmation of pregnancy, surrogates refused to acknowledge any internal sign from within their bodies that could signify the result, urging their intended mothers to seek the answer within themselves. Masha, a surrogate, emphasised this point:

---

[3] Because IVF is subsidised by the national health insurance and consequently does not present an economic challenge to the couple, most of the intended mothers interviewed had gone through at least 10 attempts before turning to surrogacy.

[4] See Schuz, chapter 3, this volume.

[5] See Sandelowski, Harris and Holditch-Davis (1993) for ethnographic exploration of a similar process among couples waiting to adopt.

I told Tova (her intended mother), 'I refuse to get nervous while we wait for an answer. I will not walk around thinking "did it work or didn't it?" for two weeks, and then be disappointed. You can get nervous, you can do the waiting, I am just going to pretend everything is normal.' So she asked me, 'but do you feel something? Do you think you are pregnant?' And I said to her, 'Do you? It is yours, do you think it took?'

Likewise, surrogates narrated an instinctive feeling from the start of the pregnancy identifying it as different from those they had experienced before. While one surrogate maintained that 'it isn't the same womb' carrying this pregnancy as the one that had carried her own child, another surrogate claimed that she did not feel this baby move inside her at all, unlike her own children who 'moved inside me all the time.' Comparing intuitive knowledge of their 'own' bodies in pregnancy with the surrogate pregnancy thus served as another strategy toward the same goal.

Elsewhere (Teman (2001a)) I have expanded upon this phenomenon, showing how surrogates use the idea of the pregnancy occurring outside of their own body to conjure up a 'third body'. By locating the pregnancy in this 'third body', they ease its transfer to the intended mother's embodied space. This 'third body' acts differently from their own bodies during pregnancy because of cramps and birth pangs that appear in different parts of the body and at altered intensities. Moreover, they identify this pregnancy as different because of the differing length in time of the gestational period and hours in labour, as well as the different responses of their bodies after giving birth, such as immediate weight loss and stunted production of milk.

As a result of this process, surrogates narrate the way that this disembodied internal knowledge of the pregnancy locates itself within the intended mother's body. Orna, a surrogate, claimed that she did not gain a significant amount of weight during the surrogate pregnancy and that her stomach remained small throughout, while her intended mother gained thirteen kilos and looked bloated 'like she was pregnant herself'. By emphasising the intended mother's sympathy pains, surrogates demonstrate how the intuitive-physical knowledge that they had recognised as part of their own 'real' pregnancies is now developing in their female partner.

As the gestational period progressed, both women often marvelled at the miraculous manner in which the intended mother seemingly 'knew' of the foetal movements in the surrogate's body. Masha vouched that her intended mother, Tova, would call her 'knowing' that the baby inside her had just kicked, or that she was feeling cramps in her left side. 'I asked her how she knew,' Masha recalled, 'and she said, "what do you think? I feel it too." ' When prompted on this subject, Tova added: 'I would wake up with cramps in my back, and I would know that she was having cramps. I suffered through this pregnancy with her.'

Through time, this exchange led most of the intended mothers to experience couvade symptoms and to virtually embody the pregnancy. Ayala, an intended mother, internalised the pregnancy to such an extent that she questioned whether her surrogate had 'known' the pregnancy to the same degree that she, Ayala, felt by proximity:

> From the very beginning I felt pregnant, from the minute they inserted the embryos, I felt like it was my body going through it . . . Not only on an emotional level but also on a physical level it affected me. I really had the same feelings she did—I felt it. It was really like they say a man whose wife is pregnant goes through it. I too really felt all the nausea when there was nausea and the heartburn when there was heartburn. I don't know about her but I really felt what she was going through . . . outside of the feeling of responsibility and pains on an emotional level, I felt really connected to her.[6]

The increasing legitimacy of her inner knowledge of the foetus became so convincing to one intended mother, Rivka, that she claimed she'd actually 'felt pregnant' during this period:

> You know what, I say to Orna that it is lucky that, you know, those hysterical pregnancies (fake pregnancy), it is lucky that I didn't have one of those . . . but the transferring part and the feelings, I felt exactly the same (as a pregnant woman). Maybe that's what gives me the push to say, yes, I was pregnant, and not through a surrogate. Because I felt exactly what she felt.

By constructing 'intuitive knowledge' as a source of 'knowing' the pregnant body, surrogates and intended mothers work together to make their partnership in the pregnancy more equal. They even out the surrogate's privileged place in 'knowing' the foetus by collaboratively constructing their own authoritative knowledge which aligns all intuitive and embodied connection between the foetus and the intended mother. In the following section, we will witness how the technological viewing technique of foetal ultrasound is brought in to this effort as well.

4. THE KNOWING MACHINE: TECHNOLOGICAL KNOWLEDGE

Eugenia Georges (1997:93) claims that 'ultrasonography can act as an especially potent facilitator in the production and enactment of authoritative knowledge.' Brigitte Jordan (1997) claims that when machine-based claims conflict with the woman's own bodily experience, the latter is negated in favour of the unquestioned status and authority of medical knowledge. Consequently, women are specifically excluded from techno-childbirth, denied any input into their labour experience, and given the message that the only knowledge that counts is that of the doctor.

I argue that this hierarchical distribution of knowledge in technologically mediated situations is inverted in surrogacy when the surrogate herself uses technology to extract herself from the pregnancy experience. Instead of negat-

---

[6] Ayala published a personal journal of her experience with surrogacy in a daily newspaper. Her journal appeared in Maariv daily, weekend supplement.

ing the knowledge that she has of the state of her body (Jordan (1997)) techno-medical knowledge is adapted as a source for legitimating the fictional reality that the two women are constructing between them. The techno-medical knowledge of the pregnancy is also communicated in a structure that actually encourages the intended mother to believe in the internal messages that her body is giving her.

By technological knowledge I refer to surrogate and intended mothers' accounts of their encounters with ultrasound technology. Like in all births in modern-day Israel, repetitive scanning is a routine part of surrogate pregnancies, only more intense than in regular pregnancies. Although both women discussed ultrasound in their narratives, it seemed to be more important to intended mothers as it served to confirm the existence of the baby for them and enabled them to act out the culturally prescribed role of soon-to-be mother.

Ultrasound extends the sensory abilities of the intended mother and adds the dimension of 'seeing' to the inherent 'knowing' discussed above.[7] In this way, ultrasound served as a proxy for the pregnancy experience, giving intended mothers the opportunity to become more relevant to foetal progress and to move to centre stage beyond their 'stage-hand role' vis-à-vis the surrogate's 'leading lady role' (Sandelowski (1994)). The intended mother's greater 'knowing participation' in the pregnancy via ultrasound enabled surrogates to take a step back, deriving a type of vicarious pleasure from watching the intended mother bond with the technological image of the foetus.

Consequently, all the surrogates interviewed saw importance in having their intended mother accompany them to every ultrasound appointment. These outings strengthened the surrogate-intended mother relationship, bringing them closer together by making intended mothers feel more like partners in the pregnancy. The technological medium thus reinforced the intuitive connection already established by the women through their own indigenous sources.

One surrogate claimed that she saw the ultrasound as an event in which her intended mother could take part in the pregnancy:

> It was important to me that she be present at all of the ultrasounds, for instance. Because it was important to me that she go through the whole experience and that she see the whole experience . . . I have no problem with a woman coming in [to the vaginal ultrasound, E.T] . . . and she said to me before we went in, if you don't want I won't come in, I'll wait outside. I said no way. About those things, I made sure that she took part in everything. Because it is really important to me that she go through and feel the whole experience exactly as I do. That is the way I wanted it, that she be my partner, as much as possible.

Likewise, all of the surrogates interviewed for this study dismissed their intended mother's concern over witnessing the vaginal ultrasound, in which their most intimate parts are exposed. Surrogates erased all sexual embarrassment

---

[7] See Sandelowsi (1994) for a discussion of how ultrasound leads to the greater involvement of fathers-to-be in 'normal' pregnancies.

from their accounts of these situations, making their own subjectivity invisible. Accordingly, Orna, a surrogate, dismissed her intended father's shyness at seeing her partially unclothed during an ultrasound by assuring him that he was not seeing her—Orna, the woman. Extracting her presence from the scene, she told him that all he was seeing was a 'stomach' that separated him from his child:[8] 'I said to him, don't be shy, just remember, this is yours (pointing to her stomach). Don't even think about this stomach, it is nothing, just a stomach, only think about what is inside it.'

Ultrasound provides visual access to the foetus *in-utero*, enabling the intended mother[9] to conceptualise the foetus for the first time apart from the surrogate. As she lays in the supine position and is scanned, while her intended mother (or couple) stand with the doctor,[10] the surrogate symbolically becomes a silent participant, a transparent medium for technological viewing of the foetus.

Interestingly, while ultrasound has been critiqued for opening the inside of women's bodies for visual inspection, leaving their body boundaries thoroughly transparent (Van der Ploeg (1998)) here it is this same transparency that is used by the women themselves to define the maternal subject. The ultrasound presents the foetus as an individual entity, alone on the screen, as if removed from the surrogate's body. This visual dislocation of the foetus from the surrogate's body aids her in disengaging herself from the pregnancy while providing the couple with a direct mode of communication with the foetus on screen. Instead of merely demoting the surrogate's body to a secondary order of significance (Georges (1997:99)), ultrasound enables her to promote the intended mother's bodily and visual experience to a privileged place of significance and to support her own emotional disconnection.

Surrogates rarely mentioned their own participation in ultrasound, focusing instead on the intended couple and their excitement at seeing the image of their future child on screen. None relayed personal excitement at seeing the foetal image, claiming boredom and disinterest, or narrating an excitement centred entirely upon their intended mother's happiness. Masha asserted that she did not pay particular attention during ultrasound appointments, claiming: 'Mostly

[8] See Teman (2001a) for an exploration of surrogates' use of commodity metaphors as a method of disconnecting from the pregnancy.

[9] In most cases the intended mother attended the ultrasound viewing alone with the surrogate. In a handful of cases the intended father also entered the ultrasound, and in other cases the intended father waited outside the room or behind a curtain. See Ivry (2002) for a discussion of Israeli men and the way that they relate to their wives in pregnancy.

[10] When the women are treated through the national health insurance clinics then the ultrasounds are mainly carried out by female ultrasound technicians who have been specially trained in foetal scanning. It is common for the doctor to enter and exit the room while the scanning session is taking place. When the woman is treated by a privately paid physician, the physician will usually do the scans his/herself in order to give them, as one physician told me, 'the full package'. Nearly half of the couples whom I interviewed chose to hire private physicians, claiming that this pregnancy was too 'yakar' (a Hebrew word meaning both 'dear to the heart' and 'expensive') to trust the regular clinic doctors.

he [the doctor] would talk to her [the intended mother]. I didn't really need to know.'

Mitchell and Georges (1998) state that it is customary during ultrasound for the pregnant woman and her partner to smile, laugh and point to the screen, bonding with the technologically produced 'blur'. Acting out this cultural prescription themselves, intended mothers told of interactions between themselves and the doctor, as though the surrogate had not been present at all. The surrogate's effort to make room for the intended mother to act out the culturally expected reaction to foetal ultrasound was mutually constructed in unison with the doctor and the technology itself. In all of the interviews, it was evident that the doctor or ultrasound technician had a central role in encouraging the intended mother to 'bond' with the foetal image onscreen by focusing deliberate attention on her.

Sarit, an intended mother, attested to the way that the doctor encouraged her and her husband to take on parental responsibility for the moving image on the ultrasound screen:

Usually he [the doctor] would speak to us [her and her husband] during the ultrasound. Especially in the early stages, because you are focusing on the child, and the child is ours. He would say to us, here, you see, his eyes are like this and his head is a little bit wide, it looks like his father's head, and stuff like that.

Sonographers took on active roles in transferring maternal subjectivity from the surrogate to the intended mother. Similar to the description given by Sarit's doctor above, their depictions of the foetus passed through a cultural sieve. The doctor, by describing the likeness of the foetus to the intended father, reassures the couple of their parental claim over the foetus and encourages them to bond directly with the image onscreen (Mitchell and Georges (1998)). Moreover, by communicating primarily with the couple and not with the surrogate, the sonographer uses the authoritative knowledge that grants him the ability of 'knowing' how to decode the bleeps on screen in order to increase the intended mother's involvement in the pregnancy and minimise the surrogate's embodied, privileged access to the foetus.

Ultrasound photos also played an important role in constructing the intended mother's maternal claim. All of the surrogates interviewed asserted that the ultrasound photos went straight into the intended mother's baby album, while they assured me that they felt no inclination to keep copies for themselves. 'Why should I keep a copy?' Masha, a surrogate, reflected, 'I have ultrasound photos of my own kids. I don't need one of hers. And when I know that the doctor needs to look at them, I just call her to bring them along.'

During my first interview with her, Riki, an intended mother, asked me if I wanted to 'meet her twins'. Puzzled, I followed her to the refrigerator, where a recent ultrasound photograph was pasted at its centre. Stroking the photograph lovingly, she explained: 'This way I can wish them good morning, and put them to sleep at night.' Through these symbolic representations of the foetal bodies,

Riki was able to establish a direct link of communication with her awaited twins, keeping them close to her, in her own home, even while they developed in another woman's womb. Yael also attempted to embody the pregnancy by keeping the ultrasound images with her at all times. She carried them in a small envelope in her purse, removing it delicately to show them to me as though the photos were part of the awaited child.

The ultrasound photos complete a new hierarchy of knowledge created through technological intervention in surrogacy. By giving sonographers the power of clinically interpreting the sonogram and controlling distribution of technologically produced knowledge of the foetus, foetal ultrasound makes embodied knowledge of the pregnancy less exclusive and more dependent upon technology (Sandelowski (1994)). Consequently, sonographers achieve a privileged position that allows them to intervene in the social relationships of both women to the pregnancy. By focusing on the intended mother during scans, they shape her into a more equal 'knower' of the foetus. This process is finalised in the intended mother taking home the souvenir images of the foetus. Her possession of this foetal artefact finally makes her into the direct disciple of the technological knowledge of the pregnancy.

Contrary to prior research, this hierarchical distribution works towards the same aims that the women themselves co-create intuitively. While in many cases, such as the 'normal' technologically managed childbirth described by Brigitte Jordan (1997), the competition between indigenous and technologically derived knowledge leads to the woman's internal knowledge being overridden, this case emerges differently. These women's expressed knowledge about their bodies is not ignored, denied or replaced by another conflicting version of reality. Rather, these two types of knowledge collaboratively produce and maintain the same fiction together—that the 'real' body that is connected to the pregnancy belongs to the intended mother. Thus, machine based and intuitive records of the pregnancy do not serve to negate one another but serve as a resource for justifying the woman's own bodily claim.

The surrogate's transparency and disrupted oneness with the foetus during ultrasound enables her to show her emotional distance from the pregnancy and to emphasise the intended mother's strong connection to the foetus. Viewing the foetus and maintaining foetal pictures minimises the intended mother's distance from the foetus, equalising her position with the surrogate and giving her the opportunity to enact culturally defined maternal scripts and claim her foetus in yet another way.

5. KNOWING THROUGH MEDICINE: MEDICAL KNOWLEDGE

The involvement of medical practitioners in the pregnancy follows a similar path. Doctors, nurses and the bureaucratic protocols seemed to direct the construction of a similar reality. Using their privileged knowledge, they constructed 'the patient' as an ambiguous entity that combined both women in it while providing legitimation of the intended mother's maternal claim. I now expand upon this construction of the intended mother as a hybrid patient and the way that this fiction encourages the women to engage it as an additional source in their own collaborative effort. Riki, an intended mother, explained how important it was to both her and her surrogate that she be present at the doctor appointments and be the main actor in them:

> She refused to let the doctor begin his check-up without me. Even when I was thirty minutes late one time, she made him wait. She said that this is Riki's baby and that she had to be here.

Surrogates also seemed to actively define the intended mother as the recipient of medical care, demanding her presence at every check-up. Rinat, a surrogate, remembered the day that the embryos were implanted in her womb:

> She [the intended mother] was late, and I kept making the doctor wait. I said, she will come. She will come. And the poor thing was stuck in a traffic jam. In the end she arrived at the last minute before he couldn't wait any longer.

In both cases above, the doctor is a co-conspirator who collaborates with the women in their effort to designate the intended mother's status in the pregnancy. One surrogate, who was in the beginning stages of surrogacy, asked me if I knew of any 'sympathetic' doctors that could accompany her and her intended couple through the process. 'I want a doctor who understands,' she said, 'who can make her [the intended mother] feel like she is going through this.'

Intended mothers cited their doctors' encouragement, with one woman asserting that, 'He always treated me like I was the patient, even though it was she who was pregnant.' Sarit, an intended mother, described a scene in which the doctor conducting the embryo implantation gave rise to her first maternal feelings:

> I saw how they inserted the embryos into her womb, and that was really the first time that I felt like a mommy. I got there a little late, and they had already laid her down on the bed. Then the doctor said, here comes the mommy. And when he said that I got very excited, because I really did feel right then like a mommy.

In her description, the doctor aids Sarit in encompassing the procedure as her own, promoting her identification with a procedure carried out on the surrogate's body. Pronouncing her the 'mommy' while implanting the embryos in the surrogate's womb lends an air of legitimacy to Sarit's internal feeling of connection to the pregnancy. Elsewhere (Teman (2001b)) I discuss the way that surrogates draw upon medical knowledge in order to disclaim maternity. They use images of hormone injections and the creation of embryos in unnatural settings to support their claim that the surrogate pregnancy has been generated by the doctor, therefore 'proving' their claim that no 'natural' feelings of attachment to the foetus are pre-destined to arise in them from this 'artificial' pregnancy. This strategic borrowing of medical authoritative knowledge also aids them in emphasising the 'natural', bio-genetic basis of the pregnancy for the intended mother, aiding her in claiming maternity for herself.

Israel's state medical policies also play a part in this construction. Because fertility treatments are subsidised by Israeli national health insurance for childless couples, they are bureaucratically considered as belonging to the intended mother. Both the hormonal treatment aimed at increasing the intended mother's egg supply, as well as hormone injections for preparing the surrogate's womb for embryo insertion are considered by the state to be fertility treatments for one patient—the intended mother. Intended mothers were usually the ones to call the clinic for the results to the pregnancy test, and in more than one case, a doctor had personally called the intended mother to deliver positive results to his long-standing patient, who would then inform her surrogate.

The medical system structures surrogacy so that the intended mother has more medical knowledge of the pregnancy than the surrogate does. Again, it is exactly this hierarchy that enables the surrogate to invert the situation in her own interest and equalise her and her intended mother's participation in the pregnancy. While one surrogate informed me that the doctor had 'two files stapled together. Two files that were one'; another surrogate claimed that she had 'no file, I was only part of her (the intended mother's) file.' This evidence of the need for the two women to merge in order for the process to succeed led Orna to explain: 'My body could not do it without hers.'

The unitary patient construction was evident in other ways as well. Doctors prescribed medical prescriptions and appointment referrals in the intended mother's name, and she would buy the medicines and dispense them to the surrogate. Intended mothers often described themselves as middlemen between the doctor and the surrogate. 'I was the connection between the doctor and her from the time we began the process until the third month of the pregnancy,' Sarit, an intended mother claimed, 'most of the time she didn't even need to come with me. I would go to the doctor and then give her what she needed.'

Orna, a surrogate, saw the doctor's referral practices as a channel through which responsibility for the pregnancy could be delegated to her intended mother:

> All of the prescriptions have to be on her name, because she has to pay for them. She pays the money. It is just as if I give you acamol (paracetamol), but it was bought on my name. So what? But if you go to buy medicine that is on someone else's name, they won't give it to you. So you buy it on your name, and then you give to someone else, then what do they care, after you bought it, its your responsibility. But the check-ups were in my name.

Obtaining and delivering the required medical drugs was consistently regarded by surrogates and intended mothers alike as the intended mother's responsibility. By managing their interactions with the medical practitioners, intended mothers were able to make use of this third source of authoritative knowledge in their pursuit of maternal identity. Surrogates routinely stepped

down from the jobs of scheduling doctor's appointments and making the associated necessary arrangements, leaving all such considerations to their female
partners in the pregnancy. Such responsibility serves to legitimatise the 'inner
knowing' that they already sensed. Sometimes the intended mother's heightened
knowledge of the foetus through these three channels lead to leaky identity
boundaries for the women, who become unsure which one of them is the
patient. Riki said:

> There were tests that were for me, like the amniotic fluid test, because I am older and
> she wouldn't have needed it regularly at her age. So whose name do we put down? It
> is her pregnancy, but my test. So each time we would put down a different name, one
> time hers, one time mine . . .

Sometimes, this heightened sense of identification with the surrogate's body
gives way to the intended mother imaginatively constructing her own body as
physically connected to the surrogate, conjoined at the stomach gestating the
foetus. Dalit, an intended mother who was interviewed in a national newspaper,[11] relayed that:

> I felt that she, who is carrying my child, she is the closest thing to me. As if we were
> two halves of one stomach that unifies us. I fully believe that that is the way a rela-
> tionship should be with a surrogate—without estrangement and not only through
> social workers.

In the same article, Dalit claimed that their doctors, unlike some friends and
family, encouraged this shared body phenomenon:[12]

> Many people had a hard time digesting the relationship that formed between us. They
> warned us not to get too attached, maybe because we are talking about a process that
> is still relatively new in Israel. But the doctors that accompanied us actually got very
> excited [about our relationship]. I, anyway, proceeded according to my heart.[13]

In her words, Dalit shows how intuitive knowledge and medical authoritative
knowledge coincide in the construction of the singular subject. Dalit herself
'proceeded according to her heart', although she also mentions her doctor's
approval of this hybrid fusion. On a procedural level, both women are admitted
to the hospital and remain together throughout the period up to and through the
birth. While Blyth (1994) has pointed out that in English surrogacy births the
surrogate can usually pass off the intended mother as her friend and thus receive

---

[11] Dalit was interviewed in Yediot Ahronot daily, 'Seven Days' weekend supplement, 17–9–99,
in an article entitled 'Twenty Seven Weeks.'

[12] The shared body phenomenon is discussed in full elsewhere, in Teman (2000) 'Being One
Body', unpublished manuscript.

[13] Dalit's words echo a phenomenon recorded by Heléna Ragoné (1994) among the surrogates
and intended mothers that she interviewed in the United States. Because in traditional surrogacy the
intended mothers that Ragoné interviewed had no genetic connection to the foetus, they upturned
notions of biological kinship by claiming they had conceived the child 'in the heart'. Here we see that
Dalit proceeds in the surrogacy relationship according to her instincts and not according to what is
expected by others. She conceives the relationship 'in the heart'.

permission for her to stay with her throughout the birth, in Israeli situations the immediate medical staff is informed that it is surrogacy and treat it according to a special protocol. From the surrogacy narratives of this period, it became clear that the medical staff actively interacted with the women in shaping them into 'one patient'.

Rinat described how the head nurse co-conspired with her to construct her and her intended mother as a combined patient:

> I said to her, when they hospitalised me, 'you are going to be hospitalised with me.' And she was with me in the hospital. On the weekend she stayed with me in the hospital. Thursday, Friday and Saturday she was in the hospital. Next to me in the same room. Yes. They gave us a room alone. And when a nurse came who didn't know about our story, she started to yell. So I said to her, 'who are you yelling at.' Right away I said to her, 'Do you see her, that is me.' And she said, 'But you. . . .' And I said to her, 'Do you see her, she is me.' So she didn't understand what it was and she went to the head nurse and said to her, 'In that single room two women are sleeping.' And she answers her, 'Yes, I know. Those are two women who are one. They are two that are one.' And then she sat down and explained it to her.

Rivka, an intended mother, also described how the doctor encouraged this hybridity by preparing 'them' for giving birth:

> Afterwards, when we went down to do the monitor, then (the foetus) didn't move. So they said okay, you have to go eat (plural),[14] go eat (plural), and then come (plural). They were always speaking in couple (form). Because of that, it also gave me the feeling (that I was giving birth myself). Go eat, maybe while you (plural) eat she will move (the foetus).

The doctor's use of the Hebrew plural form to relay instructions for the pregnant body made Rivka feel like she was half of his 'patient'. Accordingly, when I asked their doctor about how he related to the two women, he affirmed his part in constructing their hybridity, claiming that: 'I would relate both to the surrogate and to the intended mother, both as individuals and as one together.'

The heightened sense of identification with the surrogate and the feeling of being half of 'one patient' led Ayala, an intended mother, to narrate a scene where she virtually gives birth to her twins:

> They gave her (the surrogate) an operation (Caesarean section) and I sat outside and I got up and sat down and at one point I fainted. I lost consciousness and collapsed on the floor for eight, nine, ten minutes. And it ends up that exactly at that same moment they extracted them (the twins) from the womb. And everyone said to me, 'here you gave birth to them just now.' And at that very second I hadn't known what was going on inside and she had gone in already at seven thirty. Eight, nine, ten minutes. They (the medical staff) elevated my legs and extracted our foetuses, I mean they took our

---

[14] Rivka describes the doctor speaking to her and her surrogate in the plural Hebrew form for 'you' (Atem) instead of the singular form for 'you' (At).

babies out, so I was still on the floor. And two women took me to a side room and brought me the children and I burst out crying.[15]

In Ayala's account, it is the medical staff that actively encourages her to make the connection between her fainting spell and the birth of her children. Once the child has been born, an agenda of separation replaces the former oneness, and the medical staff hands the newborn immediately to the intended mother. The surrogate is then given a room in the gynaecological ward while the intended mother is given a room in the new mothers' ward. Surrogates are now not allowed to see the child without the intended mother's permission, a rule that the nurses strictly enforce. A state social worker arrives to intermediate between couple and surrogate. Both the intended mother and the surrogate receive identity bracelets with the newborn's name and the newborn is fitted with one on each arm.

Irma Van der Ploeg ((1998) p. 105), in her study of the New Reproductive Technologies, claims that the NRT's create a hybrid patient by fusing the separate individualities of couples into a hermaphrodite, unitary body. She sees this new 'individual' patient as a deliberate erasure of female individuality for the purpose of legitimately conducting invasive medical procedures on women's bodies, often for the benefit of other individuals that her body contains—the foetus and her male partner. The female patient herself is thus demoted to the bottom of the power structure that exists in her body.

Returning to the case of medical intervention in surrogacy as described above, it is possible to shed light on the motivation of the medical staff in creating a hybrid patient between the two women until birth and the subsequent separation of the shared body into individual entities. The hybrid patient emerges as a method for treating the ambiguous situation that surrogacy presents, being an effective mechanism for making treatment more direct and efficient. Thus, health practitioners are able to structure the surrogacy situation—having only one patient, instead of two, throughout—by treating the two women as one during the pregnancy, and promoting their separation after the birth.

6. CONCLUSION

In this paper, I have shown how surrogates and intended mothers collaborate with one another in producing their own interactive ways of 'knowing' the surrogate pregnancy. The women define motherhood as embodied, intuitive knowledge of the foetus and locate that knowledge—through bodily and rhetoric constructions—as external to the surrogate's pregnant body and as part of the intended mother's embodied space. Ultrasound technicians and doctors

[15] Interview with an intended mother, by Liron Meir, Final paper for the course: Anthropology of the Body, Hebrew University of Jerusalem, 1999.

actively participate in this relocation of motherhood by associating all techno-medical authoritative knowledge connected to the surrogate pregnancy with the intended mother.

As a result, the authoritative knowledge in surrogacy does not follow the classic top-down distribution of power in technological childbirth described by Jordan (1997). Instead of being the helpless victims of the medicalisation of childbirth, surrogates and intended mothers actively co-create meaning in surrogacy in collaboration with representatives of the techno-medical realm. Surrogacy thus provides a framework in which types of authoritative knowledge regularly characterised as oppositional work together toward the same goal. Women's bodily knowing and techno-medical knowing are set in an interactive, collective process of constructing meaning together.

The question remains as to why surrogacy presents such a conceptual threat to women, health practitioners and the state that they would all work together to achieve analogous interpretations of surrogacy. The collaboration can be seen as a collective effort to find a containable solution to surrogacy's anomalous connotations. This is accomplished by achieving a singular definition of the maternal subject that is easier for all to handle, decipher and read (Hartouni (1997)).

These three forms of knowledge work together to invert the threatening association of families pieced together from different wombs, eggs and sperm, replacing it with traditional biogenetic kinship, in which maternal claims are established through the body. In this manner, all of the parties involved work to eliminate the inconsistency between the pregnant yet non-maternal surrogate and the maternal yet non-pregnant intended mother. By confirming the intended mother's maternal subjectivity and connection to the pregnancy all along, they make surrogacy seem to confirm, rather than challenge, the Jewish-Israeli cultural belief system.[16]

The collaboration also emerges as a cultural coping technique for diffusing the conceptual threat that surrogacy presents to Israeli culture by moulding this inconsistent phenomenon to comply with Israeli society's pronatalist core. The state regulation of women's reproductive bodies under the surrogacy law can be seen to represent the symbolic control of the Israeli body politic, and the roles of health professionals in solving the anomalies of surrogacy can be seen as an effort to aid the state in maintaining normative boundaries around reproduction.[17] This, of course, is part of the role of institutions. As anthropologist Mary Douglas ((1986:63); Hartouni (1997:125)) put it, 'Institutions bestow sameness; they turn the body's shape to their conventions.' They attempt to convention-

---

[16] See Davis-Floyd (1990) for an example of how the technocratic belief system of American society emerges as a solution to the anomalies of childbirth.

[17] See Amir and Benjamin (1997) for an exploration of how this works in hospital abortion approval committees, and Weiss (forthcoming 2002) for how the Israeli body politic controls the individual bodies of its citizens from before birth, through soldierhood and even in death.

alise and contain diversity or to render difference socially legible (Hartouni (1997)) consequently maintaining the national, religious and social structure.

National goals also affect the female actors' collaboration with these institutions. In a country where women are regarded as gatekeepers of the national collective (Amir and Benjamin (1997)), surrogacy holds the possibility of affecting both of these women's place in the collective. Surrogacy threatens to stigmatise the surrogate as deviant of her natural, national maternal duties (Teman (2001b)) even as her gestational labour acts to bring the intended mother into the realm of normative Israeli womanhood. By creating a flow of indigenous, technological and medicalised knowledge between them, centring maternity and the pregnant body in the intended mother's embodied space, these women collectively recompose maternal subjectivity across their bodily boundaries and consequently turn any threats to the 'traditional' view of motherhood and family on their head.

By redirecting the pregnancy away from her body and towards the intended mother, the surrogate circumvents the cultural paradox that surrogacy presents: the denial of her supposed 'natural' procreative urges and maternal instincts in a culture that valorises women mainly for their motherhood. She incorporates the voices of doctors and nurses into her narrative, as well as the textual and photographic representations of the pregnancy, in order to lend 'concrete' evidence and legitimacy 'proving' that she is not denying maternity in the least. On the contrary, she proves that not only she, but also the intended mother, the doctors and the state all regard this pregnancy as not belonging to her, and that even her body 'knew' it was not hers. She thus reinterprets her seemingly deviant actions in terms of creating motherhood for another woman, a purpose that is one with the nation's pronatalist ideology and not subversive of it (Teman (2001b)).

Together, these women co-scripted a body with a specific social message, generating a dialogue about self and other (Colligan (2001)) by making the intended mother's marginal body more normative. This enables her to move from the marginal status of non-mother to the normative status of woman/mother in Israeli society (Kahn (1997)) through a process that threatens the surrogate with further marginality. Their mutual effort to defy the threat of deviance thus created an interspace that held emancipatory possibilities for both of them (Colligan (2001)).

These women show that women's bodies are not simply entities to be acted upon, but can participate in a 'conjoined agency' (Colligan (2001)) and in a co-authoring of their roles as mothers and members of the nation-state. The act of constituting the body in surrogacy is not a passive but a deliberate attempt by these women to direct the gaze of society where they want it directed (Peace (2001)). It is a personal as well as a political statement liberating the objectified body with an alternative, interactive form of female power.

Acknowledgement: I wish to thank my advisors Professor Meira Weiss and Professor Eyal Ben-Ari of the Hebrew University Anthropology Department for their support, encouragement, guidance and helpful comments throughout the stages of this project. I would also like to thank Don Seeman, Tamar Rapaport, Edna Lomsky-Feder, Lauren Erdreich, Svetlana Roberman, Tsippi Ivry, Limor Samimian, Adi Kuntsman, Avi Solomon, and Rhisa Teman for helping me think through earlier drafts of this paper. A final thanks to Rachel Cook for her editorial comments and to all of the women who shared their surrogacy stories with me.

REFERENCES

Amir, D and Benjamin, O, 'Defining Encounters: who are the women entitled to join the Israeli collective?' (1997) 20 *Women's Studies International Forum* 639.

Baslington, H, 'Anxiety Overflow: Implications of the IVF surrogacy Case and the Ethical and Moral Limits of Reproductive Technology in Britain' (1996) 19 *Women's Studies International Forum* 675.

Benshushan, A and Schenker, JG, 'Legitimising Surrogacy in Israel' (1997) 12 *Human Reproduction* 1832.

Blyth, E, 'I wanted to be interesting. I wanted to be able to say "I've done something interesting with my life": Interviews with surrogate mothers in Britain' (1994) 12 *Journal of Reproductive and Infant Psychology* 189.

Colligan, S, 'The Ethnographer's body as text and context: revisiting and revisioning the body through anthropology and disability studies' (2001) 21 *Disability Studies Quarterly* 113.

Davis-Floyd. R, 'The Role of American Obstetrics in the Resolution of Cultural Anomaly' (1990) *Social Science and Medicine* 31, 175–89.

—— and Davis, E, 'Intuition as Authoritative Knowledge in Midwifery and Home Birth' in R Davis-Floyd and C Sargent (eds), *Childbirth and Authoritative Knowledge: Cross-Cultural Perspectives* (Berkeley, University of California Press, 1997).

—— and Sargent, C (eds), *Childbirth and Authoritative Knowledge: Cross-Cultural Perspectives* (Berkeley, University of California Press: 1997).

Douglas, M, *How Institutions Think* (Syracuse, NY, Syracuse U Press, 1986).

Farquhar, D, *The Other Machine: Discourse and Reproductive Technologies* (New York and London, Routledge, 1996).

Gailey, C, 'Ideologies of Motherhood and Kinship in US Adoption' in H Ragone and F Winndance Twine (eds), *Ideologies and Technologies of Motherhood* (New York, Routledge, 2000).

Georges, E, 'Fetal Ultrasound Imaging and the Production of Authoritative Knowledge in Greece' in R Davis-Floyd and C Sargent (eds), *Childbirth and Authoritative Knowledge: Cross-Cultural Perspectives* (Berkeley, University of California Press, 1997).

Hartouni, V, *Cultural Conceptions* (Minneapolis, University of Minnesota Press, 1997).

Ivry, T, *Pregnancy in Japan and in Israel* (Hebrew University, Jerusalem, PHD Thesis, forthcoming 2002).

Jordan, B, 'Authoritative Knowledge and Its Construction' in R Davis-Floyd and C Sargent (eds), *Childbirth and Authoritative Knowledge: Cross-Cultural Perspectives* (Berkeley, University of California Press, 1997).

Kahn, S, *Reproducing Jews: The Social Uses and Cultural Meanings of the New Reproductive Technologies in Israel* (Phd Thesis, Harvard University, 1997).

Macklin, R, 'Artificial Means of Reproduction and Our Understanding of the Family' (1991) *Hastings Center Report* 21 5–11.

Mitchell, L and Georges, E, 'Baby's First Picture: the Cyborg Foetus of Ultrasound Imaging' in R Davis-Floyd and J Dumit (eds), *Cyborg Babies, From Techno-Sex to Techno-Tots* (New York, Routledge, 1998).

Peace, W, 'The Artful Stigma' (2001) *Disability Studies Quarterly* 21 125–37.

Ragone, H, *Surrogate Motherhood: Conception in the Heart* (Boulder, Westview Press, 1994).

Sandelowski, M, 'Fault Lines: infertility and imperilled sisterhood' (1990) *Feminist Studies* 16.

—— 'Separate, but Less Unequal: Fetal Ultrasound and the transformation of expected mother/fatherhood' (1994) *Gender and Society* 8 230–45.

—— Harris, B, and Holditch-Davis, D, 'Somewhere out there: Parental Claiming in the Pre-adoption Waiting Period' (1993) *Journal of Contemporary Ethnography*, 21 464–86.

Shalev, C, 'Halakha and Patriarchal Motherhood—An Anatomy of the New Israeli Surrogacy Law' (1998) 32 *Israel Law Review* 51–80.

Stanworth, M, 'Reproductive Technologies and the Deconstruction of Motherhood' in M Stanworth, (ed), *Reproductive Technologies: Gender, Motherhood and Medicine* (Minneapolis, University of Minnesota Press, 1987).

Teman, E, 'Technological Fragmentation as Women's Empowerment: Surrogate Motherhood in Israel' (2001a) *Women's Studies Quarterly* 31.

—— 'The Medicalization of "Nature" in the "Artificial Body": Surrogate Motherhood in Israel' (unpublished manuscript submitted for publication, 2001b).

Van Der Pleog, I, *Prosthetic Bodies: Female Embodiment in Reproductive Technologies* (University of Amsterdam, PHD thesis, 1998).

Weiss, M, *The Chosen Body: The Politics of the Body in Israeli Society* (California, Stanford University Press, forthcoming 2002).

18

Still Giving Nature a Helping Hand? Surrogacy: A Debate about Technology and Society

MARILYN STRATHERN

1. INTRODUCTION

NUMEROUS DEVELOPMENTS MARK the period since this book was first conceived.[1] Among non-scientists, one has been the emergence of commentary on the explosion of ethics committees and ethical protocols across Europe which accompany applications of new science, especially in the medical field. It is as though we had suddenly become aware of the fact that scrutiny of interventions in medical contexts (ethics committees of the kind found in hospitals) has become a paradigm for diverse multidisciplinary reviews dealing with public reactions to science (commissions of enquiry, governmental working parties, expert consultations).[2] This is all part of a wider phenomenon of scientific accountability (Nowotny, Scott and Gibbons (2001)). But while proliferation of occasions and bodies concerned with the 'application of science' has been going on for several years, for some, at least, the *realisation* that these forms of governance are a force in their own right has taken time to surface.

It is a truism of present concerns with technological innovation that science and technology race ahead while society and its views lag behind, never quite catching up. We can think of many ways in which this is true. But in one profound sense it is untrue. To a social scientist, and especially to an anthropologist, science and technology are part of modern society, and social views are

---

[1] This is a version of 'Reproducing the future', a talk given to the European Molecular Biology Laboratory, Heidelberg, November 1998, in the Science and Society lecture series. The case draws on Strathern (1998), which offers a rather different context, and repeats material found there. (That touches on American data, but with some small exceptions here I restrict my comments to developments in the UK. When I refer to Euro-American I mean that my remarks apply to cultural continuities broadly identifiable across Europe and North America.) This chapter was first published as a paper with the same title in the *Journal of Molecular Biology* (2002) and is reprinted from that source by kind permission of the publisher, Elsevier Science.

[2] Eg, Siegler (1999) on the US experience; for a wider context in the UK see Rose (1999); for an anthropological glance, Strathern (2000). Medical ethics committees are not the only antecedents. The Warnock and Glover Reports (Warnock (1985); Glover (1989)) are classic examples coming out of parliamentary and quasi-parliamentary procedure.

already embedded or sedimented in them. Nor is science a special case, as the example I have just given shows. My comment was on the interpretation of extra-scientific activities, the proliferation of ethics committees in forums where scientists meet non-scientists. Changes in the ethical terrain within which science operates have been going on all the time, until we suddenly seem to find ourselves on a 'new' social map which needs interpretation. We are already there, the social innovation has already happened: it is the commentary which lags behind.

It is important to take commentary for the activity it is. Whether in meetings of specialists, or more widely in 'hybrid forums' (Callon (1998:260)) or the agora to which Nowotny, Scott and Gibbons (2001) refer,[3] the communication of findings and issues is meant to engage different segments of society. What is involved is a process of translation across domains of knowledge: society interrogating itself. Usually we are not aware of social innovations until they become the focus of such commentary—in the media or whatever—so that the innovation that has already taken place becomes the innovation that is now subject for comment. One cannot independently 'see' that prior process of change. However, there are moments which afford glimpses of it. These include moments when public discussion finds itself up against issues which already seem to have been resolved and, refusing to be dislodged further, point to changes which have already happened.

I wish to go back to a past moment of discussion and trace one such process. It offers a salutary example for how we might understand future commentaries, for future ways in which science will find itself in perhaps unexpected ethical terrain. It happens, incidentally, to be both evidence of the process of commentary and to address it directly in addressing the role of interpretation in social life. There is another reason for revisiting this material. When social scientists contribute to debates of public concern over new technologies they help 'heat up' already 'hot' situations (Callon (1998:260–61)), which may or may not be a desirable thing to do. Some argue that the scholar's job is to negotiate and thus further stir 'epistemological turmoil' (Barnett (2000)). But social science also has concerns of its own. Suppose the object of interest were not the technology but the society. The new technologies can be approached for the light they throw on more general social formations.

2. DESCRIPTION AND INTERPRETATION

In 1995, the chairman of the Norwegian Natural Science Research Council and a professor of mathematical logic addressed himself to the topic of the relation-

---

[3] *Agora* (after the Greek) describes 'the new public space where science and society, the market and politics, co-mingle' (Nowotny, Scott and Gibbons (2001:203)); the participants they have in mind are largely the articulate products of an enlightened educational system.

ship between the social and natural sciences. He chose economics and anthropology as his paradigmatic social sciences. There is common ground, he argued, between the natural and social sciences in their search for structure and explanation. However, he observed of social anthropology that:

> When one describes the dynamics of a process, one must bear in mind that an act can be both *described* (externally observable) and *understood* (carry an intentionality or meaning). Neither dimension can be reduced to the other (Fenstead (1995:63), my emphasis).

I would just add that an act can be understood in the sense of carrying an intentionality or meaning *which is communicated to others*, that is, it enters a discourse shared by the actor and other persons in his or her social field. And if neither dimension can be reduced to the other, each also implicates the other. A commentator describes (observes) the act and understands (interprets) the intention at the same time. The converse also holds: thus anthropologists try both to understand the act in the context of other acts and observe how the actors understand what they are doing. They are interested in people's interpretations. Fenstead goes on: an act, he says, may have material consequences independent of the actor's intention or meanings. This is the point at which the anthropologist will talk of the social or cultural contours of discourse. Such discourse offers a language which people in turn use in making their own interpretations.

Needless to say, the language is likely to be edited. This was striking in the case of the two biological fathers reported in the *Los Angeles Times* in 1998. Under the title 'Gay parenting gets a hi-tech helping hand', we are told:

> Thanks to in-vitro technology, a West Hollywood couple is due to become parents of the world's first two-father child. [The clinician] expects the one-mother, two-father child to be entirely healthy. . . . 'We have done all the necessary animal testing. It works in mice, it works in rhesus (monkeys), and it's working now with [the child]. Every new advance is scary to some people, but look at the benefits. There is no way under heaven this couple could have a child together otherwise'. [The two men] concurred. 'Gay couples have always wanted to be parents—real biological parents.'

In this context the ideas are ones already in place: the intending parents use an analogy with the heterosexual couple who has a natural child—same vocabulary, same sentiments—in order to create an image of real biological parents. Yet the image of biological parenting is rather startling for what it edits out: it ignores the original logic of joining, which in heterosexual coupling is the joining of opposites,[4] and ignores the fact that with two eggs required for separate

---

[4] In the short-lived 'virgin birth' furore (Silman (1993)) women who sought fertilisation outside the context of any kind of sexual relations with a man were excoriated not just for wanting to create fatherless children but for ignoring the symbolism of cross-sex union.

fertilisation before being fused the mother's contribution is a kind of reverse twinning.[5]

It would be trite to say that new technologies stimulate new social phenomena and vice versa—the child with one genetic mother (from two maternal eggs) and two genetic fathers (combining in one complement of chromosomes) along with the evident desire of the gay couple to be parents. But novelty is measured against what is allowed to pass as unchanged. There is very little contention over what is old in this case, namely continuing to use the term 'father' for the male parent. Innovation is revealed precisely because a new version (the gay parent) has been made out of an old phenomenon (the father). The completely new phenomenon (the process of parental division and fusion) is not brought into the image of what parenting is to mean. Relegated to 'the technology', it leaves the notion of 'biology' intact.

Contained in the interpretation of this event is a vision of future possibilities. One purchase we have on the future is how in the past people have dealt with new possibilities and new technologies, how the once new has *had* an impact. I go back to events that took place in the late 1980s/early 1990s—significant in Britain as a time of public debate surrounding the Human Fertilisation and Embryology Act 1990 (Morgan and Lee (1991)) which set the legislative tone of regulation in the field and has been something of a model for legislation elsewhere in Europe (Forvargue, Brazier and Fox (2001)). They involved the possibility of fertilised eggs ('embryos') living outside the womb leading to improved implantation procedures so that the egg may be returned not to the woman who has ovulated but to another woman altogether. Maternal surrogacy emerged as a 'new' arrangement[6] which took advantage of this technological innovation, and there is something to be learned from its reception.

But I wish to derive another lesson. I use the case of maternal surrogacy as a folk model for the role of commentary itself. Forcefully, it depicts a relationship between two kinds of factors—those which are evidently dependent on others and those which appear to have their own autonomous trajectory. The difference is between what calls for understanding, and thus interpretation, and what seems self-evident, and therefore a matter of observation or description.[7] In the eyes of policy makers that becomes the difference between what requires regulation and what must be taken as a given fact of life. For the two sides of

---

[5] Several eggs were obtained from the woman who was to carry the child; they were fertilised by sperm from both men. Two female embryos, each thus 'fathered' by one of the men, were then fused, forming a 'combined embryo, in which cells fathered by the two men were intermingled' (*Los Angeles Times*, 1 April 1998).

[6] An 'old' concept (one woman having a child for another) re-made anew through technology.

[7] I use 'description' in the general sense intended by Fenstead; it can of course contain the same contrast within itself. The distinction (between description and interpretation) is itself part of a Euro-American model of knowledge, but rather than unpacking it I here run with it. (The same could obviously be said of the distinctions and elisions of Nature/Technology/Biology/Society.)

Fenstead's act can also be taken as two sides of the phenomenal world. That is what some of the debate over surrogacy shows us.[8]

3. A FIFTEEN-YEAR-OLD DEBATE: SURROGACY

Early techniques in assisted conception, procedures such as *in vitro* fertilisation and embryo transfer, made it possible to separate the procreation of an embryo from its gestation. This gave rise to all kinds of possibilities for infertile couples. It included the possibility of finding substitutes not just for parental genetic material but for the womb. The nub of surrogacy agreements, as they came to be called, was the intention of a woman gestating an embryo/foetus to hand the child when it was born over to other persons, preferably a couple. The commissioning couple were typically the intending parents of the child to be.

For a period there was considerable terminological fluidity around the designations of the various parties, and differences within English between British and American usage. Early on a contrast was established between partial and full surrogacy, between the woman who bore the child contributing both uterus and egg and contributing the uterus alone.[9] In the USA, the former was also called 'traditional surrogacy', and the latter 'host' or 'gestational' surrogacy (Ragoné (1994:73).[10] With technological improvements and increasing demand, gestational surrogacy became more widespread, and the designation became common usage in English.[11] Gestational surrogacy is the arrangement I deal with here, but with a rather different part of the epistemological turmoil.

Perhaps we should not be surprised that the New Dictionary of Medical Ethics (Boyd, Higgs and Pinching (1997)) defines surrogacy as follows: 'the use of a third party to assist a couple in conceiving and bearing a child when the commissioning woman is either lacking a uterus or is unable to use her own uterus for medical reasons.' However, if we go back to when surrogacy was being debated in the British Parliament, when it was one among a tangled skein of 'hot' issues at the time, we find a specialist in health-care law noting just the opposite definition:

---

[8] I should make it clear that almost all of what I say is by way of cultural commentary. It may require me speaking as though I were giving an opinion or stating a norm, but the speaker is not me—I am describing opinions and norms which arise in Euro-American discussions about the assisted reproduction techniques. Part of the anthropologist's concern is to describe the contexts or domains in which ideas flourish (the 'culture'). Culture we may consider as a field in which ideas, concepts, practices, values are recognisable and thus replicated across domains. When they become unrecognisable to one another, we are in a new cultural field.

[9] 'Full surrogacy' did not mean that the birth mother was more a mother but that she was more a surrogate. (Haimes (1992:120–22)) laid out the number of relational permutations that—in the early 1990s—could be derived from gestatory and genetic parentage.

[10] She retrospectively applies the term 'gestational surrogate' to both the UK Warnock Report on Human Fertilisation and Embryology (1985) and the Report for the European Commission on Reproductive Technologies (Glover (1989)), though neither used the vocabulary at the time.

[11] See elsewhere in this volume.

> By surrogacy . . . I mean an understanding or agreement by which a woman—the sur-
> rogate mother—agrees to bear a child for another person or couple. Of course *this*
> *popular understanding* immediately encounters the objection that it is the person . . .
> who takes and rears the child rather than she who gives birth who is properly the sur-
> rogate. The woman giving birth is the mother (Morgan (1989:56), my emphasis;
> author's emphasis removed).

The objection came from those who wished to defend the legal understanding
that the mother of a child is the one who gives birth to it. In the English law of
the period, the woman who bore the child was the child's legal mother, and her
husband the child's legal father. (Intending parents could make a case for adoption if, among other conditions, the child were genetically related to at least one
of them.) The objection was that in popular understandings parenthood had
become defined as 'genetic' and was ignoring the authenticity of the gestational
and therefore birth mother. Contemporary OED definitions of the English term
'mother' (woman who has given birth) and 'surrogate' (one who acts in the
place of another) supported the complaint. The surrogate would be the woman
who subsequently acquires a child to which another has given birth. But the
reverse view, which the dictionary encoded, was entrenched popular usage. For
popular usage was determined to have it the other way round. It was the term
'surrogate' which became irrevocably and stubbornly tied to the woman who in
these circumstances bears the child. I am going to suggest that beyond the
genetic issue there were other interesting reasons for that stubbornness.
Classification had already taken place. Already sedimented in public discourse,
public usage showed an openness to new possibilities long *before* they became
overtly debated.

4. INTERPRETATION IN CONTEXT

The reasons why the term surrogate will go on being used for the woman who
carries a child on behalf of another lie beyond the immediate debates themselves. They have a cultural purchase that is not directly affected by the course
of the debates. In brief, the term draws attention to the role of interpretation in
explanations of human life.[12]

Two dimensions of the broader context are crucial here, Euro-American in
cultural terms, enlightenment in historical reference and modernist in epoch. I
relate them as axioms.

1. Society is built both on and after the facts of Nature: it exploits, moulds
   and imitates Nature all at once. At the same time: (1.1) Nature has its own
   self-regulatory trajectory, and Society therefore both regulates and is reg-

[12] In so doing the term makes explicit a mode of understanding the world which I take as wider
than simply English-language usage: it is more generally characteristic of twentieth-century Euro-
American cultures. Wagner (1975) is one of the classic statements in anthropology.

ulated by circumstances beyond itself; (1.2) Society's own systems of communication are self-regulatory and 'natural' to itself.
2. Such bifurcations lead to perceptions of different orders of reality. (2.1) Interpretation implies the ability to see relationships between orders of reality, so that one set of phenomena can be related to another. (2.2) This perception itself exists in a dialectical relationship with what is accepted as a self-signifying condition requiring or allowing no interpretation.

To expand: much is invested in seeking the context and reasons for social institutions. Whether in the realm of 'natural' or 'social' affairs, people aim to make explicit the conditions of existence. If Euro-Americans thus presuppose that human activity includes efforts to interpret and hence represent the world, then language, symbolism, and the way people express themselves all create orders of reality built on and after other orders of reality. Indeed signification is held to afford infinite possibilities in the further relationship it creates between what is given and what is subject to human intervention. So Euro-Americans create meaning by dividing phenomena into those whose meaning is self-evident or self-signifying and those whose meaning has to be made explicit by reference to what is being signified, and here they become conscious of the act of interpretation itself.

The figure of the surrogate mother (in gestational surrogacy arrangements) makes explicit the relationship between gestation and other factors in childbirth. The meaning of surrogacy is thus established *by reference* to those other factors and to those circumstances where gestation is part of a self-evident maternity. It is—among other things—an act of signification. Now gestation on the part of the birth mother may be interpreted as 'more' or 'less' biological and as 'more' or 'less' indicative of authentic motherhood, depending on the context. It itself is not diagnostic of surrogacy. The diagnostic issue is that one woman is perceived to be carrying a child *for another* woman[13]—and this is a specific representational strategy. In acting on behalf of another woman, she represents a facet of motherhood but is not otherwise the mother. She is a stand-in, occupying the place of the mother for a while, discharging an important function, but always in reference to another person who by implication is the eventual parent. It is precisely because she stands in for that element that otherwise defines motherhood

---

[13] In effect, the woman usually carries the child 'for' a couple—but of that male-female couple she specifically stands in for the female. The Glover Report (1989:67) captures it: 'The term "surrogate" implies that one woman replaces another in her role as mother,' although as we shall see there is a critical difference between two modes of 'replacement'. Note that the Warnock Report (1985:42) was also clear ('Surrogacy is the practice whereby one woman carries a child for another with the intention that the child should be handed over after birth') *until* the possibility of the carrying mother not being the genetic mother arose. This could lead to argument 'as to whether the genetic mother or the carrying mother ought *in truth* to be regarded as the mother of the child' ((1985:44), my emphasis). The popular view supported the definition adopted in the 1985 Surrogacy Arrangements Act which banned commercial surrogacy (' "Surrogate mother" means a woman who carries a child in pursuance with an arrangement' [S1]), the one piece of legislation stemming immediately from the Report.

that she is the surrogate. Popular English-speaking usage was immediately clear on this.

In short, this is the folk model. It borrows from the law in the sense that the arrangements depend on the agreement of the gestational surrogate to bear the child for the commissioning couple, not for the commissioning couple to rear the child for the birth mother. To the ordinary person, the intentions underlying the relationship are clear. Contest only arises when *the relationship* between the surrogate and the woman on whose behalf she is bearing the child breaks down. (I refer to the fact of relationship, not to its conduct.) The relationship in question is at once social, between persons, and conceptual, between different significations of what the persons are doing. When gestation is claimed to be definitive of her own motherhood, the surrogate is no longer a surrogate.

However, it is my interpretation of the folk model. This is not how people generally talk about surrogacy. They cut through the potential turmoil with a very simple device: making a distinction between the mothers. The surrogate is not, by definition, the 'real' mother. The debate over who is the real mother seems to have been won before it was ever argued. And that is because of her counterpart: *what was certain was that the surrogate could* not *be the real mother*. This piece of instant popular wisdom was not to be given up easily. It remained a point of clarity amid all the questions that continued to be asked about the apparent doubling of the maternal contribution.

5. THE ENIGMA OF THE REAL

Everything about 'reality', including its own concrete-sounding imagery, would suggest that the surrogate is a by-product of what we know in advance as real. The observer/interpreter (anthropologist) would, we have seen, put it the other way round. In terms of popular categorisations of these issues, the surrogate role is quite straightforward: one person stands in for another. The designation points to or signifies the fact that the real mother must be another person than herself. But on what grounds is the other person a mother? *The enigmatic role turns out to be that of the 'real' parent.* That is, when one has to explain and interpret what is real, one opens the self-signifying up to signification. It is how to determine what is real that becomes open to doubt.

The enigma was already there in the objection Morgan brought up. Surrogacy does not seem to lead to agonising scrutiny of what makes a woman intend to act on another's behalf; the question of who might be the real mother may well do so. The definition of surrogacy belongs to the world of agreements and contracts between persons (cf Dolgin (1997) on status and contract in surrogate motherhood from a US perspective); the real mother, by contrast, is established by an appeal to some inherent characteristic, for example, the wish or intention, the 'biological drive', to be a parent. In short, the objection noted by Morgan arose not from ambiguity surrounding the definition of surrogate, but from ambiguity in respect of the real or natural mother.

This was acted out in legal disputes at the time where, and they have been much publicised,[14] a woman who has agreed to act as a gestational surrogate then wishes to claim the child as hers, that is, makes a claim to be the real mother. In other words, the stand-in claims she is not a stand-in after all. One claim to reality *substitutes* for another.

What do I mean by substitute? We might say that the real world created by the possibilities of new reproductive technology inevitably substitutes for a real world whose possibilities were tied to other means. In the same way new knowledge substitutes for old: it constitutes an order of reality in its own right. This 'taking the place of' another, is different from 'standing in' for another. It is the difference between what is seen to require interpretation by reference to another person or order of reality (surrogacy) and the supplanting of one by another (substitution). In the case of surrogacy there is always an interpretative move (the one mother makes sense in reference to the other), while in the case of substitution, no further interpretation is necessary. The difference is no more nor less than *the visibility of the relationship between them* (that is, the two women). The 'surrogate mother' is a surrogate as long as her relationship with the 'other' mother is intact; should she claim the child to be 'hers', however, she then substitutes for that other woman. For to desire to be a mother is generally taken as requiring no further justification or interpretation.

The logic is supported by attendant substitutions. Compare the altruism of surrogacy with that of ovum donation. In making a gift the donor alienates her rights to the eggs; the eggs may still carry her identity, but she cannot dispose of them further, and in popular parlance neither donor nor recipient is a surrogate. Rather, donated eggs substitute for the commissioning mother's eggs.[15] And, in Euro-American cultures, a gift-giving is a complete act that requires no further interpretation. The act of gifting—culturally understood as altruism—is self-signifying; it points to itself. When the surrogate substitutes her own maternal impulse (to have a child) for altruism (to bear a child for another) this is understandable; indeed the generosity is generally approved. Surrogate mother, 'real' altruist.

However, the same self-signifying logic, that is, action which requires no interpretation, occurs in another social domain which brings emphatic

---

[14] Primarily in the period leading up to the 1990 Act, see Morgan (1989); Wolfram (1989). Commentary continued to pour in from the USA, and particular stories were widely reported in the British press (see, eg, the cases detailed by Dolgin (1997)).

[15] In both UK and American usage, when all that is at issue is the donation of ova, the gestational mother is taken to be the natural mother of the child she bears. Thus an intending mother who receives eggs by ovum donation is not called a surrogate, any more than the egg donor is. (The Warnock Report recommended that the birth mother using a donated egg should be the mother recognised in law.)

disapproval.[16] Here the real meaning of her actions may be thrown into doubt. For her very willingness to act as a surrogate may already carry a substitutive possibility of another kind. In the place of a desire to help there may instead be a desire for money. When the surrogate substitutes a commercial impulse for a maternal one, it too may be understandable but is invariably put into negative light. For there is nothing surrogate about commerce. Profit is thought to contain its own rationale: acting for profit in and of itself need require no interpretation. Indeed the market is an end as well as a means, for it is regarded as a political regulator in its own right. I suspect that the equivocations surrounding the commercial possibilities of surrogacy arrangements turn in part on the substitutive and thus displacement effect that money introduces. Surrogate mother, 'real' profiteer.

The British Human Fertilisation and Embryology Bill 1990 was intended to set up, as it did, a licensing authority for certain treatments of infertility and associated embryo research. While the Government's position was that both treatment and research should be encouraged with multiple benefits in view, it drew back from allowing the market to intervene as a mechanism for regulating supply and demand. An explicit provision in the Act debarred the donors of gametes from being able to profit from the donation (section 12(e)) and persons who wished to seek an order to be treated as parents of a child from either donated gametes or a surrogacy arrangement could not do so if money had changed hands (section 30(7)). The commercialisation of surrogacy by third parties already involved a criminal offence. Whatever the range of needs, market-led possibilities were rejected in favour of only permitting surrogacy arrangements on a private basis. In the background was the idea that only such a context would sustain the value of altruism that made the agreement between surrogate and commissioning mother socially acceptable. In seeking money, of course, it was assumed that the surrogate was primarily interested in that and not in the relationship between herself and the other mother.

It would seem that the altruism (if only minimally the altruism sealed in a contract) that otherwise justified surrogacy could be displaced by other orders of phenomena which then appeared as 'the real thing'. That might be either maternity or commerce.

6. FOUNDATIONS

But if the impulse to motherhood appears to require no interpretation, why should the 'real' mother appear the more enigmatic of the two? By itself motherhood is not enigmatic. But precisely because its rationale is ordinarily taken

---

[16] I am stabilising these ascriptions for purposes of exposition. The same act can of course be taken now in a self-signifying mode (figurative) and now in a referential or interpretative (literal) one. The interest is the way the popular usage of the term surrogate has stabilised this dialectic with respect to gestational surrogacy.

for granted, a given, motherhood appears problematic at the moment when it becomes the subject of questioning. When disputes arise as to who is the real mother, the category is thrown open to potentially endless interpretation. In such circumstances appeal is frequently made to further givens, that is, further taken for granted and unquestioned grounds which will bulwark the once unquestioned grounds now being contested. The former may appear as *foundations* for the latter.

In popular parlance, 'real' motherhood has its foundations both in biology and in the social recognition of biology, so the real mother always has either nature or society on her side; by the same token, when a 'surrogate' acts on behalf of a real mother it is because the real mother's claims are already there. Thus a commissioning mother can be considered a real mother, whether by nature (some commissioning parties can also claim a genetic tie; all can claim the natural desire to be a parent) or society (through seeking legal support for their claims or demonstrating they can provide the child with everything that defines good parenting). So where is the enigma? The enigma rests in the very necessity to conserve the foundations on which the real thing is established. Competing foundations take away their own axiomatic (and thus foundational) status. Here the foundations being propped up are the authority of society and of nature.

I touch briefly on two conserving strategies,[17] the first to do with the evidence that nature produces of and about itself, and the second with the regulating role of society. As sketched earlier, Euro-Americans take society's capacity to organise and regulate the social world as its own self-evident foundation in the same way as nature is known by its self-regulating properties. Part of that regulatory activity involves making explicit the relationship between these different orders of reality.

The evidence nature produces of and about itself: there is of course a history to be traced in the sequence that has turned 'nature' into 'biology' and biology into 'genetics'. What is enigmatic is how one should understand (interpret) the real thing. Disputes over carrying and birth motherhood show the point at which biology ceases to be an axiomatic foundation for motherhood—not because 'social' motherhood is opposed to 'biological' motherhood, but because *what is biological about biological motherhood* has to be made explicit. This is what makes the claims of the real mother enigmatic. How will the real thing show itself? On what will it be founded? Is it still biology, and what do we mean by that? Is the desire to have a child as much a biological function as the ability to bear one? Or the ability for mothering in the same sense as 'fathering' (begetting)? If the foundation for biogenetic kinship is taken to be the genetic tie, the appeal to biology may be understood as an appeal to genetic connection. The foundation of all life in genes seems to need no further interpretation. Indeed if

---

[17] And they are also conservative: foundationalism endures in folk models where it is discarded in analyses and interpretation in the human and social sciences.

popular usage is stubborn on the issue of who is the surrogate, it is also stubborn on the significance of genes. The UK Clothier Report (1992) which followed closely on the Human Fertilisation and Embryology Act (HFE Act), opened with this statement: 'Genes are the essence of life: they carry the coded messages that are stored in every living cell, telling it how to function and multiply and when to do so' (1.1).

There is an important sense in which technology is self-signifying: when it operates as an enabling process. When we ask *how* it is sustained as self-signifying, then—as in the case of motherhood—we start looking for and thus querying its foundational rationale. I return to this in a moment. Here I remark that it can enable another self-signifying process. Procedures which assist gestational surrogacy allow an intending couple who have no uterus to claim the evident value of genetic parentage. Writing a decade ago, one eminent figure in clinical medicine envisaged a new question (Weatherall (1991:29)). Ethical problems could be seen on the horizon: 'as we become more efficient at predicting the genetic make-up of individuals, how far will we be justified in offering parental choice?' What kind of choice, Weatherall asks, should a parent have to bring a defective child into the world? That choice is of course subsumed in the prior choice by which parenthood is in the first place claimed on a genetic basis. Do we glimpse a dimension that begins to make the genetic tie enigmatic? Insofar as the genetic (biological) tie takes precedence only by having been actively sought out, it is no longer a given of parentage; it has been selected as one among other possible routes. The case of the two fathers would bear that out.

Note that Weatherall's warning about the long term, that future developments in molecular biology might raise fundamentally new ethical issues, already drew together scientific and non-scientific ('ethical') factors. This leads us into society as an object whose foundations must also be conserved, and into the second strategy.

When surrogacy cases are debated in terms of a contrast between the genetic and the gestational tie, asymmetry is assumed; one or other must take precedence. Indeed, if surrogacy always implies such an asymmetry (it points to 'the real thing' elsewhere), this is also true in the relationship between technology and biology where technology simply assists biological process. At the same time technology is regarded as in a relationship of sorts with society. Technology is seen to be built on and derived from the same materials that nature uses (it assists biology) but with the further input of human ingenuity and human intentions for it which are geared to social purposes. Here its foundational rationale belongs to society.

For as long as social ends remain stable, technological innovation does not, in this Euro-American (modernist) view have to mean social innovation. On the contrary, as in the promotion of the nuclear family, new procedures may fulfil old goals: the application of technology is taken to have a foundation in social values it leaves unchallenged. Certainly in a society that values individual well-being, it is considered morally proper for technology to be turned to the ends of medical welfare. This is largely the basis on which developments in gene therapy, for instance, were justified. At the time when, in early 1990s Britain, the legitimacy of surrogacy arrangements was being debated, gene therapy pinpointed further possibilities in the medical applications of genetic knowledge. Provided the (old) social foundations remained stable, however, genetic technology could continue on its (new) trajectory.

Weatherall's warning came from *Science and Public Affairs*, a joint publication of the British Association for the Advancement of Science and the (British) Royal Society. In 1991 the magazine published a multidisciplinary discussion[18] intended to allay anxiety by clearing away confused thinking. His opening paper pointed out that it was difficult to predict long-term outcomes, and this was the context of his warning; in the short term, however, the position seemed clear:

> Our new-found ability to manipulate our genes is giving rise to a certain amount of public concern. In fact the application of human recombinant DNA technology *does not raise any fundamentally new ethical issues*, at least not yet. . . . Genetic screening and prenatal diagnosis have been accepted procedures for many years; our new technology will simply increase the number of diseases that can be avoided in this way . . . Organ transplantation is quite acceptable; replacing defective genes is, in essence, no different to replacing whole organs (Weatherall (1991:28), my emphasis).

New technology, then, but old practices. New possibilities for human health but no new ethical issues because the kinds of decisions individuals have to face have already been encountered in clinical medicine. The new field simply highlights existing issues. The discussion was attended by members from the Committee on the Ethics of Gene Therapy which presented its report to the British Parliament the following year (Clothier (1992)).

The report was requested precisely because, among other things, it was acknowledged that gene therapy may 'introduce new and possibly far-reaching ethical issues which have not previously had to be considered' (1.11). The presumption of the report was that before gene therapy was introduced into medical practice it must be ethically acceptable; for instance, such therapy must stand the tests of 'safety and effectiveness in relation to other treatments' (1.12). However, its general finding was that the basis for an ethical position already exists. It offers the tentative view that 'gene therapy should initially be regarded as research involving human subjects' (8.3). Somatic cell therapy was directed to the specific individual with a disorder, and the conditions for such an application of genetic knowledge were met by already established guidelines for research with medical patients (such as preserving the subject's rights and carrying out procedures with respect to the subject's well-being).

---

[18] At a meeting organised by the Royal Society under the title 'Embryos and Ethics', a small-scale example of a kind of 'hybrid forum' (see above page 282) becoming increasingly common.

Somatic cell gene therapy will be a new kind of treatment, but it does not represent a major departure from established medical practice, nor does it, in our view, pose new ethical challenges (8.8).

The foundational status of society's regulatory capacity was conserved.[19]

This returns me to a point made at the beginning. Current medical ethics presumably provided a foundation for ethics in the area of gene therapy because it already embodied the values of society thrashed out through much deliberation and discussion. So the finding of no new ethical issues was based on already established practice. Like popular usage of the term surrogate, perhaps we glimpse here another absorption of new ideas into a form ('no new ethical issues') that was already sedimented in discourse.

7. TECHNOLOGY AND SOCIETY

In the field of assisted reproduction, the relationship between technology and nature—or biology—seems for all the world like the two components of maternity that have now entered popular parlance, the social and the biological; this in turn is like the two components of biological motherhood made explicit in surrogacy, genetic and gestational.

Reproductive technologies are regarded as facilitating biological process, above all as 'assisting' conception (see, for example, Franklin (1999:135–36)). (They do not assist nurture or those after-birth body processes some have regarded as equally biological in nature.) Insofar as techniques focus on conception, they focus on the fertile union of male and female gametes and on the viability of the embryo. In this, artificial insemination, *in vitro* fertilisation or other practices such as GIFT (gamete intra-fallopian transfer) simply *stand in*, so the justification goes, for natural body processes. Not themselves natural, they make up for natural impairment in the same way as the woman who acts on behalf of another's motherhood is a surrogate for her capacity to bear a child. We could consider them surrogate processes.

What makes a surrogate mother like a mother yet not the real mother is the fact that she assists the real mother to overcome a particular impairment. While her gestation of the child is a complete substitute for the commissioning mother's role in gestation, by itself it is an *incomplete* act that only makes (interpretative) sense when seen as part of the total social process by which the real mother is created. (If there were no 'real' mother to receive the child, her act by itself would be meaningless). In the same way, medical technology is like the natural processes it assists yet is not the natural process itself. Again, techno-

---

[19] Of course, what appears to be an unequivocal foundation can in turn be open to doubt. The processes of regulation may also be in need of regulation. Thus it is acknowledged (3.8) that different codes of practice and means of regulation have evolved to cover different areas that treatment may force together.

logical intervention attends to some particular bit of the whole developmental sequence that creates a child; each act of assistance as such is only given meaning, however, by a successful outcome that is simultaneously a natural one—an egg is fertilised, a child is born. (If there were no encompassing 'natural process', the interventions would have no outcome).

This commentary on the two conservation strategies brings an interesting realisation. It is not just that technology can appear now an adjunct of nature, now an adjunct of society, but assisting nature *is* also assisting society. In the epoch of which I talk, each could appear foundational to the other.[20]

The folk model of surrogacy enables us to clarify certain aspects of the science/society debate as it has appeared in the recent past. Specifically, I have drawn a parallel with how technology gives birth, with what kind of mother it is. Surrogacy offers a depiction of a relationship between factors which are evidently dependent on others, and factors which appear to have their own trajectory. If the surrogate who keeps her agreement is an uncontested surrogate, so, too, technology. As long as technology is simply 'giving nature a helping hand' (cf Hirsch (1999:102)), then it appears akin to natural resources which can be put to the benefit of society. As one speaker in the debates surrounding the passage of the British Human Fertilisation and Embryology Bill said: 'research and experimentation are a natural part of the development of the human condition' (quoted in Franklin (1999:145)). But the discourse faces both ways. By the same token, technology (and pari passu science) appears to be fuelling a runaway world when its aims are presented as a substitute for society's, and it seems to be the only real thing there is.

REFERENCES

Barnett, R, *Realizing the university in an age of supercomplexity* (Buckingham, SRHE [Society for Research into Higher Education] & Open University Press, 2000).
Boyd, K, Higgs, R and Pinching, A, *The new dictionary of medical ethics* (London, BMJ Publishing group, 1997).
Callon, M, 'An essay on framing and overflowing: economic externalities revisited by sociology' in M Callon (ed), *The Laws of the Market* (Oxford, Blackwell publishers/The Sociological Review, 1998).
Clothier, CM, *Report of the Committee on the Ethics of Gene Therapy* (London, HMSO, 1992).
Dolgin, JL, *Defining the family: law, technology and reproduction in an uneasy age* (New York, New York University Press, 1997).
Edwards, J et al., *Technologies of Procreation: Kinship in the Age of Assisted Conception,* 2nd edn (London, Routledge, 1999).

[20] (But a foundational model separates out nature and society again). The argument may be pursued in Strathern (1992) and Franklin (1999); the realisation is an analytical performative or obviation (Wagner (1986)). These chimera (nature, society etc.) are of interest today for the lessons they may hold for current conceptualisations of a biosocial world.

Fenstead, JE, 'Relationships between the social and natural sciences' (1995) *European Review* (3) 61.

Forvargue, S, Brazier, M and Fox, M, *Reproductive choice and control of fertility*: Report to European Commission, DG XII Concerted Action programme on biomedical ethics (Manchester, Centre for Social Ethics and Policy, Manchester University, 2001).

Franklin, S, 'Making representations: the parliamentary debate on the Human Fertilisation and Embryology Act' in J Edwards et al, *Technologies of Procreation: Kinship in the Age of Assisted Conception*, 2nd edn (London, Routledge, 1999).

Glover, J, *Fertility and the Family: The Glover Report on Reproduction Technologies to the European Commission* (London, Fourth Estate, 1989).

Haimes, E, 'Gamete donation and the social management of genetic origins' in M Stacey (ed), *Changing Human Reproduction: Social Science Perspective* (London, Sage, 1992).

Hirsch, E, 'Negotiated limits: interviews in south-east England' in J Edwards et al, *Technologies of Procreation: Kinship in the Age of Assisted Conception*, 2nd edn (London, Routledge, 1999).

Morgan, D, 'Surrogacy: an introductory essay' in R Lee and D Morgan (eds), *Birthrights: Law and Ethics at the Beginning of Life* (London, Routledge, 1989).

Morgan, D and Lee, R, *Blackstone's Guide to the Human Fertilisation and Embryology Act, 1990. Abortion and embryo research: the new law* (London, Blackstone Press Ltd, 1991).

Nowotny, H, Scott, P and Gibbons, M, *Re-thinking science: Knowledge and the Public in an Age of Uncertainty* (Cambridge, Polity, 2001).

Ragone, H, *Surrogate Motherhood: Conception in the Heart* (Boulder, Westview Press, 1994).

Rose, N, *Powers of freedom: Reframing political thought* (Cambridge, Cambridge University Press, 1999).

Siegler, M, 'Ethics committees: decisions by bureaucracy' in H Kuhse and P Singer (eds), *Bioethics: an anthology* (Oxford, Blackwell Publishers, 1999).

Silman, R, (ed), *Virgin birth* (London, Academic Unit of Obstetrics and Gynaecology, Whitechapel, WFT Press, 1993).

Strathern, M, *After Nature: English Kinship in the Late Twentieth Century* (Cambridge, Cambridge University Press, 1992).

—— 'Surrogates and substitutes: new practices for old?' in J Good and I Velody (eds), *The Politics of Postmodernity* (Cambridge, Cambridge University Press, 1998)

—— (ed), *Audit cultures: anthropological studies in accountability, ethics and the academy* (London, Routledge, 2000).

Wagner, R, *The invention of culture* (New Jersey, Prentice-Hall, 1975).

—— *Symbols that stand for themselves* (Chicago, Chicago University Press, 1986).

Warnock, M, *A Question of Life: The Warnock Report on Human Fertilisation and Embryology* (Oxford, Basil Blackwell, 1985).

Weatherall, D, 'Manipulating human nature' (1991) *Science and Public Affairs*, The Royal Society BAAS 25.

Wolfram, S, 'Surrogacy in the United Kingdom' in LM Whiteford and ML Poland (eds), *New approaches to human reproduction: social and ethical dimensions* (Boulder, Westview Press, 1989).

Index